To Isabel

good wishes

The Greatest Love Story Ever Told – and then some!

The Gospels retold for teenagers

Rosie Rushton

Rosie Rushton
2011

kevin mayhew

kevin mayhew

First published in Great Britain in 2011 by Kevin Mayhew Ltd
Buxhall, Stowmarket, Suffolk, IP14 3BW
Tel: +44 (0) 1449 737978 Fax: +44 (0) 1449 737834
E-mail: info@kevinmayhewltd.com

www.kevinmayhew.com

9 8 7 6 5 4 3 2 1 0

Hardback
ISBN 978-1-84867-396-0
Catalogue No. 1501286

Paperback
ISBN 978-1-84867-392-2
Catalogue No. 1501285

Cover design by Rob Mortonson
© Image used under licence from Shutterstock Inc.
Edited and typeset by Free Range Book Design & Production Limited

Printed and bound in Great Britain

About the author

Rosie Rushton is the author of more than forty best-selling books for teenagers and young adults. She has been a youth officer in her local church and for several years was a Governor at a C of E secondary school and is a Lay Reader.

Her great loves are swimming in the sea, going to the theatre, reading, sharing meals with friends, exploring new forms of worship and reverting to childhood with her six grandchildren. She is rather less keen on dusting, bigotry and being sensible.

In the biographies at the front of previous books, she stated that her ambition was to write the book that has been pounding in her head for years. *The Greatest Love Story Ever Told – And Then Some!* is it!

She now has two new ambitions: to visit China and to learn to sing in tune. She holds out rather more hope for the first than the latter.

PART ONE

Mary's Story

CHAPTER ONE

Rooftop revelations

'She's not like the other girls.'

'My Rebekah says her daydreaming is getting worse than ever – she left her bucket at the well yesterday and just ambled off, humming to herself.'

'That's all she ever does – talk to herself and sing and skip about! She's fourteen, for heaven's sake – way too old for that kind of behaviour.'

'She'll have to get her act together once she's in Joseph's house – hardworking man like him won't be doing with an airhead for a wife!'

As their peals of laughter rang out over the sound of her neighbours' grinding stones, Mary drew back from the doorway, glad that they hadn't spotted her – and more than a little annoyed at their perception of her. Airhead indeed! She did more thinking than the rest of her friends put together – and not about the boys in the next village either. And so what if she liked to sing and compose songs in her head? She got that from her mother and sometimes, when the pain of missing her was almost too much to bear, she would hum the songs that they had sung together while Anne taught her to grind grain or knead bread. That morning, she had been close to tears; there were so many questions she needed to have answered, and there was no one she could ask. Her cousin Leah was kind enough, in a brisk, don't-get-under-my-feet sort of way, but on the few occasions that Mary had tried to voice her feelings, Leah had looked at her as if she was mad and told her to stop being fanciful and get on with her chores. All that the other girls in the village seemed to want was to be betrothed like her and have a home of their own; they thought she was weird because she wanted to talk about why things were as they were, and what the world might be like where the Romans came from and . . . oh so many things. Things her parents would have encouraged her to explore, things Anne, her mother, would have woven stories about. But her parents weren't here and even her prayers brought Mary little comfort right now; knowing that her mother rested with God was one thing – but somehow it didn't fill the hole in her chest or ease the tightness in her throat.

Especially today. The fourth anniversary of her mother's death and still the pain was as sharp as ever. Leah was not one to talk about Mary's parents; she believed that the past was the past and it was only the present that mattered. Mary often wished that it had been cousin Elizabeth who had taken her in; Elizabeth had been Mary's mother's favourite relative, always smiling and seeing the best in everything. But Elizabeth and her husband Zechariah didn't live in Nazareth and it had been her father's wish for Mary to be brought up where he had been born and where his ancestors had lived for generations.

Thinking of her parents, Mary could once again feel the burning of unshed tears behind her eyes, and the persistent throbbing of the headache that had niggled at her since she awoke that morning was making her feel nauseous in the increasing heat.

Rebekah's mother had been right in one respect: Mary wasn't like the other girls. For one thing, her parents had been fiercely protective of her – after many miscarriages and stillbirths, the arrival of Mary had been more than they had dared to hope for. Their home, built of the white limestone quarried from the nearby mountains, was conveniently situated on the outskirts of the village, a fact that made it easy for Mary's mother, who had always been a very private and introverted person (some in the village went as far as to call her stuck up) to keep her treasured infant away from any family in the area who displayed the merest hint of illness or whose way of life was a somewhat liberal interpretation of the law of Moses. And when Mary's father Joachim dropped dead in the field two weeks after Mary's sixth birthday, Anne clung to her even more fiercely, never letting her out of her sight, and devoting every waking moment to her precious daughter.

So when her peers – Anna, Rebekah, Judith – were running up and down the streets, collecting pebbles for their games of jacks or climbing the neighbouring hills to gather flowers to decorate their hair, Mary had been close at her mother's side, learning her letters, memorising the uses of the plants and herbs that grew on their small patch of land, and listening to the songs her mother loved to hum softly as she worked. On their journeys to the well, Mary would eye the other children shyly, but while they ran off from their mothers, shrieking and laughing, one look from Anne kept Mary obediently at her side. It did little for her relationships with her peers, but she became an excellent eavesdropper, soaking up the chatter of the village women and storing it away to ponder on as she lay on her mattress pretending to be asleep.

And then one day her mother got sick. The rash that started on her chest spread over her whole body, which jerked and thrashed as the fever gripped her. Within two days, she was dead. Mary was alone.

It was Leah, Joachim's first cousin, who took her in. Unlike the other villagers, she didn't worry about contagion or wait to see whether Mary too would succumb to the fever, but quietly led the sobbing child down the hill to her own tiny house, knowing that of course, no food could be prepared in a home where there had been a death, and understanding that even a grieving ten year old needed a good meal each day. Leah's two daughters were both married, her husband Samuel was set in his ways and somewhat demanding, and despite grumbling a lot to her neighbours, secretly she was happy to have another youngster in the house; someone who would look up to her, obey her and hopefully make herself useful now that every joint in Leah's body seemed to scream out in protest whenever she bent down to sweep or lift a bucket.

And, she muttered to her friend Deborah, hopefully the child would now lead a more normal life – would play with the other children and get some colour into those pale cheeks.

Four years on, Mary still felt like an outsider; the other girls all had their own cliques and while they weren't unkind to her, they still viewed her as different; they laughed at the way she would suddenly go off in a trance in the middle of a conversation, whispering to herself or smiling in what they called 'that weird way'. They felt slightly embarrassed by her penetrating questions about things they never gave more than a passing thought to – heaven and hell, the purpose of life, why some people were born healthy while others, like Naomi's youngest, could neither see nor speak. But what bewildered them the most was that she wouldn't talk about her betrothal or join in the giggling speculation about what it would be like to be a wife.

A wife. As she slapped the thin flat circles of dough she had been kneading for the past half hour onto the hot stones in the fire, she thought yet again about what Leah had said to her that morning.

'Soon it will be time, child – time for you to leave us and go to the house of your betrothed. You are indeed a fortunate young woman. Joseph is a good, reliable man, his business is thriving thanks to his hard work, and he will expect . . .'

And as her cousin, bent now from the pain in her back, listed the duties of a good Nazarene wife, Mary had done what she always did when the thoughts in her head became too overwhelming. She kept her head bowed, she nodded compliantly while all the time praying silently and fervently in her head.

'Oh Lord my God, I know I am a dreamer and I'm sorry that I get into trouble for having what cousin Leah calls stupid fancies . . . but please my God don't let my life be boring. Let me do something – anything – that will make some sense of why you kept me alive and took my mother and father away. Let it all have been for a good reason.'

She wasn't sure that she should pray to Yahweh in that manner, but her mother had always told her that God knew the thoughts of her innermost heart and so he must surely know her dreams too. And since her mother had also assured her that everything she was and ever would be was part of Yahweh's great design and that he loved her with a love greater than anything she could possibly imagine; well, then, was it so very bad to ask him if she could be something more than just Mary, orphan of Anne and Joachim, grateful recipient of the charity of Samuel and Leah?

'God will have some special purpose for you, my child . . .'

Mary's mother's words rang in her head, blotting out Leah's oft repeated instructions on the correct way to prepare wool for spinning.

'. . . perhaps you will be a great storyteller.' And at this point, her mother would always chuckle. 'Heaven knows, you have enough imaginings in that little head of yours!'

It was true. Mary loved stories; she had grown up with them. Her father had begun teaching her the basics of the Torah, the stories of Abraham and Isaac, Moses and Elijah as soon as she could sit still enough on his knee to listen – but it was the wonderful word pictures that her mother would weave while teaching Mary to press olives or grind barley – stories about great women of the past; Esther, Deborah, Ruth, Jael that had fired Mary's imagination the most.

'Tell me more, tell me more,' she would beg, and her mother would pull her closer and begin the story again, always with the same words.

'Well, I don't know any more, not for a fact, but you know what I think?'

And then she would describe the way Esther looked, what Deborah liked to wear, what made them angry and what they did when they had a spare hour to themselves.

'I'm only imagining, of course,' her mother would point out repeatedly, but Mary didn't care. Imagining brought her heroines to life, imagining made her believe that just possibly amazing things really could happen to ordinary people.

'I want to be like them,' Mary would say. 'Brave and clever. And important.'

And on the days when her chores seemed endless and all she wanted to do was wander off by herself and daydream, she would pout and frown and mutter under her breath, 'I bet they didn't have to spend all day doing boring stuff like making oil and feeding chickens.' And her mother would place her hands on her shoulders and fix her steely grey eyes on hers.

'Just remember one thing,' she would whisper. 'Whatever God has for you to do, be it crushing an olive or teaching a child or saving a nation . . . that is what you do. It is not for us to question God's will for our lives.'

That, thought Mary to herself with a sigh now, as she flipped the flatbread over on the coals, is all very well. But surely God had got enough women to get married and bear children and milk goats; did he really need her to do the same as all the others? She knew that wasn't really the problem; of course she wanted a home and a family, but the truth was that she was scared. She wanted time to stand still; she was frightened of becoming a wife. Leah constantly repeated to her the teachings of the wise Solomon on the subject. That a good wife does her husband good, and not harm; works wool and flax with willing hands, rises in the dark of the night to provide food, spins, weaves and never, ever 'eats the bread of idleness'.

Mary sighed. These were all the things she was bad at; there was no mention of making music, singing songs or telling stories. What if she messed up? What if she didn't please Joseph? What if the food she cooked wasn't to his liking? And what if he too laughed at her – or worse, got angry with her? And the other stuff . . . the things her friends whispered about? The thing you did if you wanted a family. That sounded scary, far more scary she thought than leading an army into battle like Deborah, or standing up to the king like Esther.

Not that Joseph wasn't kind – he was, of that she was sure. OK, he was older than her, nearly twenty-one in fact – and quiet, withdrawn even; she couldn't imagine him bursting into song or dancing on the spot. But when he had come to Samuel's house for the betrothal, he had spoken with a deep, soft voice reminiscent of her father's, and Leah had said that his smile lit up his whole face when he looked at her. Mary didn't know whether that was true, of course; she had kept her eyes firmly on the floor. To be honest, it wasn't so much Joseph she feared; it was herself. She wanted to stay just as she was. She didn't want to give herself to anyone at all. She thought that if she did, she might just get lost and never find the Mary that was hidden inside.

That's why her friends thought she was strange. Perhaps they were right. Perhaps this restlessness, this constant dreaming of something that seemed just out of reach but which she was sure was there – maybe it was all the result of what Leah called her overactive imagination.

From outside she could hear the chattering of Rebekah and Joanna as they passed her house on their way to take food to the men who were planting in the nearby fields, and for a moment, she was tempted to join them. Without even the slightest breeze from outside blowing through the narrow doorway, the heat in the kitchen was becoming intense. She lifted her arm and mopped the sweat from her brow with her sleeve. She knew it would not be long before Leah was back from the marketplace, expecting Mary to join her in sorting and carding the last of the wool from their three goats. Even listening to Rebekah's gossiping and Joanna's obsession with Benjamin would be preferable to that.

Lifting the baked bread from the coals and setting it to cool, she peeped out of the doorway. No sign of Leah as yet. If she could just get some air, lie down for a few minutes, perhaps she would feel less agitated.

She climbed up the steps onto the flat roof and gingerly touched the floor with her toe. The fresh coat of clay plaster which Samuel had applied the week before in preparation for the coming of the rains had hardened and Mary saw that Leah had begun spreading out the laundry to dry in the sun once more. Even up here, the air was heavy with the threat of thunder. Across the street, Aphia and Tirzah, the children of Tabitha, Leah's closest friend, were bowling a hoop and shrieking with delight; in the distance, Mary could see the stooped backs of the workers in the field, diligently plucking weeds from the furrows.

She lay down on the matting spread in the far corner and closed her eyes, rubbing her temples with her second and third fingers in the hope of easing the pounding. Somewhere in the distance she could hear the faint strains of a lute, its notes obliterated from time to time by the angry barking of a dog. For the first time that day, she felt her whole body begin to relax. Her eyelids became heavy, and the tightness in her chest eased. She slept.

'No! What . . . who?'

Suddenly she was alert, every fibre of her being taut and ready to jump to her feet. Except that she couldn't move. As she opened her eyes, the brightness of the noonday sun was so dazzling that all she could see at first were black spots dancing across her field of vision. She put her hand to her forehead to shield the light but the light didn't go away.

And then she saw him. Or thought she did – but it couldn't be. She was still dreaming. She had to be. Because what she thought she could see was an angel. And angels didn't stand on the roofs of humble houses in Nazareth.

'Hello, Mary. Mary, you are wonderful, beautiful . . .'

No, it couldn't be an angel. Angels didn't do flattery. It was a man. And he shouldn't be here. She opened her mouth to scream but no sound came out. She tried to scramble to her feet, but her legs were leaden, as if anchored to the dusty floor by an iron weight.

'Hush, Mary, it's OK, God is with you. There is no need to be frightened. God has sent me to you.'

Suddenly, the panic left her to be replaced by a huge wave of guilt and shame. Her mind was flooded with the memories of her prayers to God that morning – all those requests for how she wanted her life to be. And now she was to be punished – and rightly so, because what was it her father used to say? Wait patiently for God's plan and never question his purposes.

The angel Gabriel was sent from God to Nazareth, a town of Galilee, to a virgin named Mary, who was engaged to Joseph, a descendant of David. The angel, as he approached her, said 'Greetings, favoured one. The Lord is with you.'

Luke 1:26-28

'I'm sorry, I . . . God . . .' She tried to close her eyes, to avert her gaze from the shining face of the angel but it seemed as if her body and her will had left her.

'Listen to me, Mary. You are going to have a baby – a son, who you must call Jesus.'

So I am dreaming, Mary thought and almost laughed out loud. A baby indeed! That was one thing she knew for sure couldn't possibly be true.

'God has chosen you to be the mother of his son . . .'

'What . . . ?'

'Your son will be great; he will be called the Son of God and he will claim back the throne of your ancestor David.'

'No . . .' Mary pinched her wrist as hard as she could to make herself wake up. When she drew blood, she knew she was awake. For a moment she thought her heart had actually stopped beating in her chest.

'. . . and he will reign forever – his kingdom will never, ever come to an end!'

'But . . . how? I mean, I've never, that is to say – I mean, I'm a virgin.'

The angel smiled gently and slowly nodded his head.

'With God all things are possible. This child will be conceived not by earthly means, but through his power. His Holy Spirit will come upon you so this baby will be holy – the Son of God! God has chosen you, Mary – chosen you to be the mother of his Son.'

He heard me, she thought. He knows me. He knows I wanted to do something, be someone. But this? Can this really be true?

'God has chosen me?' she whispered.

'He has. And what is more, in case you didn't know, your cousin Elizabeth is six months pregnant.'

'No! But she's old and besides, everyone knows that she's . . .'

Mary hesitated, reluctant to voice the shameful truth, the secret that suggested Elizabeth was being punished by God.

'Barren? That's what people thought, but they'd reckoned without God! I told you, with God nothing is impossible.'

And in that moment, Mary knew. She heard the words but more than that, she felt their truth. It was as if her whole body was suddenly flooded with warmth, as if liquid honey was running through her veins. She was still scared out of her wits, a thousand questions crowding one upon another in her mind, and yet despite all that, there was a knowing, an awareness that this truly was God's plan, his plan for her, Mary – the one 'not like the other girls'.

'Mary?'

The angel seemed fainter now, the light not so dazzling.

'Mary?' That questioning tone again.

Mary took a deep breath.

'I am God's slave girl. I'll do whatever God wants,' she said softly. 'This seems too amazing to get my head around, but yes – I pray it happens and that I turn out to be worthy of all this.'

> Behold, I am the handmaid of the Lord; let it be to me according to your word.
>
> *Luke 1:38*

She bowed her head, overcome by her own emotions.

And when she looked up, ready to ask the angel one of the many questions buzzing in her brain, he had gone.

'Mary? Mary, where are you?' Leah's voice carried up to the roof and she didn't sound happy.

'Coming!'

Mary took a deep breath in an attempt to stop the trembling that had seized her the instant the angel departed. She swallowed hard, fixed what she hoped was a calm expression on her face and ran down the steps and into the house. It only took a second for her to realise why Leah was so angry.

'You foolish girl!' Her cousin gestured towards the bread that Mary had left to cool. One torn chunk lay on the wooden platter; the rest was a mass of crumbs.

'How many more times do I have to tell you?' Leah sighed. 'Those scavenging dogs will take anything within reach. Why do think we have shelves?'

'I'm sorry, cousin. I was stupid.'

'All that flour wasted – and our last shekels gone to those . . .' Leah bit down on her lip, resisting the urge to utter her true opinion of the Romans' latest tax raid on the village in front of her impressionable relative.

'I'm sorry,' Mary repeated. 'I will make some more at once. There is a little flour left in the sack.'

At the thought of more hours in the stifling kitchen, Mary's eyes filled with tears. Leah's face softened and she stepped closer to Mary. 'What is it, child? Are you sick?'

Mary shook her head. 'No – no, I just feel a little faint . . .'

What else could she say? She couldn't get her head around what was happening, never mind put it into words to someone like Leah.

'It is your monthly time,' Leah asserted in her all-knowing way. 'That would account for your being so thoughtless. Am I right?'

You couldn't be more wrong, Mary thought, shaking her head.

'Well, any day now, then,' Leah declared. 'I know the signs. Forget the bread – take this goat's milk to old Sarah. She's still ill, poor soul, hasn't left her house for days. You'll be safe – it's her legs, nothing contagious.'

Leah eyed Mary closely. 'You're well enough to walk the two miles, aren't you?'

'Oh yes, yes, absolutely!' The chance to escape for an hour – two, if she could pretend that Sarah had kept her talking – was too good to miss. 'And I'm so sorry about the bread.'

She snatched up the pitcher of milk, and stepped out into the street. As soon as she was out of sight of Leah's house, she slackened her pace to a mere dawdle and allowed the thoughts that were hovering on the dark edges of her mind to come to the surface.

She was going to have a baby.

She was going to have a baby and she wasn't married.

She was going to have a baby who would be God's own son.

She couldn't explain it. She didn't understand it. But she believed it with all her heart.

She also knew that no one else would believe it for one second. How would she explain it to Leah and Samuel? What was even worse, how would she explain it to Joseph?

She stopped dead in her tracks. If she continued on this path to Sarah's house, she would have to cross the marketplace and walk close by Joseph's workshop and she couldn't face that. She turned, retraced her steps for a few yards and took a narrow, stony track up the side of the hill. It wasn't an easy walk; the ground was uneven and she had to be careful not to jiggle the pitcher of milk, but there were few people about and little to disturb her thoughts other than the bleating of a few sheep and the reedy piping of one of the shepherd boys' flutes from beyond the brow of the hill. She hesitated briefly at a bend in the track, her eyes fleetingly resting on the cave on the opposite incline; the cave holding the tomb where her parents rested.

'O Lord my God, what should I do? Please, please put the right words in my mouth, so that the people I care about won't get angry or be ashamed when I tell them about all this. Lord my God, guide me.'

She repeated the words, mouthing them silently as she crested the brow of the hill and turned to walk down to the tiny hamlet where the widowed Sarah lived.

Sarah might be old, incapable of moving more than a few steps, and with failing eyesight, but, Mary thought, as she sat on a low stool at her feet, she certainly had all her marbles. She had remembered that it was four years ago that Mary had been orphaned, and had patted her head and murmured a prayer for the rest of the souls of Anne and Joachim. She had been almost girlish in her enquiries about the handsome Joseph and made some rather racy remarks about Mary's forthcoming marriage.

'And your dear cousin Elizabeth,' she murmured now. 'What news of her?'

Mary, lost for words, hesitated.

'I know, I know, my dear, you must miss her,' Sarah went on, squeezing Mary's hand. 'Leah told me that you used to visit her with your mother every year . . .'

'I did,' Mary nodded. 'From way back when I was a baby. Every year until . . .' Her voice faltered.

'Well, now you're not a baby any longer but a soon to be married woman!' Sarah declared, clapping her hands so that the folds of wrinkled skin on her arms wobbled like tent flaps in a high wind. 'So you will be able to travel with Joseph and visit again!'

She rubbed her eyes. 'I remember when I was a young woman, first married to Jacob and we travelled up to . . .'

But Mary wasn't listening. The old woman's words seemed like an answer to her prayer.

Elizabeth. If what the angel had said really was true and Elizabeth really was going to have a baby – and it had to be true, didn't it, because angels never lied – then maybe Elizabeth would believe that Mary truly was pregnant by God's Holy Spirit. And Elizabeth was sensible – she would help Mary work out how to tell people, how to cope with everything that was going to happen.

It wouldn't be easy to find a way, but she had to go there. She had to spend time with the one person with whom she could be totally herself.

And she had to do it soon.

So what has that got to do with me?

1. Mary felt like an outsider, someone who was seen as 'different' and who didn't fit into her peers' perception of what she should be like. Put yourself in her shoes and discuss how you would feel and then, more importantly perhaps, imagine you are one of her friends. What motivated them to think she was 'weird'? How often do we look at someone, and assume things about them without ever bothering to find out the reality of their lives? What can we do to prevent that kind of behaviour in the future?

2. Mary's mother had taught her that 'whatever God has for you to do, be it crushing an olive or teaching a child or saving a nation . . . that is what you do. It is not for us to question God's will for us.' How do we know what God wants of us? What did Mary do when she reflected on her future? Do we believe that we have no choice, that our lives are predestined and we can't alter them? When we face a challenge that seems to overwhelm us, what do we tend to do? Who do we go to for help, and most importantly, how do we decide who to listen to and whose advice to reject? Is there any way we can possibly know we are doing what God wants?

3. This is the first of many appearances of angels in the New Testament. Do we believe in angels? Do we see them as shining white beings with wings, or do we believe that angels come in many different guises? What made Mary sure that the angel was indeed from God? How do we make our judgements on what is from God and what is not?

4. Mary accepted her heavenly assignment with grace and faith. In her shoes, many of us would have tried to rationalise the experience or put it down to an hallucination, a dream or even stress. In our twenty-first century world, how ready are we to believe that God sends us messages too? And if we are not, why is that?

5. Mary prayed that God would help her find the right words to tell her family about her pregnancy. She prayed through her problem. Notice that Mary's prayer wasn't only for herself; she wanted to

find a way to make this enormous revelation easier for her family to cope with; she wanted to save their embarrassment. We know that we can pray, and we frequently do; how deep is our faith that God hears our requests and our cries of desperation? When we get a quick answer, we are happy; when it seems that our prayers go unheard, we think God has ignored us. How do we pray when we have a problem? Fancy words from a book? A cry from the heart? Persistent, ongoing prayer or just one attempt and then a tendency to say 'Forget it!'?

CHAPTER TWO

Sharing the secret

'How many more times do I have to tell you – you're being ridiculous!'

Leah churned the goat's milk in its goatskin with even more vigour than was needed, her lips pressed in a firm line.

'All this nonsense about visiting Elizabeth – as if!'

'But Leah,' Mary pleaded, 'Mummy visited her every year and always told me that love in a family is the most important there is.'

'That is true,' Leah nodded, 'and when you are with Joseph in a few months' time, he will no doubt take you there.'

'But surely, it would be unreasonable of me to expect him to leave his workshop and give up good earning time to accompany me?'

She noticed Leah hesitate and pressed on without drawing breath.

'And you said you thought I was looking pale . . .'

'Indeed you are – in fact I've been really worried about you these past few weeks – which is one reason to stay here where I can keep an eye on you!'

'I think,' Mary whispered, 'that I am troubled because I know my mother would wish me to do what is right – and I feel somehow that Elizabeth too misses her and needs to see me.'

She added a silent plea for forgiveness to Almighty God; she wasn't lying, but then again, she wasn't exactly being honest. It was three weeks since the angel's visit and for the last ten days, she had struggled to hide the nausea that swamped her for the first two hours after rising; had covered the pools of vomit outside the house with straw or washed them away with precious water – but she knew she couldn't carry on like that much longer; already Leah had commented on her lack of appetite at breakfast and since the days were cooling, Mary couldn't blame a touch of heatstroke for her refusal to touch the honeyed figs which were her favourite treat.

'But . . .'

'Mary, enough! Get these idle thoughts out of your mind and go and feed the chickens. And I don't want to hear another word on the subject.'

In the end, ironically, it was Joseph who had come to her rescue. He had visited the house to deliver a new stool for Leah – the old one proving incapable of holding her increasing weight – and to discuss the date when Mary would move to his home and officially become his wife.

'The sooner the better,' Mary had heard Samuel say. 'She has some notion in her head about travelling to visit her aunt in Kerem! She says that dear Anne would have wanted it, but it's impossible . . .'

'But why? It seems a good idea,' Joseph had interjected, as Mary, listening from the stairway, held her breath. 'She is, after all, following the teaching of Solomon, that great and wise writer of the proverbs – to honour the wishes of her parents.'

'Well, yes but . . .'

'And as it happens, my neighbours, Jacob and Milcah, will be travelling there in two days' time with their children – what better opportunity for Mary to make the visit? Then as soon as she returns, we can be married – by then I will have finished work on the house.'

'But I need . . .'

'And I am sure Milcah could do with her help on the journey,' Joseph went on. 'Those children of hers are something of a handful, let me tell you!'

It was settled. To argue with the man about to marry one's foster child was unthinkable, and one look from Samuel told Leah that he would give his consent.

A week later, as the travellers reached the crossroads where they would part company, Mary realised just how accurate Joseph's assessment of Milcah's children had been! She would, she vowed, make sure that her son behaved himself a whole heap better.

On a rooftop overlooking his village, Zechariah sat, stylus poised over his wax tablet. At the sound of laughter from below, he took a deep breath and began to write

> The child Mary has arrived. Well, no longer a child, I suppose – one forgets. I should go down to greet her – in a minute I will, but it is somehow less stressful to sit here on the roof than to have to try to make someone new understand me, to see the bewildered expression and the embarrassed shifting of eyes. And anyway, Elizabeth will be chattering away to her; better that I leave the women to it for a time.
>
> It will be good for Elizabeth to see Mary, to have someone to confide in; these past weeks have been so extraordinary, so beyond anything she, or indeed, I could ever have imagined. The power of God – it is beyond human describing.
>
> Elizabeth is particularly fond of Mary – having no child of our own, she has always taken the closest interest in the offspring of our relatives and friends, hiding her own longing and pain beneath an outpouring of love and dare I say, spoiling, to any child that comes near her! When parents grumble about their wayward sons or the fact that their daughters are sulky or behaving in an indiscreet manner, Elizabeth is the one to set them straight, to gently remind them to delight in what they are doing, not moan about what they're not. She's wise, my Elizabeth.

Zechariah paused in his writing, flexed his arthritic fingers and put his wax tablet on the floor at his feet, balancing the stylus carefully to prevent it from rolling away. Sighing, he gazed out from the rooftop of his home at the limestone hills, shimmering in the late afternoon sun. He had made several attempts over the past months to write down what had happened to him that day at the Temple, and every time he gave up in despair, knowing that he wasn't being one hundred per cent honest and yet fighting the realisation that if he was to write anything for this unborn child of his to read one day, it had to be the full, unvarnished truth.

Taking a deep breath, assured by the muted murmur rising from the room below that he would not be disturbed for a while yet, he picked up his stylus.

> That day in the Temple at Jerusalem – oh, how I wish I had not doubted even for that fleeting moment. Had I not questioned God's purpose, His plan – well, I would still be able to speak. Instead here I am, unable to carry out my priestly duties and constantly having to use sign language to make myself understood. Elizabeth is so patient; but I can see she longs to have a two-way conversation once again! Well, at least now Mary is here, she will have that pleasure. Mary may be thirty years younger than Lizzie, but she's got an old head on those shoulders of hers.
>
> I still feel ashamed; I had so longed and prayed for that day – the day when I, Zechariah, priest of the Abija division of the Temple service corps, would be chosen by the drawing of lots to enter the inner sanctuary, the Holy of Holies to burn the incense. When it came, I was over the moon, so honoured to be the one to serve God in this way. And then I messed it all up.
>
> I had travelled from my home here to the Temple in Jerusalem. The journey had been uneventful; and yet on the way, as I heard my companions speak of their families, their children, and in one case, a grandchild born just the day before – well, I remember wondering whether God was punishing us, Elizabeth and I, by ignoring all the years of prayer and devotion and sacrifice. But once I got to Jerusalem, and the day for the ceremony dawned, I put my grief behind me, conscious only of the honour that lay ahead.
>
> I had taken the incense into the inner sanctuary; outside the people were praying. Listening to the familiar chanting

of the age old prayers 'May the merciful God enter the Holy Place and accept with favour the offering of his people,' I suddenly felt a lightness of spirit, an overwhelming sense of the presence of God; the pain in my back which so often made me groan in agony seemed a mere shadow of its former self, and my hands were steady as those of a man half my age.

I prepared to light the taper and that was when I saw him, standing at the right-hand side of the altar, gazing straight at me, iridescent, fluid, yet recognisable. An angel. I remember I cried out loud, dropping the lighted taper which brushed against my bare left foot. (I have the mark to this day.)

'Don't be afraid, Zechariah. God has heard your prayer.'

My heart was pounding so loudly in my chest that I could hardly hear his words.

'Your wife Elizabeth is soon to be pregnant – you are going to have a son!'

Pregnant? A son? I remember thinking that either he or I were crazy and since angels come from God and are above such things, it must be me. For one thing, Elizabeth was barren – all those years of trying to conceive a child, praying incessantly, and nothing. And now her monthly cycle had all but stopped – it was ludicrous, a complete impossibility. I opened my mouth to speak, but the angel's voice grew stronger and more insistent.

'You must call the baby John . . .'

John? But surely a firstborn son would be named after me? That was my first thought. And if not me, then at least after my father or grandfather.

'This child will bring you joy like you have never known before – joy that everyone will share because they will sense and know that he is one of God's special, chosen men.'

At that, my pounding heart actually missed a beat. Of course, all my life I had prayed fervently that I could do something, anything, special for God and now it seemed as if that prayer was being answered. But it was all so bewildering . . .

'And because of this,' the angel continued, a mite sternly I thought, 'he must never drink wine or spirits – not that he will need them because he will be, from the moment of his conception, filled with God's Holy Spirit!'

The angel's face was so radiant with joy and laughter that had I been in my right mind I too might have smiled and shared in the wonder of that moment. As it was, my head was spinning and I feared I might actually pass out.

'John will grow up to do amazing work for God – he'll be the kind of guy who can get God's message across to people in ways that they will really take on board,' the angel went on.

From outside, the sound of the crowd faded as the prescribed prayers were over; they would now be expecting me to reappear at any second. They would have to wait.

'Because of that, people will be more prepared for the coming of God's Son, the Messiah, which is . . .'

'Wait! Stop!'

Even now I can hear the impatience, the irritation in my voice and the shame and the regret will be with me till the day I die. You know what I said?

'This just doesn't make sense! How can it happen? I'm old, and my wife is past childbearing age. What you're talking about is impossible!'

It was as if the radiance on the angel's face was suddenly clouded. Even the timbre of his voice changed, and the exhalation of his breath turned the air around me suddenly cold.

'I am Gabriel,' the angel said slowly, 'I come from God especially to give you this message. But you won't believe me. And so, from now until your son is born you won't be able to utter a single word. You will be struck totally dumb.'

I opened my mouth to apologise, to plead forgiveness, but I could not make a sound. Not even a guttural groan in my throat. Nothing.

'You say that the time is past for childbearing,' the angel sighed. 'But you're looking at time in a worldly way. Everything I've told you will happen. It will happen in God's time and because God has chosen to make it happen.'

In an instant the sanctuary was empty. And I was alone.

The people outside thought I was ill as I staggered out into the sunlight. They pestered me with questions but of course, I couldn't answer and back then, I hadn't learned to speak with my hands as I can now. But they got the message about one thing.

'He's had a vision!' someone shouted, and then they all took up the cry.

I went home. And when I saw Elizabeth, I broke down. I wrote down everything that had happened, and you know what? She took my hand, she led me to our sleeping space, lay down and wrapped her arms around me.

'Maybe even the Lord will need some help from you,' she smiled. And in her face, I saw total trust – the trust that I had lacked.

Within days, Elizabeth knew she was with child. I didn't ask how. I believed.

Zechariah sat for several moments in deep reflection. Then, shaking his head and pulling at his beard he began silently to weep. From below, the voices of his wife and their visitor could be heard rising in excitement; but for him, this moment demanded something different.

He sank slowly to his knees and prayed.

'My child, my child . . . oh Mary!'

Elizabeth finally released Mary from the rib-crushing hug in which she had enveloped her the instant she stepped over the threshold, and holding her at arms' length, gazed at her with eyes glistening with tears of joy as waves of heat coursed through her body.

'Elizabeth, I have to tell you something . . .' Mary stammered, dropping her eyes and taking a deep breath.

'Oh Mary, you are so, so blessed – and the baby you're carrying . . . he is – what can I say? God's gift to us! And now you, the mother of my Lord – you're here in my house? What have I done to deserve so much joy?'

Mary looked up in astonishment. Elizabeth's arms were lifted heavenwards and the smile on her lips lit up her whole face.

'But . . . how did you know?'

'The second you called my name, the baby – my baby – somersaulted inside me, like a child bouncing with joy! Oh Mary . . . you too – you too have been chosen by God. I don't know *how* I know; I just do! I am right, aren't I?'

Mary, close to tears, nodded.

'What you just said . . .' she stammered.

'Mary, those words just came to me – this child you are carrying – is from God. And you believed and you obeyed . . . oh Mary! You truly are more blessed than anyone I know!'

She grasped Mary's hands and twirled her round, breaking out into peals of laughter.

'Isn't God the most amazing, the most wonderful Father of us all?'

Then, at the sound of footsteps on the outside stairs, she stopped and leaned towards Mary.

'Quickly, let's go outside – let's go for a walk. Zechariah – well, there's a lot you need to know before you see him. And I haven't been further than a few yards from the house for what seems like a lifetime! Come on, before he comes down . . .'

Elizabeth tired quickly. They had only walked a quarter of a mile or so up the uneven hill path before she was out of breath.

'Just give me a few minutes,' she panted, easing herself onto a smooth rock and rubbing her back. 'And then we'll talk.'

Mary walked a short distance, and gazed out over the Judean hills to the high plateau where the city of Jerusalem could be seen faintly through the heat haze. To her left a carpet of blue flax waved in the gentle breeze, its stems turning yellow as the harvest time drew near. The air was heavy with the threat of thunder; a small lizard scurried off a nearby rock as Mary's shadow fell across it and it ran across her toes before disappearing under a convenient stone.

The sense of overwhelming peace that flooded her senses took her by surprise; ever since the angel had visited her, she had felt quite calm about bearing this precious baby – for it was God's child, and he would care for it – but it was a calm that receded rapidly every time she thought about Joseph, about the chattering of the village women, and about the way Leah and Samuel would take the news. Would they think she had gone crazy? Or that she was lying to cover up some unspeakable behaviour?

And then it hit her.

God had chosen her. Out of all the women in the world that he could have picked, he had wanted her to be the mother of his son. And because of that, he would make it alright. Whatever happened, it would be his plan and all she had to do was go with the flow. She was in his hands.

She closed her eyes, lifted her arms way above her head, stretched and felt all the tensions and anxiety of the past ten days fall away from her like the skin falling from a ripe fig.

She began to sing softly to herself, the words springing almost unbidden to her lips and fitting a tune she remembered her mother humming as she milked their goats, the song of Hannah.

> 'I feel such joy, such wonder and happiness
> about the way God has chosen me, just an ordinary girl.
> An ordinary girl, a simple kid
> – but the luckiest girl alive!
>
> The luckiest girl, the luckiest girl, I'm the luckiest girl alive!
> No one is ever going to forget what God –
> the holy, one and only, amazing God – has done for me.
> Never, ever will they forget it!

What God has done for me.
His compassion and understanding wash over us all
like a vast tsunami of love,
never ending, generation after generation,
whenever we turn to him.'

She paused, catching her breath and gazing out over the surrounding countryside with eyes blurry with unshed tears.

'He has always done amazing things
– his power sorts out the boasters and deceivers;
tyrants and cruel men don't stand a chance
when he is on the case,
but the innocent, those who have committed no crime
but who constantly suffer at the hands of others.
They can rely on him one hundred per cent to save them.
He nurtures and nourishes everyone who is in need,
but he doesn't show his face
to those who focus on feeding themselves
and themselves alone.
And look at what he has done for Israel; century after century,
he has given such gifts, been so merciful.
It's all just as he promised, way back in Abraham's time
and right through to this moment now!'

She spun round as a hand touched her shoulder.

'Always the little songbird!' Elizabeth smiled. 'And now I must tell you what's been going on around here over the past months. I was about to say you won't believe it, but of course you will. For God has not been idle with us, either. It was when Zechariah was on temple duty . . .'

'I can hardly take it all in!' Mary gasped, when Elizabeth had finished speaking. 'Your son will be God's messenger? And mine . . .'

She faltered, hardly daring to say the words out loud.

'Mine will be God's own Son. He will be the Message.'

They sat there, two pregnant women, one with skin wrinkled and dotted with age spots, the other fresh faced with eyes the colour of snail shells, and stared at one another. Then, without speaking they joined hands, closed their eyes and held their two futures out to their God in prayer.

So what has that got to do with me?

1. Still on the theme of prayer, Zechariah had been asking God for a child for years and years. Why did God leave it till now to send an angel? Why couldn't he have reassured him way back that one day he'd have a son? Why do you think God sometimes keeps us waiting for a long time before showing us his plans for us?

2. Zechariah was astonished when the angel said that the child should be called John. Immediately he started questioning why the baby would not bear his own name. To us, it may seem extraordinary that after such an amazing revelation, he was thinking about the trivial things – extraordinary, perhaps, until we think of our own reactions. Think about and discuss times when a huge opportunity or challenge faces you and instead of looking at the big picture, you worry or argue over detail. Why do we all do this from time to time?

3. Contrast Zechariah's response to the angel with that of Mary. He says 'How *can* it happen?' Mary asks 'How *will* it happen?' Zechariah says it is impossible. Are we so immersed in the secular, scientific, technological world of today that we can't bring ourselves to believe that God can and does still work miracles? Does this make you angry because you can think of a hundred things you would like God to do for you, your family or friends that he appears to ignore completely; or does it give you hope that in fact he knows every last detail of your needs and aches to fulfil them – in his time?

CHAPTER THREE

Getting the message

> By now Elizabeth's waiting time was over for the time had come for the baby to be born – and it was a boy.
>
> *Luke 1:57, Living Bible*

Elizabeth's baby was born the day before Mary was due to go back to Nazareth. He was a big, lusty boy with a shock of dark hair standing erect on the top of his head.

'He's beautiful,' Mary whispered, squeezing Elizabeth's hand (although secretly she thought him rather ugly, red and scrunched up and angry looking and was convinced that her son would be a great deal more handsome).

'He is, isn't he?' Elizabeth nodded, gazing lovingly at the baby. Zechariah, still robbed of the power of speech, knelt in a corner, silently mouthing a prayer of thanksgiving and turning repeatedly to smile at his wife.

'And think,' Elizabeth whispered to Mary, 'in just a few more months, you too will be cradling your precious gift.'

Mary's hands went instinctively to her stomach, rounded now and visible to even the most untrained eye as that of a pregnant woman.

'And when I get home . . .' For a moment, her voice faltered.

'And when you get home,' Elizabeth interjected emphatically, 'everything will be as God intends. All will be well, child; all will be well.'

Mary nodded. They had discussed this many times and always the same conclusion had been reached. God would sort it.

Mary knew it was true, but knowing it didn't stop her stomach churning at the thought of facing Leah and Samuel. As for Joseph . . .

Suddenly all she wanted was a hug from her mum.

'I shall miss you so much!' Elizabeth exclaimed, hugging Mary tightly to her. 'But you will come next year, yes? With Joseph?'

'If he . . . I mean . . .' Mary stammered.

'Next year with Joseph.' Elizabeth held Mary's gaze as she repeated the words. 'Go in peace.'

Mary climbed up onto Jacob's laden cart, and sat next to Milcah. She had wanted to stay with Elizabeth until the naming ceremony of her baby but Zechariah was adamant that she should take the opportunity to travel with people known both to him and her own family and of course, she had no choice but to bow to his decision.

Zechariah, one arm resting lightly on Elizabeth's shoulder, watched as the cart trundled out of sight. Then turning to his wife, he cupped her face in his hands. If only he could speak! He pointed to the child in her arms, then to his own heart, and then lifted both arms in the air and nodded.

Elizabeth understood at once. Smiling, she turned and together they went into the house. Laying the sleeping baby on a mat in front of them, they bowed their heads and once again offered thanks to God. Anyone passing their doorway would have witnessed a scene of perfect tranquillity. What they could not have imagined were the thoughts and feelings raging inside each of them.

'Lord, I'm sorry – how many more times must I say it? Please give me back the power of speech. You said that when my son was born I would speak but still not a sound utters from my throat. Will John grow up not knowing the sound of his own father's voice? Please Lord. Please.'

'I shall miss her so much, Lord. I know I'm a chatterbox, and I know that there is much joy to be found in silence – but oh Lord my God, with Zechariah mute and my time not yet come to mix with the women again . . . Lord, let him speak. Please. If, of course, it's your will. Please could you make it your will? Thank you.'

'Such a fast recovery . . .'

'You are indeed blessed, Elizabeth . . .'

'Such a handsome boy . . .'

Elizabeth sat cradling her son, still shrieking in fury at the pain of his circumcision, as the villagers gathered round her.

'And his name?' Eunice, one of the older women, asked.

'John,' Elizabeth replied.

'John? John?' Eunice retorted. 'What sort of name is that? There is no John in the child's ancestry. Zechariah would not allow that . . .'

'You speak as if he is not here,' Elizabeth replied mildly, turning to her husband who was scratching furiously at his wax tablet. 'Zechariah?'

He held up the tablet and began to mouth the words written on it.

'His name is John.' His voice echoed round the room.

For an instant no one spoke – and then the room was filled with the babble of excited voices.

'He's got his voice back!'

'It's a miracle!'

'After all this time, and he sounds just as he always did!'

Elizabeth leapt to her feet and hugged her husband.

'As the angel said,' she whispered. 'May God be praised.'

When the guests had left, talking nineteen to the dozen about all they had witnessed, Zechariah picked up the sleeping baby, walked out of the house and stood several metres away, rocking slowly back and forth on his heels. At first, Elizabeth felt irritated – she had only just got John off to sleep; she was still weary from the birth and the excitement of the past few days, and the last thing she needed was for her husband to disturb him before she had had the chance to sit down, just for a moment or two. But when she heard his deep, gravelly voice and saw him standing, face upturned to the heavens, she knew that this was not the moment to interrupt.

She edged to the doorway and listened.

'Lord my God, it's true, isn't it? It's happened. You're coming to save, just like the prophets in the past said you would. We're really going to be saved, aren't we? Saved from our enemies and all those people who've hated and despised us for so long!'

Elizabeth held her breath. She saw the tears glistening on her husband's cheeks but still she didn't move.

'Lord, you've never forgotten your promise to us, have you? Not even when things seemed hard – even when we thought we were in trouble, we weren't, not really – because you were there. We are so lucky to be the ones you have called to serve you. From now on, we needn't be frightened, or worried by the hollow threats of people who hate us – we are free and longing to serve you for as long as we have breath in our bodies!'

As Elizabeth watched, she felt a lump in her throat. Never had she seen an expression of such joy on Zechariah's face, never had he looked so free from anxiety and tension. And it was catching! Despite her age, and the aches and pains and the soreness from the birth, she wanted to jump for joy and clap her hands and tell the whole world that with God in charge, everything comes right in the end!

She was about to call out to her husband, when she heard him speak again.

'And you, John my child, will be called a prophet of God on high.'

He looked down at the baby and gently kissed his forehead.

'I feel it – I feel your destiny deep in my heart. You too are called, I just know it; called to pave the way for the coming of the Lord, called to spell out to people just what it means, just what they need to do to be saved. What a privilege, little one, to tell people that through him they will be saved and all their sins forgiven. Our God is so gentle and forgiving; because of him this country of ours will be restored and a new era, a heavenly time, will break into our world, shining the light of the love of God on people who right now see only gloom and sadness – and leading us all – rich and poor, strong and weak, everyone – into ways of peace together.'

He bowed his head and for several minutes stood motionless and silent. Suddenly, the peace was broken by the frantic bawling of the baby in his arms. Elizabeth smiled. Her son John would, she knew, one day be a great man serving God in whatever way he was called – but right now he was an eight-day-old infant who wanted only one thing. Food. And he wanted it now.

So what has that got to do with me?

1. Mary lived in an age in which she had 'no choice but to bow to' Zechariah's decision about when and with whom she should travel. Society today doesn't put such constraints on women and we have come to take it for granted that we can do pretty much what we like as long as it is within the bounds of the law. How does this affect our choices? Do we consider how our behaviour will look to, or affect, others? Has our freedom made life easier, or more difficult? There are still countries and faiths today in which women are subjected to the will and the decisions of men over issues far more challenging than when to travel. Consider what sort of life restrictions you would find the most challenging? Choice of career? Of what to wear? Of being able to worship openly? Of being educated in a co-educational environment? Of being able to go out with a guy or a girl regardless of their religion, colour or economic status?

2. Mary faced a huge challenge when she left Elizabeth's house to return home and yet she and her cousin had always come to the same conclusion – God would sort it. Do we find it hard to believe that God is still in charge, just as he was then, and if so, why? What is it about our lives today, two thousand years on, that make it hard for us to 'wait and see' what God will do?

3. Zechariah got his voice back when he had written the name of the child on the wax tablet. Why not as soon as the baby was born? What was it about writing his name down that made the difference?

4. The first thing Zechariah did when he regained his voice was to praise God. His words form the Benedictus which is part of the church's liturgy today. But what do they say to us? Can you pick out two or three phrases which apply to the way you would thank God for something he had done for you?

CHAPTER FOUR

A step into the unknown

'You've done wonders with the house, Joseph!'

Eli reined in the ox cart, laden with water jars and newly baked pots, and gazed admiringly as Joseph hung the new wooden door on its leather hinge.

'You've practically doubled its size,' Samuel, Eli's twin brother remarked, with just a hint of jealousy. 'You must have been working flat out.'

'Mary's going to be blown away when she sees it,' Eli said. 'Assuming she ever comes home, of course.'

He leaned down from the cart and gave Joseph a friendly punch on the shoulder.

'You don't know what might be happening . . .'

'Mary will be home any day,' Joseph cut in abruptly, hoping that he sounded more confident than he felt. 'Which is why I need to get on, OK? See you guys around.'

Eli, who had always been an easy going sort of guy, grinned, flicked the leather rein and ordered the ox to shift himself.

'If she needs any more pots you know where to come!' he laughed.

'You bet!' Joseph smiled, already regretting his snappiness.

'So do you think Mary's ever coming home?' he heard Samuel mumble to his brother above the rattling of the cartwheels. He strained his ears, but Eli's reply was swallowed up in the noise of the marketplace.

Suddenly he felt a huge weariness come over him. Every muscle in his body had been aching for the past three days, and his brain felt fuzzy from lack of sleep. Building the second room onto his tiny house in addition to meeting all his usual orders for carpentry and repair work had been time consuming, and hadn't been helped by the unseasonable rain or by the fact that the Romans had demanded another wodge of cash from him in the latest of their raids. They said it was a tax on new building but that was the first he'd heard of such a thing and guessed it was just a device thought up by some ambitious centurion to gain favour with his commander. Not that there was any point in resisting. A flogging at the hands of the Romans could render a man incapable of work for weeks.

All he wanted now was for Mary to come back so that he could take her into his home and begin their future. Despite his weariness, a smile danced across his face. Mary. Mary. He savoured the word as he had done so many times before.

He remembered the day that he had first seen Mary. Well, possibly not the first time his eyes had seen her, but the first moment that she had stirred something inside him. It was shortly after his mother, now living in a world of her own, shut off from reality and unaware of who he or anyone else actually was, had been taken by her sister Lydia to live with her ten miles away. Joseph, torn between relief that he no longer had to leave his work to find her when she wandered off and guilt at the fact that she would be better cared for by someone else, had flung himself into his work. On the death of his father, the carpentry business had become his; his brother Cleopas was the clever one, away in Jerusalem keeping accounts for traders in tin and metal, but that sort of life held no appeal for Joseph. Ever since childhood he had known that his hands had a power of their own; he could mend things, make things, create shapes in his head and then render them in wood and stone – and doing so made him feel alive, fulfilled. It was more than a job; it was what, he was sure, God had made him for.

He had been walking to Abdeel's house to carry out repairs on a broken cart when he'd seen her. She was ambling along the path, swinging an empty bucket in her hand and humming softly under her breath. Two of the village girls, Rebekah and Judith, arms linked and chattering nineteen to the dozen, were with her and as Joseph drew nearer, he saw them nudge one another, glance at him coyly and then drop their eyes, giggling and whispering. Then he realised that Mary had stopped, and was gazing into the distance, almost as if she were in a trance. Rebekah and Judith walked on, but still Mary stood in the middle of the path, motionless. He had stepped off the path onto the grassy hillside to edge past her when his foot caught a stone and he stumbled, the tools in his leather bag rattling against one another.

Mary had gasped and spun round, snapping out of her reverie. Seeing it was Joseph, her face relaxed and she had smiled. At that point, Joseph's heart began behaving in ways unknown to him till then, leaping into his throat and then plunging down into his guts.

'I didn't mean to startle you . . .'

Even his words had raced up and down the scale like those of a kid whose voice was breaking.

'Leah's always saying I need startling into action,' she had laughed. 'So in her book, you've just done me a big favour.'

With a small wave of her free hand, she had turned and hurried down the path to rejoin her friends.

Joseph had watched until they all disappeared out of sight.

That was when he made up his mind that one day, Mary would be his. He had never changed his mind.

Stretching now, and massaging his aching shoulders, he glanced up at the sun. Nearly midday and he'd promised Simon that he would finish the work on his roof today. Breaking off a hunk of bread and spreading it with curd cheese, he stuffed his mouth full, tossed the remainder into his toolbag and headed for the other side of the village.

If he hadn't been on the roof of Simon's house, putting the finishing touches to the fresh plaster, he wouldn't have been there when Mary returned with Milcah's family. But from his vantage point at the end of the main street, he had caught sight of the dust being thrown up by the wheels of the cart, and heard the cries of some of the younger village children as they ran up the road to meet their friends. His first reaction had been to down tools and run down the stairs at the side of the house and go straight to Leah and Samuel's home to greet Mary. But good manners and an awareness that Mary would want some private time with her cousin prevailed – or was it, he asked himself a dozen times later that day – was it God who stilled him and made him wait and watch?

And so he sees the cart pull up outside Leah's house; watches as Samuel and Leah hurry from the doorway to greet Mary. Sees Mary struggle down from the cart, her shawl clutched tightly round her. Smiles as the neighbours come out to greet her, calling her name, eager to hear news of Elizabeth. Feels his chest swell with pride – and yes, with desire – as the girl he is soon to make his wife moves slowly towards the door.

And then he spots little Abigail, Simon's granddaughter, toddle up to Mary and tug at her arm. Mary turns instinctively to hug her, and her shawl blows open and falls to the ground.

And all the calling and the welcoming stops. For a moment, no one moves. Mary stands motionless, Leah's hands dart to her mouth, from somewhere a woman's voice gasps, 'No!'

Then Samuel utters a low guttural cry, turns and strides back into his house gesturing to Leah to follow him, a gesture she has no choice but to obey. The village women clustered together, whispering behind their hands. Joseph moves to the edge of the roof, peering down to see what has caused this abrupt change of mood.

'Leah!'

As Mary calls her cousin's name she steps forward and he sees. The curve of her stomach, plain to see as the wind caught her dress and blew it back. No. No, this isn't happening. Not Mary, not his Mary. He runs down the outside staircase and hovers by the corner of the house. On the breeze, he catches the mutterings of some of the women nearest to him.

'With child . . .'

Everything in him screams a silent 'No!' No, don't you see, it's not that – it's just a slight increase in weight, perhaps Elizabeth has been overfeeding her – maybe she didn't work so hard in Zechariah's house and . . .

But then Mary glances around her at the murmuring women and slowly but firmly places both hands protectively on her stomach. With that gesture, in that moment, any attempt on his part to think rationally flies out the window.

He draws back, desperate not to be seen, turns and begins running blindly in the opposite direction. Runs and runs, his tools abandoned on the roof of Simon's house. Runs till the stitch in his side vies in intensity with the pain in his heart. Eventually, way beyond the village limits, he veers off into an olive grove and sinks to the ground clamping his hands to his face and pulling at the skin of his cheeks. No, no, no! He wants to be sick, he wants to hit someone, he wants to grab hold of Mary and shake her and make her tell him what she had been thinking of. But his Mary – she couldn't have, she wouldn't have . . . A thousand images begin tumbling through his head. Did she meet some opportunist lout in Kerem? But surely Elizabeth and Zechariah would have kept her close to them and besides, no Jewish boy known to such a priestly family would dare . . . oh dear God! The Romans! Did one of them do this to her? Had she been raped? He had heard stories of lascivious Roman soldiers who . . .

He bangs his fists against the side of his head. So that's that, then. He must divorce her, of course – no self-respecting Jewish guy can be seen to have any dealings with a woman who allowed herself to . . .

But what if it wasn't her fault? What if she was powerless at the hands of some brutal thug? Even as he asks himself the question, he knows the answer. No matter what the circumstances, she is soiled goods. Tarnished. Trash. The sooner he rids himself of her the better, because one thing is certain; his business would suffer if he was seen to hesitate, to be weak, to even think of associating for one day more with a girl who was no longer a virgin.

He leans back against a rock, and it's only then that he realises that tears are coursing down his cheeks, and that the palms of his hands are bleeding where he has dug his nails into the flesh. He must go back. He must go straight to Samuel and declare the betrothal to be at an end.

But not yet.

Not till it's dark. He doesn't want to add to the family's shame; if he can just do it quietly and with dignity, suggest perhaps to Leah and Samuel that they send Mary back to Elizabeth until the fuss has died down . . . she's so gentle, Mary – she wouldn't stand a chance here, against all the gossip and worse; he isn't stupid, he knows that there's every chance that she'll be stoned, chased out of the village, her family shunned and treated like lepers.

How could this be happening? A few hours ago, he was planning a new life, the possibility, if God was gracious, of having children, dreaming about being with Mary forever and now . . . nothing but an empty future.

Suddenly, his grief turns to red hot, burning anger. To hell with being kind, to hell with waiting so that the family won't be shamed. He'll go now, he'll say the words that bring an end to his betrothal and he'll shout them loud from the rooftops. Mary didn't think about him so why should he bother about her feelings now?

As he scrambles to his feet, the ground appears to rise before him and then spin. He sinks down again, nauseous and faint. Running in the heat, he tells himself – stupid. He closes his eyes, and breathes deeply. If he just rests for a minute or two – then he'll go, but right now, he's so tired, so, so weary.

> Because Joseph her husband was a righteous man and did not want to expose her to public disgrace, he had in mind to divorce her quietly. But after he had considered this, an angel of the Lord appeared to him in a dream . . .
>
> *Matthew 1:19, 20*

Joseph's eyes were heavy with sleep when he sensed someone dropping to the ground beside him. He stirred, as a hand was laid on his shoulder.

'Don't look so worried . . .'

'You don't have a clue,' Joseph muttered, opening his eyes, and then closing them rapidly as the world spun even faster. 'If you were in my shoes . . .'

'Joseph, Joseph, you're a descendant of David, right? So put all thoughts of denouncing and divorcing Mary out of your mind right now! The baby that your beloved Mary is carrying isn't the result of anything bad or immoral that's happened to her . . .'

'What? What do you know about Mary and . . . ?' Forcing his eyes open, he tried to frame the words but suddenly his lips wouldn't move. The man seemed to be shimmering in a heat haze; in fact he didn't really resemble any of the men from these parts, he was more like . . .

God's messenger. Did the man say that? Or did the words just frame themselves inside his head.

'The child has been conceived by God's Holy Spirit. It's all been planned by God. Mary is carrying God's son.'

God's son? This wasn't making any sense. The sun must have got to him more than he realised.

'She's going to have a little boy, and you will be his earthly father. You must call him Jesus – because he will be the one who saves people – saves them from all their wrongdoing and misguided ways and sinful behaviour.'

The man lent towards him, so close that Joseph could feel his breath on his cheek, felt it drying the moisture of his tears.

'All this is happening so that what the prophets said might be brought to fruition,' he went on. 'You remember? "A virgin will be pregnant and bear a son, and they shall call his name Emmanuel, which means God with us."'

Remember? Of course he remembers – what Jewish guy whose parents had brought him up in the faith wouldn't know about the prophesy, about the Messiah who would save them. But here, now? How could that be?

The man touched Joseph's arm.

'And God is with you, Joseph. He has chosen you, just as he has chosen Mary. So put away your fears, ignore the gossips and do as God wants. It's OK. Do not be afraid.'

It's OK, it's OK, it's OK . . .

The words rang in Joseph's ears, each time growing fainter.

'But . . .'

Thank goodness, he could speak. He said bolt upright and looked around.

The man had gone. And the ground where he had been sitting bore no imprint. The grass was as straight as it had always been.

The sun was sinking behind the hills and still Joseph sat there. He had tried telling himself it was just a dream; he had argued that maybe the effect of the sun and his lack of sleep had made him hallucinate.

And every time he almost managed to convince himself that it was all rubbish, those words seemed to be whispered on the wind.

'God is with you . . . it's OK, it's OK, it's OK . . .'

'OK God, so tell me this; am I going mad?'

His words echoed over the silent hillside and the answer came silently. Suddenly he knew what he had to do. He jumped to his feet, dusted the dried grass from his tunic, buckled his sandals and headed off back to the village. Striding down the main street, he looked neither to left nor right, but focused his eyes on Samuel's house, acutely conscious of the stares of men herding their animals into shelter for the night.

For an instant, he hesitated at Samuel's doorway – then, deciding that this was not the moment for social niceties, he walked boldly in.

'Joseph!' Leah, eyes red rimmed, hastily pulled her head covering over her face. 'I – Samuel – he is on the roof . . .'

But Joseph's eyes were not on Leah, and he hardly heard her words. Mary was sitting in the corner of the room, knees tucked under her and hands folded in her lap. At the sound of his name, she raised her eyes and looked straight at him. Her lips trembled but her piercing blue eyes remained locked on his and in them he read her silent plea.

'Please, believe.'

'Mary.' His voice cracked slightly as he spoke her name.

'Sir.' Mary's reply was decorous.

'I must speak with your guardian – with Samuel,' Joseph said. 'To arrange . . .'

'. . . the annulment.' Samuel appeared in the doorway, hands clenched together and head bowed. 'We understand. The shame that has been brought on this house . . .'

'No!' Joseph cut in. 'I've come to make the arrangements for Mary to move to my home. The new room is almost complete. We must set the day of the marriage.'

It was late by the time Joseph left Samuel's house, a time when normally the street would have been empty of all but a few late returning herdsmen or travellers seeking shelter for the night. The clusters of women hovering in the street did their best to look as if they were there purely by chance – brandishing brooms to sweep outside their doorways, or calling to invisible children – but the nudges and the whispers told Joseph exactly what their main source of interest really was.

'Joseph, dear Joseph . . .' It was Priscilla, the village loudmouth, who crossed the street, her face contorted with the effort of combining what she hoped was an expression of pure compassion with an overwhelming eagerness to hear every detail of Joseph's agony and anger. 'You poor man . . .'

'She will be dealt with.' Joshua, the burly famer whose olive groves supplied the surrounding area with oil and who saw himself as the mover and shaker of the community, threw an arm around his shoulder. 'You can count on that.'

'Little slut!'

'ENOUGH!' Joseph wheeled round and faced the growing cluster of villagers. 'Mary is my betrothed. Tomorrow we will marry.'

'Marry? After she's . . . Joseph, you're insane!' The babble of their protests came at him from all sides.

'What kind of man takes a whore as his wife?' Joshua jeered. 'A wanton . . .'

He choked on his words as Joseph grabbed him by the throat and thrust his elbow into his rib cage.

'Shut it!' he shouted. 'If you – if any of you – ever say one word, one syllable, against Mary ever again, you will have to answer to me.'

'But Joseph,' Priscilla ventured, 'the shame, the . . .'

'The only shame we need to worry about, Priscilla, is the shame of going against God's will. And this child is . . . is . . .'

His courage failed him. He released his grip on Joshua and shoved him away.

'And this child is to be reared as my own. The subject is closed.'

With that, he turned and walked as fast as he could without actually breaking into a run until he reached his own home. Sinking to his knees, he beat the side of his head with his fists, and rocked back and forth.

'Lord God Almighty, I don't know how to do this. But if this really is your doing, and your will, then Lord all I pray is that you will give me the strength, that you will take away these feelings of anger and fear so that I can be what it is you want me to be. I'm scared, Lord. Scared of tomorrow, of what might happen to Mary – to me. Lord be with us, I pray. Please.'

So what has that got to do with me?

1. Why do you think the author switches from the past to the present tense as Joseph watches the return of Mary, and keeps us in the present tense until he falls asleep?
2. Today, pregnancy outside of marriage is not deemed to be a problem by large sections of society, but in Mary's time it was shameful. Why would God put her in this difficult position, and why would he choose to inflict the situation on Joseph? Could it be that he chooses strong individuals to carry out his will in the hardest situations? Are we able to look at huge, and unwanted, challenges in this light?
3. As Joseph battles with the thought of Mary being pregnant by someone else, what signs of his innate sense of justice do we see? What questions does he ask himself that tell us that he is the kind of guy who tries to think things through? What happens when his anger finally gets the better of him and he decides to denounce Mary from the rooftops? What prevents him doing this? Do we remember any situations in which God has 'taken us to the wire' before intervening?
4. When the angel asks Joseph whether he remembers the prophesy about the coming of the Messiah, Joseph's first thought is 'Surely not here, not now?' Why do we often feel reluctant about believing that God could actually use us to fulfil one of his plans? Why do we believe that much of what we read in Scripture applies to another place, another time, another people? Could it be fear of it applying to us? Could it be our own feelings of inadequacy, a belief that God couldn't possibly think of involving us? And if so what can we do about these feelings which just might be shutting our ears to God's word?
5. Frequently in the Bible, angels (God's messengers) tell people not to be afraid. We are tempted to think 'Yeah, right! What's not to be scared about?' Challenging situations bring up feelings of fear in most of us. How do we react when people tell us not to be afraid but to trust in God? Does this help when our loved ones are sick or

dying? When we, or one of our parents, lose a job or get chucked out of school? When money is so tight that we can't even afford to go out with our friends? When everyone else at school has a best mate and we're always on our own? Think of a situation about which you are currently fearful and discuss how the words 'do not be afraid' make you feel right now.

6. Joseph faced a crowd who were 'on his side'. It would have been easy for him to accept their sympathy, have second thoughts about taking Mary as his wife, and go back on the decision he'd had such a struggle to reach. Sometimes standing against the crowd is really hard; especially in situations where to agree with them would mean having a whole group of people ready to fight our corner. What gives Joseph the strength to go against the conventions of his day? What situations can you think of that would put you in a similar position? And who are the people most likely to be like the neighbours in Nazareth?
7. When Joseph returned home, he prayed to God. He doesn't use fancy words and he doesn't try to pretend that he is someone he is not. He admits that he is scared, and fearful and he prays for strength. How often do we feel able to go to God and let it all out? Shout at him? Cry with him? Do we think we have to use a prayer book, or use long words? If so, why?
8. 'Joseph was a righteous man' – what evidence is there of his 'righteousness' in this chapter?

CHAPTER FIVE

He comes!

> In those days Caesar Augustus issued a decree that a census should be taken of the entire Roman world. (This was the first census that took place while Quirinius was governor of Syria.) And everyone went to his own town to register.
>
> *Luke 2:1-3*

'I can't leave you here, Mary, not with the way things are.' Joseph ran his fingers through his matted hair and chewed his lip. 'There's nothing for it – you must come to Bethlehem with me.'

For once, Mary was grateful to the Romans and their dictatorial way of doing things. Her first few weeks as Joseph's wife had been far from easy; many of the village women cut her dead when she went to the well, and only a handful deigned to speak as they passed her doorway. Joseph, too, had had to put up with snide remarks from several customers at his workshop.

'Mary?' Joseph's voice was taut with tension. 'Are you listening? Do you understand what I'm saying?'

'Of course,' Mary nodded. 'The Emperor has called for a census and everyone has to go back to their birthplace – so we're off to Bethlehem!'

'You make it sound like a pleasure trip!' Joseph grunted. 'Normally, I'd suggest you stayed with Leah but – well, she's not been well, Samuel's getting more frail and I don't want to leave you unprotected. On the other hand, it's a five day journey and you've only got a few weeks before the baby . . .'

'A few weeks!' Mary laughed. 'We'll be back in plenty of time – plenty of time for you to finish that beautiful crib!'

Joseph smiled and laid a hand on her shoulder.

'I do love you, Mary,' he whispered. 'Now I must get on – there's a lot to get ready and we can't afford to waste time.'

Just ignore it, Mary told herself sternly. It's far too soon. You've just got cramp from sitting on the donkey too long.

'I think I'll walk for a bit, Joseph,' she called over the clattering of the donkey's hooves on the rutted track. 'I need to stretch my legs.'

Joseph helped her down and eyed her anxiously. 'You're OK?'

'Fine,' she replied, biting the inside of her cheek as another twinge gripped her. 'Let's keep going – is that Bethlehem over there on the hill?'

Joseph nodded. 'Another hour and we'll be there,' he said encouragingly. 'We'll go straight to my cousin Benjamin's house and you can rest.'

Rest. That would be good. The journey had been more taxing than she had anticipated. At first, they had found lodgings on the way – at Megiddo, and Ibleam, and even at Shechem, although that place was crowded and smelly and not a comfortable place to be. But by the time they reached Shiloh, the road was heaving with people heading for Bethlehem, and they had been forced to sleep outside; or rather not sleep, since the carousing and noise from some of the families nearby prevented anything but the lightest doze. She was tired; bone weary.

Now these pains were gripping her, getting worse by the hour. Surely it was too soon? But it was in God's hands. He wouldn't let anything go wrong. He would know it wasn't time yet. Wouldn't he?

Half an hour later, as the water gushed down her legs, Mary realised beyond a shadow of a doubt that it was time.

'Joseph! Help me!' Her knees buckled under her as a pain more intense than any she had ever known took her breath away.

'Mary, what is it? What's wrong? It's not – it can't be – not the baby?'

Mary, unable to speak, merely nodded and gripped his hand with all her might. 'I've got to lie down,' she gasped as the pain eased. 'How far is it to Benjamin's house?'

'It's the other side of the town,' Joseph replied. 'About a mile.'

'I can't go that far,' Mary groaned. 'The pains – they're getting worse.'

'But you said we had a few weeks to go and . . .'

'Well, clearly I was wrong,' Mary retorted. 'That, or this baby has other ideas. God's in charge, remember and he . . . Aarrgh . . . !'

'We will find the *kataluma*,' Joseph told her, trying to keep the panic out of his voice.

Mary's heart sank. Everyone had a *kataluma* of sorts – a small room on the flat roof, or a corner set aside to offer accommodation to passing travellers, but she knew that at this busy time every private household would be full. The alternative would be one of the campsites and that she just couldn't face.

'I don't want to be in a crowd,' Mary pleaded. 'Please – just find a cave, a shack, anywhere – but please, hurry.'

Between pains she stumbled along at Joseph's side, gripping his arm and biting down hard until she drew blood from her lower lip.

The instant they reached the first house on the outskirts of the town, Joseph banged on the door, only to realise too late that it was barred from the outside and weeds were already growing in the crevices of the wall.

He ran ahead, shouting for help while Mary, panting for breath and reciting every prayer she had ever learned, lent against the donkey, who conveniently seemed more interested in a clump of grass than his mistress's distress.

'Help me, please! I can feel the baby, it's coming, I know it's coming . . .' Mary cried.

'Now don't you worry, my dear!' An elderly woman, as wide as she was high, bustled over to Mary, cast an experienced eye over her and turned to Joseph, who was following meekly behind.

'What were you thinking of, dragging this poor lass about in her condition?' the woman demanded. 'Honestly, you men – you don't have a clue!'

'Aaaargghh!' Mary's cry of agony froze any reply that Joseph might have made. Wrapping his arm around her, he took all her weight and together they stumbled along following the woman around the back of a small house.

'I'm Shamira,' the woman said. 'And you're lucky – I'm a midwife!'

'Really?' Relief flooded Mary's face. 'Could we . . . ?'

'I can't have you inside,' Shamira went on apologetically. 'My husband's mother died last night and our *kataluma* is full of relatives and besides, you'll need food and . . . anyway, you can stay here.'

She gestured to a crumbling stone shelter built onto the side of the house.

'Matthias built that in the days when we had more animals than we could manage downstairs,' she sniffed. 'But these days, what with the taxes and the Romans and . . .' Her words were drowned in another groan from Mary, whose face was beaded with sweat.

'It's coming . . .'

'I'll get water. You . . .' She poked Joseph in the ribs. 'Lay her down on the straw, and I'll bring blankets.'

'Thank you, thank you so much,' Mary gasped.

'Don't you bother thanking me,' the woman smiled. 'Just you get on and deliver that baby. My, but it's in a hurry to get here. I shouldn't wonder if it's a girl – they always come fastest.'

'Oh no, it's a boy . . .'

'Bless her,' the woman whispered to Joseph. 'Hope over experience, that's what that is. I know these things. Let's hope she's not disappointed. I'll go and get that water.'

> And there were shepherds living in the fields nearby, keeping watch over their flocks by night.
>
> *Luke 2:8*

'I'm getting too old for this,' Zebulun sighed, pulling his sheepskin mantle more tightly round his shoulders. 'My bones ache at the best of times and this cold just makes matters worse.'

'Oh stop moaning,' Asher muttered. 'It's not like we have any choice in the matter. Don't see the master deciding to come up here and watch his own sheep!'

'I said last week it was time to take the sheep down from the hills but would any of you listen? Oh no – you knew best. I said we were in for a cold spell. I could tell it from the state of my knees.'

Asher ignored him and looked up at the cloudless night sky, peppered with stars.

'You know what? There's something odd about the sky tonight . . .'

'Oh, you're not going off on one of your fanciful star gazing moments, are you?' Zebulun teased. 'I don't know what you see in lying on your back night after night imagining pictures in the sky! No wonder you lost that ram last week – you're supposed to concentrate . . . my God! What's that?'

He pointed a grubby finger upwards and then flinched, and threw his arm across his face, shielding his eyes from a sudden burst of piercingly bright white light.

Asher leapt to his feet, and grabbed his crook, waving it frantically and backing off as a figure appeared out of the light. From behind them came strangled cries as some of the younger shepherds who had been sitting on a rock playing jacks jumped to their feet.

'Don't be scared!'

The figure seemed amused at the commotion he had caused.

'Who . . . what?' Zebulun appeared to have lost the power of coherent speech.

'He's . . . got . . . wings,' Asher stammered grabbing Zebulun's arm. 'It's an angel!'

The angel smiled.

'I've come to give you wonderful news,' he said. 'Not just for you, for everyone in the world! Tonight, over there, in Bethlehem, David's own city, the Saviour, Christ the Lord, has been born!'

The men stared at the angel open-mouthed. Two of the boys who had been playing crept nearer and one of them – Justus, always the brash and confident one – took a deep breath.

'Is this for real?'

The angel turned to him.

'You'll know it's for real when you see him; you'll find him wrapped in swaddling clothes and lying in a feeding trough.'

At that he rose up with hands heavenwards, his fingers splayed outwards. For a moment it looked as if sparks were flying upwards and then, suddenly, the whole sky lit up and a host of angelic beings streamed above their heads. The sounds of the night – the bleating of the sheep, the distant howling of a wolf, the trickling of a stream over nearby rocks – were all blotted out by the joyful calls of the angels.

'Glory to God in the highest and on earth, peace on all on whom his gift of love rests.'

The light in the sky grew brighter and brighter until the shepherds could no longer keep their eyes open – the glare was too much.

Then, suddenly, silence.

The skies were empty, just a few stars twinkling in the black expanse.

'Tell me that just didn't happen,' Asher said.

'It did,' Zebulun breathed.

'So come on, let's go!' Justus urged them. 'Let's see whether we're all going mad or whether there is a baby in Bethlehem.'

'We can't just leave the sheep,' Asher protested. 'You want to lose your job?'

'Well, I'm going,' Justus said. 'Timothy! Tim-oh-thee! Benjamin – over here.'

He called to the two youngest boys who were standing, wide-eyed and shaking, staring at the sky.

'Watch the flock,' he ordered. 'Mine, not just yours – all of them. We're going down into the town.'

'He's so beautiful.'

Mary gazed at the squalling baby and touched his cheek with the tip of her finger. Shamira had left them, having done all that was necessary; cutting the cord, bathing the baby and rubbing salt on his body to cleanse him from risk of infection.

It was the salt rub that had caused him to yell. And as Shamira swaddled him in linen cloths that she had brought from the house, his protests had grown even louder. Mary undid her robe and put him to her breast. The crying ceased in an instant.

'Jesus,' Joseph murmured, watching him suck furiously. 'You shall call his name Jesus.'

There were tears in his eyes.

'Hello, little Jesus,' Mary whispered. 'I'm your Mummy.'

She glanced up as Joseph turned and walked to the door of the shelter, his back to them both.

'Joseph?'

Nothing.

'Joseph, what is it?'

Joseph sighed, turned and came towards her. Dropping to his knees beside her, he stretched out a tentative hand and took one of Jesus' tiny hands in his huge, calloused one.

'What am I to do?' he asked. 'I want to be a father to him. But I can't be. I'm not his father. God – God is his father. I feel – well, I guess I feel redundant.'

'Now listen to me,' Mary replied firmly. 'Jesus is God's son, we know that. And God chose you to be his father here on earth. Day by day. Good times and bad. We're *in* God's hands, but we have to *be* God's hands too.'

'So – you think he'll look on me as a dad?' Joseph didn't sound convinced.

'Of course,' Mary said. 'Who will it be who teaches him the Torah? Who will it be that plays with him, makes toys for him . . .'

'I could make him a horse with wheels, and maybe when he's a bit bigger, a hoop. He could help me in the workshop and . . .'

Mary burst out laughing. 'Maybe not just yet,' she smiled. 'Joseph, you're going to be a brilliant father.'

She bit her lip and looked up at him. 'I just pray that God will show me how to be a good mother to his son,' she murmured.

'Seems like you're doing the right thing,' Joseph smiled. 'Look, he's fast asleep. You look exhausted; let me lie him down over here and then you can get some rest.'

He took the baby gently from Mary's arms and carried him over to the stone feeding trough against the opposite wall. Scooping fresh straw with one hand from a pile under the manger, he filled it to the brim and laid Jesus down. The baby didn't stir.

'And now, sleep,' he said turning to Mary. 'If we . . . what on earth . . . ?'

Joseph spun round as a shadow fell over them. Standing in the doorway to the shelter were five scruffy, weatherbeaten men and a couple of young boys. Their sheepskin mantles were grimy, and the older men were panting heavily.

'I'm sorry, you can't come in,' Joseph began, eyeing them with a certain amount of distaste. 'My wife . . .'

'There's a new baby, right?' Zebulun cut straight to the point. 'We're sorry, sir, but we were told to come.'

'Told? By whom?'

Zebulun dropped his eyes and shifted his weight. 'OK, now don't go thinking we're crazy or anything but there was this angel . . .'

'He's not lying,' Asher cut in briskly.

Joseph nodded slowly. 'An angel,' he smiled. 'They do get about a bit, don't they?'

'Joseph!' Mary stifled a giggle and turned to the shepherds. 'You've come to see Jesus? He's over there, but please be very quiet. He's sleeping.'

The men tiptoed self-consciously towards the manger and peered in.

'He's so small,' Asher murmured.

'Do you think this is the right baby?' another asked tentatively. 'I mean, the angel said he was Christ the Lord.'

He dropped his voice and nudged Asher in the ribs, jerking his head in the direction of Joseph and Mary.

'Those two don't look like a lordly lot to me.'

'Angels don't get it wrong,' Justus broke in assertively.

'Oh, like you have a lot of conversations with heavenly beings, do you?' Zebulun murmured. 'But no. You're right. Remember what else the angel said?'

The others nodded.

'This baby would be a Saviour for us all,' Asher replied. 'For us all. And that must include the likes of us because why else would the angel choose to come to us?'

'He is,' Mary broke in gently, stifling a yawn, 'a gift from God. And thank you for coming to see him.'

'And now,' Joseph said firmly, 'I must ask you to leave. My wife needs to rest.'

'I can't wait to tell that lot in the village about this,' Asher interjected. 'This will make them sit up and take notice. Won't be so eager to turn their noses down at us now, will they?'

'I'm sure they'll manage it,' Zebulun remarked ruefully. 'But I don't care – God chose us, not them! Praise be to him!'

So what has that got to do with me?

1. The Christmas carol that we all learn as children speaks of 'Little Lord Jesus, no crying he makes'. How unrealistic is that? If Jesus came to earth in human form, he came with all the human reactions – and have you ever come across a baby who doesn't yell when it's hungry or needs a cuddle or a nappy change? Why do we sanitise the Christmas story? Mary went through labour and that's a painful process. Do you think people relate better to the story when they realise that everything Mary and Joseph and the baby experienced is the same as the things we experience today? Think about aspects of the story of the Nativity as told by the author that don't appear in the Bible. Why do you think the author wanted to explore the minor characters and their reaction to what was happening?

2. When Joseph expresses anxiety about his role as a father to Jesus, Mary says 'God chose you to be his father here on earth. Day by day. Good times and bad. We're *in* God's hands, but we have to *be* God's hands too.' In what ways can we be God's hands today? What about being his ears and eyes? If you think about the past week, when do you think you were being hands, ears and eyes for God? Can you think of occasions when you might have missed the opportunity to be just that? And if so, what stopped you?

3. Over and over again in the story of Jesus' life, it is the ordinary people who feature as being vital to the fulfilling of God's purpose. Sometimes we try to be modest about our own God-given gifts; we underestimate what we could achieve because we will all, always, know people who are cleverer or more confident than we are. But God uses every one of us if only we will let him. What would be your first step towards letting God use you? Think of one thing that you believe he could use right now, today? Don't be modest – say it like it is!

4. Throughout the Bible, we read of people praising God out loud and yet sometimes we feel embarrassed about vocalising what God has done for us. It seems fine to mutter a prayer of thanks

under our breath, but quite something else to dash around school or our workplace or down our street, telling everyone we bump into that God's done something stunning in our lives. Why are we like that? Do you feel embarrassed about speaking of your faith? Many of us do – why is that? Why is it commonplace in some cultures and faiths to speak openly of faith every day and yet for many Christians it is a bridge too far? When someone rubbishes Christianity or says that God doesn't exist, how does it make you feel? How do you respond? Would you like your response to be different?

CHAPTER SIX

Another journey

'Benjamin, you've been so generous to us!' Joseph slapped his cousin affectionately on the shoulder. 'As soon as we are back from the Temple, we will pack up and be out of your way, I promise!'

'There's no rush,' Dinah, his wife, smiled. 'It's been so lovely having you and the little one here – I just wish you'd come straight to us after Jesus was born.'

'How could we?' Mary protested. 'For seven days I was unclean and . . .'

'Well, if you ask me,' Dinah said sternly, 'there are some rules that shouldn't apply to family. I mean, you out there in that shack . . .'

'We were fine,' Mary assured her. 'Shamira took good care of us.'

'Yes, she is a good woman,' Dinah agreed. 'But I'm glad you came to us as soon as you could.' She picked Jesus up and gave him a hug. 'I shall miss you, baby.'

'Don't worry – when we come to Jerusalem for the Passover, we'll call in to see you,' Mary smiled. 'I promise.'

'Now you just take care today,' Benjamin added. 'And may God go with you. You have enough money for the sacrificial doves?'

Joseph nodded. In truth, it was a struggle; nearly seven weeks away from home had meant no income. He had never planned to be away for that long but once Mary had given birth, she couldn't leave the house or travel until she was purified.

'A great moment for you,' Benjamin continued. 'Last month, you named your son at his circumcision; today your wife attends her purification and you present your firstborn son at the Temple. A wonderful day!'

For a moment a shadow passed across Joseph's face as a mixture of emotions took him by surprise. This precious baby was God's son and yet all he could afford to offer at the temple was a couple of pigeons; money just wouldn't stretch to doves, never mind a whole lamb. He knew that would be enough for Mary to be declared clean again by the priest but he wished he could have done better.

And then there were those words of Benjamin's – words spoken in all innocence. 'Your firstborn son.' Mary's son, God's son – but not his. And yet, he was to be the child's father here on earth. Could he do it? What if . . .

Mary touched his hand, and nodded at him encouragingly. Looking into her trusting eyes, he smiled. 'Indeed, Benjamin,' he said. 'Indeed it is a wonderful day.'

When the time of their purification according to the Law of Moses had been completed, Joseph and Mary took him to Jerusalem to present him to the Lord (as it is written in the Law of the Lord, 'Every firstborn male is to be consecrated to the Lord'), and to offer a sacrifice in keeping with what is said in the Law of the Lord: 'a pair of doves or two young pigeons'. Now there was a man in Jerusalem called Simeon, who was righteous and devout. He was waiting for the consolation of Israel, and the Holy Spirit was upon him. It had been revealed to him by the Holy Spirit that he would not die before he had seen the Lord's Christ. Moved by the Spirit, he went into the temple courts. When the parents brought in the child Jesus to do for him what the custom of the Law required, Simeon took him in his arms and praised God, saying: 'Sovereign Lord, as you have promised, you now dismiss your servant in peace. For my eyes have seen your salvation, which you have prepared in the sight of all people, a light for revelation to the Gentiles and for glory to your people Israel.' The child's father and mother marveled at what was said about him. Then Simeon blessed them and said to Mary, his mother: 'This child is destined to cause the falling and rising of many in Israel, and to be a sign that will be spoken against, so that the thoughts of many hearts will be revealed. And a sword will pierce your own soul too.' There was also a prophetess, Anna, the daughter of Phanuel, of the tribe of Asher. She was very old; she had lived with her husband seven years after her marriage, and then was a widow until she was eighty-four. She never left the temple but worshiped night and day, fasting and praying. Coming up to them at that very moment, she gave thanks to God and spoke about the child to all who were looking forward to the redemption of Jerusalem.

Luke 2:22-38, NIV

'Mary, are you OK?' Joseph took his wife's arm and eyed her anxiously. 'You're very pale.'

'No, no, I'm fine,' Mary assured him, adjusting the shawl around Jesus as the breeze strengthened. 'I was just – well, it's been a big day – my purification and Jesus' being consecrated . . . and . . .' She faltered.

'There's more to it than that,' Joseph replied. 'I know you too well – something's troubling you.'

'No really . . .'

'Was it something the priest said when he took you to one side?'

He stopped, tipped Mary's chin with his finger and smiled gently. 'It was, wasn't it? Come on, spit it out.'

'He said . . .' She hesitated. 'He said that Jesus had been chosen by God and that he will save many souls.'

She dropped her eyes. It wasn't the whole truth, but she knew that Joseph was still struggling to take on board everything that had happened in the past few months and she didn't want to burden him with worries about what the future might hold for them all.

'Well, that's wonderful, isn't it?' Clearly Joseph wasn't taken in. 'What else?'

Mary thought fast. How could she tell him that Simeon had said people would speak out against her beloved son. How could she utter those frightening words – '*and a sword will pierce your own soul too*'. 'That old lady,' she murmured. 'The one who kept watching us and pointing us out to everyone, saying . . .'

'. . . that child over there is the gift of God, the Saviour of us all!' Joseph finished. 'She was Anna.'

Mary looked at him in surprise. 'How do you know?'

'While you were in that huddle with Simeon, I asked one of the other priests. To be honest I felt a bit conspicuous standing there, with her pointing and nudging people and smiling from ear to ear at everyone.' He sighed. 'The priest said she lives in the temple – spends all her time praying and fasting. He clearly had a huge amount of respect for her. He said she was one of the truly faithful.' He looked at Mary. 'Was that what was troubling you?'

'I knew she was talking about the baby,' she admitted. 'And I feel bad. I should have taken him over to her but . . . well, I just wanted to go. Is that really bad of me?'

Joseph put his arm around her shoulders and gave her a hug. 'Of course not,' he said. 'You were right. It's been a long day. Let's go home.'

From Simeon to my dear grandson

I saw them climbing the fifteen steps that lead up to the Gate of Nicanor – and I knew. This was the child. This was the infant I, Simeon, priest of the Temple, had been shown by the Holy Spirit; the child that God had promised to show me before my time to go to him came around.

Now I guess that sounds strange to you, my dear boy, because heaven knows, we see enough babies here. And there was nothing to single this one out from all the others. Don't get me wrong: he was a cute enough little chap, and the parents clearly idolised him, but he was just another Jewish babe to look at. But still I knew.

Oh yes, I can hear you thinking 'Grandfather's gone off on one again,' but this is so important that I have to write it down for you. You have to try to understand. You see, in that moment, everything that had happened in the previous seventy-eight years was as nothing. As the child's mother handed her precious bundle to me for the ritual of the law to be carried out, her eyes met mine. In them I saw it all; the love of God, the love of the child, the weight of responsibility, and the knowledge, buried deep but always there, of the pain to come. And the reason I could see it had nothing to do with me; it was a gift of insight given to me by God.

My voice cracked as I blessed the child – the emotion was almost too much to bear. I remember that the words just poured from my lips, almost without my thinking them first.

'God, you can let me, your servant, die now. Release me in peace as you promised. With my own eyes, I've seen your salvation; it is now out in the open for everyone to see. A God-revealing light to the non-Jewish nations, and of glory for your own people Israel.'

I remember that Mary and Joseph seemed speechless with amazement at what I was saying; Joseph, poor chap, looked somewhat out of his depth! He reminded me a bit of your father, God rest his soul. Anyway, I blessed them both and then I took Mary a few steps to one side. I didn't really know how to put what I had to say to her, but the Holy Spirit urged me on. I took a deep breath.

'Mary,' I said. 'This child is chosen by God – to destroy and to save thousands of people in Israel. He will be a visible sign from God – yet many will speak against him and misunderstand him and by their behaviour, show themselves up for what they really are.'

She was watching me closely, her eyes shining with unshed tears. She was completely still, but I noticed that the edge of her sleeve shook as her hands trembled. I knew I had to tell the whole truth. I didn't want to but God drove me on and the words poured out.

'Sorrow, like a sharpened sword, will break your own heart.'

For an instant, I held Mary's gaze. Then I laid my hand on her head, blessed her again, turned and left them. My job was done.

Samuel, my dear, only grandson, my time is nearly over. Already I feel the strength leaving my body, and even the effort of putting stylus to tablet is becoming too much. I have written this for you because you are blessed. Blessed to live in the time of the Saviour. Tell the news. Tell your children when you have them.

Enough. My love and blessings, Samuel, on you and all you love and will love. Simeon.

As they had approached the village of Nazareth, weary after the journey home from Bethlehem, Mary had felt the apprehension rising. Her heart beat faster, and her stomach swirled with nausea reminiscent of the early days of her pregnancy. Joseph, too, she knew was feeling the pressure; the anxiety as to how the villagers, their friends, would treat them now.

'It's Mary! Mary's back!' Rebekah's shouts brought others running from doorways – Anna and Judith, Deborah and then, hesitating for just an instant, Leah. Without realising what she was doing, Mary drew the sleeping Jesus closer to her breast, gently flicking away a fly that had landed on his arm.

'Mary – oh Mary!' Leah ran towards her, stumbling as she almost tripped over her own feet. 'Are you alright? And the baby? The birth? I said you shouldn't go but would you listen? No of course not – and all those days we had worrying until we had news . . . but oh, come, let me see him.'

Mary handed Jesus to her cousin and glanced up at Joseph.

'And you, Mary? Are you eating well? The child needs good milk and . . .'

'Leah, relax!' Mary laughed. 'I'm fine, Jesus is fine . . .'

'Jesus? That's his name? Jesus. Jesus.' She nodded. 'Yes, I like it. Jesus will do very well, very well indeed.'

'Can I hold him? Please?' Judith pleaded.

'No, me first!' Anna protested.

'All in good time,' Joseph cut in. 'But now, we're going home. We've had a long journey and Mary's tired and . . .'

'Joseph.' Leah's voice shook.

He turned enquiringly towards her.

'Thank you,' she whispered, so softly that even Mary had difficulty hearing her words. 'Thank you for – well, for everything, for taking care of Mary. And I'm sorry.'

Mary prayed that Joseph would understand what a huge effort it was for Leah to apologise.

Joseph stepped forward and clasped her bony hands in his. 'I will take care of her, and of her – our – son for as long as I have breath in my body,' he said.

Joseph had never missed celebrating Passover in Jerusalem, and when Jesus was sixteen months old, he took his family with him. The previous year, when Jesus was still a baby, Mary had stayed at home; the child had been fretful and the weather unseasonably cold and wet, and everyone agreed it would be wrong to expose Jesus to the risk of disease and chill.

So this trip was doubly exciting – not least because they planned to keep their promise and spend a few days in Bethlehem with Benjamin and Dinah. Joseph had sent word to them by one of the traders whose cartwheel he had mended the week before; he needed no reply – he knew how thrilled his relatives would be to see the baby.

'He's not a baby any more,' Mary had laughed. 'He can walk – well, OK, stagger, and he babbles away nineteen to the dozen . . .'

'And he says "Abba",' Joseph said proudly. No matter what, Jesus saw him as Daddy and that was enough for him.

'And he says it far more often than he says "Mama",' Mary smiled, and then sighed.

'Don't worry,' Joseph urged. 'He'll be saying that every day soon and . . .'

'No, no, that's not what I was thinking,' she replied.

'What then?'

'Just . . . oh, nothing. Come on, we need to pack.'

Their arrival in Bethlehem after the Passover celebration was less joyous than they had hoped. The moment Dinah saw them she broke down in tears.

'It's Benjamin,' she sobbed. 'He took a fever and now that's passed but he's . . .' She paused, clearly searching for the right words.

'He's what?' Joseph urged gently as little Jesus clutched at his leg.

'Different,' Dinah sighed. 'He forgets things; he asked me only this morning what I was doing in his house.' She shook her head anxiously. 'And yesterday, those hateful Romans came careering down the street demanding their latest handout . . .'

Mary had never heard Dinah sound so bitter.

'. . . and Benjamin, my strong, go-getty Benjamin, he was whimpering in a corner like a little child.'

'We will go,' Joseph said. 'You have enough to cope with . . .'

'No! Please stay, at least one night. Only . . .'

'Yes?'

'Benjamin insists on sleeping on the roof – when he is down here he says the walls are closing in on him. So I'm afraid I must ask you to sleep here.' She gestured to the corner of the room where rolled sleeping mats were stacked. 'It's just that I can't risk upsetting . . .'

'Of course we will sleep down here,' Mary assured her. 'And don't worry – we will be gone first thing in the morning.'

'And now,' Dinah smiled, wiping her eyes and crouching down to Jesus' level, 'let me take a look at this little fellow. Oh Mary, but he's beautiful . . . !'

It was pitch dark when Mary woke with a jolt. 'Joseph? Joseph!' She nudged her husband in the ribs.

'What? Who . . . is it Jesus?'

'No, he's fine – he's asleep. But there's someone outside.'

'What? Oh Mary, this is Bethlehem – there's always someone coming and going. For that you wake me up?'

'No, listen!'

Joseph sighed and propped himself up on his elbow. From beyond the wooden door, slightly open because of a broken hinge, came the sound of voices, getting louder by the second.

'You're right – and they're strangers.' Joseph was on his feet, fastening his tunic. 'Can't understand a word they're saying.'

'Get rid of them,' Mary urged. 'They'll only wake Benjamin and you know what Dinah said about how easily he gets upset.'

Joseph opened the door a fraction wider, and then took a step backwards. 'Who . . . ?'

'Please, we mean you no harm. We have come because of the star. The child?' The man who spoke was strangely dressed, and his belted tunic and full sleeves were of a rich material, albeit covered in dust and grime. Behind him stood a cluster of other men, none of whom said a word. 'Please – the baby?'

'What are you saying?' Joseph found the man's attempt at Hebrew hard to understand.

At that moment, Jesus woke up and whimpered.

'Yes!' The man's face lit up and he turned to his companions. 'This is right. He is here!' He stepped into the room, bowing respectfully to Joseph.

'I don't think . . .' Joseph stammered.

'It's alright.' Mary sounded calm. 'They've come to see Jesus, I'm sure of it.' She sat on a low stool and lifted Jesus onto her lap. The visitor dropped down onto one knee, and looked up at his companions. At once, they did the same. The toddler bounced up and down with satisfaction at being the centre of attention.

'Me – I called Melchior. He Caspar, he Balthazar.' Melchior gestured to his companions, and then nodded to the shorter of the three. 'Caspar?'

The man turned and took a bag from his friend's hand. Opening it, he drew out three boxes, richly encrusted with jewels. Both Mary and Joseph gasped in amazement.

'These gifts we bring for him your baby in honour of.'

The sentence structure was all wrong but Mary got the message. 'For Jesus? These are for him?' She used hand gestures to help him understand.

The man nodded. 'Is gold, is frankincense, is . . . is . . .'

Joseph leaned forward and sniffed. 'Myrrh,' he murmured, looking at Mary. 'That's myrrh. How odd . . .'

Mary said nothing. She looked at the three men, and then down at the baby who was happily playing with a tassel on the visitor's tunic. 'Thank you,' she whispered. 'But . . . how did you find us?'

More gestures were needed before the visitor understood. When he did, he clapped his hands and burst out laughing. 'The star of course!' he chuckled.

'You followed the stars?' Joseph asked. 'But . . .'

Melchior waved a hand in the air to stop him. 'No – new star. Big. Over house.' He moved towards the door, indicating to Joseph and Mary to follow him. The night air was crisp and the sky was cloudless. A carpet of twinkling stars spread across the heavens like a twinkling trail left by a giant snail. But as their gaze followed Melchior's pointing finger, they saw one huge star, brighter than all the others, right above Benjamin's house. 'The star,' Melchior whispered. 'Like we told Herod.'

'Herod?'

That was one name that needed no translation.

'You have come from Herod?' Joseph sounded alarmed, and seized Mary's arm, backing off from the man.

'Come from long way away, Persia' Melchior corrected him. 'And now – now we go home.'

He turned to his companions and spoke rapidly in a language that neither Mary nor Joseph had ever heard before. One word, however, kept cropping up. Herod.

'No go to see Herod again,' Melchior said, struggling to find the right Hebrew words. Joseph too was struggling; even though Aramaic was his first language he knew Hebrew from his temple worship but Melchior's accent was so thick that he couldn't grasp everything he was trying to say.

'Have seen the child – he will be very great. Very great king. Yes?' He looked at Mary. 'A great king,' he repeated. 'We worship him.'

The three walked backwards out of the room and into the night. Mary and Joseph looked at one another, and then at the sleepy toddler sucking his thumb on Mary's lap.

For several moments neither of them said a word. Mary lay Jesus down on his mat. Joseph picked up the three gifts and wrapped them in a piece of the sacking that he used to cover the donkey.

'I just don't understand . . .' he murmured.

'We don't need to,' Mary replied softly. 'God will tell us all we need to know. Come – sleep. You know how grumpy you get if you're tired.' She took his hand and smiled up at him. 'Jesus won't want a grumpy Abba in the morning, will he?'

They both lay down and shut their eyes. But it was some time before either of them slept.

> When they had gone, an angel of the Lord appeared to Joseph in a dream. 'Get up,' he said, 'take the child and his mother and escape to Egypt. Stay there until I tell you, for Herod is going to search for the child to kill him.'
>
> *Matthew 2:13, NIV*

'We must go!' Joseph was on his feet packing their few possessions into the panniers when Mary woke up. It was still dark and Mary's eyes were heavy with sleep.

'In the morning, yes, but . . .'

'No, now!' Joseph's voice was stern, his eyes clouded with anxiety. 'I have had a dream. God spoke to me – he said that Herod means to kill Jesus.'

'Oh my God . . .' Mary scrambled to her feet.

'We have to leave and go to Egypt . . .'

'But that's three days away . . .'

'You think I don't know that?' Joseph snapped. 'You think I want to do this? But God told me and when God speaks . . .'

'Yes. I know. You're right. Tell me . . .'

'We have to go to Egypt,' Joseph repeated. 'Strange, isn't it? My namesake Joseph was sold by his own brothers into slavery in Egypt and now I . . . ah well!' He took a deep breath. 'Thankfully, one of my distant cousins lives near Gezer – his ancestors were there during the great captivity and God has been good to them. I will find work . . .'

'You mean, we'll be there for a long time?' Mary asked hesitantly.

'We will be there until God tells us different,' Joseph sighed. 'Mary, I don't get it but I know this is out of our hands. God, only God, knows what the future holds.'

'What about Dinah?' Mary asked, as she gathered Jesus' clothes together. 'We can't just leave . . .'

'Write her a note.' Joseph gestured to the wax tablet propped against the wall. 'Just say . . . give her God's blessing and say that the child was fractious and we left early to save disturbing Benjamin. And hurry. We have to go before it is too late.'

He paused. 'I must find a way to get a message to my brother Cleopas – he will deal with my business. Find someone to watch the premises . . .' The worry was etched on his face as he took the wax tablet and added a few words. 'Dinah will get word to him, I know she will,' he said.

Minutes later, they were outside, Joseph holding the sleeping toddler. As they began to move down the street, Mary's eyes turned heavenwards and she stared once more at the bright star. 'Oh Lord my God go with us,' she prayed. 'Keep us strong. Show us the way. Keep your Son safe. Help us, Lord. Help us.'

When Herod realised that he had been outwitted by the Magi, he was furious, and he gave orders to kill all the boys in Bethlehem and its vicinity who were two years old and under, in accordance with the time he had learned from the Magi. Then what was said through the prophet Jeremiah was fulfilled: 'A voice is heard in Ramah, weeping and great mourning, Rachel weeping for her children and refusing to be comforted, because they are no more.'

Matthew 2:16-18

Days later, those cries to Yahweh for help echoed through the streets of Bethlehem. The people didn't know it, but Herod's fury at discovering that the wise men had left without reporting the whereabouts of the newborn king to him, was without parallel in the memory of anyone at court – and that was saying something, since Herod was a man given to violent mood swings and episodes of terrifying rage.

Determined that no one should usurp his throne – a throne that he knew was not rightfully his – he ordered the immediate slaughter of every boy under the age of two in Bethlehem and the surrounding countryside.

Three days later, as Joseph and his family crossed the Wadi El Arish and entered Egyptian territory, safe from Herod's jurisdiction, blood flowed in the streets of Bethlehem and a cloud of grief and pain enveloped the entire town. Shortly afterwards, Herod left Jerusalem and within a short while, he died.

Once again, God spoke to Joseph in a dream.

'You mean, we can go home?' Mary's face lit up with joy. 'Now?'

'Now,' Joseph told her. 'We're going home to Nazareth.'

So what has that got to do with me?

1. Mary heard things that she probably would have preferred not to know about. Why was it necessary for Simeon to say what he did? Would it have been kinder for him to keep his thoughts to himself? In what sort of situations do we struggle to decide whether to give someone news they might not like and when to keep it to ourselves? What part does God play in guiding us in such situations? Think of any time when you have not known whether to tell someone something or keep it to yourself – perhaps when a friend is being cheated on, or you have to admit that you can no longer sustain a relationship with someone? How did Simeon deliver his news? What can we learn from him?

2. Here we have two characters, Simeon and Anna, who have devoted their lives to God. How do we view monks and nuns, especially those in silent orders? How do we see their role in the modern world? If you have never had a conversation with someone living a monastic life, try to arrange to do so (not with a silent order, of course!). Many houses welcome visits by people of any age, and some offer quiet days – or noisy ones – where you can learn more of the reasons they have chosen, or been chosen, to live the way they do.

3. Contrary to the images on Christmas cards, the Magi didn't visit Jesus in the stable. The Bible says they came to 'the house' and that Jesus was a 'child'. Can you discover other Christmas card images or traditions that are not actually mentioned in the Bible? Do we really know the names of the Wise Men or how many there were?

4. Yet again Joseph has a dream that threatens to turn his entire life upside down once more. Think about it; he's told to go at once to a foreign country, to leave his flourishing business and his friends, not knowing when or if he will return. He leaves because of the threat to his son; how many places in the world can you think of where people are forced to flee their homes because of war, tyranny

or persecution? How would this story speak to a refugee? How hard is it for us to accept that even in situations such as these, God knows what he is doing? Does he always seem fair to us? And when he doesn't how does that affect our faith?

5. The story of Joseph being sold into slavery forms the basis of the popular song 'Joseph and the Amazing Technicolor Dreamcoat'. You can read the whole story in the Book of Genesis.

6. Joseph would have probably managed to find work in Egypt as there were colonies of Jews in several Egyptian towns and some of his distant relatives lived there. However, leaving his thriving carpentry business without being able to go back and make plans for someone to take care of it would have been a huge upheaval. What events in our recent or current history can you think of that have put people in this sort of position? Where do you think God is at such times?

7. The Massacre of the Innocents, as the killing of all the children under the age of two is called, has been depicted in films with scenes of horseman galloping through the streets slaughtering toddlers. It is tempting for us to say that such things couldn't happen today but sadly they do – genocide is still a tragic evil in our society. Lust for power can make people commit atrocities – and some of them are not so visible as outright slaughter. Can you think of evils perpetrated around the world today that lead to the death of innocent people? Where is God, do you think, in these circumstances? Again, how does the evil done by others make us question God's purposes? What helps to keep our faith in him intact? When we feel our faith wavering, what do we do?

CHAPTER SEVEN

Lost and found

As she watched her son on his hands and knees, hunting for a nail that his father had dropped in the dusty workshop, Mary couldn't help wishing that time would slow down. Tomorrow, they would be going, as they did every year, to celebrate the Passover, only this time Jesus was no longer a child. He was twelve; a youth on the threshold of adulthood.

Watching him now, images of the last ten years since their return from Egypt flashed through her mind. 'Look, Mummy – I made it myself!' The tiny, lopsided wooden boat that Jesus proudly showed her when he was – how old? Five? 'Found her, Mummy, I found her!' Her eight-year-old son, flushed with pride and covered in mud, carrying an equally dirt-encrusted lamb, one of their neighbour's flock that had gone missing two days earlier. 'I'm working with Dad!' He was ten when Joseph considered him old enough to undertake the fifty-minute walk to Sepphoris, the Gentile city being rebuilt by Herod Antipas; and where Joseph had the job of crafting doors for the new synagogue. The boy had been so excited and had come back full of stories about the bustle and vibrancy of the city.

'Why? Mummy? Why are people like that?' That was the question her son had posed as, on the way home from market one day, he saw a group of men encircling a young woman, kicking her and hurling stones at her head. Remembering that moment, Mary felt again the anguish of facing that question. She had seen an image of how it might have been for her; saw herself lying there, hands clasped over her head, ineffective against the hail of pebbles and rocks. It could have been her blood soaking the ground, her death only moments away.

'They think she has done something bad,' she stammered, as Jesus fixed his dark brown eyes enquiringly on her face. 'But even if she has, they shouldn't take matters into their own hands like that.'

Jesus had turned and stared angrily at the crowd. 'And do you think, Mummy, that none of them have ever done anything wrong?'

'I'm sure they have – we – well, most of us do wrong at some time in our lives.'

For a moment, he hadn't said a word. Then sighing deeply, he took her hand. 'We must tell them,' he said. 'Make them stop.' He had tugged at her hand.

'Jesus, no. Stand back, keep moving. Come on.' Even if she had gone with him, it would have been too late. The woman was dead.

From that day, her son changed. He was still as loving to her, as helpful to Joseph and as willing to help their neighbours as he had always been; but he grew quieter, more thoughtful and began asking penetrating questions, many of which Mary found impossible to answer. As soon as he had been old enough to sit still and listen, she had explained to him that he was very special; that God had chosen her to be his mother and Joseph to be his father but that God, his heavenly father, had important plans for him. She had never been sure he had understood; but the day after the stoning of the woman, she had once again sat down and called him to her.

'Jesus, you remember how I have often told you that God chose . . .'

But this time, instead of sitting at her feet and listening, he interrupted. 'I know, mother. I know.'

'Yes, but . . .'

'Mother, I know. My Father in heaven has told me.'

Their eyes met and it was Mary who dropped her gaze first. In that moment she knew that her son would never be wholly hers ever again. Indeed never had been wholly hers. She wanted to weep, for fear, for loss, for simply not understanding what would happen. But she didn't weep. Instead, she did what she always did in moments of emotion or doubt. She climbed to the roof, knelt down and prayed.

The journey home from Jerusalem after the Passover was always a time Mary enjoyed. It wasn't only the Temple worship and the Passover meal itself, commemorating the deliverance and Exodus of the children of Israel from slavery under Pharoah in Egypt, that she loved, important as that was. It was the travelling home from the city that gave the whole event a sense of holiday and rest from the daily chores.

It was a chance for the women, walking at the front of the long column of travellers, to catch up with friends and relatives from all over Galilee before they all went their separate ways. The fact that their husbands were by tradition bringing up the rear, well out of earshot, allowed for a freedom of speech and laughter that might otherwise have been thought frivolous.

'I can't get over how Jesus has grown!' Mary's cousin Elizabeth sighed as they joined the other women who were setting up resting places for the night.

'John too,' Mary nodded. 'And just think – next year they'll both be attending the Passover as grown men. Thirteen in a few months time . . .'

'Time goes so fast,' Elizabeth sighed. 'One minute they are little babies, the next . . .' She paused, and clasped a hand to her chest.

'Elizabeth, are you alright?' Mary knew it was a stupid question; it had been obvious for the past three days that her cousin was far from well. There was a greyness about her complexion, an unnatural rapidity to her breathing and as for her appetite, it was non-existent.

'I'm fine, just give me a moment.'

'You should ride with Zechariah,' Mary declared. The old priest was even more infirm than his wife, and Elizabeth had confided in Mary that he knew his days were numbered.

'He insisted on one more Passover journey,' she had murmured the first day in Jerusalem. 'I tried to dissuade him, but he wouldn't take any notice. Thank goodness he's riding in Isaac's cart.'

'At least John is with him,' Mary had reassured her. But now, seeing the pallor on her cousin's face, she wished that John was here to care for his mother.

'There!' Elizabeth said suddenly, straightening up. 'I'm fine now.' She began walking slowly alongside Mary. 'Now what were we saying? Oh yes – the children. Between you and me . . .' She dropped her voice as a cluster of chattering women drew level with them. '. . . I worry about John.'

'Worry? Why?' Mary asked. 'He's certainly a strapping lad and . . .'

'Yes, but he's such a thinker . . .'

Mary burst out laughing. 'Isn't that a good thing? Remember what Judith was saying, about how her three lived to play and never paid attention to learning? You're lucky . . .'

Elizabeth smiled. 'Oh, I know – it's just that he spends so much time on his own, doesn't really mix with the other boys in the village. And the things he says . . . sometimes he sounds so much older than his years, not at all like an ordinary boy of twelve.'

Mary nodded and took Elizabeth's arm. 'We both know, Elizabeth, that our sons are not just ordinary lads . . .'

Elizabeth nodded slowly. 'You're right,' she sighed.

'Jesus speaks of God with such knowing,' Mary went on. 'Such . . . such intimacy. And John . . . ?'

'He said to Zechariah the other day: "One day I will see the Messiah."'

The two women looked at one another for several seconds, their fingers touching. They both nodded. The truth was there inside them yet the enormity of it made words impossible. Minutes later, they caught sight of Joseph, striding towards them smiling broadly.

'You two still chattering?' he laughed. 'I'm surprised you have anything left to say to one another.'

'We were talking about our boys,' Elizabeth explained.

'Speaking of which, where is Jesus?' Joseph asked. 'He's really too old to be hanging out with the women all the time.'

'He hasn't been with us all day,' Mary said. 'I assumed he was with you.'

Joseph shook his head. 'I haven't seen him since we left Jerusalem. Surely you've been keeping an eye on him?'

'You've just said he's too old to be with us,' Mary pointed out, a mite acerbically.

'Sorry,' Joseph replied. 'I guess he's off somewhere with the youngsters . . .'

'There's John,' Elizabeth interrupted, picking up her skirt and waddling over to him, stumbling a little on the uneven ground. 'John, have you seen Jesus?'

The boy shook his head. 'Not today.'

'Malachi, Daniel, over here a minute!' Joseph beckoned to two of the boys with whom Jesus often spent time back in Nazareth. 'Have you seen Jesus?'

'No. We were looking for him. We wanted him to play Hounds and Jackals with us.'

Joseph smiled to himself. Jesus loved to play checkers, as the game was also known, and was rather good at it.

'He said he would,' Daniel added. 'But we haven't seen him all day.'

'Oh my God . . .' Mary gasped.

'Mary, calm yourself,' Joseph said. 'He'll be somewhere daydreaming no doubt. You know what he's like. I'll go back up the hill, and you ask around all the families down here. We'll find him, don't you worry.'

As the hours passed and night fell, Mary grew more and more panic stricken. None of her friends had seen Jesus all day; Joseph had walked back the way they had come for a good ten furlongs but there was no sign of him.

'First thing tomorrow, we must go back to Jerusalem,' Joseph declared.

'Tomorrow?' Mary gasped. 'But he's all alone somewhere, it's night-time, what if . . . ?'

'Mary, Mary, listen!' Joseph reasoned. 'He's a sensible boy. If he's lost, he'll find a cave, or some form of shelter, and wait till morning. And think – there will be other travellers from first light – it's not as if the roads will be deserted.'

'Exactly!' Mary cried. 'And what if someone harms him, what if . . . ?' She broke off. She couldn't voice her deepest fears, not here among all the sympathetic glances from other mothers, and the excited whispers of their children. What if, she thought, choking back tears, what if Jesus, God's own son, was hurt? Or worse? And it was all her fault?

All night, as Joseph slept a fitful sleep at her side, she prayed. At first light, they set off, retracing their steps. Every one of the twenty miles felt like a hundred, every hour without finding Jesus seemed like a week. Every time they peered into a ditch and didn't find their precious son with his head smashed in, they uttered prayers of thankfulness; every time they peeped into a cave or searched a stable and found it empty except for cattle and fowl, they fought back tears of fear and frustration. When they got to Jerusalem late that evening, footsore, weary and growing more and more worried, there was still no sign of Jesus.

The city was dirty. The litter left behind after the influx of worshippers had not yet been cleared and hordes of flies swarmed around Mary and Joseph as they tramped the streets. On every corner, Roman soldiers paced or stood, eyes alert for the slightest sign of civil disturbance. Mary and Joseph kept their eyes down, pausing only to ask passers-by if they had seen a young boy with curly hair and a healing scar on his left hand. No one had.

'The Temple,' Joseph said. 'That's the only place in the city he knows. He has to be there.'

The Temple was the jewel in Jerusalem's crown, the beating heart of the Jewish nation. With its white walls and gold-covered sides that glinted in the sun, it had always taken Mary's breath away, no matter how many times she saw it. But today, none of that registered. The beggars, the aggressive salesmen and the tradesmen bargaining at the tops of their voices had fascinated Jesus just days before; maybe he'd lingered by a fruit seller, or one of the trinket sellers and forgotten the time.

But still, there was no sign of him. Darkness fell. Joseph urged Mary to eat, but every mouthful stuck in her throat. They snatched a few hours sleep in a *caravanserai* – or at least Joseph did. Mary did not sleep a wink.

The next morning, they returned to the Temple Mount. Its vastness hadn't seemed threatening before, but now, as her eyes scanned every corner, every column, every palisade, it seemed like a huge, overcrowded noisy monster waiting to devour them. The Court of the Gentiles alone was three times the size of Nazareth, and now that the Passover was finished, the money changers were back in the colonnaded portico, changing foreign and local currency into Tyrian shekels, the only acceptable coins for temple offerings.

'My son, have you seen my son? A smallish boy, brown hair . . .' Time and again, Mary, now with tears streaming down her dust covered cheeks, forgot protocol and grabbed people by the arm.

'A boy? A young boy?' An elderly scribe with a roll of parchment under his arm leaned towards them.

'Yes, yes, my son – have you seen . . . ?'

'There's a boy in the Court of the Women,' the man said. 'Been there for ages – clever little chap.'

Mary ran in the direction he had pointed, her sandals slapping on the tiles beneath her feet.

'Thank you!' Joseph called and then ran after her.

'It's him, he's here, oh thank you God!' Mary dashed into the midst of the scribes and teachers seated in a circle, dropped to her knees and grabbed Jesus by the shoulders. She hugged him to her, but he pulled away and stared at her in astonishment. Then he turned back to face the teachers.

That did it. Mary blew. 'What were you thinking of? We have been out of our minds with worry,' she stormed. 'We thought you'd been hurt, or attacked or . . .'

'But you must have known I would be here, in my Father's house?' Jesus sounded genuinely puzzled.

'How could we have known?' Mary retorted. 'I thought you were with your father, and he thought you were with me and . . .' The words caught in her throat as the implication of what Jesus had said suddenly hit her. His Father's house. He didn't mean Joseph.

'I have to learn, there is so much . . .'

Mary felt a pang of guilt at her outburst. Jesus had a destiny; and she was just a small part in it.

'Your son is a credit to you!' One of the Pharisees stood up and shook Joseph's hand. 'He enquires, he reasons – you know something?

I'd like to teach this boy. Bring him back when he is older. I promise you I will see him right.'

'Thank you for caring for him,' Joseph replied non-committally. 'And now, we must return home.'

'I'm sorry you were worried, Mother,' Jesus said on the way home. 'You mustn't fear for me. My Father takes care of everything.'

Mary smiled and patted his shoulder but said nothing. What could she say? She knew that from now on, the future was out of her hands. All she could do was be there. And love him. Always and forever.

So what has that got to do with me?

1. Whenever Mary faces a problem, she prays – but notice that she isn't so holy that she doesn't panic! It's not worrying and doubting and fearing that is wrong, it's blotting God out so he can't reach us that does the damage. When you think of Mary praying, what do you see in your imagination? A devout woman in spotless blue robes kneeling with hands clasped? Or a frantic mother turning to God and repeating over and over 'Keep him safe, please keep him safe!'? Both images are valid; there are times for serene, reflective prayer and times when we cry out to God in our moments of deepest need. The important thing is to invite him into our darkest moments as well as into our times of calm and happiness. When do you find it easiest to pray? Hardest? When do you simply find it impossible to frame any words at all? What do you do then?

2. The story of Jesus in the temple can bring out a lot of fairly strong reactions in people – particularly parents! Jesus sounds so cocksure, so dismissive of the anxiety he has caused his mother and father. Perhaps the way to understand it is that the Gospel writer wants us to see that Jesus is completely focused on God. He is 'about his father's business' in the words of the older translations of the Bible. Think about the things that you are really passionate about – perhaps sport, music, potholing, rock climbing – and think how much time and dedication it takes to become thoroughly immersed in all the techniques and skills needed. This passage, far from making Jesus seem distant, should serve to remind us how human he was; he was soaking up the teaching of the rabbis. He didn't know it all yet; he was human and he had to learn as a human child did. God gave him fully divine knowledge when the time was right.

3. When Mary is reflecting on Jesus' childhood, she remembers various episodes. Which of these are memories that Jesus uses himself during his ministry?

4. In an earlier chapter, Mary feels an outsider. Here we have Elizabeth worrying that her son John is an outsider too. She doesn't feel he is like a 'normal' boy of twelve. Thinking of life today, what do you consider to be 'normal' for a boy of twelve? What characteristics would make you think someone was 'not normal'? Why is Elizabeth worried even though she knows deep down that God has singled John out? Do our perceptions of 'normal' restrict our relationships with other people and if so, in what ways?

Part Two

CHAPTER EIGHT

One moment of fear

Twenty-one years later

Reuben sat in the shadows on the corner of the deserted street, his mantle wrapped round his shoulders, his eyes scanning furtively from left to right. He picked up a stone and would have hurled it in fury at the two laughing, joking soldiers passing just a few yards in front of him, but he wasn't a fool. Lying low had never been as important as it was today.

He hadn't slept all night and now as dawn broke he had escaped the rancid smell of an overcrowded room and the nightmare-driven cries of his friends, for fear that the old demons would overwhelm him once again. If they did, then at least they'd do it without an audience.

It was never meant to be like this, he thought. It was meant to be the beginning of something great, something that would change the world. That's what they had all believed. Just a week ago they had been cheering and celebrating, certain that this was the moment – and now . . . over. Finished. All of them made to look like fools.

Perhaps that's what they were, he thought miserably. Fools. Fools to have believed, fools not to have done something to make him see sense. Jesus was a great guy but there was no dodging the fact that he attracted trouble like flies to a sheep's carcass. He'd done amazing things, he'd talked a good story but he'd got the ending all wrong. All those promises, that wonderful vision of a different future – gone. Vanished. Meaningless.

It was over. Jesus was dead and that was that.

And yet . . . there had been times he would never forget, gifts given to him that no one could ever take away. The world might still see him as the ugly, stunted, deformed boy with the big head and the short little arms, but they didn't know the half of it. With Jesus around, he'd felt he belonged, that he had a purpose. With him gone, what kind of future lay ahead? Esther would be OK, Caleb would survive on his wits but as for him . . . That's when he remembered.

The words spoken to him on a hillside in what seemed another world and another time. Jesus' words – spoken just for him. He heard them again as clearly as if they were being spoken now.

But it was ridiculous – he couldn't. He wasn't like the others. Esther could do it, Caleb definitely. But him? No way.

He tried to push the thought out of his mind, but that one memory unleashed a dozen others, not just the horrific, gut-twisting scenes from the day before, but all of it. The fears and the joys and the downright terrifying bits. All of it – right from that very first moment he saw him, that day three years before, down by the River Jordan . . .

CHAPTER NINE

Hope – and hatred

Reuben

In those days John the Baptist came, preaching in the desert of Judea and saying, 'Repent, for the kingdom of heaven is near.' This is he who was spoken of through the prophet Isaiah: *'A voice of one calling in the wilderness, prepare the way for the lord; make straight paths for him.'*

Matthew 3:1-3

It was hot, hotter than it should have been for the time of year. Although it was still early in the day, not a breath of air stirred the surface of the water and the leaves on the few acacia trees were motionless. The ground I was sitting on was hard as a rock, and not even the pressure of my toes made any mark in the baked dust. There was the sort of heaviness in the air that precedes a violent storm; but as yet there were no dark clouds looming on the horizon and even if there had been, I doubt any of us would have noticed. Not while he was talking.

'Repent, for the kingdom of heaven is near!' His voice bounced off the limestone crags and reverberated around the crowd. 'Turn to God – the Lord is coming!'

I'd heard about John – well, everyone had. He wasn't exactly the kind of person to keep a low profile. He was wild looking with hair that stood out in great matted tufts round his gaunt face, and eyebrows that were grey with the dust of the desert edge. His tunic was made of rough hair and to be honest, it was pretty filthy; but when he opened his mouth, all that faded away and all you heard were the words pouring over you, his voice urgent and compelling. Even the few Roman soldiers who were ambling up and down through the crowd, giving the odd prod to a foot here, an elbow there, would occasionally stop dead in their tracks and turn, mesmerised by the thundering tones and sheer energy of the man.

'Come and be baptised, wash away your sins and be forgiven!'

Forgiven. Just like that? Was it really possible? If I, Reuben son of – no, I won't even mention his name – if I went down there, walked into the water and let him do it, would I be like other people again? After fourteen years, was it that simple?

Some people said – not to my face, but my hearing's acute – that I was like I was because of some sin that my parents had committed. They never said what that was, and, of course, I couldn't ask. Well, my mother wasn't around any more to get forgiven, and my father – well, I hoped like hell he was dead too; but could I get forgiveness by proxy? Could I walk into that river and ask for baptism and then maybe, come out . . . Come out what? Looking like other people? Hardly. Able to speak so that people understood me? Unlikely. And yet . . . what was there to lose? If it worked and life changed, great; if it didn't, at least I'd be cool for a few minutes.

I was about to get to my feet when there was a commotion behind me and five or six pompous looking men rode up on mules, the long blue fringes on the corners of their mantles blowing back in the breeze.

'Pharisees and flaming Saducees,' muttered an elderly man to my left. 'This should be interesting. Wouldn't want to take them on myself but him . . .' He pointed to the preacher.

'Well, if he's fool enough to mess with them, he'll live to regret it.'

It was, I thought, highly unlikely that the ragged-looking preacher perched on a rock in the water would be stupid enough to argue with the Saducees and Pharisees. They were the toffs, the ones who lorded it over everyone else, telling them what to do. The Saducees were so up themselves, it wasn't true; I'd heard people say that they didn't believe in angels, or in demons, or in life after death – one guy said that he reckoned the only thing they did believe in was themselves. No way would this Baptist guy take on any of them.

One of the newcomers dismounted and looked around, clearly hunting for someone to grab the reins and take care of his animal. I was on my feet in a trice – the chance of earning a coin or two was just too much to resist. As I stretched out my hand to take the reins – trying to ignore the expression of revulsion on the face of the mule's owner, John waded along the water's edge and was standing only inches from me, eyeballing the leader of the group.

'You have come for baptism?' he challenged him.

Two of the men burst out laughing. 'Are you crazy?' the older one sneered. 'We have no need of baptism – we are the descendants of Abraham. We are favoured people, chosen of God.'

'You snakes!' John thundered, startling the mule so that I had to jerk it to a standstill. 'Do you think you're going to escape God's punishment just by claiming Abraham as your ancestor? It's what you do, and how you live now, today, that matters, not who you're descended from and let me tell you . . .'

'You are not in a position to tell *us* anything . . .'

'Unless you live in a productive and fruitful way, you're just going to be tossed to one side and destroyed in an instant!' His voice obliterated their protests, as he turned again to face the crowd.

'Not so fast!' Another of the group held up his hand and stepped closer, a conciliatory expression on his face. The others glared at him but he waved them away and focused on John.

'Listen, we just want to know who you are. We have a job to do. We have to report back to those who sent us.'

'I am not the Messiah, if that's what you're asking,' John replied.

'So who are you? Elijah?' This Pharisee seemed to be genuinely interested.

John shook his head. 'You want to know who I am?' he shouted. 'Well then, since you're so good at reciting the law and the prophets to anyone who will listen, just you remember the words of the prophet Isaiah: *"A voice crying in the wilderness, prepare the way of the Lord!"*'

'So are you him?' someone in the crowd yelled out. 'Are you the one we have been promised?'

'Is he really? Is he the one who's coming to save us?' The murmurs of the crowd grew louder and people began scrambling to their feet and moving towards the river. I was immediately on the alert – crowds drop things and one advantage of being small is that you can sink to the ground and retrieve all manner of stuff in a trice.

'No, no! Listen to me! Listen, I say!' John looked agitated as he scrambled onto a rock a few feet into the river and stretched out his arms to the crowd. 'I'm nothing. It's the one who is coming after me – he's the one you are waiting for, a man far, far greater than I am. In fact, I'm not even fit to carry his sandals.'

The murmuring grew louder.

'Coming? Coming when?'

'Listen, I am baptising you with water – but when he comes, he'll baptise you with the Holy Spirit.'

You could tell by the grunts and mutterings all around that the rest of the crowd were as bewildered as I was.

'He'll sort out those of you who live good and fruitful lives from those who ignore God's commands. He will . . .'

'So what must we do?' someone shouted. 'Tell us straight.'

'If you have two tunics, share with someone who has nothing to wear,' he replied. 'If you have food, give half of it to someone who is hungry.'

Like that was going to happen! Now I can tell you a thing or two about hunger, and yes, folk have fed me – but never one of those rich guys. It seems to me it's the people who don't have much who share with others, not that lot who've got more than they could possibly need.

'What must I do?' A small, overweight man stumbled towards John. 'I'm – well, I – I'm a tax collector and . . .'

His words were drowned out by the jeering of those nearby. You couldn't blame them; they're a devious lot, those tax collectors, creaming off money and keeping it for themselves. I wouldn't give them the time of day. Mind you, the man had guts, I'll give him that. He could have kept quiet.

John held up his hand and at once the crowd fell silent. 'I will tell you exactly what you must do,' he said. 'Do your job, yes. But don't go collecting any more than you are required to.' He turned to a couple of Roman soldiers patrolling the shore. 'And you – don't go around accusing people falsely and . . .'

'Enough!' The leading Pharisee spat on the ground, and snatched the reins of his mule roughly from my hand, gesturing to his companions that they were leaving. I stretched out my hand and stepped in front of him, fixing an expression of what I hoped was pleading humility on my face. There are times when not being able to speak is a real inconvenience, especially when you don't have the advantage of good looks to work in your favour.

'Out of my way, cretin!' I stumbled as he shoved me violently to one side, gashing my knee on a sharp stone. I winced and bit down on my knuckle in an attempt to blot out the pain.

'Hey! Leave him alone!'

You could hear the gasp of the people around me as a lean muscular guy with broad shoulders and a voice like two rocks grating against one another stepped between me and the Pharisee. Ordinary people didn't go messing with the likes of the Pharisees and the lawmakers. Not if they valued their safety.

I looked up and instantly saw who it was. It was Andrew, one of the fishermen from Bethsaida, a little fishing village on the edge of Capernaum. You get to know a fair few people when you live the way I do (and you get to avoid a whole heap more) and Andrew was one of the best. He was a big bear of a man, with unruly hair and hands the size of platters; he was also something of a soft touch, someone on whom I could rely to give me a meal and somewhere dry to sleep whenever I pitched up in his village.

Capernaum itself was rich in pickings for someone like me; there was a small garrison stationed there as well as a customs house which meant that traders were always passing through. I never hung about with Andrew for long although to be fair, he would have looked after me; he'd provided for an old beggar for months till the man died and he'd have done the same for me. But the thing is, I had always made it a rule not to stay anywhere more than a week or so at a time because for every decent person like Andrew who gives me food or even a couple of days work, there are a dozen more in the same place who fear that I bring them bad luck or who shrink back from my disfigurement and just make me angry. And angry is the one thing I cannot afford to be.

'I said, leave him!' Andrew shouted as a second Pharisee prodded me with his foot.

'Andrew, back off – don't get involved!' A smaller, wiry man with anxious eyes tried to drag Andrew away, but he just shrugged him off. His face looked familiar but I was in too much pain to give it much thought.

The Pharisee glared at them both through narrowed eyes. 'Move it!' As he urged the mule forward, the animal's front hoof caught my shoulder as I lay on the ground and I yelped in pain. Instantly Andrew was on his knees beside me.

'Are you alright? Let me look . . .' he began. Just then the Pharisee flicked his whip in Andrew's face, dug his heels into the mule's side and barged his way into the crowd. As they scattered out of his path, he yanked at the reins and wheeled round again.

'This man,' he yelled, gesturing to John who was standing at the water's edge, 'is a troublemaker. Pay attention to him and you go against all the law and the prophets.'

With that he broke into a fast trot, all but one of his cronies following on behind him with lip curling sneers on their faces. But the one who had asked John to explain who he was lingered for a moment, chewing his lip and looking as if he really wanted to stay behind.

'Nicodemus!'

He jolted out of his reverie as the leading Pharisee reined in his horse and shouted at him. With that he took one last look at John, and rode after them. That kind of broke things up. A lot of the crowd wandered off, some more hurriedly than others, and even some of those who had been standing on the riverbank waiting for baptism seemed to change their minds, and backed off, eyes cast down.

'Listen, listen to me!' Now John was running along the water's edge, arms waving. 'The one who is coming will sort out types like them. It'll be just like a farmer with his pitchfork, sorting out the good grain and tossing the rubbishy chaff away.'

As he reached the point where I was crouched on the ground, still rubbing my shoulder, he paused, and for a second it seemed he was looking directly at me.

'Do you want to be chaff? Do you want to be burned in the fire? No, I tell you, you . . .' Suddenly the words froze on John's lips. He stopped dead, gazing open mouthed over my shoulder. The expression on his face was one of total wide-eyed amazement.

I turned and at once saw who it was that John was watching. The man walking slowly through the crowd towards the river wasn't any different to look at from a dozen others in the crowd – same dark curly hair, bushy black eyebrows and the beginnings of a growth of beard on his chin – but it was the way he moved that was so astonishing. He walked with long slow strides, his head nodding in rhythm with his steps as if he were mentally reassuring himself of where he was going. Despite the people hurrying past him in their eagerness to get home, occasionally brushing his arm, he just kept moving forward, not looking to left or right, his eyes fixed on John's face. It was as if he was oblivious to everything and everyone except the dishevelled guy standing on the rock.

John's arms dropped to his side, and he fell to his knees in the shallow water. I glanced up at Andrew, but he'd forgotten I existed. He too was motionless, watching John.

'Is it – you?' John's voice, so recently taunting and loud, was a mere whisper but as I said, my hearing is the one faculty I have that works overtime. 'Jesus? It's been so long . . .'

So he knew this stranger. Yet he looked as if he'd seen a ghost. This I thought could prove interesting. I scrambled to my feet, wincing slightly at the pain. I edged nearer, on the pretext of rinsing the blood off my leg.

'Is it really you who . . . I mean, you are the one?' John was asking.

'Baptise me, John.' Jesus' voice was steady and gentle.

John shook his head. 'I – I can't . . . I mean, it's me who needs baptism from you, not the other way round – you are in no need of forgiveness. What are you doing coming to me?' John, the confident, fearless preacher seemed bewildered – out of his depth almost.

Jesus smiled. 'Just do it, – the time is right,' he said. 'It's all part of God's plan.'

Of course, once God was mentioned John came alive again. He scrambled to his feet, his eyes suddenly alight; I noticed that he too had a cut knee, dripping with blood; he must have cut it on a jagged rock. He took a couple of steps into the river and then hesitated, but as Jesus nodded encouragement, he turned and walked out into the deeper water, Jesus following him. When they were several cubits out John laid his hand on Jesus' shoulder and plunged him into the Jordan.

> As soon as Jesus was baptised, he went up out of the water. At that moment, heaven was opened and he was the Spirit of God, descending like a dove and lighting on him. And a voice from heaven said 'This is my Son whom I love; with him I am well pleased'.
>
> *Matthew 3:16, 17*

It seemed as though he was under the water longer than the others had been. John's eyes were closed and he was mouthing something – a prayer I guess, his hand holding Jesus down under the water. I was beginning to think the poor guy would drown, when suddenly he broke the surface and I swear you could hear the great sigh that escaped from his lips. Relief I suppose at being able to breathe again. His hair was dripping, of course, his robe stuck to his body, but unlike all the others who had been similarly half drowned, he made no attempt to wipe his face or shake the water from his beard. He just stood there.

Then, suddenly a stiff breeze blew up out of nowhere, ruffling the surface of the water and blowing the dust around our feet. In the distance there was a rumble of thunder, and I saw John and Jesus look up at the sky – I guess they were looking for rain clouds but when I glanced up there were none to be seen. John lifted up his arms to the sky and then embraced Jesus.

'This is my beloved Son who delights me!' I turned to see who had spoken.

'Who was that?'

'Did you hear . . . ?'

Everyone around was looking to see who it was that had spoken.

'Is it him? Is it really him?'

I turned, thinking that Andrew was talking to me, but he was simply staring at Jesus. I touched his sleeve and mouthed a thank you. He looked at me distractedly, then put his hand in his pocket and tossed me a couple of leptons. Cool – not a fortune, I grant you, but it meant I'd eat that night. I closed my fist over them and as I turned back, the man called Jesus walked past me up the hill. And as he went by, he paused and for the briefest instant, his eyes met mine. He inclined his head very slightly to one side, and then smiled. It was the gentlest and yet the saddest smile I had ever seen (not that many people smile at me at all) and for some reason I wanted to cry.

'Look, all of you!' John shouted suddenly. 'The Lamb of God – the one who comes to make sense of everything!'

One thing was sure: John wasn't making any sense at all. At that moment, Andrew broke into a run, the smaller guy panting after him. He caught up with Jesus and touched his sleeve. Jesus turned.

'What do you want?' he asked, but not in a grumpy or officious way. He sounded genuinely concerned to know. For a moment, Andrew said nothing and when he did, it wasn't an answer to Jesus' question.

'Teacher,' I heard him say, 'where are you staying?'

Jesus smiled and opened his arms. 'Come and see,' he said.

The two men glanced at one another and then back at Jesus.

'Thank you, Rabbi,' Andrew said. And with that the three men walked briskly through the crowd and disappeared over the crest of the hill. Just like that.

It was about three hours later when I saw Andrew again. I had just been to the village to buy some bread and was feeling fairly replete having also managed to pinch a bit of curd cheese from the back of an unattended cart, when I spotted him ahead of me on the path, just at the point where it forks.

'I could have stayed all evening,' he said to his companion, 'but I've got to get back.'

'Me too,' said his companion, 'I've been away long enough – James will be furious as it is . . .'

'And by the look of the weather, the fish will be plentiful,' Andrew went on. 'It'll be all hands on deck for the next few days.'

At that, my ears pricked up. Fishing – that's a good thing to get involved in because it means food and work, even for someone like me. Hired hands were always needed, and I may be small – stunted, some say – and I may look pretty weird, but neither of those things matter if you're helping to repair a sail, or mending a net or running errands. I'd helped out once before and only been cuffed behind the ear once so I thought I'd give it another go. So I lumbered along the path and finally caught up with them and asked if I could go with them. By 'asked' I mean I gestured and mimed and Andrew finally got the message and laughed and slapped me on the back, which I might add knocked me over. Then he looked worried, but I grinned and scrambled to my feet and gestured that I was fine.

'Haven't seen you for ages,' Andrew said. 'Still good at mending nets?'

I nodded, and he smiled, and jerked his head in the direction of the narrow path that led back to the town. I glowed with happiness not so much at the thought of some company and a bit of work, but because Andrew treated me like a normal boy.

The welcome we got when we reached Andrew's home near the lake shore was not exactly the warmest on offer.

'Oh, you've graced us with your presence, have you?' A stocky man with thin eyebrows and dark, darting eyes strode up to us.

'Listen, Simon, the most amazing thing . . .'

'The most amazing thing is that you imagine we can mend nets, scrub down boats, fish the lake, get the order over to the Roman garrison, while all the time you're idling . . .'

'We've seen the Messiah!'

Well, that took the wind out of Simon's sails, I can tell you. I was pretty dumbstruck myself – or would have been if I wasn't already. The Messiah? We all knew, even those of us with precious little learning, that one day he would come, this promised one, the one who would make things right, get rid of the Romans, re-establish justice and be the mightiest king and ruler ever. What was it they called him – the lion of Judah? And here was Andrew saying that he'd seen him. Did he really believe that the man at the lake had been him?

'You've seen . . . ?' Andrew's brother stammered. 'Where? When?'

'He came to the river to be baptised,' Andrew replied. 'Today. And he invited us to talk with him and what he said was . . . Simon, you have to come. Now. You have to come and meet him.'

'Andrew, how many pretend messiahs have there been? Preachers come and go and . . .'

'No!' Andrew interrupted. 'This one is different.' He turned to me. 'You saw him didn't you?'

Simon Peter's gaze fell on me and his face puckered into a frown. 'What are you doing here again?'

'He's been knocked about by a damn Pharisee,' Andrew said. 'He . . .' Andrew stopped in mid-sentence. 'You know, I've never found out your name. What is it?'

I bent down and wrote 'Reuben' in the dirt.

'Reuben?' Andrew sounded astonished, although whether at my name or the fact that I could write a few words, I wasn't sure. He turned back to Simon.

'Reuben was there – he saw it all.'

'You did?' Simon questioned, and the note of disbelief was unmistakable.

I said nothing. Andrew had been good to me, letting me go with him, and no way was I about to jeopardise supper by indicating that I hadn't a clue what he was going on about. Sure, there had been that guy who looked at me . . . but he wasn't a king, no way. Actually he was no different from anyone else, except for . . . well, that kind of determined, focused attitude he had.

'Reuben, listen,' Andrew said urgently. 'Go back – see if you can find him and bring him here. I know, I just know . . .'

No way. I gestured to the sinking sun, casting long shadows over the lake. I rubbed my stomach, I pointed to my mouth, I conjured up a couple of tears.

'OK, not you, and not now. But tomorrow,' Andrew declared. 'Tomorrow I'll go and find Jesus. That's his name. Jesus.'

'Tomorrow,' his brother stressed, 'you'll be mending your nets and helping me mix pitch. Messiah indeed! Here in Galilee? As if!'

In the end, no one went anywhere the following day. Or for several days afterwards. Andrew and Simon's mother fell ill that night, with a high fever and vomiting. The following day, Simon was puking his guts up, by evening his wife, Abigail, and Andrew were both laid low and within forty-eight hours half the village were groaning and writhing in agony. I didn't get it – which was pretty good because it gave me a chance to prove how useful I could be. The few men who were well enough to fish brought home a sizeable catch, just as Andrew had predicted, and I helped to swab down the boats and generally do the grotty jobs no one else wanted. That's when I remembered where I'd seen the other guy who'd scuttled off with Jesus. He was another John, the son of Zebedee; and he was getting a raw deal from James, his brother, who wouldn't stop going on and on about how much work he'd had to do because John skived off to hear the preacher.

'And now father's ill, and we're all behind and heaven knows how we'll manage,' he kept muttering. Of course, that was great for me; they even let me help with sorting the fish – fish with fins and scales good to keep, fish without tossed away – and gave me bread and a sizeable piece of tilapia as a reward. It was all going so well for me. And then . . .

'Get out of my way, dwarf!'

The boy who shoved me to one side was younger than me but much larger. I'd seen him around and the sneer on his face had told me he was one to avoid. Sadly, I hadn't seen him coming. I didn't move. I focused on the fish heads I was tossing into a wicker basket.

'I said move it, runt!' And he kicked me. Where it really hurts a guy, whatever size you happen to be.

'What are you doing here, you waste of space?' he shouted, kicking me as I rocked backwards and forwards on the ground. 'What are you? A dumb waste of space, that's what. Rubbish! Trash!'

And I knew in an instant what was going to happen. All the old feelings, and all the old symptoms. That memory . . . I knew I had just a few minutes to get the hell out of there.

I clutched my nether regions and staggered to my feet. I wanted to run but the agony was too much. I stumbled away, my gait worse than ever because all my effort was going into hanging on till I was out of sight. The pain in my groin made me want to vomit, and my vision was blurred with tears.

'Hey you!' I heard someone call. 'Where do you think you're going?'

I took no notice, staggering on and turning a corner.

'Get back here!' The shouts were fainter now. Grateful for the pain of the stitch in my side, I stumbled on. Sometimes, though not often, running until I dropped with exhaustion was one way to beat this thing. I took another path out of the village, and panted my way up a hillside. As the pain eased slightly, I broke into a run and as I ran, I scraped my nails up and down the palms of my hands. It didn't help. It wasn't enough.

'Runt, runt . . .' The boy's words rang in my ears and then the voice changed. Deeper now, snarling, spitting. His voice. My father's voice – the voice of the man who threw me away. That did it. I sank to the ground, my curled fists banging my head harder, harder. I grabbed a sharp stone, and gripped it as hard as I could. Its sharp edge invited me. I sliced it down my right thigh, then the left. I slashed it across my arm. The blood ran. And my tears followed.

It was worse this time. Generally speaking, a few sharp slashes, a decent flow of blood and a deep sleep sorted out that red and black spiked demon of rage that lived deep inside of me. Every few months it would break out of the chains of self-control and blanked-out memory with which I incarcerated it, and try its hardest to drive me demented. Ripping at my flesh let it escape and then it would leave me in peace for a while.

This time was different. The exhaustion that drove me into the nearest cave and wrapped me for a short while in sleep was still there when I woke, my cuts smarting and burning, my tongue furred and my head throbbing as if a hundred thousand bees were fighting to escape through my ears. But worse than all that was the hollow in my heart – the knowledge that, once again, I had blown it. All I wanted – all I had ever wanted – was to belong somewhere, and stupidly, for a few days I had thought that maybe, if I kept my nose clean and made myself useful, I could muck in with Andrew and the other fishermen guys down by the lake for a bit longer than usual. A month maybe, even the season. But now . . .

'What good are you to anyone, you weirdo?'

My father's voice echoed round the cave as clearly as if he himself were standing in front of me.

'Do us all a favour and die!'

Try as I did to block out the memory, banging my head on the wall of the cave and clamping my hands over my ears, I was back there, a struggling kid of – what? I don't know, six, maybe seven – trying so hard to manhandle a leather bucket of water, to be helpful, to get my father or one of my brothers to smile, to tell me I was doing well. But when your arms are so short that your hands hardly reach the top of your ribcage and your legs bow outwards, you might as well not even try the heavy lifting stuff. I didn't know that then. I was trying to do something to make them love me.

When the water spilled all over the drying grain at the doorway of our house, my father lost it. Again. He swept me up, hammered a fist into my face. I made all the sounds in my throat that I could, grunts, gargling noises, the odd word 'Abba, No,' trying so hard to say I was sorry. It just made him even angrier. He lifted me higher and threw me, as if I were no more than a handful of discarded olive stones, onto the ground. I sobbed, hoping that someone would come and stop him. No one did. Everyone, it seems, was afraid of my father. I'd heard people mutter that our family were tainted, devil people, that God's wrath had finally come on the house with the death of my mother and the arrival of me, the twisted, deformed, grunting child who killed her. Mustering all my strength, I grunted as loudly as I could. He kicked me again.

'Shut up,' he hissed. 'Shut up, or I'll make you shut up.'

I guess I should have taken the hint. But I grabbed his ankle, looked up at him pleadingly, tears streaming down my face. He picked me up. It was getting dark. He strode out of the village, and walked for a long time with me over his shoulder, muttering oaths under his breath. As my eyelid swelled, my eye closed; my lips were caked with drying blood, and my leg throbbed from the pain of my father's kicks. Suddenly, he slammed me down on a rock in the middle of nowhere.

'I don't ever want to see your ugly little face again,' he hissed. 'Your mother died and what for? A runt like you. You come back and I'll kill you. Get it?'

I grunted, made a few guttural pleading sounds, trying so hard to make a word come out of my throat. He kicked me.

'Shut up!'

He turned and walked away without a backward glance. I shut up. I've shut up ever since.

So what has that got to do with me?

1. John the Baptist was marked out by God from the moment of his conception to fulfil a special purpose. Hard as we may find it to believe, God has also given each of us a purpose for our lives. It may not be headline-grabbing stuff; it may not change the world. Our purpose might be to change just one life. Think about the gifts and talents God has given you, not just things such as being good at maths, or a brilliant musician, or the fastest sprinter in the athletics club, but the gift of being a good listener, an eager volunteer, a caring friend. Sit down with a good friend; tell them the gifts that you see in their lives – chances are you will come up with something that they don't even think of as a God-given gift! Then let them do the same for you.

2. John the Baptist called people to repent. What does the word 'repentance' mean to you? If you say 'turning away from sin' you are halfway there; if you add 'turning to God!' you've got it in one! We all sin – fact. Everyone – and that includes teachers, priests, politicians, the man in the corner shop, your best friend – everyone. If we say we believe and then just go ahead and live however we like, that's not repentance; if we live a morally upright life but refuse to have a personal relationship with God, we don't experience his wonderful forgiving and reconciling grace.

3. What do you think of when you hear the word 'sin'? Is it just the big stuff, like murder and theft and violence? What about lying, cheating in exams, gossiping, breaking promises, spreading rumours . . . ? The main thing is not to beat yourself up about your sins, but to ask God to help you beat them. He will; his forgiveness is not rationed. All you have to do is ask.

4. John told the people that if they had two tunics they should give one to someone who had none, and that they should give half their food to someone who is hungry. These ideals are familiar to us today. How easy do we find it to do that? Do we in the modern world have too much of everything – too many clothes, too much to eat, too many gadgets and appliances? If so, would

it make any difference if we cut back? Does John's message go deeper than simply giving away a jacket we've grown out of or popping a box of groceries to Harvest Festival? What makes us want to accumulate things? What are the underlying feelings that make us feel safer when we have 'stuff'?

5. John's calling was to point the way to Jesus. We too are asked to point others to Jesus. Discuss how we might do this. Are we sometimes reluctant for fear of seeming 'holy-holy'?

6. Andrew went to Reuben's defence and some people thought he was crazy to challenge the Pharisees. Do we find it easier to sit on the fence or keep a low profile, rather than attract attention to ourselves by speaking out for others? Do we pick and choose the type of people we stand up for? Are we tempted to side with those who might, in the end, be useful to us?

7. When Andrew and his companion asked Jesus where he was staying, he replied 'Come and see.' This is Jesus' invitation to us: Come and See. How do we do that? How do we help others to come and see Jesus? Note that Jesus didn't give them a job at this point; he didn't put any conditions on their visit, or quiz them about their motives: he just invited them to find out more. Does the church make it easy for young people to find out more? Does RE in school relate to the questions that enquirers really want answered? What would make it easier for you to come and see?

8. The pain of his father's abuse remained with Reuben constantly. His way of dealing with it was to hurt himself. At the time he had no one to turn to. Had he lived today, he could have sought help and support from teachers, youth leaders, doctors, friends . . . If you feel any sort of inner pain and feel isolated, alone or ashamed because of it, share it with someone you trust, ring ChildLine or the Samaritans. No one, ever, should have to manage pain or grief or fear or guilt on their own. Don't let anyone make you believe you deserve it – you don't.

9. A lepton was the smallest of all the coins – worth less than 1p in today's money, yet it meant that Reuben could eat. What do you think 10p would buy in a developing country of the world today? Sometimes we are tempted to think that because we only have a small amount to give, it's not worth doing. It is. Always. What may be our small change may make the difference between life and death to a street child in the developing world.

CHAPTER TEN

Coming back

Then Jesus was led by the Spirit into the desert to be tempted by the devil. After fasting for forty days and forty nights, he was hungry. The tempter came to him and said 'If you are the Son of God, tell these stones to become bread.' Jesus answered 'It is written, Man does not live on bread alone, but on every word that comes from the mouth of God.' Then the devil took him to the holy city, and had him stand on the highest point of the temple. 'If you are the Son of God' he said, 'throw yourself down. For it is written "He will command his angels concerning you and they will lift you up in their hands, so that you will not strike your foot against a stone."' Jesus answered him 'It is also written "Do not put the Lord your God to the test."' Again, the devil took him to a very high mountain and showed him all the kingdoms of the world and their splendour. 'All this I will give you' he said 'if you will bow down and worship me.' Jesus said to him 'Away from me, Satan! For it is written "Worship the Lord your God and serve him only."' Then the devil left him and angels came and attended him.

Matthew 4:1-11

Hunger is a greater driving force even than fear. After what seemed like an eternity of living on locust pods, a few berries, most of them with blight on them, and the odd wild herb, and scrounging bread on a good day from a passing shepherd, I knew it was time to get on with my life. The cuts on my legs were beginning to scab over and they could easily be shrugged off as the result of a nasty fall. My bruised scalp was hidden by my hair and the sleeves of my tunic covered the worst of the arm injuries. With a bit of skilful miming and a few bright smiles, no one need be any the wiser. And the memories . . . well, they would have to go back where I'd shoved them for the greater part of my life. Buried deep inside, locked up and boxed away where no one could get at them.

My deepest regret was that I couldn't go back to Andrew and the crew. Not because of the injuries but because of the way I'd run off. No way could I face them. It was a shame because for the first time ever, I'd felt comfortable there; not with the little thug who assaulted me, of course, but the others – they were OK. But now they probably despised me, thinking that I'd run off because I was scared of their illness when in reality that was the least of my worries. Now I was desperate to know if they were all OK.

I struggled to work out which way to go. After that first night, I'd wandered like someone in a trance, taking the nearest paths and when they ran out, tramping through the scrub and sleeping far more than normal. That's always the demon's parting gift; overwhelming fatigue and a don't-care-what-happens state of mind. Now, with hunger gnawing at my guts, I managed to get a grip and make a plan. I looked at the sun, figured out which way was north, and headed off. I could go anywhere, I told myself bravely. Maybe to Sepphoris; easy to survive there on scraps and a bit of stealing or even get to fetch and carry on one of the many building sites. Or perhaps Nazareth, or Cana . . . I'd survive. I was gutsy. I could do it. Or perhaps, just perhaps, I could venture back to Bethsaida and . . . but no, they'd never take me back now.

It was as I made my way down the stony path, slippery from overnight rain, that I saw him. At first I didn't realise who it was; the sun was in my eyes and all I could see was a figure standing on a jagged promontory a couple of furlongs away. I shaded my eyes with my hand and squinted. If it was a shepherd, I was in luck; he might give me a bit of bread or at least a swig of wine. I stumbled closer, crouching behind rocks until I knew it was safe to be seen.

Suddenly, I heard a strangled cry. The guy struck out his arm as if pushing something huge away from him. Then he turned and began striding towards me. I scurried behind a large rock. He must have heard the scrabbling of my feet, because he stopped dead in his tracks, his head to one side as if trying to detect where the sound had come from. As he did so, I saw that it was him. The Jesus man. The one from the river.

He began walking and within minutes was so close that I could see the filth on his robe, which hung on him as if made for someone twice his size. His face was more gaunt than I remembered and frankly, he didn't look well. And yet, he was walking so purposefully and with such energy that I thought he must have someone very special to get to in a hurry. I waited until he was a furlong or so ahead of me and then I followed him.

Now I had a purpose. Now I had a chance to get back in with Andrew. No matter how furious he might be with me, I had some news that he really wanted to hear. He had been so eager to get his brother to meet this Jesus guy. If I could tell him just where to find him, it might be enough to make him overlook the rest of it and let me hang around for a few more days.

I followed Jesus all the way to the river. He went back to the very spot where he'd been baptised by John. There was quite a commotion when he got there, I can tell you – John bounding up and down the shoreline telling people that this was the Saviour he'd been speaking about, the one he'd been told by God that he would recognise by a dove descending from the heavens.

But Jesus walked over to him and murmured something in his ear. John stopped his shouting, turned and walked along the shore with Jesus, their heads bowed in earnest conversation. I didn't hang about. I went straight to the village. The news I had for Andrew wouldn't wait.

Andrew gripped me by the shoulders, squatted down on his haunches by the prow of his beached fishing boat and gazed at me, those huge bushy eyebrows meeting over his nose as his forehead puckered in an anxious frown.

'What happened? Why did you run away?' His voice wasn't angry, just puzzled.

I had rehearsed this moment in my head. No point trying to explain about the bully – what was done was done and I'm not a telltale. I gestured enthusiastically in the direction of the lake, mimed splashing water over my head, and then, for good measure, held my nose and did a pretty good imitation of plunging under water.

'You went back to John? You wanted to be baptised?'

The enthusiasm in his voice was reward enough for me. I didn't deny it, but I didn't nod either. I simply smiled.

'He's still there?' Andrew asked eagerly.

This time I nodded and wrote in the dirt 'Jesus'.

Andrew's eyes widened.

'You saw him? The Promised One?'

I nodded. I didn't know who had promised what to whom, but Andrew seemed pleased with me and that was good enough for me.

'With John?'

I nodded again.

'Wait – I'm coming! Just let me clear these nets and then . . . Simon Peter! Over here!' he bellowed along the shoreline to where his brother was spreading nets out to dry. He ambled slowly over tossing a cork float from one hand to the other.

'What is it?'

'Reuben's seen him. Today. We have to go, Simon Peter, before it's too late.'

Maybe Simon Peter had got over his foul mood, or maybe the illness had left him too weak to protest, but he simply sighed, tossed his gutting knife to one side and nodded curtly. I would have followed them, but just then the smell of grilled fish hit my nostrils and the saliva gushed into my mouth. Jesus could wait; it was nothing to do with me anyway. Right now, I had one aim; to fill my grumbling stomach until it could hold no more.

'Hey you two! Where are you going? Food's ready!'

Andrew grabbed a couple of slabs of bread and rammed a charred fish between them, gesturing to Simon Peter to do the same.

'Well, come on,' he said nudging me. 'Get your food and hurry up – you're coming with us aren't you?'

I stared at him. He sounded as if he actually wanted me with them.

'I mean, you've been baptised.'

I grabbed a fish, scalding my fingers as I did so. Slipping the largest slab of bread I could find into the belt of my tunic, I turned to follow them.

'You know what? This is just typical!' James, Zebedee's grumpier son, wiped his mouth on his sleeve and glared up at Andrew. 'First you disappear every few days to listen to this Baptizer chap; then you start filling John with all sorts of ideas about him – and now you're roping Simon in! And who's left to do all the hard graft? Me!'

'Come with us,' Andrew suggested. 'Reuben will show us exactly where he is.'

James looked at me briefly, as if surprised to see me there at all. He'd never really engaged with me; he would often cast a glance in my direction and then, when our eyes met, he would look away and busy himself with something. People do that – I guess they don't know how to react to someone who can't talk to them. Some think they might catch something off me, others assume I'm a bad lot and that's why I'm the way I am. A few even think I'm stupid but that's one thing I'm not. Maybe if they realised just how not-stupid I was they might think twice before ignoring me.

'Huh!' James grunted. 'Another false messiah appears and you are so gullible that you think this is the real one. How many have there been? Ten? Twenty?'

'This one is different . . .'

'Thanks, but no thanks. You may have your head in the clouds, but we have to take the fish to Magdala for salting tomorrow.'

'But . . .'

'But nothing,' James interrupted. 'There's only one thing I'm interested in right now and that's making a living.'

As soon as we reached the river, I could see that things had changed. Oh sure, John was still there and he was still preaching but the fire seemed to have gone out of him. To be honest, he seemed less desperate to get the message across, more at peace somehow. The crowd was smaller too and for a moment, I thought we were too late. I couldn't see Jesus anywhere. And then suddenly John leapt onto a rock, raised his arm and pointed towards a grove of trees.

'There, you see? The Lamb of God!'

And you know what? He smiled. John, the firebrand, the hellfire preacher with a voice like thunder and an expression of perpetual doom, actually smiled. His face had an expression of pure joy on it – as if he'd seen someone coming towards him bearing a huge platter of food and it was all for him.

I shielded my eyes from the sun, and peered in the direction of John's gesture. There he was, Jesus. He was leaning against a tree trunk, talking to an elderly woman and swigging water from a goatskin carrier. I was trying to fathom out what John meant by calling him a lamb – it seemed like a pretty odd way to refer to a grown man since all the lambs I've seen are helpless, bleating things – when I realised that Andrew was striding up to him, bold as you like. I glanced up to see whether Simon would follow him, but he was rooted to the spot, his forehead creased in a frown.

Andrew said something to Jesus and within seconds they were both heading back our way, the woman staring after them as if wishing she could go too. Now, don't ask me why, but I scooted backwards and disappeared behind a bush. I think I was scared – this Jesus was obviously someone pretty high up in the rankings round here, and all my past experience told me to keep well out of the way of people with power. No one noticed I'd slipped away – no surprise there, then. But I was still within earshot, and through the gaps in the leaves I caught glimpses of the three men.

'This is my brother, Simon,' Andrew said eagerly.

Jesus smiled, placed a hand on Simon's shoulder and looked him straight in the eye.

'You're Simon, John's son?' he said. 'Well, I have a better name for you. From now I'll call you Cephas. Cephas the rock.'

He had a bit of a nerve, I thought. There's nothing wrong with the name Simon. Who did this guy think he was? Not that Simon Peter seemed to mind. He positively beamed from ear to ear and murmured 'Master, Master,' over and over like someone in a trance. And with that, the three of them walked away, Jesus doing all the talking and Andrew and Simon Peter hanging on his every word.

Whatever, I thought, yanking the fish and bread, half squashed by now, out of my belt and biting down on it. Don't look back. Don't check that I'm OK. See if I care. But I did.

The following morning I got down to the shore of the Sea of Galilee really early, hoping that James or John would be so rushed off their feet bringing the catch in, what with Andrew and Peter being away, that they'd give me some work – and hopefully, breakfast. There was no sign of them on the beach and within minutes, I had spotted their boat still way out on the lake. Several other boats were beached and unattended – which was just perfect for me. Glancing rapidly to left and right, I struggled to winch myself up and into the first boat – which is not an easy exercise when your arms are half the length of most people's and your feet turn inwards. After three attempts, furtively looking over my shoulder all the time, I managed it and crouching down, I began scouring the hull for any tiddler or sprat that might have slipped through the net. Fish is at its best cooked but believe me, raw fish is better than the gut ache that comes from an empty belly.

I had just found a tiny fish caught between two boards at the bottom of the boat, when I heard voices. I jumped and hit my head on the bench in the middle of the boat. Muttering expletives, I peered over the edge. It was them. Jesus, Andrew and Peter.

The dazed look had vanished from Peter's face and he was purposefully striding out ahead of Jesus and Andrew, straight towards my boat – well, his boat actually – and muttering about having work to do. I threw myself back down on my stomach. I had to think fast – very fast. If he found me messing around in his boat – well, just let's say it wouldn't do my hope of hanging around any good at all. Just at that moment, while a dozen excuses were chasing each other through my mind, the boat started to rock from side to side. There was a thud and I rolled across the deck.

'Hey, Philip, watch what you're doing!' Peter shouted. 'You want a hand there?'

Another fishing boat had smacked into the side of the one I was hiding in, splashing water all over my back.

'Philip, for pity's sake . . . !' Peter yelled.

I held my breath. I'd seen this Philip guy when I'd been this way before – you couldn't miss him really because he was always bouncing around, interrupting conversations with unending questions about everything, and being teased by the others for being clumsy. If Peter would just concentrate on helping Philip with his boat, maybe I could climb over the side and get away unnoticed. Andrew and Jesus were ambling way behind, so deep in conversation that I doubt they would have spotted me if I'd been six feet tall with shoulders like Goliath.

'Sorry,' I heard Philip say ruefully. 'I'm just not cut out for this – just because Dad was a fisherman, why do I have follow in his footsteps? There has to be an easier way to earn a living.'

'So come, follow me!'

That wasn't Peter's voice – and it was too deep and musical to be Andrew's. I squinted, and peered through a crack in the wooden slats of the boat's prow.

Philip looked up, his hands still resting on the prow of the boat. 'What? Who are you?'

'Come,' Jesus repeated, stretching out a hand. Andrew, nodding furiously, beckoned to him. Hesitantly, Philip walked over to them and the three of them stood there, heads together, muttering. Then suddenly, Philip broke into a run and sped along the beach, stumbling on patches of shingle in his impatience.

'Nathaniel! Nat!'

A man I hadn't noticed before on any of my previous visits appeared from round the side of one of the small houses at the back of the beach. He had black curly hair and a complexion much fairer than the other guys. He was carrying a scroll in his hand, and he looked pretty miffed at being disturbed.

'What is it?' I heard him ask Philip.

'Nathaniel Bartholomew, guess what! We've found him! He's here! The anointed one, the one promised to us – he's actually here and . . .'

'Philip, slow down. You're not making any sense,' Nathaniel Bartholomew sighed.

'We have found the one that Moses wrote about, the man the prophets said would come. It's Jesus . . .'

'Jesus?'

'Yes, Joseph's son, from Nazareth!' Philip gabbled.

'Nazareth?' he laughed, giving Philip a gentle shove on the shoulder. 'Come off it – do you honestly think anyone that important is going to come from third-rate little Nazareth! A town where the Romans have a garrison? I don't think so!'

'Come and see for yourself if you don't believe me!'

Sighing, and hitching his tunic Nathaniel walked over to Jesus, who was still standing far too close to Peter's boat for me to feel comfortable. I had pins and needles in my legs and my shoulder had something sharp sticking into it, but I didn't dare move a muscle for fear of being discovered. Luckily my eye was still pressed to the crack in the boat, and thankfully no one was looking this way.

As Nathaniel Bartholomew approached Jesus, Andrew and Peter, Jesus stepped forward, a broad grin on his face.

'Here is a true man of Israel – a man without a trace of deceit or pretence in him!'

Nathaniel's mouth dropped open.

'What do you mean? Where do you know me from?' he asked. I guess he was going through that embarrassing moment when someone recognises you and you don't have a clue who they are.

Jesus smiled. 'I saw you once while you were still under the fig tree,' he replied, 'before Philip called you.'

Fig tree? I thought. There are no fig trees round here. Whoever this man was, he was clearly good at talking in riddles.

Nathaniel dropped to his knees. 'Master, Teacher – you are . . . you *are* the Son of God! You are the King of Israel!'

This was getting ridiculous. King? Hardly! Not, of course, that I had ever met a king, but I'm not stupid and I knew that kings didn't wander around Galilee chatting to fishermen and talking about fig trees. They lived in palaces and ate off gold plates and ordered people around all day long. And as for being the son of God . . . well, that was even more bizarre. The guy wasn't bad looking, but god-like? No way!

At that moment, Jesus threw back his head and roared with laughter – and that wasn't exactly the sort of behaviour one expects from gods either.

'Oh Bartholomew,' he chuckled. 'Do you really believe who I am just because I said I saw you under the fig tree? This is just the start – you are going to see so much more!' He sighed, the laughter fading away.

'Before this is all over, you – all of you – will see heaven opening up and God's angels coming down here to the Son of Man and going back up to heaven again.'

Suddenly – and I don't know where it came from – I remembered a story I had heard, maybe from someone in the village, when I was still a little kid. It was about this guy Jacob who had a dream about angels coming down ladders – or something like that. I remember I had wanted to go up that ladder, to find out what was at the top.

Nathaniel stared at him. 'Master,' he said. 'I want to learn more, I want to understand. But right now I have to go to Cana – my birthplace – there is a wedding . . .'

'I too,' Jesus smiled. 'We will walk together.'

At that point, they moved away and I couldn't hear any more. Gingerly, holding my breath, I struggled to a kneeling position. I was about to stand up when I heard Andrew's voice.

'Wait! Where's Reuben? Where's the little chap?'

I froze.

'He found you again for us, Master,' I heard him say. 'And he's on his own and – well, I can't just walk away . . .'

I wanted to leap to my feet, wave my arms in the air – anything to attract his attention and get to go along. But I didn't. Why? Because I wasn't at all sure about this Jesus. Because not only did he seem a bit crazy, with all the talk of angels popping up and down from heaven and seeing people under fig trees, but he was having this weird effect on Philip and Nathaniel. And yes – because they were all talking in riddles and it was going straight over my head and if I did show up, I'd be the odd one out. The thick one, the cretin. Again. So I stayed put.

'Are you coming with us?' Philip asked Andrew.

Andrew opened his mouth to reply, but Peter was there first.

'Oh sure,' he said. 'Like the fish are going to catch themselves. We have work to do.'

But all the time he was protesting he didn't take his eyes off Jesus.

'Well I must go – it is my duty,' I heard Nathaniel say. 'I was born in Cana and my cousin's daughter is marrying . . .'

I saw Jesus lean towards him and murmur in his ear. Then he clapped Philip on the back, and the three of them began striding purposefully along the beach and out of sight. Andrew and Peter returned to their work. But neither of them looked remotely at ease.

So what has that got to do with me?

1. No one saw Jesus in the wilderness so we can only assume that at some time in his ministry he told the disciples what had happened. Or maybe he simply discussed temptation with them – we don't know. What we do know is that Satan is real, and that we too face temptation all the time. Has anyone tried the 'If' style of temptation on you? You know the sort of thing: 'If you loved me, you would . . .'; 'If you don't do that, you're a wimp . . .'; 'If you don't do that, you can't be in our gang.' How hard is it to resist these kinds of temptation? Is the fear of rejection, or of being laughed at or excluded stronger than our desire to do what's right? How do we fight the temptation? When we think we can rationalise doing something wrong, we can be sure that the devil is trying to block God's purpose. The first temptation was to turn stones into bread. Which temptations that we face are similar to this? What is the essence of the second temptation, to throw oneself down from the temple? How do we face this temptation today? The third temptation was all about getting power and position. Can you think of any temptation you have faced that is similar?
2. What lessons about how to resist temptation does Jesus teach us in this passage?
3. When Reuben thought he could lock his memories away where no one could get at them, he was wrong. God is always there in the depths of our pain, shame, fear and self-loathing; he loves us through it and he aches for us to come and talk to him, to give him that pain so he can take it and transform it. Sounds great, doesn't it? But it's hard. What are the things that block us from looking at our hurt full in the face? Why does it seem that boxing them up and locking them away is the best way to move on? And why doesn't it work?
4. What did Jesus use to resist temptation? What message does that have for us?

5. Reuben says that James didn't really engage with him. *'He would often cast a glance in my direction and then, when our eyes met, he would look away and busy himself with something. People do that – I guess they don't know how to react to someone who can't talk to them. Some think they might catch something off me, others assume I'm a bad lot and that's why I'm the way I am. A few even think I'm stupid but that's one thing I'm not. Maybe if they realised just how not-stupid I was they might think twice before ignoring me.'* Have you or anyone you know had an experience like that? What makes us wary of people who seem different from us, whether physically, mentally or through a choice of lifestyle? How can we cope when we are on the receiving end? How do you think God feels about these kinds of reactions?

6. Nathaniel cannot imagine 'anything good coming out of Nazareth'; Reuben had a set idea of what a king would look like. We can understand Reuben's confusion but it seems Nathaniel's remark was pure prejudice. How often do we judge by appearances? Or hang on to a preconceived idea of what a Christian should be like? What *do* we think a Christian should look like, or sound like? Are all Christians the same? In what ways may they differ and in what ways must they be the same in order to call themselves Christians?

7. Jesus called Peter by the name Cephas. Cephas is Aramaic and means the same as the Greek 'Peter' The Rock. How do you think Peter might have felt?

8. Reuben didn't show himself when Andrew was looking for him because he was afraid he wouldn't understand what they were talking about and he would be made to look stupid. When have you resisted doing something for fear of not getting it right? Has this ever applied to your faith journey? Do you ever feel that everyone else at church, or in the RE class, or even in your family, 'know it all'? Has it ever occurred to you that maybe by your questions you will be giving them a gift – they won't have all the answers and you may be the one who encourages them to search!

9. When Jesus said that he had seen Nathaniel Bartholomew under the fig tree, he was not talking about an ordinary tree. 'Under the fig tree' meant studying the Torah – the books that we now know as The Old Testament. If Nathaniel was doing this out of sight of Jesus, he would have been amazed that Jesus knew about it. And what if he had been reading about Jacob's ladder and then Jesus made reference to it? How amazing would that be? How do you think you would have reacted?
10. You can read the story of Jacob's ladder in Genesis Chapter 28 verses 10-22. It was a story that would have been as familiar to Nathaniel as the story of the Nativity is to us.

CHAPTER ELEVEN

Searching for a safer way

Esther

It was at that wedding in Cana that I first saw Jesus. Not that I took much notice of him at the time. I had too much on my mind, like getting the hell out of there – and fast.

The job at Cana had all seemed so good to start with – almost too good to be true. Which as it turned out, it was. When my father took up with that woman, I thought things would get better. They didn't. What's more, I made the big mistake of confiding in her – well, she went on and on about how she wanted to be a mother to me, so how was I to know it was one big lie? Anyway, when I couldn't stand it any more I took off. I walked all the way from Tiberias to Nazareth, where my grandmother lived, only to discover that she had died two weeks before. I kind of lost it – I spent days sobbing my heart out, and wandering around in a daze. I'd pinned all my hopes on living with her and now . . . well, everything seemed hopeless. And then a woman called Judith who lived down the street, took pity on me and took me into her house and fed me. She told me I should go home – and that's when I told my first lie. I said my father was dead. I even drummed up some tears and wrung my hands and tried to look sorrowful.

'And you don't have any other family?' Judith sounded genuinely concerned.

'No.' The second lie. Well, what was I supposed to do? Tell her about my hateful stepmother – the one who didn't believe me, who called me every name under the sun and tipped goat shit on my food so I couldn't eat it? Or perhaps mention my sister, the one who upped and disappeared when I was just four years old? The one who promised to come back for me – but who never did? Hardly.

'No, no one,' I had whispered, putting on the rather timid, feeble voice that I used when I wanted to get people onside. It was, I thought at the time, the right decision, because that was when she told me that her brother worked as a steward for a young man in Cana, a village five miles from Nazareth. This man was about to be married and Judith had heard from her brother that a serving girl was needed urgently since the wedding was only a week away.

'The last one was up to no good, let me tell you,' Judith sighed. 'Ran away she did, in the middle of night, taking a whole cheese and a pot of date honey with her. Disgraceful!'

She had patted me on the head and smiled.

'But you seem like a good girl, Esther,' she said. 'How old are you?'

I had just had my twelfth birthday, but I was tall for my age. 'Nearly fourteen, Madam,' I lied.

'Perfect!' she exclaimed. 'I will come to Cana with you and speak for you to my brother. It's his job to take on new servants. It'll be a good position for you.'

'Thank you,' I whispered.

'Your grandmother was a good woman,' Judith sighed. 'And she thought the world of you. She never stopped talking about you.'

That was when my tears became real.

It didn't take me long to get why the other girl had done a bunk. It wasn't that the work was never-ending – I expected that with only a few days to go to the wedding celebrations. And it wasn't the food – that was better than I'd had at home. The master, Yanai, was a kind man, even though he seemed permanently agitated as he rushed about giving orders for the wedding feast and his mother, an elderly woman who lived with him, was lost in her own world and wanted only a smile and her favourite barley cakes to keep her happy. The problem wasn't with any of them. It was Nathan, the steward.

At first, he was really friendly, constantly asking me if I was settling in to my new position, whether there was anything he could do to make me feel more at home. Of course, I said no, everything was fine, which it was but I would have said that anyway, because you never know when people like that are setting a trap for you. Raise a complaint and they'd be off to the master and have you out on your ear, soon as look at you.

Then the third morning I was there, while I was spreading linen out on the flat roof to dry ready for the wedding feast, he came up and started chatting to me. At first, he was just leaning against the balustrade, moaning about the master, saying that he wasn't a patch on his father, who had died the year before, and how this one was always checking up on Nathan's work and wanted things done differently.

'Newfangled ideas, ridiculous money-making schemes,' he muttered. 'And as for taxes and duties, well, he insists on sorting all that himself – I'm not good enough, oh no! Me, who managed his father's affairs for years . . . Well, if you ask me he's miscalculated the tax on . . .'

I didn't really listen. To be honest, all that kind of stuff goes over my head. When you don't have money, you have no need of understanding the rules that govern it.

'I hope the new mistress will like me,' I murmured, interrupting Nathan's moaning. 'I mean, if she doesn't take to me . . .' I guess I was thinking of my stepmother and how people can hate you just because you choose to tell the truth.

I should have kept my thoughts to myself. In an instant, he had grabbed hold of my wrist, and was pulling me towards him.

'I've taken to you, my lovely,' he rasped, 'and if you are a good girl and do as I say, I'll make sure you're OK, no matter what.'

Fear coursed through my body and bile rose in my throat. I struggled to release myself from his grip, but he was a big man and within seconds he had clamped his fat, moist lips on mine.

'Lord my God, save me,' I pleaded silently in my head as Nathan began tearing at my tunic.

'Nathan? Nathan! Where is that wretched man!' The master's voice rang out from the courtyard below.

'Damn him!' Nathan loosened his grip on me and tipped his finger under my chin. 'Later, my lovely – and don't think I don't mean it!'

With that, he ran down the stairs without a backward glance. I was shaking from head to foot, at first with fear, and then, when I heard Nathan's smarmy, simpering tone to the master down below, with rage.

'Excuse me, sir,' he said. 'I was just on the roof admonishing the new girl – can't have your household disrupted by substandard work, sir. I'll need to keep a close eye on that one.'

And I knew he was speaking loudly in order that I would get the message. After that, I tried to avoid Nathan at all costs but everywhere I went, he would appear. His hand would snake across my back, only to drop to his side the instant he heard someone coming. One minute he would be telling me how pretty I was and offering me a fig or date from the food store; the next reminding me that he had it in his power to send me packing at a moment's notice if, to use his words, I didn't please him. I would have made a run for it there and then, but I couldn't do that to the master. He was, I realised by the second day, one of those really anxious types; he was about nineteen, and what with his father being dead, and his mother not in her right mind, I felt sorry for him. To leave him in the lurch so close to the wedding would be cruel and besides, the next girl might not be as on the ball as I was.

Because what Nathan didn't know was that with a past like mine I had a few tricks up my sleeve to keep him at bay until I could make a run for it. Smear poisonous nettles over your face and arms, chafe your skin with pumice and complain of disordered bowels and stomach cramps, and it's amazing how fast a man will disappear. Then there are the blessed seven days every month when a woman is spared – and by a combination of those two excuses, I was safe. But I knew it wouldn't be for long.

On the day of the wedding, the bridegroom left with his men friends to go to the bride's house. I watched as they weaved their way down the street, their lighted torches flaring and guttering in the stiff breeze.

I would have loved to have been at the bride's house when he arrived and lifted her veil, I would have loved to have followed the procession through the streets. But I had work to do before they arrived back for the feast.

I had discovered that there was a bit of a worry about this meal. There seemed to be plenty of food on offer to me, but the master's manservant and Nathan both grumbled that there was insufficient and that the master was far too eager at inviting guests and not eager enough to pay for an appropriate quantity of delicacies.

For the first two hours I was rushed off my feet, weaving in between the dancing girls, balancing platters of food, scanning the tables to make sure no one was without drink, and all the time keeping an eye on the bridegroom's mother who had a tendency to wander off or begin to undress herself for no apparent reason. She should have had a maid all to herself, but the word among the field hands was that money was tight and only the most essential staff had been kept on. At least the master looked as happy as a kid in clover, beaming at his new wife as if he had just created her all by himself and popping sweet almonds into her mouth and positively drooling over her. For a moment, I paused and half closed my eyes, wondering what it would be like to have someone look at me as though I were the only person in the entire world who mattered. Like that was ever going to happen.

'Esther?'

I was on my way back to the kitchen to replenish supplies when a woman touched my arm.

'It is Esther, isn't it?' She was quite an old woman, at least forty-five, with streaks of grey in her hair and fine lines round her eyes and mouth.

'Yes, Madam,' I stammered, wondering what on earth I'd done wrong. 'Was there something you needed?'

'No, no, this is all wonderful,' she laughed. 'Judith asked me to find out how you were doing – I live close by in Nazareth. Judith and I have known one another for years and your grandmother lived opposite my house.'

'Are you . . . ?' I hesitated. It wouldn't do to get this wrong.

'Mary,' she replied. 'I am here with my family; that's James and Joses, talking with the bridegroom, and over there, that's Jesus – and two of his friends.' She gestured across to a table where a group of men were sitting, laughing and drinking wine and making more noise than the rest of the guests put together.

'My grandmother told me about – she talked of you,' I finished lamely.

'Many people talked about me,' she laughed and then looked thoughtful. 'And I believe many more will talk of my son Jesus.'

She shook herself and touched my arm. 'I remember your grandmother well,' she smiled. 'She was a dear friend of my cousin Leah. So – I can tell Judith you are happy here?'

For a moment, I wanted to tell this lovely lady the truth – that no, I wasn't happy, that I hadn't been truly happy for years, that I wished every hour of every day that I could be anywhere but here, and be anyone but me. But how could I say any of that? For one thing, Nathan was Judith's brother; she had found me the job out of the kindness of her heart, and she probably didn't have a clue what he was like. So I just smiled and nodded.

For a moment, I thought Mary was going to say something else – but just then, everything started to go wrong.

'What do we do? He'll be furious!'

'They're all asking for more and I don't know what to say.'

'Don't look at me – I'm just hired for the day!'

The servants were in a huddle, casting furtive looks over their shoulders.

'Esther, what's going on?' Mary asked. 'Find out what the problem is.'

She smiled encouragingly and I went up to Caleb, the only one of the male servants I had spoken to since arriving. He was a little older than me, about thirteen I guessed, and looked strikingly different from anyone else I knew. His skin was paler, his hair fair with a tinge of auburn and there wasn't the trace of a sprouting beard on his smooth face. He was actually pretty fit in a foreign looking kind of way.

'What's happening?' I asked him.

'The wine's run out,' he said, running his fingers through his hair and chewing his lip. 'What do we tell him?'

He jerked his head in the direction of Nathan who was hovering by the bridegroom's table, all oily charm and ingratiating smiles. Caleb pretended to be a really cool, laid back guy; he was always joking and teasing the other servants and bragging about how one day he was going to be right-hand man to the wealthiest landowner in Judea; but right then he looked like a scared kid. I went back to Mary.

'The wine has run out, Madam,' I said as respectfully as I could. 'And they don't know what to do. The master . . .'

'Don't do anything for a moment,' Mary said. 'Come with me.'

She walked over to the table where her son was sitting with me tagging along somewhat reluctantly. Knowing what a furore there would be when the master found out about the wine, I really wanted to be as far away as possible.

'They have no more wine,' she said, touching Jesus' shoulder and speaking in a low voice.

'That's not our business, Mother darling,' he said, patting her arm. Then he dropped his voice, took her hand and leaned towards her. 'My time hasn't yet come.'

Mary touched his shoulder gently. He sighed, squeezed her hand and shook his head ruefully. Mary walked over to the servants, and after a minute, Jesus got up from the table and followed her.

'Do whatever he tells you,' she instructed the servants and then walked back to her seat and began chatting to her neighbour as though nothing was wrong.

Now I admit I should have gone ahead with the clearing of empty platters, refilling the bowls of olives and making sure that the fresh batch of bread was ready to be cut and served. But I didn't. I wandered over to where Jesus was standing, and loitered a few feet away, pretending to watch the dancing. His two friends, who had had more than their fair share of wine, bounded up to him and were about to drag him away, but he just turned and looked at them and they stopped dead, and seemed to sober up in an instant.

'Fill those jars with water,' Jesus said, pointing to the six stone water jars lined up by the wall.

Well, that would go down well, I thought to myself. Rowdy guests were hardly going to take that lying down. Judging by the expressions on their faces, his friends thought much the same thing.

The servants looked at him as if he was mad, then shrugged their shoulders and did what he said.

'Now,' he said, 'draw some out and take it to the steward.'

It was all I could do to hold my tongue. Taking a jug of water to Nathan at this stage in the feast and announcing that it was all there was to drink? He would hit the roof, and what's more, blame anyone but himself for the miscalculation.

I watched Caleb's face as he poured some of the water into a pitcher.

'Aaah . . .'

At his cry, the other servants peered into the pitcher and then stood back, open mouthed, staring first at one another and then at Jesus. Jesus' friends leaned over and looked at the water as well and then jumped back – I mean, literally *jumped.* From where I was standing I couldn't see what the fuss was about – unless there was a scorpion in the pitcher, of course. It happens sometimes. But clearly that wasn't the problem, because instantly Caleb picked up the pitcher and took it to Nathan.

'Sir – er, um . . .'

'Yes, what is it, you blundering idiot?' Nathan snapped in his usual charming fashion.

'Sir – would you taste this? Just to make sure . . .'

Nathan didn't have to be asked twice. He took a huge gulp and smacked his lips.

'My lord!' he said, turning to the bridegroom. 'This wine – I'm – that is to say, you instructed me to serve the wine you purchased last week, so why – why save this fine wine, the best I've ever tasted – why save it till last?'

Wine? But it was water. I know it was. I saw them taking it from the stone jars with my very own eyes. I looked across at Mary, who was sitting calm as you like. She smiled at me and beckoned me over.

'You're sad, my dear.' It wasn't a question.

'I – um – no, I . . .' I was still reeling at the sight of wine being poured into goblets where seconds ago there had been water.

'And you have bruises . . .'

'I'm clumsy, Madam,' I stammered, instinctively brushing my hand over my cheek. Out of the corner of my eye I could see Nathan approaching, his eyes fixed on me. 'It's nothing. It's not important.'

'Anything that hurts us is important,' she said solemnly. 'Now, I have a friend who needs a girl who can . . .'

'Esther! You are not here to get above yourself and talk to the honoured guests, you are here to work. Now get back to . . .'

'I asked her to come to talk with me,' Mary said calmly, fixing her eyes on Nathan's bloodshot ones and then turning back to me.

'Remember what I've just said,' she smiled. 'And we will talk later.'

Only we didn't. Because Nathan got to me first. And this time I knew there was only one thing to do.

'Esther!'

I leapt two feet into the air, my heart pounding in my ears. I'd been spotted. Nathan had woken up – and despite the pitch black darkness of the hour before dawn, he'd seen me. I felt sick. I whirled round, my excuse ready-made on my lips. But it wasn't Nathan. It was Caleb.

'Esther, wait!'

Caleb grabbed my wrist, and instinctively I wrenched away, turned and began to run. He ran after me.

'It's OK, it's OK,' he panted, 'I'm not going to hurt you. Please, wait!'

I slowed my pace and turned to eye him warily.

'You're running away, aren't you?' he said.

'No, of course not!' I retorted. 'I was just feeling a bit faint and . . .'

'It's OK, I'm not about to tell anyone,' he assured me, glancing furtively over his shoulder. 'I'm doing the same.'

My mouth dropped open.

'Are you crazy?' I whispered. 'Why on earth would you do that? You're Nathan's right-hand man – his favourite!'

Which had nothing, of course, to do with Nathan's good nature, and everything to do with the fact that Caleb always covered up for Nathan when he was sleeping off a drinking binge or disappearing off to the village in the evenings.

'Ssshhh!' Caleb said, putting his forefinger to his lips and beckoning me. We crept across the courtyard, through the arch and onto the road, our pace quickening as we crested the hill and dropped out of sight of the house. Not until we reached a small olive grove did we speak.

'So,' I asked, still whispering, 'why are you doing this?'

'Oh come on!' he exclaimed. 'After what happened today, do you really think I'm going to hang around there?'

'Nathan didn't . . . ?'

The words froze on my lips. I hadn't intended to say them – the shame was bad enough without verbalising what had happened. Caleb's gaze seemed to penetrate right through me and he let out a long, slow breath.

'He hurt you.' It was not a question. His hand brushed my arm and I flinched and stepped back.

'It's OK,' he whispered.

But it wasn't and I knew he knew that too.

'I'm not going because of Nathan,' he said. 'Although now I wish I'd landed a few punches on him before I left. You're not the first girl he's . . .'

I turned my face away and he had the good grace to change the subject.

'I'm going because of the guy at the wedding – Jesus, is that what they call him?'

'You know him?'

'No, but I saw what he did. Esther, those jars were full of water – I helped to fill them myself. And he turned it into wine! The man's a marvel.'

'So it really was wine? Not just pomegranate juice thrown in, or . . .'

'Esther, believe me, it was the best wine ever! Nathan said in all his years he'd never tasted anything like it and heaven knows, he's had enough to be a good judge!'

I shivered, although whether from the cool night breeze or the thought that any man could magic water into wine I wasn't sure.

'Don't you see?' he went on eagerly, pulling two barley cakes from his pocket and handing one to me. 'Get work with a guy like that and you'd be made for life!'

He bit into the cake and licked crumbs off his lips.

'I overheard him say that he was going to Capernaum,' he went on eagerly. 'So that's where I'm off to.'

'But the master? He'll send someone after you, and then you'll be in all sorts of trouble,' I protested. 'Whipped and . . .'

'Then I mustn't get caught, must I?' he laughed.

'But what about money . . . ?' I ventured.

'Oh, I've got a few bits and pieces put away,' he grinned, rummaging under his tunic. 'Things like this.'

I gasped. Glinting up at me from the palm of his hand was a bronze brooch with a glistening red stone in the middle, a gold pin and several coins of pretty high value.

'Where did you get all that?' I gasped, although I wasn't sure I wanted to know.

'Let's just say that people are careless and I've got sharp eyes,' he said. 'So anyway, I'm off – there's at least an hour before dawn. What about you? What's your plan?'

Plan? Suddenly the enormity of what lay ahead hit me and to my horror, tears filled my eyes. I had no plan other than to put as many furlongs between myself and Nathan as I possibly could. That's when the old yearnings rose up again – the longing to have someone, anyone, who would love me and care for me, someone I could mean something to.

'You mean the world to me, Esther, you know you do!' My sister's voice echoed in my memory and in an instant I was back there, a tiny child, sitting on her lap while she braided my hair. 'Whatever happens, you have to remember that. Promise me?' And because at the time I knew no better, I nodded.

I guess she had hoped to get away without anyone knowing but I woke up that night and found her pallet empty and I ran outside and there she was, halfway down our street and running, her injured foot dragging in the dirt and making a sweeping sound. To this day, I don't know what instinct told me not to call out to her but I ran as fast as my four-year-old legs would carry me and it wasn't until I stumbled on a pothole that I made a sound.

'Esther, no!'

She was running back to me in an instant, scooping me up off the ground and hugging me close.

'Go home, sweetheart, right now,' she said firmly after a moment, setting me back down on the path.

'But where are you going?' I whined.

'On a special errand,' she said. 'But I'll be back, I promise. I'll be back and then I'll take you with me.'

'Really?'

'Really – only you have to keep it a secret, OK? You mustn't tell Father or – or her – or anyone. If they ask if you've seen me, you say no, not since our evening meal.'

She rubbed her bad foot rhythmically the way she always did when she was anxious. She was anxious a lot of the time. I remember looking at her doubtfully. No one took any notice of what I said anyway.

'Esther, do you hear me? Do you understand?' She shook me gently.

I nodded.

'So tell me – have you seen me?'

I took a deep breath. 'Not since our evening meal.'

'Good girl!' She hugged me again. 'Now go, quickly, back to your bed.'

I turned.

'And Esther?'

'Yes?'

'I love you so much – and I will come for you. I promise. You do believe me, don't you?'

'Yes,' I had said, nodding furiously. And I had.

But she never came.

'Esther? Esther!' Caleb was prodding my arm and I jerked myself back from my reverie and turned to face him. 'You don't have a plan, do you?'

I shook my head.

'So come with me,' he urged. 'This Jesus – he had friends with him, and family – you could get work with one of them, I'm sure of it.'

Suddenly I remembered Mary. How kind she'd been and how she said she wanted to talk to me later. Remembering it felt like a sign. If I went with Caleb and found Jesus, then I might find Mary too.

'I'll come,' I murmured. 'But I'm scared.'

Caleb smiled. 'No need to be,' he said. 'I'll look after you.'

I'd heard those words before. My heart began pounding.

'No, I . . .'

'Esther.' Caleb's voice was soft. 'Trust me. I won't touch you. I promise.'

Slowly I nodded.

'Let's go,' I said. 'Fast.'

So what has that got to do with me?

1. The wedding was the setting for Jesus' first miracle; but one of the wonderful truths about this story is not just that Jesus did a miracle, but that he cared enough about the host of the feast to rescue him from embarrassment in front of his family and friends. He cared enough not just to make wine – but to make the very best wine. Have you ever wondered if God cares enough about the little things in your life? Have you wondered whether he cares about any of the everyday things in life, or have you assumed he is only interested in how often you read the Bible, or say a prayer, or go to church? God cares about every aspect of our lives, right down to the tiniest detail. Next time to you talk to God, share with him the things that niggle you – your struggle with school or college work, difficulties with your Saturday job boss, family fallings-out. What is the hardest part about talking to God? Is it that you don't think he hears? Or that you can't hear him? God speaks to us in many different ways: sometimes through the words of friends, something we read in the Bible or see on a poster; the theme of a TV programme that just seems to address our issue when we most need it. God uses whatever reaches out to us as individuals!

2. Caleb set off to follow Jesus because he thought he would be 'made for life' – which of course, is true for all followers, but he saw it simply in terms of money and prestige. What makes us take the first tentative steps towards finding Jesus? Because we have heard what he is like? Because we think he's a magician who will make our life easy and give us everything we want? Or because we feel something in our life is missing? Because someone has spoken to us and touched a chord?

3. Esther took a hard decision. She left an abusive situation to go into the unknown. Do you think what she did was right? Did she have any other options? It is hard for us today to understand her plight – today there are support agencies, school and university

chaplains, family doctors, all of whom can offer help and guidance. Esther relied on the support of Caleb as she fled. What other consideration influenced her decision to go to Capernaum?

4. In reaching out to Esther, Mary showed kindness to a comparative stranger, and did so in a gentle, unthreatening way. Can you think of instances when you struggle to find the right words to help a friend in obvious need? What can we all learn from the imagined words the author has put in Mary's mouth?

5. Caleb clearly had jewellery that wasn't rightfully his. His excuse was that he had found it. What is your reaction to this? Can you understand why Caleb kept it? What about Esther's reaction or lack of it?

CHAPTER TWELVE

A friend in need

Reuben

When John rebuked Herod the tetrarch because of Herodias, his brother's wife, and all the other evil things he had done, Herod added this to them all: he locked John up in prison.

Luke 3:19, 20

'They've taken him!'

'He's in prison!'

'How can they do that? He's done nothing wrong!'

I was cleaning the gutting knives when Philip and Nathaniel Bartholomew arrived back early one morning, talking over one another as they poured out their news. The first thing I noticed was that Jesus wasn't with them – and to be honest, I was glad. I thought that now things could get back to normal. How wrong can you be!

'Who? What? Who's been arrested?' Andrew asked, as he and Peter grabbled to haul in one of the circular nets full of squirming fish.

'John the Baptist,' Philip panted. 'They just came and grabbed him and marched him off. We heard it from a group of his disciples who we met on the road – and you know what? They said that he didn't even try to resist.'

I could hardly believe my ears. John the firebrand letting someone arrest him and not putting up a fight? Surely not?

'They said he was causing a public disturbance,' Nathaniel Bartholomew explained.

'Apparently, he'd been mouthing off about Herod, saying that he should never have married his brother's wife,' Philip broke in. 'He said that he was wrong to divorce his own wife, and to cause Herodias to divorce her husband.'

'Well, of course it's wrong!' Nathaniel retorted. 'It's against our law but I'd have thought he would have done better just to keep his mouth shut!'

'And Jesus? What did he say? Was he there?' Andrew asked, aghast.

Nathaniel Bartholomew shook his head and perched on the gunwale of the boat.

'No,' he replied. 'He was . . . oh, so much has happened that I don't know where to start.'

Jesus went to Nazareth, where he had been brought up, and on the Sabbath day he went into the synagogue, as was his custom. And he stood up to read. The scroll of the prophet Isaiah was handed to him. Unrolling it, he found the place where it is written: 'The Spirit of the Lord is on me, because he has anointed me to preach good news to the poor. He has sent me to proclaim freedom for the prisoners and recovery of sight for the blind, to release the oppressed, to proclaim the year of the Lord's favour.' Then he rolled up the scroll, gave it back to the attendant and sat down. The eyes of everyone in the synagogue were fastened on him and he began by saying to them, 'Today this scripture is fulfilled in your hearing.'

All spoke well of him and were amazed at the gracious words that came from his lips. 'Isn't this Joseph's son?' they asked. Jesus said to them, 'Surely you will quote this proverb to me: "Physician, heal yourself! Do here in your home town what we have heard that you did in Capernaum."

'I tell you the truth,' he continued, 'no prophet is accepted in his home town. I assure you that there were many widows in Israel in Elijah's time, when the sky was shut for three-and-a-half years and there was a severe famine throughout the land. Yet Elijah was not sent to any of them, but to a widow in Zarepath in the region of Sidon. And there were many in Israel with leprosy in the time of Elisha the prophet, yet not one of them was cleansed – only Naaman the Syrian.'

All the people in the synagogue were furious when they heard this. They got up, drove him out of the town and took him to the brow of the hill on which the town was built in order to throw him off the cliff. But he walked right through the crowd and went on his way.

Luke 4:16-30, NIV

'He's right,' Philip nodded. 'If you had seen what happened the other day . . .'

'Which we didn't, on account of being here working our fingers down to the bone . . .' Peter cut in.

Philip appeared oblivious to his thinly veiled sarcasm.

'See, after we left here we went to Cana for a wedding and on the way – well, it was amazing . . .'

'Jesus stopped and talked to people, and if you'd heard him – it was like no preacher I've ever heard before,' Nathaniel Bartholomew burst out. 'People actually followed us begging him to say more.'

'And at the wedding – well, you won't believe this . . .'

I strained my ears as they huddled together. I couldn't catch everything they said but it was something about a pitcher of water turning into wine! I could hardly suppress my laughter – it was obvious they had been blind drunk and seeing things!

'He did that?' Andrew exclaimed. 'That proves it – he has to be the one!'

How was it, I wondered, that these guys who were, let's face it, not stupid – who bartered and bargained and were the first to seize new business opportunities – how could they be so stupid?

'Anyway,' Philip went on, clearly wanting to be the one to tell the rest of the story, 'after the wedding, Jesus went to Nazareth and we went with him . . .'

'Instead of returning here to help . . .' Peter began.

'Peter, be quiet,' Andrew snapped. 'Go on, Philip.'

Good on you Andrew, I thought. I like a good story and so I shuffled a bit nearer, still pretending to be intent on my job, which was fastening new cork floats onto the edge of Andrew and Peter's newest net. It was a laborious task but it did mean I could listen to every word.

'You see,' Philip went on, 'Jesus wanted to worship with his mother and brothers on the Sabbath, so we went to the synagogue. It was packed – lots of the people who'd followed him crowded in there as well as the usual worshippers.'

'That was when he stood up to read from the scroll,' Nathaniel Bartholomew interjected eagerly. 'The words of Isaiah the prophet about freedom for prisoners and recovery of sight for the blind and . . .'

'Release for the oppressed,' Peter interrupted. 'Which, I might add, seems a long time coming.'

It always amazes me how people know all this clever stuff. Me, I believe in Yahweh, of course I do, but those complicated teachings that they spout in the synagogue – well, most of them go over my head. I used to go to the synagogue once in a while – creeping in at the back and hurrying off the instant it was over, but of course, there was no one around to arrange my bar mitzvah or explain anything to me so I gave up. I miss the chants and prayers, though; they're kind of warming and safe.

'Anyway,' Philip was saying, cutting in on my thoughts, 'Jesus sat down and everyone looked at him, waiting for his teaching – and do you know what he said? Well, no, of course you don't. He said "Today that passage you just heard has come true, here, in this very place."'

'But that would mean . . . ?'

'He actually said . . . ?'

Andrew and Peter spoke in unison.

Philip nodded.

'He *is* the one,' he breathed. 'The one who is going to deliver us all from the hands of the Romans.'

'I knew there was something about him,' Andrew said. 'Didn't I say so, Peter?'

Peter didn't reply but I noticed he had stopped what he was doing and was listening intently.

'So what happened then?' Andrew urged.

'All hell let loose,' Nathaniel Bartholomew replied ruefully. 'Someone suddenly jumped up and said . . .'

'*Surely this is old Joseph's boy*,' Philip butted in, perfectly imitating the accent of a Nazarene. '*The one we've known ever since he was toddler?*'

'Mary, his mother, was in the women's court and people said she nearly fainted when people began muttering and jeering,' Bartholomew added. 'They kept asking how a carpenter's son could pretend to know all this stuff.

'It got quite nasty,' Philip said. 'But Jesus remained completely calm and he didn't even tell them to shut up. He just said that he knew that the last place a person gets proper recognition is in their own home town, among the people who've known them and taken them for granted for years.'

'And he told that story about Elijah and the widow in Zarepath. He said there were loads of widows in Israel but that God chose to send the prophet to help a Gentile woman.'

At that, Andrew and Peter gasped out loud and I almost dropped the float I was handling. Yahweh was God of the Jewish people, not the Gentiles. I knew I didn't keep half the laws and regulations I was supposed to – and probably there were a whole heap I didn't even know about – but I knew that the Gentiles didn't keep any of them and compared with us Jews, they were terrible people.

'And,' Nathaniel Bartholomew broke in, 'he reminded them that despite there being hundreds of lepers in Israel, it was Naaman, who came from Syria, that the prophet Elisha healed. When he said that, everyone went ballistic.'

I'm not surprised, I thought to myself. I was right to think this Jesus was trouble.

'But he's right,' Andrew mused. 'I'd never thought about it that way.'

'Well, his neighbours didn't think much of it, I can tell you. They hounded him out of the synagogue,' Philip said. 'Chased him out of the village – his own village, can you imagine that?'

'So what did you do?' Peter demanded.

'Well, we . . . I mean, it seemed sensible to keep a bit of a low profile, you know, what with . . .'

'It looked,' Nathaniel Bartholomew added, 'like they might actually do him physical harm, kill him, even . . .'

'But he gave them the slip,' Philip said triumphantly. 'I'm not sure how, but one minute the crowd were ranting and raving, and the next they'd lost interest, turned back and Jesus was nowhere to be seen.'

'Then what happened?' Andrew asked.

Nathaniel Bartholomew and Philip looked at one another.

'We came back here,' Nathaniel Bartholomew said. 'I have business to attend to and . . .'

'. . . and my wife is soon to have her child,' Philip added. 'But I can't stop thinking about what Jesus said and . . .'

'Well,' Peter cut in, 'perhaps you could think about it somewhere else? Some of us have work to do.'

It was early afternoon two days later when I heard the commotion. To be honest, I had skived off – I was in a foul mood, and justifiably I reckoned. Ever since Philip and Nathaniel had returned, it was as if I had become invisible. Oh, they still gave me jobs to do and there was still some fish and a few olives and a hunk of bread for me at mealtimes but I can honestly say that not one of them made eye contact with me all day. It was Jesus this and Jesus that and he said this and he thinks that . . . and even when I pointed out to Peter that two of the weights on his net were coming loose, he just tossed it at me and turned away. That's when I thought – well, let's just say I tossed it aside and stomped off. Mend your own flipping net, I thought.

There was a place I used to go when I wanted some peace – or when the bad feelings threatened to overwhelm me and make me slice my skin again. It was up on the hillside overlooking the lake, a tiny cave-like space between three boulders, just large enough for me to squeeze into but far too small for a normal-sized person to even think of attempting. That's where I was that afternoon when I heard the babble of voices.

Cautiously, I peered out from between the boulders and almost gasped out loud. Jesus was striding out, just a few yards from where I was hiding, and behind him, six or seven men, talking nineteen to the dozen. Yet further back, another dozen or so followed, more hesitantly, whispering among themselves.

'What does he mean when he says the kingdom of heaven is close by?' I heard one mutter.

'I haven't a clue,' another said. 'But this thing about repenting – you know, I kind of feel he's talking to me. That business with my neighbour . . . I mean, I do feel guilty about doing him down like that.'

At that moment, Jesus stopped dead in his tracks and turned to face them.

'You're right to think about what I said,' he announced. 'It's time to change your life. God's kingdom is here. Come!'

He beckoned them on and began walking briskly down the slope towards the lake. Several men hurried after him, but others lingered.

'Change our lives? What's he on about?' said one. 'I have a wife, six children, fields to manage . . . what's to change? I'm tired of this! I'm going back home.'

'Me too,' said another. 'I only came along because you encouraged me . . .'

'Yes, well, we all make mistakes! I'll stick with our village rabbi – you know where you stand with him! And he doesn't make impossible demands either!'

They turned and moved away, still muttering.

By now Jesus was almost at the lakeside, too far off for even my acute ears to catch what he was saying. In my curiosity, I forgot all about my bad mood and squeezed out of my hiding place and slithered down the hillside. Scurrying along behind the row of houses, I picked up one of the smaller wicker baskets (the large ones were too unwieldy for me to manage) and sauntered down to the water's edge as though I'd been working there all day. I had seen that James and John were in their father Zebedee's boat preparing for the night's fishing and fixing my most humble and willing expression on my face I raised my hand to them to let them know I was ready for work. But all the time I was watching Jesus out of the corner of my eye.

Simon Peter and Andrew were on the shore, grappling with one of the cast nets. Andrew had flung the net into the water but it hadn't opened completely when it landed, which meant the fish wouldn't be trapped underneath so they were pulling it in to try again. Simon Peter cast the net again and this time it was a perfect throw.

'Yes!' he cried. 'That should catch the little blighters!'

I heard Jesus laugh and turned my head slightly. 'Come and follow me,' he called to them.

They stopped, amazed at the sight of him.

'Come, follow me,' he repeated, 'and I will teach you to catch people, not fish!'

'Jesus!' I heard Andrew gasp, nudging his brother. Both of them stopped stock still and stared.

It was like looking at a stone carving. Neither Jesus nor Andrew nor Simon Peter moved for what seemed like minutes. Then as one, Andrew and Peter let go of the net and walked slowly up to Jesus. He laid a hand on each of their shoulders and then embraced them both, and began walking slowly along the shore towards the place where I was standing, Andrew and Peter following him. As for the net, it was left drifting in the water.

They never, ever left their nets. It was just not done. And I could see that their boat hadn't been swabbed, there was still a couple of baskets of fish from the day before to be put on the wagon to go to Magdala for salting – and yet there they both were, heads bent, talking in low murmurs to Jesus and acting for all the world as if they had nothing to do for the rest of the day.

'Reuben, can you bring us some floats?' James called from the boat. 'Fast as you can!'

I turned and walked back to the store at the top of the beach.

'James, John, will you follow me as well?' Jesus' voice carried on the breeze. Well, I knew the answer to that one; there was no way that the brothers would waste one hour of money-earning time in their father's business – a business that one day would be theirs (and by the look of Zebedee lately, that wouldn't be too far in the future). They were hard-headed businessmen as well as skilful fishermen – everyone spoke of them as being at the top of their trade. I had overheard Nathaniel say that the fish they supplied was favoured by the rich and elite as far away as Jerusalem – so much so that they transported cratefuls of biny fish for every feast day throughout the year.

I picked up three or four floats and turned to go back to the boat – and almost dropped them in my amazement.

James and John were out of the boat, splashing through the shallow water like eager children on a day's holiday. In an instant, they too were being embraced by Jesus.

'Come!' I heard Jesus say and with that they all walked along the beach towards Peter's house, leaving Zebedee and the hired hand gawping after them.

Well, of course, I was quick to seize the opportunity. I signed to Zebedee that I was free to help. But he wasn't looking at me. He was standing in the prow of the boat, staring at his sons as they walked away without a backward glance.

It didn't take me long to decide that it was time for me to move on. The catches had been getting smaller and smaller over the past couple of weeks, and the men were using their own sons and the longest-standing hired hands; the casual labour had been sent away and there was little for me to do, except dodge the sneers of the local thug and to try not to get upset when a toddler or baby burst out crying at the sight of me. It was hard enough in the evenings to hear chattering and laughter coming from the houses and to know that I would never be part of a real family, but now this Jesus had turned up, everything had changed. The guys who had stuck with him that afternoon were welcomed into Peter's house like old friends; Peter himself had been transformed from a work-centred guy to someone who appeared to want to do nothing but talk and talk with Jesus; and when I had crept up later that evening I could tell just from the smells that they were feasting and drinking and having a great time. Oh, I guess I could have hung around, and Andrew or one of the others would have given me some food; but I would have been outside, a charity case, their 'good deed for the day'. So I went into Capernaum town.

It's not a huge place, and not as busy as Sepphoris but because there are always traders passing through, it's pretty good for doing a little light thieving and I was in that frame of mind. The buzz I got from pinching fruit off a stall under the very eyes of the market trader, or palming a slice of goat's cheese off a plate in the tavern while the diners were arguing about the price of timber, stopped me from letting off steam by cutting myself, and that had to be a good thing.

I stayed there for several days. There was an empty, half ruined house down one of the rundown alleyways on the edge of the town, where I and a few other wanderers used to bed down. These were guys who were in no position to look down on me – Aaron, gentle and sweet, but with the understanding of a four year old; Hillel, who despite his blindness could play his lute so sweetly that he was never short of a few coins; and old Mordecai, whose left arm and leg were useless as pieces of rag, and who spent his days begging alms at the synagogue door. We shared out our pickings from the day and in a strange way, waking up to see them all lying there first thing in the morning gave me a sense of wellbeing that normal folk would have found hard to understand.

And then one evening I got back to the house before anyone else. It was just an hour or so before the start of the Sabbath and the streets were busy with people finishing up their daily work and women hastily buying last minute items before the *hazzan* called them to prayer. I had had a particularly fruitful day and wanted to offload my stash and hide the money. Food I'd share with anyone but coins – that was another thing altogether. All day the town had seemed busier than ever, with crowds of people jostling one another, many of them seeming not to have a clue where they were going, and all this made it perfect for me. Someone drops a coin – I'm there on my knees pocketing it before they even notice; traders arguing prices with visitors – I've snatched pitta bread and a handful of dates before they realise I'm under the table. As I said, being small does have its advantages.

Anyway, on this particular evening, I was about to pull out the loose brick I'd spotted days before in order to hide my stuff when I heard a noise. At first I thought it was one of the stray dogs that roamed the town, or perhaps a rat; there were plenty of those about. But dogs bark or howl and rats scuttle and scratch; neither of them sob and sniff.

The house had only two rooms, and it was when I peered cautiously through the crumbling doorway to the back area that I saw her. A girl. She was huddled in a corner, the hem of her dress caked with mud and God knows what else, and her hair matted and falling over her face.

I was about to retreat and think about what to do when she looked up and saw me and jumped to her feet.

'I'm sorry, is this your house, I didn't know where to go, I'm sorry, I'll go, please don't hurt me!'

The words came tumbling out of her like a waterfall after a rainstorm but it was the fear in her eyes that really got to me.

I shook my head furiously and gestured to her to sit down. She hesitated, staring at me. But the stare was not one of revulsion or disgust; it was simply that she didn't seem to believe that I wasn't about to chase her out with a big stick.

I pointed to my lips and shook my head.

'You can't speak?' she asked, her voice wobbly with the suppression of tears. 'Can you hear me?'

I nodded enthusiastically and smiled. Then I remembered that with an upper lip that is hooked to your left nostril, smiles can often have the reverse effect of what you hope. The girl didn't seem to be worried by it all.

I gestured to her to wait and went back to my corner and picked up the stylus I had found – alright, pinched – a few days before. There was enough dirt on the mud floor to make things easy and I began writing.

'My name is Reuben.' And then I pointed to her.

'Esther,' she said.

'Where?' I wrote. Back then, I only knew how to write a few words.

'Where am I going?' she asked. 'I – I'm looking for someone. The friend I was with – I lost him in the crowd and now . . .'

With that the tears started flowing in earnest.

I mimed eating and drinking and she got the message.

'Starving,' she said with a faint smile. 'But I don't have any money. Caleb was looking after what we had and . . .'

I made a gesture of dismissal and suggested she should sit down. I collected some of the dates and figs I had procured, along with a somewhat squashed barley cake and took them through to her. She began stuffing them into her mouth, while smiling up at me as if I had set a banquet before her.

'Thank you Reuben,' she mumbled through a mouthful of crumbs. 'Do you know . . . ?'

She stopped mid-sentence at the sound of shuffling in the next room, leapt to her feet and cringed back against the wall as if she hoped it would open and swallow her up.

'What's that?'

I held up a hand reassuringly, put my finger to my lips and went through to Mordecai and Hillel to prepare them for our new arrival. I didn't bother explaining to Aaron, because he lives in his own world, but through enough gestures and play-acting to earn me a role with a troupe of travelling entertainers, I got the message across to Mordecai and he put it into words for the blind Hillel.

'Does she have money?' Mordecai asked at once. I gave him my most withering look and shook my head.

'Then she's no use to us, is she?' he muttered.

'You want me to go.' Esther was standing in the doorway, her eyes flitting from one to another of us. The most astonishing thing was that she seemed totally unfazed by any of it – my deformity,

Mordecai's withered limbs, Aaron's gentle rocking and humming or the cavities in Hillel's face where his eyes should have been.

I shook my head and gestured that she could stay. Pointing to the sky I indicated that when the sun came up, we would look for – and then I wrote 'Friend' in the dirt. I hoped we would find him – I was almost at the limit of my written vocabulary.

'Thank you!' she exclaimed. 'If you show me the way to the synagogue, I'm sure he'll be there. But please, come with me? Because I'll have to go to the women's area and if you could just find Caleb and bring him to me . . .'

Go to the synagogue after all this time? It wasn't as though I needed to be there to beg, not with my little stash behind the broken brick. That would last me for at least a week. Besides, this Caleb was clearly some religious type who knew it all and would look down on me like scum.

I was about to shake my head when Esther came close to me.

'Thank you,' she repeated. 'Thank you so much.'

And she squeezed my hand and smiled at me. Just as if I was an ordinary, everyday boy of thirteen.

So what has that got to do with me?

1. Nathaniel Bartholomew said that he thought John the Baptist would have done better to keep his mouth shut, rather than tell Herod that he had done wrong. It is never easy to stand up to someone, particularly if they are in a position of authority or seem to be more popular or more clever than we are. It's very tempting to say nothing. Why did John insist on challenging Herod, even when he must have known the outcome? What was his motivation? What drives us on to challenge people, and what fears keep us from opening our mouths? How can we deal with this?

2. Jesus said that a prophet is rarely honoured among the people who know him best. Have you ever found that people close to you do not accept your Christian faith or way of life – sometimes when we come to Christ others mock us and think it is just a 'passing phase'. How do we respond? Is it best just to argue our point, or is there something else we should be doing to prove the difference Christ makes in our life? If you are still unsure about your faith, perhaps you could share with your group the things that would help to convince you that there was 'something to it'.

3. You can read the story of Elijah and the widow in 1 Kings Chapter 17 verses 7-24.

4. Put yourself in Zebedee's shoes. How would you have felt? Now imagine you are James or John? What was it about Jesus that made you drop everything and follow him? Remember they'd only just met him; all they knew about him was hearsay. Or was it? When we encounter Jesus – and it can happen in a hundred different ways – our response may surprise and even startle us.

5. Mordecai says that if Esther doesn't have cash on her, she's of no use to them. Before we judge him, imagine you are totally dependent on the charity of others – not just for a day or a week, but for a lifetime. Add to that the idea that you have a disability which in those days isolated you from society. Wouldn't you resent someone turning up who might want to share the tiny bit of food you had, or who might look down on you?

6. Esther appeared not to notice the disabilities of Mordecai, Hillel and Aaron. In fact, she couldn't have missed them (as we shall see later) but to her they were unimportant, just as Reuben's deformity and short stature wasn't an issue. Reuben showed her kindness and that was what she judged him by. Her gift to Reuben was greater than his gift of food to her: she treated him as though, in his own words, 'he was a normal boy of thirteen'. Discuss with your group the things that you most appreciate in the attitude of others towards you – are there things in your life that some people shy away from or refuse to discuss?

7. Some of those listening to Jesus did not understand what he meant by 'the kingdom of heaven'. Later in the book we will discover that Jesus started many of his stories with the words 'the kingdom of heaven is like . . .'. Before you get that far, discuss what you understand by those words. Is the kingdom some faraway place to be reached after death? Or is it something we can see – and be – signs of in our everyday lives. We will pursue this later!

CHAPTER THIRTEEN

Found – and lost

Esther

I knew I was safe. Reuben seemed kind, and not much older than me, but had he tried anything on I could have knocked him over with my little finger and made a run for it. The blind man – well, he'd be easy to dodge and as for the old boy, bless him, it would have taken him so long to shuffle in my direction that he'd have had no chance. So it wasn't fear that kept me awake half the night; it was the woman in the alleyway.

She had been the reason I had lost sight of Caleb. We were on the outskirts of the town, and Caleb had been stopping and asking every other person if they'd seen Jesus. Some of them had heard about him but were vague as to where we might find him; others heard his question and sneered, saying that it was obvious that this Jesus was just another misguided man with ideas above his station in life. He was arguing with one of the basket makers in the market, when suddenly there was this ear piercing, unearthly scream, high pitched on one note, and repeated over and over again.

'No, no, run, run, mustn't stop, run, run . . .'

There was a commotion further up the street; shouting and cursing and the sound of pottery crashing to the ground from a makeshift stall on the corner of the next alleyway.

'Get out of here, you crazy woman!'

'She's a thief, stop her!'

'Let her go, she's more trouble than she's worth!'

I stepped into the middle of the street in an attempt to see what was going on and then I saw her. A stick thin, raven haired woman in garish, if tattered, clothes and bare feet, dodging in and out of the jeering, sneering crowd. For a moment it seemed as if the burly man who was chasing her would get near enough to grab her, but at the last moment, she swerved like a goat being chased by a lynx, dived under the basket maker's stall, round the side of another, and down an alleyway.

I don't know why I did what I did next – or at least, I didn't know then. But I stepped out in front of the guy who was chasing her, sticking my foot in his path and tripping him up. The expression on his face was enough to set me running off too, and I fled down the same alleyway.

'That mad Ziva. Will we ever be rid of her?'

My heart missed a beat and I ran faster. The woman was ahead of me, running more slowly, and her laboured breathing was audible even from a distance.

And so was the sweeping sound as her left leg dragged behind her in the dust.

'Ziva! Ziva!'

For a second, her pace slackened. Then she shrieked, a wild frenzied cry like a hunted animal, and swerved down a narrow path between two houses.

'Ziva, wait! It's me – Esther!'

I had almost reached the path when a cart appeared, pulled by a lumbering ox.

'Whoa!'

The driver halted the cart on the corner, completely blocking the path, and began unloading sacks of grain.

I tried desperately to dodge round the side but the edge of the cart was only a couple of inches from the wall of the houses on either side. By the time I had crawled under it on my hands and knees, praying that the ox wouldn't lash out with his enormous feet, she had gone.

Of course, I went on looking. I peered through open doors, earning myself a few curses on the way; I looked for footprints in the dirt but there was nothing. In the end, with tears streaming down my face, I realised I had lost her for the second time.

Because I knew without a shadow of doubt that the woman was my sister. Grown, true, and terribly changed. But I knew there couldn't be two women of that name with a damaged foot – of that I was certain.

The other thing I was certain of was that I was completely and totally lost.

Not for the first time, I wondered whether I had been stupid to run away from Cana, from what was, after all, a job, a roof and two meals a day. At first, with the memory of Nathan's groping hands plaguing me every waking hour, it seemed like the perfect solution. Caleb was convinced that he could persuade Jesus to take him on as some sort of apprentice, teach him his magic and then he would go about the countryside earning enough money to keep both of us in wealth and comfort. He was so cheerful, so full of plans and for a while I was carried along on his enthusiasm.

I began to trust him too, especially when he gave me the gold pin.

'You haven't got anything,' he reasoned. 'As soon as we find Jesus, I'll be off and you'll need something to tide you over until you find work. But pin it out of sight – and if anyone asks, tell them your grandmother left it to you.'

I couldn't help smiling. My grandmother had never possessed one thing that wasn't essential for existence – her wedding jewellery had long since been sold to keep her alive.

Once we had put two days between Cana and ourselves I began to relax enough to start thinking rationally. I went over and over the events of that wedding day in my mind and no matter how often I tried to fit the Jesus that Caleb talked about with the man who had turned that water into wine, I couldn't do it.

If he was the sort of man Caleb thought he was, why didn't he stand up and shout about what he'd done, instead of just murmuring to the servants to mention it to Nathan?

If he was the sort of man Caleb thought he was, why didn't he perform this amazing feat in front of everyone, and then demand money from the host before allowing it to be served?

And if he really was an established magician, then why did his friends – the ones sitting round the table with him, and chatting to Mary, his mother – why did they look so gobsmacked at what was going on? As if it was the first time in their entire lives they had seen anything like it?

'What if he tells you he doesn't want an apprentice?' I had ventured to ask Caleb one day. 'He might not want to tell you his secrets.'

Caleb had laughed out loud. 'I shall just follow him around until he gives in,' he chuckled. 'Trust me, people who can do tricks love to have people grovelling to them and saying how great they are. My mother . . .'

He had swallowed hard before continuing. 'My mother once got a potion off a healer who travelled round the villages,' he went on. 'He told her that if she told all her friends how brilliant it was, he would give her the next jar for less.'

'Was it brilliant?'

'Not so you'd notice,' he said curtly. 'She was dead within a year.'

'I'm sorry,' I murmured.

'But once I find Jesus,' he went on, 'and get in with him, I'll be made. You could see he had a gang of mates around him, and I'm going to be one of those. One of his buddies . . .'

That was when I realised that Caleb was no different from me. We both wanted the same thing. We wanted to belong, to matter to someone, to be accepted. And as I wandered up and down alleyways looking for Caleb and dreading the dark that was rapidly making it harder to find my way, I wondered if perhaps he was right after all. If for both of us, our best bet of finding what we wanted, was to get in with this Jesus and his crowd.

It was when a couple of boys began following me, calling out obscenities, that I realised I had to find somewhere safe to spend the night. I dodged into the doorway of a house and they ran off, assuming, I suppose, that I lived there and that someone would chase them away. Across the alleyway, I spotted a tumbledown shack with torn sacking across the entrance. I peered in and despite the gloom could see that there were a couple of dirty mats on the floor but no one in sight. No sign of food, or water jars; nothing to suggest anyone was coming back.

Hunger was gnawing at my stomach, and the tears that I had held back for hours poured down my cheeks as I found the farthest corner of the back room and sat down, my knees to my chin. I felt swamped by a huge sense of loss; I'd lost Caleb and once again, I'd lost Ziva. It was strange: I had so wanted it to be her, and yet, sitting there in the dark, I almost hoped it hadn't been my sister because in my mind, along with the injured foot and the raven hair that were just as I remembered, there was the sound of that wild screaming, the anguished cry of someone in real torment. Ziva had always seemed to live in fear and it wasn't until I got to an age when I too had reason to fear what went on in my father's house that I began to understand; but she had never seemed mad.

Mad! That's when I remembered what I'd overheard the day before, when Caleb and I had hitched a lift on a cart. Caleb had asked if the carter had seen Jesus.

'What – him who's supposed to have turned a crazy woman sane?' the man had replied, sniffing and wiping his nose with the back of his hand. 'Nah – but I've heard it said he's round these parts somewhere.'

At the time, despite Caleb's eager whispering that Jesus clearly had more strands of magic at his fingertips than he thought, I had assumed the carter's story was just a wild exaggeration. But now, sitting in the dark and listening to the rumbling of my empty stomach, I began to wonder. If Jesus could turn water into wine, could he really turn madness to sanity?

If only I could find Ziva then maybe when Caleb caught up with Jesus . . . but what was the point of thinking like that? I'd lost Ziva, I'd lost Caleb and I hadn't a clue where Jesus was.

It was as I tried ineffectually to wipe away my tears on the sleeve of my tunic that I heard a noise in the outer room. My whole body stiffened with fear and I shrank further into my corner.

A shape appeared in the doorway. I jumped to my feet, apologies pouring out of my mouth, my whole purpose being to get past whoever it was and make my escape before they could hurt me. And that's when I saw Reuben.

At first, in the dim light, I thought he was a little kid, he was so small. But then I saw his short arms, his huge head, and the twisted lips and realised he was deformed. My heart went out to him; there was once a girl in our village back home who was like Reuben, and she was teased and taunted day in day out, until one morning she was found face down in the river, dead. People said she must have slipped from the bank into the water, but I didn't believe that. I saw her body and the expression on her face was, for the first time ever, one of peace.

Reuben was so kind, that it didn't take me long to decide that I would tell him about Ziva. Perhaps he'd seen her around, perhaps he had ways of finding out where she was living – and even if he didn't know anything at all, it would be one more pair of eyes on the lookout.

I decided to tell him the very next day.

So what has that got to do with me?

1. What are your reasons for 'getting in with Jesus'? Do you believe that following him is the passport to an easy life? If you're avoiding his invitation, why is that? Are you frightened you can't live up to his expectations? Do you imagine that becoming a Christian means saying goodbye to partying, and having fun?

2. Esther spends time thinking about Caleb's attitude to Jesus and begins to realise that the way he behaves is not in keeping with Caleb's view of him. Think back to your view of Jesus when you were a small child? Now? Perhaps you simply don't know what to make of him. When you are trying to get to know someone, what pointers do you look for to help you decide whether to get closer to them or to beat a hasty retreat? Do you apply the same things to Jesus?

CHAPTER FOURTEEN

Healings and heartache

Reuben

I didn't sleep well that night. It wasn't Mordecai's incessant snoring that kept me awake; I was used to that and most nights I only woke up when it stopped. It was knowing that through the crumbling wall Esther was as restless as I was. I could hear her tossing and turning, and I wondered whether it was with fear or cold. I had given her the blanket I normally used but in truth it was more holes than blanket and after the heat of the day, the temperature had plummeted and the night was cooler than usual for the time of year.

'Is it time?' The first shafts of dawn sunlight were spiking through the cracks in the wall when Esther's voice woke me from a half doze. 'Can we go now?'

I was about to protest that it was too early but the thought of walking through the town with Esther on my own made me keep quiet. Normally, I didn't like the Sabbath; work of any kind was strictly forbidden so there were no traders about, no stalls to steal from, and always the risk that if someone spotted me even gathering a few sticks, let alone lighting a fire, they would throw stones at me or chase me away. Funny that stone throwing didn't seem to be a sin, Sabbath or not.

'I do hope Jesus is there,' Esther said as we made our way down the dirt track towards the centre of the town. 'Because if he is, then Caleb will be too.'

She must have seen the look of confusion on my face, because she stopped dead and touched my arm.

'Haven't you heard about him? Jesus – he's the reason we've come here. Well, among other things . . .'

My mouth dropped open and I stared at her.

I pointed to my eyes and then thumped my chest.

'You've seen Jesus too?' She seemed delighted. 'Where? When?'

I began miming but she was in full flood.

'Isn't he amazing? Did you know he can work magic? He turned pitchers full of water into the best wine in the world, just like that! I saw it with my own eyes!'

My heart started thumping like a drum. So it was true. Everything Philip and Nathaniel Bartholomew had said was true.

'And there's more,' she added hesitantly. 'Some people say he cured a mad woman.'

I pulled a face and spun the index finger of my left hand round and round the side of my head to indicate that whoever thought that was mad themselves.

Esther looked devastated.

'You don't think it's true?' she asked. 'I hoped . . .'

She looked so upset that I jerked my head, shrugged and intimated that just possibly there might be something in it. Not that I believed that for one moment.

That's when she told me about her sister, about how she'd run away and how Esther was sure she was somewhere in the town.

'If you see anyone with a limp and . . .'

I nodded reassuringly but to be honest, if this Ziva was as out of it as Esther suggested, I knew she would have been driven out of town and was in all probability roaming the countryside alone.

If that was the case, her chances weren't exactly looking good.

The streets were getting busy with everyone heading in one direction – the synagogue.

'Listen!' Esther said, nudging my arm.

'He's here . . . saw him by the lake . . . you should hear the things he says . . . going to the synagogue . . . Jesus . . . Jesus . . .'

Myriad voices, a dozen different accents, but all talking about the same thing. Jesus was here. And I was going to see him.

Suddenly I thought about Andrew, Peter and the others. They would be here too – they had never missed Sabbath at the synagogue for as long as I had known them – apart, of course, from that time when they were throwing up everywhere. Now I was really nervous; what if they saw me and told Jesus that I'd run off without even saying goodbye, without a thank you for what they'd given me? Rabbis had strict rules and knew the law inside out and sideways.

The closer we got to the synagogue, the denser the crowd became. There must have been at least three times as many worshippers as any normal Sabbath, including many women; and some, I could tell by their accents, weren't from around Capernaum.

I gestured to Esther that she should go in with the women and I would wait outside.

'No!' she exclaimed, snatching my hand. 'Please Reuben, you promised – you have to find Caleb.'

I had promised no such thing but the feel of her tiny hand in my claw-like one did something to my head as well as my heart and I found myself nodding and smiling.

'He's got light-coloured hair and he's much paler than you – oh, and he's tall,' she said. He would be, I thought, envious of him already.

I pulled a face, shrugged and gestured to the crowd. There were at least thirty men answering to that description in this one part of the street alone.

'And he has a scar,' she said. 'Here.'

She drew a line under her left eye and onto her cheek with the tip of her finger.

So he wasn't totally perfect then. Good.

There was, however, still the small problem of my being unable to speak when and if I did find him. I pointed to my lips, shrugged and shook my head.

'Give him this,' she said and handed me a tiny pin.

I frowned.

'Just do it,' she said briskly. 'He'll know it's from me.'

Then, more gently, she added, 'Don't worry, you'll find him – he'll be wherever Jesus is.'

I didn't like to tell her that when you are as small as I am, all you are likely to see is a whole lot of backsides. But when she smiled at me, I decided that somehow I'd find a way to hunt down this Caleb, because that was clearly what would make her happy.

Then he went down to Capernaum, a town in Galilee, and on the Sabbath began to teach the people. They were amazed at his teaching, because his message had authority.

Luke 4:31, 32

It was after the prayer of Amidah that I saw Andrew and Peter – and Jesus was right there beside them. I had managed to find a space at the back of the synagogue between two elderly men, one of whom let me stand on the seat behind him. So I saw when Jesus stood up and began to teach.

The whole place hung on his every word. There's usually coughing and a bit of shuffling and the odd person changing position but not this time. Well, not to start with anyway.

'Believe the good news!' he cried. 'Turn away from sin and live!'

Then he spoke about a new kingdom that had arrived, a new promise that God was making to his people. He was amazing – not a bit like any rabbi I'd heard before. You found yourself not just listening, but believing everything he said simply because he spoke like someone who really knew what was what and wasn't just making up a load of stuff to make himself sound clever. And I guess I wasn't the only one who felt that way because you could hear the sharp intake of breath around the synagogue at his words – until suddenly there was a scream, an awful, guttural cry that sent shivers down my spine.

'What do you want with us, Jesus of Nazareth? Have you come to finish us off?'

Everyone turned. A wild-eyed man, with matted hair, and a filthy loincloth was pushing his way towards Jesus, shoving people aside and spitting on the ground.

'I know who you are,' the man screeched, and now his voice was high like a woman's. 'You are the holy One of God!'

Well, there was an uproar, I can tell you. Some shouted at him to clear off, others simply gawped and repeated the words 'Holy One of God?' in derision or, in some cases, awe.

'Be quiet this instant!' Jesus' voice rose above the cacophony of sound. 'Come out of him now!'

The man's body jerked and twisted and he crashed to the ground so violently that I felt sure every bone in his body would be broken.

And then he stood up. The twisted snarling expression had left his face, and he stood totally relaxed before us all. Jesus smiled at him, nodded and the man murmured something and then moved to one side, looking as normal as everyone else and a lot less agitated than many.

I couldn't believe it. I'd seen a fair few crazy people in my time – and I'd been called an imbecile by a good many more; but never once had I seen anyone recover from insanity. Esther's story might have sounded good but I thought it was just that; a story. I knew that demons lived inside people – I had my own to contend with – but to see them leave a person, just like that . . .

'What's going on?' the old man to my left asked voicing my own thoughts. 'Who is this Jesus? How come he speaks and a madman becomes sane?'

'If I hadn't seen it with my own eyes,' another said, 'I would never have believed it. That man has been raving around this area for months – and now look at him.'

He shook his head in bewilderment.

'I need to find out more about this Jesus.'

And as he squeezed past me, the guy in front of him turned to allow him through and I saw the long, silver line of the scar running under his eye and down onto his cheekbone. It had to be Caleb.

I tapped him on the arm and he glanced round, puzzled for a moment and then, looking down and seeing me, sighed impatiently and made to shove me away. So I used the old trick that we little people learn early in life. I dropped to my knees and sat on his feet.

'What the . . . ?'

I waved the pin in front of him, and then pointed to the women's gallery.

'Is that the . . . ? What are you doing with that? Give it to me!'

I wasn't stupid. I ducked clutching the pin in my fist and pointed again to the women's gallery.

'You thief . . .' His voice was at that stage where guys lucky enough to have one find it sliding up and down the scale in the most unpredictable manner. At least his embarrassment shut him up for a minute.

I shook my head violently and went on pointing. Slowly light dawned on his face.

'Are you telling me Esther's here?'

I nodded and then put a finger to each eye and drew a track of imaginary tears down each of my cheeks, and pointed again to Caleb.

'Where did you find her? She just wandered off and . . . oh I get it!'

He grabbed me by the shoulders, gripping so hard that my eyes watered with the pain.

'If you've hurt her . . .'

I shook my head again, I mimed eating, drinking – and then thought it best to ignore the sleeping bit in case he got the wrong idea. I gestured to the women's gallery yet again and prayed that he would spot Esther.

'Oh for God's sake, just tell me!' he shouted.

I pointed to my lips and shook my head. His face flushed and he let go of me.

'I'm sorry,' he said. 'Really I am. I didn't realize that you were dumb as well as . . .' He had the good grace to let the words die on his lips.

'Look, I can't come right now – I have to speak to Jesus,' he gabbled. 'Go and tell Esther – oh, you can't tell her anything can you?'

I nodded and mimed writing.

'You can write? Really?'

Honestly, just because I don't look that hot doesn't mean I don't have a brain.

'Tell her that as soon as I've spoken to Jesus . . .'

I nudged him and gestured to the doorway. He glanced frantically around the synagogue and realised that Jesus, along with most of the worshippers had already left.

'Oh no!' He looked genuinely distraught. 'I don't believe it – I have to find him. Get Esther – and . . .'

He hesitated, eyeing me up and down.

'I guess I can trust you?'

I nodded emphatically.

'If I can find out where he's going . . . I heard one of the men with him say that his mother-in-law was sick and Jesus said he'd go and visit but . . .'

I was pretty sure that he was talking about Peter; his mother-in-law seemed to be sick more often than well these days and I knew that Peter's wife was beside herself with worry. I gestured to Caleb that I knew exactly where Jesus would be going and that I'd take him there. With Esther of course.

'You will? But I can't pay you.'

he look I gave him was withering enough to get the message across. Some people you just help because you want to.

The road that hugged the edge of the lake was thronged with people, but by walking along the beach we were able to get ahead of many of them, and it wasn't long before I saw Jesus, Andrew and Peter branching away up the narrow track that led to Peter's house at the edge of Bethsaida village. I beckoned to Caleb and Esther to follow me and dodged between the clusters of onlookers in the hope of sneaking round the back of the house. I saw Peter and Jesus disappear through the doorway of the house but as we drew nearer, Andrew turned, held up a hand and began speaking.

Jesus left the synagogue and went to the home of Simon. Now Simon's mother-in-law was suffering from a high fever and they asked Jesus to help her. So he bent over her and rebuked the fever and it left her.

Luke 4:38, 39

'Please,' he said, 'my brother's mother-in-law is very sick; she has a high fever and . . .'

At that quite a few people began backing off rapidly.

'. . . and she needs quiet and rest. She is very ill.'

A murmur of sympathy rippled through the crowd.

'So please, give us some space, some time to be with her until . . .'

He left the sentence unfinished.

At that, more people began leaving, but a few sat down on the ground quietly chanting a prayer or singing one of the psalms of supplication to Yahweh.

I looked questioningly at Caleb and Esther.

'We will wait,' Caleb said emphatically. 'For as long as it takes.'

'I'm hungry,' Esther sighed.

'Don't look at me,' Caleb muttered. 'I'm not leaving here until I've talked with Jesus.'

I gestured to Esther to wait. This was something I could do for her that Caleb couldn't and if it meant helping myself to something that wasn't mine, well so be it. Within minutes I was back, handing her a fistful of dates, some pitta and half a pomegranate that someone had discarded.

'Look!' For one heart-stopping moment, I thought someone had seen me stealing from the unattended kitchen of Zebedee's house. I wheeled round, heart pounding and then realised with a great flood of relief that no one was looking at me.

They were all staring into the courtyard of Peter's house. His mother-in-law, humming softly under her breath, walked out into the courtyard and opening the door of the clay oven, took out some bread that had been baked before the Sabbath began. Then she squatted down and glancing up towards the setting sun, lit the fire, and began tossing herbs into a pot.

'But she was ill . . .'

'I know she was, I saw her with my own eyes last night and I thought she was close to the end . . .'

'What happened?'

As the astonished murmurings reached her ears, Peter's mother looked up, her eyes bright and her face free of all ravages of fever.

'Jesus healed me,' she called. 'See, I'm well!'

And with that she stood up and twirled round like an excited child.

'I knew it, I knew it!' Caleb gasped, grabbing Esther by the shoulders. 'I told you he was a magician! I have so got to get in with this guy.'

'Oh come off it,' a heavily set boy with broken teeth burst out. 'It was just a coincidence – it has to be. She was probably well on the mend and then saw she had visitors and decided to get up. My mother does it all the time – sighing and complaining to us, and then when the neighbours come she's suddenly all charm and sweetness!'

'No!' another disagreed. 'I saw her just hours ago and she was bathed in sweat, thrashing around on her mat, and talking gibberish with the fever. It's a miracle!'

'Well, I'll tell you one thing,' her companion nodded. 'I'm going right now to fetch my nephew – he's been wasting away before our eyes for weeks. If this Jesus can cure Peter's mother, then why not little Benjamin?'

'Or my Raisa?'

'I'm going to tell my husband – he's been coughing blood for days and . . .'

'Hurry! Hurry!'

The ripple of conversation ran backward through the crowd like a wave pulling away from the beach edge, and as one the crowd turned and then split, with people running in different directions in their haste to bring their friends and family before Jesus moved on.

'Come on!' Caleb cried excitedly, grabbing Esther's arm. 'Quick – follow me!'

'Where are we going?'

'Into town,' Caleb told her. 'There's money to be made.'

'What do you mean?'

'Listen, we go and find all the sick-looking people and the cripples and tell them that we know where Jesus is and that he can heal them in a trice. But we don't show them where he is till they cough up some money.'

'You can't do that!' Esther exploded. 'If anyone deserves to be paid, it's Jesus and he didn't ask that madman for a single lepton.'

She was right. I was never one to turn down the chance of earning money but not by preying on people like me – people who needed every last shekel to keep body and soul together.

'You don't get it,' Caleb said confidently. 'He'll be doing it for free to start with, just till he's made a name for himself and after that – well, he can charge whatever he likes. But we'll get in first while we've got the chance.'

'I don't know . . .' I could see Esther wavering. I grabbed Caleb's hand and shook my head vigorously, waving my arms and making a thumbs down sign to show my disgust.

'Please yourselves,' he said. 'I'm going and . . . oh! No – wait, I've a better idea.' He stared at me, his eyes widening and a great grin spreading across his face.

'You live round here, right?'

I shrugged, gesturing that I was prone to coming and going.

'So people know you?'

I shrugged again and then gave a brief nod.

'So we get Jesus to heal you – and then we go and show people what he's done and that way, they'll give us their last . . .'

I stamped my foot, spat on the ground and walked away, clenching my fists and biting down on my lip until I could taste the blood. How dare he even think of using me as some sort of sideshow? How dare he consider parading me in front of Jesus just to line his own pocket? What did he think would happen? That Jesus would suddenly add eighteen inches to my height, untwist my lip, lengthen my arms and give me a voice? I didn't think so.

'Reuben, Reuben, wait!'

I could hear Esther calling me but there was no way I was even going to turn round, especially since my eyes were blurred with unshed tears. I turned down the path that ran behind the cluster of houses and headed up the hill fighting the urge to tear at my hateful body and let the rage ooze out with the blood.

It was a good hour later, as I sat on a rocky outcrop holding my bruised head in my hands and relishing the stinging of the oozing cuts in my groin, that I saw them – crowds of people heading towards Peter's house, but moving much slower than when they had left an hour earlier. Then they had been running and shouting, pushing one another out of the way. Now it was a slow column, some shuffling painfully, some with bandaged limbs, some being carried on pallets. I got to my feet and watched. Could it be possible that Jesus would actually heal all these? The man at the synagogue had seemed OK, but then again, for all I knew he could have another fit of madness at the next cycle of the moon. And Peter's mother-in-law – maybe that man in the crowd was right. Maybe she had been on the mend after all.

But this lot – they would present him with a real challenge. What would he do when he saw them? There must have been at least forty people, limping, coughing, bent with pain. Surely he couldn't . . .

But what if he could? Would that mean that he could make me normal? Obviously not make me taller – but give me the power of speech? I tried to imagine what it would be like to speak, to be able to hold a proper conversation, to answer people's questions without having to resort to sign language or the few written words I had learnt. I visualised people looking at me, not as if I was some halfwit, but like an equal, one of them.

Before I realised what I was doing, I was scurrying back down the hill towards Peter's house. Whatever was about to happen, I had a feeling it was going to be too important to miss.

By the time I reached the bottom of the hill, the courtyard of Peter's house was overflowing with people. I half expected Peter or Andrew to come out and demand that they went away, but instead, Jesus appeared in the doorway. I had hidden behind a huge wooden barrel, from which point I could see everything that was going on, but be out of sight to all but the most observant onlooker. And believe me everyone's eyes were fixed on Jesus.

'Master, for three years my husband has been unable to walk. Touch him and he'll be well!'

'Rabbi, my father – his eyes are clouded, he cannot see . . .'

'Master, my child vomits her food and is wasting away . . .'

Jesus moved slowly among them, laying his hands on each one. Before my eyes I saw the man on the stretcher stand up and walk, tears pouring down his face; the old man crying out with delight and shouting 'My wife – I see you! I see you' before clasping her to him as she sobbed with joy; and the little girl jumping up and down and begging that her mother take her home and cook fish and make barley cakes.

On and on he went, calmly, gently, as more and more people clamoured for his attention. I could see Peter, Andrew and Philip in the doorway, their eyes glued on Jesus. I edged nearer, my heart pounding. At that moment a woman rushed up to him and fell to her knees.

'Master, my son – over there, please – he's fitting again, day after day he has these fits, help us, please help us . . .'

With two long strides Jesus was at the side of the boy whose body was writhing and jerking on the ground.

'Come out!' Jesus commanded in just the same tone of voice as he had used with the madman in the synagogue.

The boy's body lurched, his back arched and foam coated his lips.

'You are the Son of God!' the boy screeched. 'The Son of God – you are, you are . . .'

'Be silent!'

Jesus' voice echoed round the watching crowd.

In an instant the boy crumpled like a sail being loosened from the mast of a boat, all tension escaping from his body. With a huge sigh, he opened his eyes. Jesus stretched out an arm and helped him up.

'Go,' he said. 'You are well.'

After the crowd had dispersed, buzzing with excitement at everything they had seen, I looked for Esther and Caleb but there was no sign of them. I guessed that Caleb had persuaded Esther to go into town and spread the word about Jesus. It didn't surprise me but it made me angry – although to be honest, I think it was as much anger at the fact that Esther would be with a normal, good-looking boy who could talk to her and flirt with her as annoyance at the way Caleb wanted to cash in on the amazing things Jesus had done.

The door to Peter's house remained firmly closed and I guessed that with Jesus there, no one would be giving a thought to me, so I headed back to the shack I shared with Mordecai and the others. I couldn't get the images of the day out of my mind – and nor it seemed could anyone else because the nearer I got to the town, the busier the streets were. Despite the late hour, people were gathered in clusters outside their houses and it didn't take long to realise the one topic of conversation they were all sharing.

Jesus the miracle man.

'There's nothing he can't cure,' I heard a burly man say as I turned down our alley. 'Soon there won't be a sick soul or an ailing cripple in the whole of Judea!'

OK, so he sounded as if a quantity of wine had lubricated his vocal chords, but the words hit a nerve with me. *There's nothing he can't cure.* Pushing open the flimsy piece of sacking that served as a door to the shack I stared round the room. *There's nothing he can't cure.*

Could Jesus give Aaron a grown-up brain? Could he restore Mordecai's withered limbs to working order? And Hillel – surely if Jesus could restore sight to one blind man he could restore sight to a dozen of them? It seemed he could do anything. And if he could – then where did that leave me? *There's nothing he can't cure.*

It all seemed too good to be true. All my life I'd longed to be normal; to be good looking, to stand erect, to have arms that could lift heavy weights and reach high above my head. I'd dreamed of waking up to find that my harelip had vanished, that the cleft inside my mouth had closed up – that I could speak. And now, just possibly, all that might be within reach.

So why was I feeling so desperately scared?

'Have you heard about this healer?' Mordecai asked a moment later. 'Whole town's buzzing with it – load of nonsense if you ask me.'

I shook my head, pointed to my eyes, and then nodded.

'You've seen him?' Mordecai gasped. 'And?'

I threw myself into some fairly dramatic role play, miming the boy cured of fitting, and following that up with what, if I say it myself, was a pretty good imitation of the blind man seeing again and the cripple leaping to his feet.

'What's he doing?' Hillel asked.

'Trying to tell me that this Jesus cured a load of people from incurable conditions,' Mordecai laughed curtly. 'As if.'

I ignored his sarcasm and gestured that he should go to see Jesus too.

'Reuben, you're a nice kid,' he said in a patronising kind of way, 'but don't get taken in by this man. It's obvious it's all a con!'

I shook my head vigorously.

'The way I see it,' Mordecai went on, 'is that this Jesus has his accomplices, right? They pretend to be blind, or sick, or have a pain, and he pretends to cure them. Then afterwards he shares out the fees he's taken with them and . . .'

I waved my arms furiously and gestured that he didn't ask for any money.

'He doesn't?' Mordecai sounded genuinely astonished. 'You mean – people go to him, he cures them – supposedly – and that's it?'

'So what does he get?' Hillel demanded.

I kept shaking my head. I wanted to mention all that stuff about the new kingdom that was coming and how Peter and Andrew thought he was a really good guy but I was tired and there's only so far one can go with mime.

'Where is he then, this Jesus?' Mordecai asked suddenly.

I pointed in the direction of the road that led to Peter's house and then gestured that tomorrow I would show him.

'You will?' Mordecai urged. 'Take me there tomorrow?'

'And me?' Suddenly they were both sounding less sceptical. 'Worth giving it a go, I guess.'

I nodded, and it was then that I suddenly realised Aaron wasn't there. I pointed to his mat and raised a questioning eyebrow.

'Ah,' said Mordecai. 'About Aaron.'

Something in his voice made my stomach lurch.

'We won't be seeing him again,' he murmured. 'This gang of boys – they threw stones . . .'

There was a catch in his voice.

'I shouted at him to run but he thought it was a game – until a large stone hit him between the eyes. I think – I hope – he was dead before he hit the ground.'

It could have been me. That was the thought that tormented me all night. I'd had my fair share of verbal abuse in my time; I'd been tripped up, teased, bullied and yes, a few times, physically hurt. I'd had stones thrown at me but I'd learned at an early age to duck and dive in more ways than one. Poor Aaron didn't have the ability to understand that it hadn't been a game.

Mordecai said the boys were caught but he knew, and I knew, that in all probability nothing would happen to them. They had fathers and uncles and rabbis to vouch for them; people who would say Aaron threw the first stone, and that they were simply protecting themselves. Aaron had no one to speak for him – and anyway, in most people's eyes he was expendable.

Who would wash him? Who would sit *shiva* for him, the seven days of mourning that relatives always observed? I knew the answer; no one. The question that I didn't dare ponder on was this; what about me? Who would miss me if I died?

Although it was still early when Mordecai, Hillel and I set out for Peter's house, we weren't alone. The word had clearly spread and the road was busy; there were carts carrying those too infirm to walk, men carrying children with wasted limbs, old women leaning on sticks or being helped by younger relatives. When we reached Peter's house I saw Andrew standing in the courtyard looking worried. I pushed my way through the throng and tugged on Andrew's sleeve.

'Reuben!' he exclaimed, and to my dismay I saw him gaze at the blood, now congealing, that had trickled onto my wrist. I hastily grinned and mimed tripping on a stone.

'You must take care,' he said. 'Where have you been?'

I didn't have time for pleasantries. Mordecai was already beginning to mutter about wishing he hadn't come and while I guessed it was nerves, I couldn't risk him disappearing.

'Jesus?' I wrote in the dust and opened my arms questioningly.

Andrew shook his head.

'We don't know where he is,' he sighed. 'When we woke up he'd gone. Peter, and James and John are out looking – oh! Look, there they are. But . . .'

He didn't need to say it. Jesus was nowhere to be seen.

At daybreak Jesus went out to a solitary place. The people were looking for him . . .

Luke 4:42

'He says he needs some time out, time for prayer,' Peter announced. 'And then he is moving on – he says the whole purpose of his life is to spread the word about the kingdom not just here but throughout the whole of Galilee. He will be going . . .'

His words were lost as the news rippled through the crowd.

'This way, he's gone this way . . .'

'Hurry, we must find him . . .'

The crowd turned as one and began hurrying along the lakeside path.

'What did I tell you?' Mordecai was at my side in an instant. 'He's making his escape while he can – before people see through his so-called miracle cures! No wonder he's praying – praying he's not found out I guess! What a waste of a morning!'

I tried to drag him to Andrew but he was having none of it.

'Grow up, kid,' he snarled at me. 'You'd be better begging alongside me than believing all that rubbish. Now if you don't mind I'm off.'

'Wait for me,' Hillel pleaded. 'I need you to help me find a good place to sit and play.'

Perhaps I should have tried harder to make them stay, to follow the crowd and catch up with Jesus. But doubts were creeping into my mind too; what if they were right? What if Jesus wasn't all he seemed to be? I'd look a fool if I went on insisting he was a healer and it turned out it was all a trick.

I turned and found Andrew staring at me.

'Reuben?'

I paused.

'We've been talking, Peter, James, John and me,' he said. 'And well – thing is, we're going to go along with Jesus. He's going to be our rabbi – he's chosen us as his disciples.'

He looked as proud as could be but to me it seemed odd. Rabbis don't choose their pupils; it's the other way round. But then again, not many people go about curing insanity as easily as plucking an ear of corn.

'Just imagine – he's chosen us! We're going with Jesus,' Andrew repeated.

My heart sank. That meant I'd have to find someone else to latch onto and there weren't that many people as kind as Andrew.

'I thought that while we were away you could help out,' he went on. 'The hired hands will be needed on the boats but you could do some of the shore jobs. There won't be much money but our mother will make sure you eat.'

He didn't need to say any more. Regular food and a place to sleep that wasn't out in the open was not to be sneered at. I nodded enthusiastically.

'Good,' he said. 'But Reuben . . .' He hesitated. 'No running off like before,' he went on. 'Promise?'

I grinned.

'Good,' he smiled. 'You had me really worried last time. So come on, let's get back to the boats and I'll show you what we need you to take care of.'

As I followed him, it wasn't the thought of pay and food that was giving me a warm glow. It was the knowledge that for the first time in a long while, someone had cared enough to worry about me.

They didn't go for a couple of days. Peter insisted they should fish for two more nights in an attempt to improve the stock of fish and ensure that no one went hungry while they were away. Zebedee would take any surplus to Magdala on the cart for salting and then the guys would leave and catch up with Jesus who was just a few furlongs away along the shore. We could see the crowds of people following him; and we picked up snippets of conversation when they returned home past our little hamlet at night.

Things didn't go well; the lake should have been teeming with fish at that time of year, but for some reason the catches got smaller and smaller which meant that Peter, whose mood swings could be quite alarming, was in a foul mood by breakfast time on the third day when the nets held little more than a few sardines and a dozen sprats. James and John were bickering between themselves, Andrew was silent and morose and to be honest the atmosphere was getting so prickly that even the hired hands began to talk of moving on to another fleet.

And that's when Jesus came back. Well, Jesus and about three hundred others.

'Peter!' he exclaimed, clapping him on the back. 'So good to see you!'

Immediately Peter brightened.

'Master! You're back!' He glanced around. 'And so many people!'

I wondered whether he was doing a quick calculation about just how much fish he might have been able to sell them had he managed to catch more.

Jesus nodded.

'The thing is, I need to talk to them – and there's no way they can all hear me standing here. So – I'll get into your boat, and if you just push off from the shore a few yards, that would be a perfect solution!'

I half expected Peter to protest that there was work to be done, but he simply clambered into the boat and did what Jesus asked.

Jesus began speaking and everyone fell silent. He spoke about turning away from everything that was bad and corrupt and embracing a new life where love and peace were what mattered. He said that the time had come when the poor would have a voice, where blind people would see and prisoners would go free. Personally, I thought that was about as likely to happen as me waking up and discovering I was six feet tall, and there were a few in the crowd who muttered and shuffled and clearly seemed to think he was crazy; but there were far more who were fired up with enthusiasm, cheering and hugging one another, some even with tears in their eyes.

And then the most extraordinary thing happened.

'Peter,' Jesus said, loud enough for all of us to hear. 'Put out into the deeper water now, and let down the nets for a catch.'

Peter looked at him in astonishment.

'Master, we've been at it all night and we haven't caught anything.'

Jesus said nothing, just inclined his head and smiled.

'But,' Peter said, 'because you want me to, I will do as you say.'

Now that was a first. Peter was one of the most experienced fishermen; he knew those waters like the back of his hand, and he knew that if there hadn't been shoals of fish a few hours earlier when it was dark, there certainly wouldn't be any now. I thought he was probably humouring Jesus because he was a visitor to these parts and courtesy demanded it.

He beckoned to Andrew to bring the nets and, with James and John and Philip all watching as if they had taken leave of their senses,

Peter put out into the middle of the lake. The crowd began to drift off, talking earnestly in clusters, and occasionally glancing over their shoulders at the boat, alone on the lake as the sun climbed higher in the sky.

And then there was a shout.

'James, John, quickly!'

The brothers, who were in their boat scrubbing it clean, looked up.

'The catch – we can't manage it on our own!'

There was a collective gasp from the crowd, and people began running to the water's edge straining to see what was happening. I put my hand up to shield my eyes from the sun. Peter and Andrew were both straining to hold onto the net and even at that distance I could see the fish thrashing about and the net bulging dangerously.

James and John immediately pushed off from the shore rowing as fast as they could to come alongside the other boat. Between them they managed to haul the net up and no sooner had they tipped the fish onto the floor of the boat, than the net on the other side was hauled up and was equally full of fish. By the time they had finished, both boats were full, the weight of the catch causing each boat to lie dangerously low in the water.

As they came ashore, the noise was deafening. Some people were cheering, others were pushing forward to peer into the boats as if they still couldn't believe their eyes. Let's face it, everyone in the area knew how poor the catches had been in previous weeks; it affected all of us and for this to happen – well, it was a miracle. Andrew was beaming from ear to ear, and James and John were looking as proud as if they had personally arranged for the fish to be there. Even old Zebedee looked more cheerful than I'd seen him in ages.

It was as Jesus waded ashore through the last few feet of shallow water that I saw Peter. He wasn't leaping about in excitement like everyone else, he wasn't giving orders for the sorting of the fish or even shouting at the hired hands to fetch the knives and start sorting and cutting. He was on his knees at the water's edge and his shoulders were shaking. At first I thought he was laughing.

But he wasn't. He was crying.

Jesus was at his side in an instant. I edged closer pretending to be looking for something I had dropped.

'Lord – go away!' Peter choked on the words and waved his hand as if to send Jesus packing. 'I'm such a sinful, wicked man!'

Now that I couldn't get my head around. OK, so Peter might be a bit taciturn at times, a bit volatile at others and yes, he was always impetuous and impatient – but wicked? No way. Unless of course, he'd done something that none of us knew anything about.

Jesus squatted down so that his eyes were on a level with Peter's.

'Don't be afraid, Peter,' he said. 'Remember what I told you – from now on, it's going to be people you'll be catching, not fish.'

'Me?' Peter asked. 'You really mean – YOU want me?'

Jesus nodded.

'You,' he said. Then he leaned towards Peter and I couldn't hear what he said – but I saw the light in Peter's eyes, and the way he scrambled to his feet and clasped Jesus' hand.

And I thought that I had never seen anyone switch from despair to joy so quickly in my life.

After that, they went. Peter, Andrew, Philip, James, John – all left and followed Jesus. And you know the strangest thing? There was more work for me now than there had ever been; not just with the boats but helping the women who'd been left to cope with things at home, fetching, carrying – I was busy all day. I was well fed, and I had shelter every night.

So why as the days passed did I become so restless? So discontented?

Why did I wish that Andrew had asked me to go along with him?

And why did my thoughts keep going back to Esther and Caleb, to Mordecai and Hillel? I was far better off with Zebedee and the hired hands than I would be roaming the streets with them.

But Esther and Caleb might have found Jesus. They might, I thought jealously, be one of his gang by now. That's what Caleb was aiming for after all.

They were probably all mates together while I was stuck here, the charity case, the one that people took pity on to ease their own consciences, not because they really wanted to be my friend. The little thug in the village who had beaten me up before was doing his best, along with a couple of his hangers-on, to make my life a misery and even Zebedee was waspish with me, denying me jobs that I knew I could cope with because he said he needed a fully grown man like his absent sons, not some pint sized kid.

One night about ten days after Jesus had left, I knew that it was going to happen again. The tension had been building inside me all day, the anger growing like a red hot piece of charcoal in my chest. When sleep eluded me, I snatched a fish hook from the storeroom and took it back to the shack where I slept. I took a deep breath, shut my eyes and held it poised above my thigh.

'Don't do it. Jesus will come back to you.'

I nearly jumped out of my skin, dropping the fish hook and spinning round, my heart thumping. Who was there? Who had seen me? The shack was completely empty.

I went to the door and peered out. No one. Nothing.

I went inside, picked up the fish hook, and then dropped it again. The feeling had passed. All I felt now was an overwhelming tiredness. I lay down on my mat and as I closed my eyes those words drifted gently through my mind.

'Jesus will come back – to you.'

So what has that got to do with me?

1. The Gospels are full of stories about Jesus driving out demons. Reuben describes his demon as taking the form of a huge anger and grief that makes him want to cut himself. The man in the synagogue may have been psychotic or suffered from delusions – but Jesus drove out the demons and restored him to full mental health. Today, we might see demons as making people depressed, violent, or turning them to some form of abuse of alcohol, drugs or other substances.
2. When Jesus healed Peter's mother-in-law, some of the onlookers thought it was a coincidence; they assumed she was on the mend already. Do we believe in the possibility of miracles? When something unexpected happens, do we label it a coincidence? Remember, coincidences are just miracles in which God chooses to remain anonymous!
3. Caleb is still thinking about himself and about the money he reckons he can make. What does his suggestion to Reuben about asking Jesus to heal him tell you about Caleb's current attitude? What is the effect on Reuben? Has Caleb taken on board the effect of his ill thought out words? How does Reuben deal with it? Can you think of parallels in your own experience?
4. When the demon shouted that Jesus was the Son of God, why did Jesus tell him to be quiet? Surely he wanted people to know that? Or was it that he wanted people to believe in him through *his* words, and not the words of the demon?
5. Reuben was just beginning to think Jesus might help him, and asks himself 'Why am I so scared?' Often we are so used to being the way we are that the thought of change can be terrifying, no matter how much we want it. Are there things about getting closer to Jesus that scare you? Why are we frightened even by things that he promises that sound too good to be true? There is always a risk in forming close relationships – one of which is that we never know exactly where it will lead us. Would it be easier to follow Jesus if we knew his plan for us in advance? If not, why not?

6. Peter agreed to push the boat out and fish again even though he thought it a crazy idea. When have you 'pushed the boat out' for someone when in your heart of hearts you thought their idea was silly? Do you think there are times when Jesus asks us to 'push the boat out' in our daily lives? How does he tell us? How do we respond?
7. Why did Peter say he was a wicked sinful man? Consider his attitude to Jesus thus far. What has changed? What does Jesus' response tell us about him, about Peter – and about our relationship with Jesus?
8. What was your immediate reaction when you read about Reuben hearing a disembodied voice telling him that Jesus would come back? How would you react if one of your friends told you they had heard Jesus speaking to them? Share reactions among your group – what was the overriding feeling? Why?

CHAPTER FIFTEEN

Through the roof

Esther

I don't think even Caleb had imagined it would be the way it was. The crowds that were following Jesus were huge; more people than I had ever seen in one place together in all my life. Sometimes when they clustered round Jesus the people at the back were so far away that they couldn't hear his words but had to rely on the people in front passing them, sentence by sentence, to the ones at the back. People had come from miles around, some even from as far as Jerusalem; and they weren't, as Caleb had reckoned, all gullible, ignorant peasants. Judging by the way some of them spoke, and the clothes they wore, they were well-off, educated people who were desperate to find out about some new kingdom that Jesus was going to set up. I guess they wanted a job in the new regime. I didn't understand a lot of what they were saying, but one thing was clear; Jesus was going to overthrow the Romans and set up a new kingdom in which everyone would be free.

And that sounded pretty good to me.

Each night many would drift away to their own homes, but there was always a hard core that stayed close to Jesus, sometimes sleeping in the open, but more often than not accepting one of the many invitations that came from people with houses large enough to provide shelter for the dozen or so that never left Jesus' side. Sometimes Jesus would disappear for a while; Caleb overheard one of his disciples saying that he needed time out to pray on his own; but it was never long before someone would shout out that they had seen him, and within minutes the crowd would be gathering once again.

After a few days, Caleb's enthusiasm for the whole thing started to wane. For one thing, his attempts to get people to pay him if he showed them where Jesus was were futile, because everyone knew where he was; news travels fast and even when he moved on, there were plenty of passers-by to point the way the crowd was heading. What's more, he hadn't managed to get anywhere near Jesus to ask him to take him on and teach him his magic. Everywhere he went, his gang of cronies went with him and even when we got quite close, they could see that neither of us was ill or crippled and they shooed us away so that Jesus could deal with those in real need. I could see their point but it certainly got Caleb really wound up.

Often when Caleb made another of his attempts to push through and get nearer to Jesus, I would hang back. I didn't like getting caught up in the middle of the crowd. In fact, I hated it. I was scared of being among so many men, although none of them looked at me the way Nathan had; I just didn't want to risk it. I preferred to remain on the edge, or when Jesus moved on, to hang back, picking up the odd bits of food and the occasional coin that had been dropped, while Caleb raced ahead. Reuben had told me to keep my eyes pinned to the ground whenever there were large groups of people and he was right; it was amazing how careless people were when their minds were on other things. So it was ironic that despite all Caleb's efforts, it was me who got really up close to Jesus first.

It was late one afternoon; we were at a small village – I forget its name but we had walked for two hours to get there – and I was doing what I had been doing every day since we left Reuben – scanning the crowds in the hope of catching a glimpse of Ziva. For once, I had a good vantage point; I had helped a woman who was struggling up the steps on the outside of one of the houses close to where Jesus was addressing the crowd. She had a screaming baby under one arm and was battling with a toddler who was throwing a tantrum to end all tantrums. To be honest, I'd only offered because she was clearly well off; her clothes and sandals were of the very best and she had gold in her ears and on her wrists. You would have expected someone like that to have a servant to care for the children and I guess she usually did because she certainly didn't have a clue about keeping the little ones quiet. In fact, she was so grateful for my help that she invited me to stay with her and to have a drink of watered wine and some freshly baked bread, and of course, I didn't refuse.

From the roof we had a clear view of Jesus, and the woman was trying desperately to catch what he was saying, so I kept rocking the baby back and forth while pulling funny faces to make the little boy laugh.

Suddenly there was the sound of a bell and the woman gasped and actually took a step back from the edge of the roof. Down below, the crowd parted – people began shouting and swearing, some of them literally turning tail and hurrying away, others brandishing their staffs and yelling 'Away! Go away!'

It didn't take long to see why. A leper was shuffling through the crowd, his hands bandaged in filthy rags, his nose eaten away, his face distorted by huge pustules. His feet were deformed by the disease; one eye was closed tight. And judging by the expressions on the faces of those nearest to him, he didn't smell so good either. And he was heading straight for Jesus.

As people backed off, a hush fell over the crowd. The only person who didn't look repulsed by the sight of the leper was Jesus. Even his disciples made to drive the man off, but Jesus stopped them with a look.

The leper fell onto his knees.

'Lord, if you want to, I know you can make me clean.' He spoke slowly, forcing the words out of a mouth twisted and deformed by the disease.

'Of course I want to,' Jesus replied. And then – and I promise you, I'm telling the truth – he touched him. Jesus touched a leper! That's against the law; even I know that. What's more, it meant that now Jesus himself was unclean.

Everyone gasped. The disciples looked at him as if he had taken leave of his senses. But when the man stood up the gasps were even louder. His face was as clean as anyone else's. The pustules had gone. His eyes were both open. He pulled off his bandages; his hands were strong, the skin without blemish.

'Master!' he gasped, choking on the word.

'Now listen to me,' Jesus said firmly, resting a hand on his shoulder. 'You are not to tell anyone about this – no one at all. Your first job is to go straight to the priest and make the sacrifice demanded by the law. You understand that?'

The man nodded but I got the impression he wasn't really listening. He kept twirling round and round, gazing at his hands, then running them up and down his cheeks.

'You must keep the law – go now and show yourself to the priest,' Jesus repeated. 'And remember, not a word to anyone.'

I didn't get that. I mean, surely Jesus would want the whole world to know what he'd done? Why keep a skill like that a secret? It simply didn't make sense.

I didn't realise I had voiced the question out loud. The mother of the children turned to me and smiled as I jiggled the baby on my hip.

'You know what I think?' she said. 'I think he wants all people to come to him to hear what he has to say, not just the ones who want healing.'

She sighed.

'Mind you,' she murmured, 'there are some things that need healing that have no visible signs.'

There was a sadness in her voice that resonated with me.

'I so want to follow him,' she said. 'I want him to teach me and . . .'

She laughed abruptly.

'But no chance of that – I'm a woman and . . .'

'And you have children,' I added nodding towards the little boy who was lining up pebbles in a row a few feet away.

She laughed again.

'Oh, these are not mine,' she smiled. 'I'm caring for them while my cousin attends a burial. Her husband is one of those who is following Jesus and where is he when he's needed? Somewhere in that crowd, while I try to manage these two!'

She touched my arm.

'Without your help I don't know what I would have done. I'm not used to little ones.'

Her voice again had that note of deep sadness.

'I'm Susanna, by the way,' she smiled. 'And your name?'

'Esther,' I replied.

Just then I spotted Caleb in the crowd, not far from the house. He was looking about him distractedly and I guessed it was me he was searching for.

'I must go,' I said. 'Thank you for the drink.'

'You are following Jesus?' she asked. 'You're very young. You are – you are alright, aren't you?'

'Yes, I'm fine, I . . . no, I'm not, not really . . . I had a job and I ran away, there was this man, and then I thought I'd found my sister and . . .'

Why I said all that, I will never know. It was as though someone invisible had put the words in my mouth and made me say them.

'Your sister?'

It all poured out – about how Ziva had run away all those years ago, and how I'd seen her in the street and then lost her, and how she had been screaming and how I was frightened for her. And all the time Susanna sat listening, nodding gently.

'And Ziva, she . . .' Susanna paused as if wondering whether to continue speaking.

She took a deep breath.

'She has a limp?'

I gasped. I hadn't mentioned her foot – talking about it would only bring back memories of how it happened.

'How do you know?' I could hardly get the words out.

'I've seen your sister several times recently.' Her lips formed a smile but that couldn't mask the pain in her eyes. 'She even worked for me for a short time, but then . . .'

My mouth was dry and my heart was pounding.

'She found another job.'

'But where? What does she do? And why . . . ?'

'Why is she as she is?' Susanna took the words out of my mouth. 'She is troubled. But she's not like that all the time – she has times of great, bouncing energy, huge joy – times when she can make everyone laugh, when she sings like a lark . . .'

'She always sang,' I murmured, and dashed a tear away before she could notice.

'And then the great rages and sadness hit her,' Susanna sighed. 'And that's when she's vulnerable – it was during one of those times that she left my service. I was sad to see her go because I knew . . .' She faltered. 'I knew life would be hard for her,' she concluded.

'They say Jesus can cure mad people,' I blurted out.

'He can,' Susanna replied. 'I have a friend . . . well, let's just say I can vouch for him.'

'If only . . .'

'It seems to me that we only have one choice,' she broke in gently. 'We must find your sister and we must take her to Jesus.'

I was sure I had misheard her. 'We?' I whispered.

Susanna nodded. 'Like I said, I had a serving girl and she left. What better thing than to have her replaced by her little sister?'

'You're offering me a job?' I couldn't believe my ears.

'On one condition.'

I should have known there would be a catch, I thought to myself. 'What?' I asked warily.

'If – when – I find a way of getting close to Jesus, you come too.'

Was that all?

'Of course,' I nodded.

'Esther? Esther, is that you up there?'

Caleb's voice had a note of urgency about it. Suddenly I felt guilty. I'd been so taken aback by Susanna's suggestion that I hadn't given a thought to how Caleb would feel about it.

'Who's that? Your brother?' Susanna asked.

'No, he was a servant at the place – he ran away with me,' I said and then immediately regretted it. I knew what she'd think.

'He's not – I mean – he left because of Jesus. He wants Jesus to teach him his magic,' I gabbled.

Susanna shook her head and laughed.

'Somehow I think he's going to be disappointed,' she replied. 'Look, go and tell him our plan – then this evening, come back with me to my house in Capernaum. It's the last one on the main street opposite the barrel maker's shop. I will be home by then.'

I moved towards the stairs and she touched my shoulder.

'And tell your friend that if he needs food or shelter, then he too should come to my house. Will you do that?'

'Do you mean it?' I asked.

'Of course,' she smiled. 'I make a point of never saying anything I don't mean.'

'This is it, Esther! Jesus is going back to Capernaum and I've found a way to be right there within touching distance of him!'

Caleb's eyes were shining.

'Apparently he's just cleansed a leper – can you imagine that? I didn't see Jesus actually do it but . . .'

'I did,' I interrupted. 'It was amazing.'

'You did? He's telling everyone that Jesus just touched him and his skin . . .'

'But Jesus said he shouldn't say a word about it,' I broke in.

'Well, that's plain crazy,' Caleb shrugged. 'People saw it – you saw it – why wouldn't he talk about it?'

'I don't know but Susanna said . . .'

'Anyway,' Caleb went on, not even pausing to ask who Susanna was, 'I met these three guys and they've got a friend who is paralysed – can't move his arms or legs at all. And they are desperate to get him to Jesus, but they can't lift him on their own. So I said I'd help.'

He grinned at me.

'First thing tomorrow, we're going to his house and then we'll carry him to wherever Jesus stays,' he gabbled. 'And of course, that'll give me the chance to persuade him to take me on. Good, eh?'

He looked so excited that I couldn't help smiling.

'I've got news too,' I ventured, and told him about Susanna.

'Nice for you,' he said, somewhat dismissively. 'Not that I'll need her help, of course. Twenty-four hours and I'll be one of the disciples. Made for life, yeah? Just imagine that!'

'So Jesus will be at Capernaum, right?'

That's where we had left Reuben. Maybe if I could go with Caleb, I could find him again. I still felt awkward about the way we had parted.

Caleb nodded.

'Well, Bethsaida actually, on the outskirts of Capernaum, where Peter and Andrew live,' he explained. 'Peter's all fired up about seeing his kids again and Philip's going to hand over his boat to his cousin so he can follow Jesus full time.'

'Susanna wants to see Jesus,' I told him. 'She said she wants to be one of his followers too.'

'Who's Susanna?'

I sighed.

'I just told you – I met her . . .'

'Oh, yes – well, she can't be a proper disciple obviously, because she's a woman but when we come this way, I guess she could provide meals for us. I've seen women bring food to Andrew, Peter, Philip, Bartholomew . . .'

He was obviously proud that he knew the in-crowd by name.

'Anyway, I've got to go,' he declared. 'My new friends are waiting for me – we've plans to make!'

'I'll see you later, then!' Suddenly I felt all at sea; Caleb had been with me ever since I ran away and if he really was going to become a disciple – well, where did that leave me? Susanna seemed a really kind person but a servant–mistress relationship wasn't the same as having a mate.

I turned, with every intention of going back to Susanna – at least I could tell her where Jesus was going to be and maybe we could walk to her house together. But as I neared the house, I saw a woman with red-rimmed eyes approach the door. Susanna appeared and enveloped her in a hug. This wasn't the time to intrude.

I walked to her house and sat down outside. I knew she would come eventually and I also knew for certain that for now this was the safest place to be.

'You know something, Esther? I really believe God sent you to help me yesterday!'

Susanna smiled at me as she piled food into a bag the following morning.

'Without you, I wouldn't have thought of taking food to Jesus but I guess the poor man has to eat even if he is a prophet!'

'Is that what he is, then?' I asked timidly as I touched the braid into which Susanna had fashioned my hair the night before. 'Like Moses and Elijah?'

'You know the stories of our ancestors?' she asked, clearly surprised.

'My grandmother told me all about them,' I explained. 'About Moses finding God in a burning bush, and about the Promised Land, and how David killed the giant Goliath and Elijah made the widow's oil last for days and days. Do you really think Jesus is like them?'

'I think he's someone very special,' she replied. 'His mother Mary is a friend of mine and when my husband was killed . . .'

She turned away, overcome with emotion.

'Let's just say that I have heard many things about him and that's why I am determined to find out for myself – and thanks to you, that begins today!'

I had to ask the question that was gnawing at the back of my mind.

'Do you want me to stay behind here in the house, mistress?'

Susanna looked at me in amazement.

'Stay here? Of course I don't.' She laughed. 'OK, I'll come clean. You're my personal maid – yes, that's what I'll call you because that's acceptable to people; but I hope you'll be my friend too?'

I nodded eagerly.

'So – where I go, you go too. Besides, we're looking for your sister, remember? Unless, that is, you've had second thoughts?'

I shook my head not trusting myself to speak.

'Right, come along then,' she said briskly. 'Let's get going!'

It wasn't hard to discover which house Jesus was visiting. The sheer volume of noise from inside, together with the ten-deep crowd circling the building, made it unmissable. I was surprised; it wasn't a big house – in fact, looking around, it seemed to me as if it were one of the smallest in the village, and in all honesty, not the best kept either. I wondered what Susanna would make of it.

'Is the Master in there?' Susanna asked a bystander.

'He is,' the woman replied, 'although if he's not squashed alive, it'll be a miracle.'

'We need to get closer,' Susanna urged. 'But I don't see how . . .'

The throng was pressing right up against the walls of the house, pushing and shoving in an attempt to get inside. Some people had climbed onto the roofs of neighbouring dwellings in order to get a good view, others were balancing on carts or climbing trees in the hope of seeing more.

'There might be a door around the back,' I suggested. Gradually we edged and pushed and shoved our away to the side of the house.

'There! Look!' Susanna pointed to a small window cut in the wall. It was hardly big enough to pass a grinding stone through, but by pulling back the thistles growing up the wall and pressing our faces against the stone we could glimpse the back of Jesus' head.

'My goodness,' Susanna breathed. 'He's even caught the attention of the teachers of the law – and look over there – Pharisees!'

She pointed to a group of three men who, with their earlocks and prayer shawls, stood out from the rest of the people crammed into the house.

Jesus held up his hand and instantly, the babble ceased and the crowd, both inside and out, fell silent. His voice was strong and resonant.

'Listen,' he said, 'the time has come, the kingdom of God is near! Repent!'

> Some men came, bringing to Jesus a paralytic, carried by four of them. Since they could not get him to Jesus because of the crowd, they made an opening in the roof . . .
>
> *Luke 5:18*

'Let us through, please, please, let us through!'

I recognised Caleb's voice at once, and standing on tiptoe strained to catch sight of him. He and three other men were on the edge of the crowd, each at one corner of a crudely made stretcher – just two poles with some sacking stretched over bound with pieces of rope. On the stretcher lay the withered and twisted figure of a young man, his face contorted with pain as the bearers jerked and tipped the stretcher in an attempt to get through the throng.

'Ssshh!'

'Go away, the rabbi is speaking!'

'Be silent!'

'Take him away – the stink!'

The crowd outside the house closed ranks and I saw a few of those at the back throwing warning glances in the direction of Caleb and his friends.

'Look! Up there – there's no one!' Caleb was pointing excitedly to the roof.

'Come on!' he cried. 'Quickly!'

'You're insane,' muttered one of his companions.

'It's no use,' the boy on the stretcher muttered. 'Just take me home.'

'Like you really think we're going to get Joshua up those steps . . . and if we do, what then?'

'Just do it!' Caleb insisted and for some reason, his friends stopped complaining, sighed deeply and heaved the stretcher up from the ground once again.

I couldn't believe my eyes. Huffing and puffing they struggled up the steps at the side of the house and onto the flat roof. Although I couldn't hear what Caleb was saying over the sound of Jesus' voice and the murmurings of the bystanders, I could see well enough.

The four men were pulling at the brushwood branches which were protruding though the dried mud plaster.

'He's amazing!' For a moment I thought Susanna was talking about Caleb, but it was Jesus she was staring at through the tiny window. 'Did you hear what he just said?'

I nodded, although all my attention had been focused on Caleb.

'Love one another . . . oh, if only that could be . . . oh my goodness!' She took a step back, aghast. 'Esther, look!'

Branches and twigs, and lumps of dried mud were showering down through the gaping hole in the roof. From inside the house, shouts, gasps and cries of dismay – not to mention some choice obscenities – drowned out the words of Jesus.

Slowly Caleb and his friends lowered the stretcher, tipping at a heart-stopping angle, down through the hole and onto the mud floor. It came to rest at the feet of Jesus.

'Look, Esther, look,' Susanna breathed pulling me nearer to the window.

Jesus squatted down by the paralysed man, and looked deep into his eyes. It seemed as if everyone in the room was holding his breath.

'Son,' Jesus said, 'I forgive you all your sins.'

The man closed his eyes and turned his head away as if in total desperation. Then Jesus turned round and eyeballed the Pharisees.

'I know what you're thinking,' he said. 'You think I'm blaspheming because only God can forgive sins.'

By the expression on their faces, you could see that was precisely what they had been thinking.

'Well, answer me this,' Jesus said. 'Which is easier – for me to say to this man that I forgive him his sins or to tell him to take up that stretcher and walk again?'

The Pharisees said nothing.

'Look, so that you can see for yourselves that I am the Son of Man and I do have the authority and power to do both those things . . .'

He paused and smiling down gently at the paralysed man he stretched out his hand.

'Get up,' he said to him. 'Pick up that stretcher and go home!'

The man's body twitched, an expression of disbelief crossed his face. Gingerly he lifted a foot, then rolled over. And then – he did it! He grabbed Jesus' hand, scrambled to his feet and with tears of joy pouring down his face, stammered his thanks.

'Go home, go into your new life!' Jesus smiled. The man picked up the stretcher, the crowd parted and he walked through, as steadily and as confidently, as if there had never been the slightest thing wrong with him.

Suddenly he dropped the stretcher, spun round and threw his arms in the air.

'I'm healed, I'm healed – glory be to God!' he cried. 'Look at me, I can walk!'

The crowd erupted – they cheered, they clapped, they hugged one another. Well, most of them did; the teachers and the Pharisees looked as if someone had stuffed their mouths full of sour lemons, and the owner of the house was gazing up at his roof with an expression of horror on his face. Jesus too paused and looked up at the hole. Three of the men had disappeared, but I saw Caleb staring down – straight into Jesus' eyes. Then, in an instant, he was gone.

'Don't worry,' I heard one of Jesus' disciples say, slapping the homeowner on the back, 'we'll fix the roof in no time.'

The owner turned and dropped his gaze to the floor.

'No, no – what is a roof compared with . . . it was a miracle. A miracle, here, in my little house! Just what kind of man is he?'

'He is our Lord,' the disciple said, and putting an arm around the owner's shoulder he led him towards the door where Jesus was talking.

'Have you ever seen anything like that?' a woman standing behind Susanna gasped. 'If I tell them back home, they won't believe me.'

'I think,' Susanna said, 'that this is just the beginning. I really do think he is the Messiah – the one who has come to save us all.'

'Well, the sooner he sorts the Romans out the happier I'll be,' the woman said. 'The taxes we have to pay – it's a disgrace.'

Susanna said nothing but just smiled and moved away. I followed her. 'Why,' she murmured, more to herself than to me, 'do I get the feeling that we are all missing the point?'

So what has that got to do with me?

1. Lepers were 'untouchable' because people feared catching the disease. They weren't allowed to live in town; often they lived on or near the rubbish dumps. Yet Jesus touched him. What does this teach us if we want to follow Christ? Is the lesson just about physical contact or is there something more?
2. What do you think made Esther blurt out her story to Susanna? What was the 'invisible' something that put the words in her mouth?
3. Susanna had told Esther she wanted to follow Jesus. In reality, she was doing that already. In what ways was she living out his teaching?
4. Caleb was eager to help the other men take the paralysed man to Jesus. What was his motive? How often do we try to tell Jesus what we want of him? And how often do we remain still and quiet and try to hear what he wants from us? Are we more ready to help someone if we think there will be a 'pay off' for ourselves?

CHAPTER SIXTEEN

Messing up?

Caleb

I should have been on a real high. The other guys were, that's for sure. One minute their mate is lying paralysed on a mat, able to move only his head and the fingers of his left hand; and the next he's walking, running, jumping just like any other person. He was whole again. And his sins had been forgiven.

That was what kept going round and round in my head. That was the reason that although outwardly I smiled and slapped Josh on the back and cheerfully dismissed his thanks for helping to get him to Jesus, in reality all I wanted to do was get the hell out of there and try to get my head together.

Who was this man Jesus? He was doing stuff that no one I'd ever heard of had done before and yet the guy was acting as if it was commonplace. He didn't even seem fazed when that stuck up lot demanded to know how come he thought he could forgive sins. You could see their point – I mean, Yahweh forgives sins, not itinerant . . . itinerant what? Healers? Magicians? Con men?

No, not that. One thing I suddenly realised for sure that day was that, whatever else he was, Jesus was no con artist. I had been wrong. I didn't have a clue about how he did what he did, but I did know this. He was for real. To be honest, when we had been carrying Joshua to see Jesus, I'd been pretty sure that this time Jesus would turn a blind eye – after all the guy was in a really bad way and had been for years apparently. And I had watched Jesus closely; he didn't use any potions, he didn't chant anything, he just talked about forgiving sins and then suddenly said 'Get up!' That was it. Nothing more.

After Josh's mates had dashed down the steps to greet him, I saw Jesus staring up at me – right into my eyes as if he was waiting for me to say something. I could have said it there and then; asked him to take me on and make me like him, but the words stuck in my throat. Which was a good thing because, of course I realised afterwards that he was obviously simply anxious to check out the roof, making sure that someone would take care of mending it. It wasn't me he was interested in at all. Why would he be?

If he was able to forgive sins – and somehow I doubted that very much – it was probably only little things like stealing a bit of food or not going to synagogue or drinking the dregs of wine when you were meant to be clearing tables. Sins like mine – well, let's just say that if he knew even the half of what I'd done in the past there'd be no chance of him even giving me the time of day, never mind letting me get close to him.

I'd heard people saying that maybe Jesus really was the Messiah, the Promised One. Now I've never been clever – not in a reading-the-scrolls kind of way. Dead boring, that stuff. But my father, in the days when he still loved me, used to say that one day a Messiah would come and turn the world upside down.

'He will set us free,' he would say. 'Not just from the Romans, but from this grinding poverty, from the way the landowners trample us into the dirt, from this life at the bottom of the pile . . . all of it. I won't live to see it, but maybe you will.'

I remember how scornful I was.

'Oh sure,' I retorted. 'It's been how many hundreds of years since someone said the Messiah would come? It's just a story – anyone with half a brain can see that.'

I'll never forget the look of desolation that crossed his face.

'Caleb, never doubt God's promises,' he sighed. 'It will happen. It will.'

The following week I did that terrible thing – the thing I still can hardly bear to think about – and my father never spoke to me again. And I went on believing he'd been deluded.

But that day, after Joshua and his mates ran off home, I realised I wasn't so sure any more.

'I've seen you around a lot – you were at the synagogue a while back, right? Are you one of us?'

It was an hour or so later, and I was sitting on the shore a couple of furlongs out of Capernaum, idly picking up pebbles and tossing them in my hands when a man I vaguely recognised touched me on the shoulder.

'I – no, no – I'm not a fisherman, I used to work at . . .'

The guy smiled and shook his head.

'That's not what I meant,' he said. 'I'm Philip, by the way – and you?'

'Caleb,' I said, getting to my feet.

'I meant, are you a follower of Jesus?' Philip looked at me intently. 'You were on the roof, weren't you? Helping that paralysed man? So you are a believer.'

'I wasn't,' I replied. 'I mean, yes, I was on the roof, but right up until – well, let's say when I woke up this morning I was anything but a believer.'

Philip nodded thoughtfully.

'And now?'

'I don't know what to believe,' I admitted. 'One thing's certain; whoever this guy is and however he does what he does, I know now he's not just some travelling magician. And I guess there's no chance of me ever getting the chance to learn how to do it myself.'

'Was that why you hung around?' Philip asked. 'So you could learn to heal?'

I swallowed hard. 'Yeah, I guess.' But I didn't add that I had thought of it as a way to make money fast. I was too ashamed.

'So join us,' Philip said, as calmly as if he'd been suggesting I should take part in their next trip to the tavern. 'Jesus would be thrilled.'

I looked at him as if he had taken leave of his senses.

'But you know nothing about me,' I protested. In my head I could hear Jesus saying 'Your sins are forgiven you.' And one thing I knew for sure: he was hardly likely to forgive mine. Not that he knew what they were, of course. Or did he?

I guess the expression on my face must have hinted at what I was feeling because Philip touched my shoulder.

'No, I don't know you,' he agreed. 'But that doesn't matter. You want to learn from Jesus; Jesus wants us all to learn from him. What's to argue about?'

He slapped me on the back.

'Listen, I've got to check my boat – while I'm away, I'm letting my cousin fish with it, but I can't do that till I've done a few repairs. You help me out with that – and then I'll take you to Jesus. He's heading into town. And with your help, we could be there in a couple of hours. What do you say?'

'Yes,' I breathed. 'Yes please.'

Little did I know what I was letting myself in for.

Jesus went out and saw a tax collector by the name of Levi sitting at his tax booth. 'Follow me', Jesus said to him, and Levi got up, left everything and followed him.

Luke 5:27, 28

'He's at Levi's house!'

Even Philip looked aghast when the rope maker pointed down the road.

'What – you don't mean Alphaeus' son, Levi? Surely not that one?'

'Yes, him! A rabbi eating with tax collectors – I ask you!' the man grunted. 'They're vermin, the lot of them, and Levi's one of the nastiest; he's been threatening me all week because I'm a few denarii short on my tax. You can't give what you haven't got!'

'He's been on my back for weeks too,' Philip said. 'Telling me that it's not his fault the catch hasn't been good and if I don't cough up soon, he'll have me taken to court. But . . .' He paused. 'If Jesus is with him, it must mean . . .'

'If Jesus is with him, he's no friend of mine!' The man turned and spat on the ground. 'That Levi would squeeze blood out of a stone given half a chance!'

Philip gestured to me to follow him and we made our way down the street, crowded with traders, to a large house on the outskirts of the town.

'Levi, of all people,' Philip kept murmuring. 'Everyone knows that tax collectors can't be trusted. I can't get my head round it.'

As we entered the courtyard, I spotted Andrew, the guy who had shooed me away when I tried to get near to Jesus. I guessed he wasn't going to be overjoyed to see me.

'Andrew!' Philip grasped his hand. 'What's going on?'

Andrew exhaled and shook his head.

'It's Levi – or Matthew as all his cronies call him – did you hear what happened?'

Philip shook his head.

'We were passing his tax booth, and Jesus stopped, marched over to him and just said "Follow me". And he got up and came with us! Just like that!'

'You mean, he left his money . . .'

'Yes – he just walked away! Have you ever seen a tax collector do that before?'

Philip was speechless and I wasn't surprised. Tax collectors milked the system for all it was worth; the Romans gave them a franchise to collect a specific sum – and did they do that? No way! They collected a whole heap more and kept the surplus for themselves.

'What's more,' Andrew went on. 'Matthew's now ordered his servants to prepare a meal for us.'

'Great,' Philip grinned. 'Let's go in before he changes his mind – I could eat an entire sheep!'

'Well, you'll be sharing it with a lot of people,' Andrew laughed, leading us into the house. 'Jesus appears to have invited all the disreputable of Capernaum!'

It was true the place was buzzing. Levi-Matthew was bustling around ordering the servants to pile food and drink on the tables,

Jesus was laughing and joking in a corner of the room with a bunch of men who looked suspiciously like moneylenders and there were even some women there who, judging by the way they were dressed, were the sort that my old master would have had me fling out onto the street in an instant. Certainly not the kind of people you'd expect to find in polite company.

'Peter, over here!' Philip called and Simon Peter, goblet of wine in one hand, looked up, grinned and pushed his way across the room to where we were standing.

'This is Caleb,' he said. 'He's – well, let's just say he's had an interesting day and he wants to find out more about the Master.'

'Welcome, Caleb!' Peter said. 'Come and meet Jesus.'

'No!' I couldn't do it. I wasn't ready. I hadn't worked out what to say – or rather, all the words I had practised in my head seemed inadequate now.

'Caleb?' Philip looked at me anxiously.

'I – I don't know . . .'

'This is an atrocity!' I was saved by the arrival of a bunch of angry looking Pharisees who seemed to be in a state of high tension.

One of them marched straight up to Andrew and planted himself squarely in front of him.

'Tell me this,' he said. 'What is this so-called rabbi doing eating and drinking and making merry with a bunch of low lives and sinners? Eh? Tell me that!'

'Look at them!' cried another, making a sweeping gesture with his arm around the room. 'Dishonest, raucous, underhand, manipulative – crooks the lot of them!'

They were shouting so loudly that everyone in the room could hear them. The buzz of conversation dropped to a low murmur as Jesus set down his goblet of wine, got to his feet and turned to face the intruders.

'You wouldn't waste your time taking a healthy person to a doctor, would you?' he asked. 'Doctors are for those who are sick, those whose health is under threat, right?'

The Pharisees frowned but said nothing.

'What I suggest you do is take yourselves away and think hard about what God meant when he said to the prophet Hosea, "I want mercy, not blind religious duty."'

The Pharisees sniffed and shuffled their feet. One of them stepped closer to Jesus and murmured, 'Go on . . .'

'You see the thing is,' Jesus continued, 'I haven't come to pander to all the religious do-gooders; I have come to invite the outsiders, the downtrodden – all the people you sneer at. That's why I'm here.'

It sounds crazy but when I heard those words my whole body tingled, my heart began beating faster, and a shiver ran the whole length of my spine. A whole host of images flashed through my mind; Reuben with his twisted body (and the way I'd looked down on him when I first saw him, assuming the worst just because of the way he looked); the leper healed and whole; the way Jesus always focused on the down and outs even when the wealthy were elbowing him and asking clever questions – and the last words my father ever spoke to me as he hurled me out of the door of our family home: 'You are the lowest of the low life and you are no son of mine!'

Jesus was saying that he was there for people like me? Was that what he really meant – or was it just drink talking? There was only one way to find out.

After Jesus had returned to his place in the corner of the room, I turned to Philip and was about to ask him whether, after all, I could speak to Jesus when a group of four or five men burst into the room.

'Andrew!' one of them called. 'How are you?'

'Eli!' Andrew replied. 'You too? And David? Terrible business about John – I can't get my head around it. But you're all still together?'

I guessed from what he was saying that these were old mates of his from the days when he and John hung out with John the Baptist. Philip had told me all about it on our way to the party.

'So now you're coming to follow Jesus? Isn't it amazing, he's . . .'

'Hang on,' Eli said. 'Not so fast. There are too many unanswered questions about this rabbi – I mean, none of it makes sense. John seemed to think he was . . . well, the Chosen One, but he's clearly not the business because . . .'

'Not the business?' Philip burst out. 'You have to be joking!'

Eli turned to him, gave him a withering look and returned his gaze to Andrew.

'Well, how come we fast, and the Pharisees fast – everyone with any love for God fasts, but . . .'

At that moment Jesus walked over to them, a broad smile on his face.

'Welcome,' he said. 'You were about to ask why my disciples don't fast?'

Eli looked somewhat taken aback, but nodded slowly.

'Well, I'll tell you,' Jesus said pleasantly. 'If you go to a wedding, and you're filled with joy at the sight of the bridegroom hosting a feast, you don't burst into tears, and wail and go without, do you? You sit down at the table and share the joy of the feast with him.'

Eli frowned.

'Don't get me wrong, fasting is not a bad thing at the right time,' Jesus went on, 'but the right time is not when there is true joy and excitement to be celebrated and shared.'

'But . . .'

'Listen – let me put it another way. If you had a tear in your tunic, would you patch it with a piece of new cloth? Of course you wouldn't – for the simple reason that the patch would pull away from the old material and make the hole worse. It's just the same with wine; who in their right mind would put new wine into an old wineskin?'

'Well, no, of course not,' Eli admitted. 'The skins would burst . . .'

'Exactly!' Jesus smiled. 'The wine would run out and the wineskins would be ruined, which is why new wine goes into new wineskins. That way, both are preserved.'

Eli pulled at his beard thoughtfully.

'So – you are saying that this is a new way of thinking and . . .'

He glanced nervously at his companions who were glaring at him in a somewhat threatening manner.

'Much to think about, Rabbi,' he murmured.

'Much indeed,' the others repeated, but their words were sneering and sarcastic. 'Much indeed.'

Jesus smiled and turned back towards the low table where Matthew-Levi was telling a joke. I don't know where I found the courage – or the audacity – from but I stepped in front of him. My knees felt like jelly and my mouth was dry as a bone.

'M . . . mm . . . Master, Rabbi, my Lord, sir . . . I mean, Teacher.'

Jesus threw back his head and roared with laughter.

'What is it? Just say it – I don't bite!'

'I . . . you . . .' Now I was this close to him, I couldn't frame a single sentence.

'This is Caleb,' Philip said, resting a hand on my shoulder. 'He wants . . .'

'Let Caleb tell me himself what he wants,' Jesus said gently. 'Caleb?'

'I want to understand,' I said. And suddenly I knew that was exactly what I did want.

'Then follow me,' he said.

'But I need to know whether . . .' I began.

'Just come,' Jesus said and then with a smile, he turned away.

'There you are,' Philip said. 'Now you are one of us. Come on, let's eat.'

This wasn't right, it was all moving too fast. What I had wanted was for Jesus to sit down, and explain how he could cure people and how he had turned that water into wine, not expect to join his gang without even telling me anything of what that meant. It was OK for Philip and Andrew and Peter and that lot; they were older, they had been working for years and probably had a stash of cash to fall back on while they wandered the countryside with Jesus. And they had each other; they'd been mates for ages. Beside them, I felt like some dumb kid. When I'd been with Esther, I'd felt like the main man, the one who was getting his life together, the organiser, but now . . . Esther!

Jesus and his friends were deep in conversation, and as Philip drifted over to them, I slipped out of the door, and sank to the ground, my head in my hands. What had I been thinking of? How could I have done that? I had just left Esther and gone – first with Joshua's mates and then off with Philip. Anything could have happened to Esther – and if it had, it would all be my fault. Just like it was all those years ago . . .

I had thought that by keeping an eye on Esther, helping her get away from Nathan, I could somehow make up for what happened with Kizia, my little sister. And now I'd messed up again. If anything had happened to her . . .

What was it Esther had been saying just before I went off with Joshua's friends? Something about a woman she had met, who wanted to follow Jesus too? What was her name? I couldn't remember. If only I had paid more attention.

But if this woman was going to tag along with the Jesus crowd, then maybe my best chance of finding Esther was to do the same. It was late now, and wherever she was I hoped she'd have the sense to find shelter. She'd done that before when she lost me and that's how she met Reuben . . . Reuben!

Maybe she'd met up with him again. He was bound to be around Capernaum surely – a guy like him would stick to people he knew if he had any sense at all. I was beginning to feel better, more in charge again. I had a plan. Find Reuben, track Esther down and then – well, maybe the three of us might go and meet up with the Jesus crowd again then. It would be easier with mates and if it all turned out to be a waste of time, well at least we would have one another. And I wouldn't look like a total idiot.

It was late and now I had a plan I felt better. No harm going back into the house and eating with Philip and the rest of them. The smell of roasted lamb, freshly baked bread and the spices in the lentil and barley stew were too much for me. I went in, sat down by Philip and nodded when he repeated the affirmation that I was now one of them. And I ate and drank and no one stopped me.

So what has that got to do with me?

1. Caleb has taken the first step towards getting closer to Jesus. What was that first step? Just four words! Does he see it as a positive step?

2. Caleb sees Jesus looking up at him but can't believe he's interested in him. Can you relate to that feeling? When are you most likely to think that Jesus can't possibly be interested in you? Caleb thinks that his past rules out any possibility of Jesus wanting to have anything to do with him. Why do we know he's wrong?

3. There is no entrance exam for following Jesus; no modules to prepare or certificates to gain. Which sounds great, but sometimes we feel as if everyone else has got it sussed and we don't understand half of what they are talking about. That's great – it's the people who think they know it all that are probably missing the point. Caleb took the first step when he admitted he had been wrong (yes, that's the answer to the first question!).

4. The Romans levied heavy taxes on the countries under their control. The Jews opposed the taxes because the money went to support a secular government and pagan gods but they had to pay. Tax collectors were very unpopular because they made themselves rich by milking their fellow countrymen. What lessons about justice and fair play can we learn today? Are there any sections of our society that could be seen to be 'milking the system'?

5. Matthew took a huge step when he left his job as a tax collector to follow Jesus: a bigger step even than the fishermen. They could go back – and did – from time to time to fish. Matthew, once he had left his franchise, had no chance to turn back. Could we leave our present way of life and follow Jesus into the unknown? Is there anything that you would find hard to give up? Are they things Jesus would ask you to give up? And if they are, what would be the stumbling block? Make sure you haven't jumped to the conclusion that Jesus is against anything that's fun; he's only

against things that harm you or other people or go against God's hopes and dreams for you.

6. Matthew responded to Jesus' call at once – not stopping to think about it. He wrote the Gospel according to St Matthew. When he first followed Jesus, he had no idea how his talents would be used; but he was used to keeping records as a tax collector and through him we have a vibrant, lively record of Jesus' life and ministry. God has a purpose for each one of us but when he first calls us we probably won't be given even the smallest clue as to what that is!

7. Sometimes it isn't until we actually open our hearts and mouths to speak to Jesus in prayer that we actually find out what our deepest desires are. Turning them over and over in our mind day after day is not nearly as helpful as turning them over to God! There are as many different ways to pray as there are people: 'Pray as you can, not as you can't'. Some people like to use set prayers written down by someone else; some like to write their own; some talk to God in conversation as they go about their daily tasks; some sit in a quiet place and meditate; trying out new forms of prayer can have some surprising and rewarding results.

8. In biblical times, wine was not kept in glass bottles but in wineskins made from goatskins. New wine expanded as it fermented which stretched the wineskin. After the wine had matured, the stretched skin would burst if more new wine was poured into it. New wine, therefore, always went into new wineskins.

9. Caleb wanted to know exactly what was expected of him, all the conditions and every detail about what would happen. He wasn't yet ready to trust Jesus and wait to see. What about us? Are we like Caleb – torn between wanting to understand and needing to know what lies ahead? How hard is it for us to trust? Have we had experiences with other people where trust was broken? If so, it is difficult to understand that Jesus will never let us down. He may not give us what we want but he will always give us what we need.

CHAPTER SEVENTEEN

Taking the plunge

Reuben

I saw them coming while they were still a good fifteen minutes' walk away – a cluster of people, hugging the shoreline path and moving steadily towards the village. I rushed into Peter's house and gestured to his wife Abigail to come out and look. She was busy kneading bread – it was only a few hours until the start of the Sabbath and everyone was working flat out to get everything ready – but Ruth, his five-year-old daughter, dashed out and then flew back into the kitchen, grabbing her mother's arm.

'Mummy, Mummy, lots of people are coming!' she shouted. 'Will Daddy be with them? Is Daddy coming home?'

Abigail pummelled the dough even more vigorously.

'He'd better be,' she muttered. 'Or I'll have something to say to your uncle Andrew. It was him that got your father into all this, you know – never mind dragging James and John along with him. Poor Zebedee – he's never been the same since . . .'

I slipped out of the house. Abigail was a nice enough woman, but once she got on her high horse about things, there was no stopping her. Mind you I could see her point; remove five able-bodied men from a community like hers and those left behind couldn't help but struggle.

'Reuben, Reuben, come with me! I'm going to see if my daddy's coming!' Ruth was jumping up and down. She knew she wasn't supposed to go far from the house on her own, and she also knew that I was the most likely person to give in to her, largely because it was easier than trying to make her understand what I was saying.

I nodded, and we set off, Ruth running ahead of me, and then stopping to beckon me to hurry up. It wasn't as big a crowd as usual; with the Sabbath due to begin most people would be finishing their work or preparing the Shabat meal. I couldn't help wondering whether for some of the earlier followers, the novelty had worn off; I knew only too well that wandering round the countryside, never knowing what was going to happen next, was something few people would do out of choice. I certainly hoped Andrew and the other guys had got this following Jesus thing out of their system; the atmosphere in the village had been less than relaxed over the past week and I realised that without the leadership of men like Andrew and Peter, the hired hands only did the minimum necessary. Zebedee seemed to have aged several years, and most of his conversation was peppered with phrases such as 'James would have put the nets down earlier' or 'If John were here . . .'. Perhaps now they'd be back for good and life would return to normal.

'Daddy, Daddy!' Ruth suddenly shouted and broke into a run. Peter ran towards her, scooped her up in his arms and hugged her tightly. I swallowed hard in an attempt to dislodge the lump in my throat. Seeing proper fathers with their kids always had that effect on me.

'Ruth!' he cried standing her down again. 'Have you been a good girl while I've been away? Have you been helping your mummy?'

Ruth nodded, hopping from foot to foot in her excitement.

'Come,' Peter said. 'We must go and tell your mother that she can expect visitors tonight.'

'Is Uncle Andrew coming?' Ruth asked. ''Cos Mummy's a bit cross with him.'

Peter laughed. 'She won't be,' he said. 'Not when she hears all that I have to tell her.'

I wouldn't count on it, I thought, watching as the two of them hurried towards Peter's house. I scanned the crowd in an attempt to spot Jesus. I figured that where he was, Andrew wouldn't be far behind. But when I did see him, I nearly fell over. He was surrounded by four or five women, all laughing and chatting nineteen to the dozen as if he was just a regular person. One of them was even touching his arm! I knew that no self-respecting rabbi would allow that kind of familiarity. Whatever this Jesus was, he certainly didn't seem to know the rules.

'Master, I have brought you a warm blanket,' I heard one of them say. 'The nights are cooler now and . . .'

'I have figs and cheese to add to the Sabbath meal . . .' another cut in.

'And I have baked bread,' said a tall, elegant woman who was clearly not short of a few denarii, judging by the gold on her wrists and ankles. 'My servant girl has it in a basket.'

All this fawning and one-upmanship was beginning to get to me, and I turned away, intending to walk up the hill at the back of the houses in order to see over the heads of the crowd and maybe spot Andrew or Philip.

'Esther!'

Hearing that name, I spun round. The woman was ushering a girl with a basket up to where Jesus was standing. It couldn't be – surely. The girl was wearing a clean dress, she had sandals on her feet and her hair was neatly braided. I couldn't see her face; she had her back to me. I edged closer, elbowing my way past people and ignoring their muttered curses. Jesus was moving on and all I could see was a mass of backsides as people jostled to get closer to him.

'Reuben!'

I looked up and there was Andrew, grinning from ear to ear.

'Reuben, good to see you! You haven't seen my brother, have you?'

I pointed towards Peter's house.

'Great,' he said. 'He'll be making the preparations then.'

He turned and called to Jesus.

'Master, this way . . .'

The crowd parted and there she was. Esther. Looking directly at me, an expression of open-mouthed delight on her face.

'Reuben!' she cried, and began to hurry towards me.

'Esther?' The tall woman frowned and Esther hesitated.

'It's Reuben, he's the one who saved my life.'

I felt that was something of an exaggeration but the look on her face gave me a warm glow.

'Please – may I . . . ?'

The woman smiled. 'Of course, and I must meet this hero!' She glanced round, obviously trying to work out which of the many guys in the crowd was the one Esther was heading for.

'Reuben!'

Esther grabbed my arm and hugged me.

'I've so much to tell you, are you OK, I'm sorry we ran off, have you seen Caleb, did you know . . . ?'

I smiled and held up my hands to slow her down.

'Esther?'

The tall woman was eyeing her quizzically.

'Madam . . .'

'I told you – it's Susanna, not Madam!' the woman said.

'Susanna, this is Reuben. He's the one I told you about, the one who helped me when . . .'

'I remember,' she said. You could tell she was a well-born woman because she managed to control the look of surprise at my appearance and turn it into a wide-eyed smile.

'Reuben, I'm pleased to be able to say thank you to your face.'

I frowned, puzzled.

'If you hadn't helped Esther she wouldn't have been near my house, she wouldn't have helped me, and I wouldn't have the best servant girl I've had in ages!' she laughed. 'What do you say to that?'

I glanced at Esther. Hadn't she told Susanna that I was mute?

'Oh. I forgot,' Esther gasped. 'Susanna, Reuben can't speak.'

'You didn't tell me,' Susanna said, clearly embarrassed.

'It didn't seem important,' Esther shrugged.

That was one of the kindest things anyone had ever said about me for as long as I could remember.

'Have you seen Caleb?' Esther asked eagerly. I shook my head and felt a stab of envy when I saw the look of disappointment on her face. I gestured to my eyes and mimed looking for him.

'If you do see him, tell him I'm living at Susanna's house – it's the one at the end of the street where the barrel maker lives.'

'And that's where we must be going,' Susanna said briskly. 'The Sabbath is almost upon us.' She paused and smiled at me. 'We'll see you again,' she said. 'You'll be following Jesus, right?'

I shook my head, and mimed that I had nets to mend and fish to gut. I pointed to the boats beached nearby.

'Please, Reuben,' Esther said. 'Susanna is sure that Jesus is going to change the way we live, he's going to make things right and . . .'

I pointed to Peter's house, I mimed eating and sleeping and I pointed to the hills and shivered.

'I guess you like it here,' Esther nodded. At least she got the message unlike her mistress. Susanna just kept staring at me as if she didn't get it at all. Some people can be incredibly slow on the uptake.

'If you don't come with us, that will be such a shame,' she said eventually. 'But we'll be looking out for you – and I have a feeling it won't be long before we see you again.'

'I hope so,' Esther said quietly. 'I miss you.'

When she said that something odd happened in my chest. My heart flipped, and I wanted to run after her, to say that I'd go wherever she wanted me to, no matter what – but common sense prevailed. At least with Andrew and Peter's household I had food and a mat in the outhouse. Why would I give that up for . . . for what?

After that, everyone dispersed back to their homes – everyone, that is, apart from the in-crowd – guys like Philip and Bartholomew and one or two others I didn't recognise but who seemed to be on pretty familiar terms with Jesus. I was pretty sure that Abigail wouldn't welcome the intrusion but to be honest I was delighted because Peter came out and asked me to help with the serving.

'You're a bit of fixture with us now, aren't you?' he smiled. And it occurred to me that something about him had changed. I couldn't put my finger on exactly what it was but there was a light in his eyes that hadn't been there before.

One of the great things about serving a meal is that you get to eavesdrop on the conversation. I wasn't anywhere near Jesus; he was inside the house and I was just attending to the needs of some of the followers who had spilled over into the courtyard, but when the solemn rituals were over, tongues were loosened and some of the stories I heard made my head spin.

> At that time Jesus went through the grainfields on the Sabbath. His disciples were hungry and began to pick some heads of grain and eat them. When the Pharisees saw this, they said to him, 'Look! Your disciples are doing what is unlawful on the Sabbath.'
>
> He answered, 'Haven't you read what David did when he and his companions were hungry? He entered the house of God, and he and his companions ate the consecrated bread – which was not lawful for them to do, but only for the priests. Or haven't you read in the Law that the priests on Sabbath duty in the temple desecrate the Sabbath and yet are innocent? I tell you that something greater than the temple is here. If you had known what these words mean, "I desire mercy, not sacrifice," you would not have condemned the innocent. For the Son of Man is Lord of the Sabbath.'
>
> *Matthew 12:1-8, NIV*

Apparently Jesus had no fear of the Pharisees: he answered them back whenever they challenged him, which to my mind seemed like inviting trouble. One guy was talking about the previous Sabbath, the week before, when some of Jesus' disciples had been walking with him through a cornfield, and they had picked some ears of corn, rubbed them in their hands and eaten them.

'There was this Pharisee,' one of the guys was saying, 'and he went ballistic – saying that they were breaking the Sabbath rules.'

'Which they were, Amos, let's face it,' another man said. 'Can't fault them on that.'

'So what did Jesus say?' another asked.

I hovered with the pitcher of wine. It was empty and I should have been refilling it but I couldn't miss the punchline.

'Well,' Amos said, 'Jesus looked at him, bold as you like, and started telling the story of David going into the temple and taking the consecrated bread for his friends to eat?'

'I never believed he really did that,' another admitted. 'I thought it was just a myth – I mean, consecrated bread is for priests only, right?'

Amos nodded. 'Yes Silas, you're right, but you see Jesus maintains that what he says is more important . . .'

'Hang on, he went further than that,' a small, chubby man who had up till then been quietly stuffing his face. '*He* said that he was the Lord of the Sabbath! I tell you, that Pharisee went purple in the face – I thought he was going to explode!'

'Jesus kept on and on about mercy being more important than sacrifice . . .' Amos added.

'Tell that to the lawmakers,' grunted Silas. 'Hey, you . . .'

He stuck out his goblet in my direction.

'Top it up, will you? All this talking's giving me a dry throat.'

I gestured that the pitcher was empty and turned to refill it from the table by the door.

Jesus left that place and went to a synagogue, where there was a man who had a paralyzed hand. Some people were there who wanted to accuse Jesus of doing wrong, so they asked him, 'Is it against our Law to heal on the Sabbath?'

Jesus answered, 'What if one of you has a sheep and it falls into a deep hole on the Sabbath? Will you not take hold of it and lift it out? And a human being is worth much more than a sheep! So then, our Law does allow us to help someone on the Sabbath.' Then he said to the man with the paralyzed hand, 'Stretch out your hand.' He stretched it out, and it became well again, just like the other one. Then the Pharisees left and made plans to kill Jesus.

Matthew 12:9-14

When I returned the chubby man was speaking again.

'Yes, but a withered hand made new in an instant – it was amazing! And still those Pharisees went on and on about how Jesus shouldn't heal on the Sabbath!'

I almost dropped the jug which I was, of course, holding in my good hand. Had Jesus really done that? My good hand was shaking as I poured the wine and it splashed onto the sleeve of one of the guests.

'Watch what you're doing!' he snapped.

'Clever though, wasn't he – you know, asking them whether if one of their sheep fell into a pit on the Sabbath, they wouldn't go and lift it out?'

'Like that's ever going to happen – they'd just send a shepherd to do it so they could remain oh-so-pure!' laughed Amos.

'Jesus said that people are more important than sheep,' replied Silas. 'And therefore if you would rescue a ewe, it must be perfectly within the law to heal on the Sabbath.'

'You know what, though,' Amos said thoughtfully. 'I reckon that Jesus is going to get himself into serious trouble if he doesn't back off. I mean, he's just one man; those Pharisees are a powerful bunch and if they don't like you – well, your days are numbered.'

'Do you think,' murmured the chubby man, 'that he really is the Chosen One, the Messiah?'

For a moment no one spoke.

'If he's not, then who is he?' Silas asked. 'He's a miracle worker, that's for sure.'

'Yes, but the way I see it is this,' Amos argued. 'The Messiah is going to save us from the Romans – and to do that, he'll have to make sure he gets in with the people at the top. All Jesus does is wander around the countryside talking about his kingdom. Talking is all very well, but he needs to have a strategy, a plan . . .'

I couldn't risk lingering any longer; already people were beginning to leave and it was my job to help clear up. Besides, I wasn't really interested in all the talk of strategies and kingdoms. What I couldn't get out of my head was the fact that Jesus had healed a man's hand. As I walked away I glanced down at my claw-like fingers, curled tightly into the palm of my hand; at the bent wrist and the disfigured knuckles. Could he? Would he? Was it possible?

If he could, then I could get a proper job – be a regular servant, not just the cheap-at-the-price hired hand, last in, first out; no longer the charity case, the person to be fed in order to make someone feel good.

Then reality hit. OK, so imagine Jesus did make my twisted hand whole. What about the rest of me? I was, as a number of people kept reminding me, a freak. Disfigured, unable to speak, a lip that was attached to my nose, and to cap it all, I was no taller than the average seven year old. Even little Ruth was only a couple of inches shorter than me. I reckoned I would be too great a challenge even for Jesus.

I was suddenly bone weary and close to tears. I slunk off to the outhouse and sank down onto my mat. As I did so I heard footsteps, and worried that Peter or Andrew were coming to tick me off for something, I peered cautiously out of the door.

Jesus was walking on his own, his shoulders sagging, head bowed. He went through the archway and turned to walk round the house and up the hill. I didn't get it. It was late. Everyone was going to bed. Why on earth would he choose a time like this to go walkabout?

> Jesus went out to a mountainside to pray, and spent the night praying to God.
>
> *Luke 6:12*

I would have followed him but my eyelids were heavy with sleep and it just seemed too much effort to move.

It was not a restful night. My dreams were a muddle of images; Aaron lying in the street, not dead but staring at me arms outstretched, as though I could help him; my father shouting 'Cretin! Imbecile!' over and over again, until the tears choked me and I woke up shaking. When I finally succumbed to sleep again, I was climbing a hill, way behind the rest of the crowd, unable to keep up but desperate to get to Esther who was at the top beckoning me on. I kept stumbling, cursing my bowed legs, tears streaming down my face.

'I miss you, I miss you,' Esther was crying and with every word she seemed to get further away.

I tried to shout to her to wait, but of course, no sound came out. It seemed that the more I tried to hurry, the slower I moved.

She was tiny now, a speck in the distance. 'Wait!' In my dream I had a voice. I couldn't believe it. 'Wait!' I shouted again.

'I'm here, I'm waiting!' I looked up. It wasn't Esther. In her place, Jesus was standing, hand outstretched, smiling as if he had eyes for no one in the world but me.

All that Sabbath day, with no work to be done, I walked. Along the lakeside, up the hill and back again, and all the time that image of Jesus was there at the forefront of my mind. Of course, I told myself, it was just a dream; a very real dream, but nothing more. Then Susanna's words would echo in my head

'If you don't come with us, that will be such a shame.'

I kept hearing Esther saying 'He's going to make things right'. Could I possibly be one of those things? I could go and see – just for a bit. After all, I didn't have to stay with Peter's family – I wasn't indentured, I was free to do what I liked. And if he and Andrew were so keen on the man they called Master, well, they couldn't object to my wanting to find out more about him, could they?

All morning I grappled with the idea. If I didn't go, I would never know; but what if I did follow him, and he saw me as the hopeless case that everyone else did? Wouldn't that be worse than never knowing?

'I've missed you,' Esther's voice was as loud in my head as if she were standing right beside me in the flesh. 'I've missed you.'

And in the end those were the words that made up my mind. I'd go because she wanted me to. That's what I would focus on. I wouldn't think about the rest of it. That way I couldn't be disappointed.

So what has that got to do with me?

1. Reuben decided to stick with Jesus largely because he wanted to be close to Esther. God uses our friends in many ways and uses us to help others to reach him. It's not all about 'preaching' and being holy-holy. What kind of behaviour from others would make you want to find out more about the person they follow? What things would put you off? How might you gently lead someone closer to God?

2. 'All Jesus does is wander around the countryside talking about his kingdom.' Why do you think some people found it hard to see Jesus as the Chosen One? If Jesus came back today, who would you expect him to be? How would you expect him to behave? How would he react do you think to drug abuse, homelessness, politicians who defraud their constituents, industries who pollute the environment?

CHAPTER EIGHTEEN

The hopeful apprentice

Caleb

I guess it served me right. For two days after the meal at Matthew's house, I wanted to die. Vomiting, diarrhoea, stomach cramps – you name it, I had it. I guess a stomach that had made do with barley cakes and the scraps for days on end just couldn't cope with the huge portions of meat, the fava beans, the honeyed almonds and my favourite, the bowls of *lebaneh,* the tastiest dish of curdled sheep's milk with yogurt and garlic and cucumber. Not to mention the wine, which just kept flowing. One thing was certain, Matthew was a wealthy man and despite all the talk about his money grabbing ways, a seemingly generous one.

Towards the end of the meal I stood up to go outside and relieve myself, and the whole room spun. Next thing I knew I was flat on my face. I could hear raucous laughter as I scrambled to my feet and staggered out of the door; but then the sound of my own vomiting blotted out everything else. I felt so ashamed and slunk away, not daring to return and look anyone in the eye.

Some time later, curled up behind some water jars, I heard Philip calling my name but I didn't make any attempt to answer. And for the next two days, I lay in a disused outhouse vowing never to touch a drop of drink or rich food for as long as I lived.

When I finally felt halfway human again, I tried to find out where they had all gone. Matthew's booth was deserted and the rumour was that he hadn't even been back to collect his belongings but had just gone off with Jesus; someone said they were heading for Hattin Hill, and I figured the only thing to do was to set off in that direction, but keep my distance; I wasn't ready yet to face the teasing and ridicule that would follow my abrupt and somewhat messy departure from the party.

It was a long walk and I was still weak and had to sit down every mile or so; the path up the hillside was steep and my legs kept turning to jelly. Worse, I felt hollow inside; not just from the sickness but from loneliness and shame. I had been so intent on doing what I wanted that I hadn't thought about Esther; and if anything had happened to her, it would be my fault. My sister had died because I hadn't looked after her well enough and now . . .

I shook myself. Esther would be fine. She wasn't four years old like Kizia, and she wasn't stupid – after all, she'd managed OK when she'd lost me before. If she saw danger, she would know how to avoid it; little Kizia didn't have a chance. I struggled to my feet and set off again, following the path as it twisted through patches of blue globe thistles and stunted broom bushes. There was no sign of a crowd of people yet in the distance I could hear voices. I kept climbing, knowing that when I reached the top I would have a view across the surrounding countryside. Eventually, out of breath and desperately thirsty, I crested the top of the hill – and stopped dead in my tracks.

There, no more than fifty yards away and with his back to me, was Jesus, surrounded by ten or twelve of his disciples. I recognised several of them – Andrew, Peter and Philip, James and John – Matthew was also there, talking to Bartholomew. On the slope that dipped away in front of them were crowds of people, their voices buzzing with excitement. I had approached from the south side of the hill – a few steps more and I would have been visible not only to Jesus and his disciples but to everyone waiting expectantly on the grassy slopes. Quick as a flash I slipped behind a gnarled tamarisk tree, its twisted trunk wide enough to conceal me from view.

'I have prayed to my Father,' I heard Jesus say, 'and now is the time. You, my friends, are no longer simply my disciples. You are apostles.'

The group looked at one another in amazement.

'You, Peter – my rock – I'm going to build on your firm foundation and you Andrew, you will spread the message too.'

He touched each as he spoke.

'James, John, you are the sons of thunder . . .'

'You can say that again,' I heard Philip murmur, 'and twice as noisy!'

'Philip . . .'

'Me, Master?' Philip gasped.

Jesus nodded.

'And you too Bartholomew, Matthew, Thaddeus, Judas, Simon . . .'

He continued naming each in the group and then noticed Thomas, sitting with his back to the others, head bowed.

'And you too Thomas,' he said, gently touching him on the shoulder.

'Me? Surely not me, Lord?'

'Yes Thomas, I need you too,' Jesus smiled.

For a moment I thought Thomas might burst into tears, but thankfully he simply stammered his thanks and joined the others.

'Now listen,' he said. 'You too must spread the Word – you too must go out into the countryside and do as I do. Drive out demons . . .'

At that I almost gasped out loud. So he did take on apprentices, he did teach people how to be like him! And if he was inviting a tax collector to be one of the select few, what was to stop me doing it too? I wanted to rush up to him there and then and say that I'd been waiting for this moment ever since the wedding at Cana; but just then he spoke again.

'Come,' he said. 'I must speak to the people. Listen carefully for this is a message for you – for everyone. This is the message you must spread.'

The group moved a little further down the slope and shielded by bushes and the occasional tree I skirted the hill until I was able to find a patch of ground just below where he was standing. As he held up his hand, the babble of conversation ceased and all that could be heard was the song of the birds and the rustling of branches. And then he began to speak.

Now when Jesus saw the crowds, he went up on a mountainside and sat down. His disciples came to him, and he began to teach them.

He said:

'Blessed are the poor in spirit,
for theirs is the kingdom of heaven.
Blessed are those who mourn,
for they will be comforted.
Blessed are the meek,
for they will inherit the earth.
Blessed are those who hunger and thirst for righteousness,
for they will be filled.
Blessed are the merciful,
for they will be shown mercy.
Blessed are the pure in heart,
for they will see God.
Blessed are the peacemakers,
for they will be called children of God.
Blessed are those who are persecuted because of righteousness,
for theirs is the kingdom of heaven.

Blessed are you when people insult you, persecute you and falsely say all kinds of evil against you because of me. Rejoice and be glad, because great is your reward in heaven, for in the same way they persecuted the prophets who were before you.'

Matthew 5:1-12

'I want you to understand,' he began, 'that you are lucky – indeed you are blessed – when you are at your wits' end, when you don't know which way to turn.'

The hills around formed a sort of amphitheatre that meant that Jesus' voice resonated clearly even to those sitting a hundred yards away. The crowd murmured and I had to admit that what he said seemed pretty stupid to me. How could being at the end of your tether be a blessing?

'Why?' he boomed and for an instant I could have sworn his eyes met mine. 'Because your emptiness lets God find his way into your lives.' He paused, his eyes scanning the crowd. 'And blessed too are those of you who are grieving, who have suffered loss, because in your pain and anguish you will be embraced by God. Blessed are those of you who don't crave position or authority but who are happy with who they are and what they have; you know why? Because you are the ones who will receive things that money and authority simply cannot buy.'

The murmuring in the crowd grew louder and a man sitting in front of me nudged his companion.

'Do you get all this, Jake?'

'Sounds a bit too good to be true from where I'm sitting,' his friend admitted. 'But be quiet, he's saying something else.'

'And listen,' Jesus shouted. 'You're blessed if you really want to get to know God, because the nourishment you will get from knowing him is far better for you than all the fine food and drink you can imagine.'

'Now he really is seriously off the wall,' Jake muttered. 'Clearly he's never been starving.'

Jesus turned, almost as if he had heard what Jake was saying, which of course, he couldn't possibly have done.

'And blessed are those of you who show compassion to others, those who see the needs of those around them and care for them. Because when you do that, you open yourselves to receive the care of God.'

He held his arms out wide as if wanting to scoop the entire crowd up in his arms. 'And blessed are those of you whose hearts and minds are free of prejudice or greed, bitterness or anger. Why? Because when you clear yourselves of all those negative emotions, you will suddenly see God in the world and the people around you.'

I shifted my position. It had been greed and anger that had made me do that terrible thing years before. This was all getting a bit too close to home for comfort.

'Lucky, too, are those who offer the olive branch, those who diffuse tempers and step in to stop fights and arguments; for that is what is asked of members of God's family. And what is more, you are blessed when people persecute you because of your commitment to God your Father.'

Now that really did cause a stir. Voices rose, and someone to my left almost had apoplexy. 'That's ridiculous,' he spluttered. 'It doesn't make sense, it's . . .'

'You want to know why I say this?' Jesus asked, raising his voice over the voices of his audience. 'Because when people take it out on you for loving God, all they manage to do is drive you closer to the kingdom. When people mock you, or challenge you, or cast aspersions on your sanity simply because you follow me, you are blessed, truly blessed! They only behave that way because the truth hurts and they don't like to feel uncomfortable.'

He waited until the murmuring died down. 'They won't like your dedication to me, but I do! Everyone who has followed the will of God my Father has faced these sorts of challenges.'

With that, he turned and gestured to Matthew to pass him a goatskin water bag. Taking a long draught, he wiped his mouth and beckoned to his disciples to move along the ridge to a rocky outcrop. I didn't want to miss a minute of what was going on but just seeing him drink had made me realise how thirsty I was and I cast around to see if there was someone who looked approachable enough for me to request a drink. Not far to my left was a group of women, two of whom had small children with them; mothers are always more willing than others to be generous, so keeping my head down so that Philip wouldn't see me, I scuttled over to them.

As I approached them, my foot caught in a tree root and I stumbled, crashing into a woman who was sitting slightly apart from the rest of the group. 'I'm sorry,' I gabbled. 'I didn't mean . . .'

'Caleb? Oh Caleb . . . it's you!'

I turned and there she was, beaming at me from ear to ear.

'Esther!'

'Oh Caleb I've been so worried about you! Where have you been? Are you here because . . . ?'

'It's a long story,' I interjected, aware that the woman I'd banged into was eyeing me closely. 'I'm so sorry I ran of. I . . .'

'Don't worry, you're safe and you're here, and that's all that matters. This is Susanna,' Esther said. 'I told you about her . . .'

'Caleb, it's good to meet you,' Susanna said. 'Any follower of Jesus is a friend of mine! Come, share some food with us. This is my good friend Joanna.'

She gestured to a well-built woman sitting to her left, who smiled at me and patted the ground beside her by way of invitation. And that's how it was that as Jesus began speaking again, I was nibbling, cautiously at first, and then more enthusiastically, on bread and smoked fish, drinking down cool draughts of water and revelling in that title, 'follower of Jesus'. For now that would be enough; to be in the crowd, with Esther, watching and listening.

For now, I was happy to imagine what it would be like when I was up there with the other disciples, telling people what to do and sounding clever. It was going to be so cool.

Jesus went on talking for a long time, and I'll be honest, some of what he said went right over my head. It was fine when he was talking about everyday stuff; like the fact that if you had salt that wasn't salty any more it would be useless for preserving food, and how if you want to light a room you don't go and hide the oil lamp under an upturned bowl.

'You – all of you,' Jesus declared, making a sweeping gesture that included the whole crowd, 'you are the salt of the earth, the light of the world. You must be the people who bring the flavour of God's spiritual food to people who have never tasted it. You must be the people who shine like beacons on a hilltop and draw people to the light. If you do that, people will see the light of God shining through you and they will praise your Father in heaven.'

'Yes,' Susanna breathed. 'Yes, yes.'

Listening to him I got that feeling I'd had before, like anything was possible; as though I could be one of these powerful amazing people who could change the world. But there were those in the crowd who didn't seem to like what he was saying.

'Never mind the fine words!' someone shouted out. 'You keep breaking the law, healing on the Sabbath, eating with . . .'

Jesus held up his hand and spoke over him.

'There's one thing you have to get straight,' he declared. 'I am not here to tear apart the Scriptures or to overturn the law and the teaching of the prophets – no way! I'm here to complete the picture, to open up God's law to everyone. God's law is what matters; it is the only law that will last for eternity.'

The man who had shouted seemed mildly appeased but Jesus hadn't finished.

'If you take God's law seriously – God's law, mind, not your own fabrications – and if you help others to see the right way to go, then you will be honoured in my kingdom. You've got to do a whole lot better than the Pharisees and teachers of the law or there's no way you'll get there!'

Oh whoops. Hadn't he realised that the guy who shouted at him was a Pharisee? And that he had friends with him?

'The law is watertight, it's stood for centuries,' the angry Pharisee shouted.

'But I'm adding to it,' Jesus proclaimed. 'You know that for generations the commandment has been that you should not commit murder.'

My throat began to close up and my heart raced. In my head, my father was yelling at me again, 'Murderer! Murderer!'

'Well, I'm saying more than that – far more. What I say is that if you show anger towards a brother, if you shout "fool!" at them – you stand to be judged. If you say spiteful words to a sister – well, you are at risk of punishment, because words can injure – in fact, they can kill.'

This was too much. I couldn't sit and listen to that – it hurt too much. I began scrambling to my feet.

'Caleb, where are you going?' Esther asked.

'I – I've got cramp from sitting still too long,' I lied. 'I'm going for a walk.'

'I'll come with you . . .'

'No! Leave me alone!'

I saw the look of pain that crossed her face and the words of Jesus echoed in my head.

'I'm sorry it's just – just the pain from the cramp. Yes, come. Thanks.'

Perhaps talking to Esther would banish all the awful memories and the black blob of guilt.

For a while we just walked round the back of the crowd, saying nothing. Jesus' voice was still clear – but I wasn't listening. The memories blotted it all out; once again I saw myself standing on the threshold of our house, a cocky, loudmouthed eight year old, yelling at his little sister. 'Shut up, shut up, shut up, cry baby!'

I saw myself walking towards her, where she sat in the corner screaming on that one, high-pitched note, her face scarlet. 'Just go and play, you pathetic little kid!' And then . . .

'Caleb? What is it?'

Esther touched my arm.

'What? Nothing, I . . .'

'Caleb, you're shaking like a leaf! What's wrong?'

'I'm fine,' I snapped. 'It's just – I was ill for a couple of days and I guess I haven't quite got my strength back yet.'

The lie seemed to satisfy her.

'Let's just sit for a bit,' she suggested. 'Your face is the colour of cold ashes!'

'Have you seen Reuben?' I asked in hope of distracting her.

'Yes,' she replied eagerly. 'We tried to persuade him to come with us to hear Jesus, but he refused. I did think . . .' She paused, and nibbled on a broken fingernail.

'You thought what?'

'Well, what with Jesus being able to cure people and stuff, I thought that if he came along, and Jesus saw him . . .'

'He'd cure him? Make him look normal?'

Esther nodded.

'There's an awful lot to cure,' I murmured. 'I mean – he's . . .'

'I know,' Esther sighed. 'It was just a thought.'

Suddenly she brightened. 'But hey, he hangs out round Peter's house – so he's bound to see Jesus there sometime, isn't he? And Jesus will see what he's like and sort it out. He's that kind of guy.'

When she said that, I found myself almost wishing there was something wrong with me. Nothing major, but just enough to attract Jesus' attention; enough to get a bit more from him than just 'Follow me'.

So what has that got to do with me?

1. Are the Beatitudes – the 'blessed are you' sayings – too close for comfort for you? Which of these sayings touches you the most? Which do you find the hardest to get your head around?
2. What sort of nourishment do you think Jesus is speaking of?
3. Look at the Beatitudes one by one and discuss their relevance for society today. Try rewriting them as a poster for your school, church group, sports club or workplace.
4. When Jesus says that everyone who follows him faces the risk of being scorned how does it make you feel? Why do you think he said something that clearly might put people off?
5. Jesus said, 'If you show anger towards a brother, if you shout "fool!" at them – you stand to be judged. If you say spiteful words to a sister – well, you are at risk of punishment, because words can injure – in fact, they can kill.' What effect did these words have on Caleb? Which parts of Christ's teaching, if any, make you feel that way?

CHAPTER NINETEEN

You too, little one

Reuben

You have heard that it was said, 'Eye for eye, and tooth for tooth.' But I tell you, do not resist an evil person. If anyone slaps you on the right cheek, turn to them the other cheek also. And if anyone wants to sue you and take your shirt, hand over your coat as well. If anyone forces you to go one mile, go with them two miles. Give to the one who asks you, and do not turn away from the one who wants to borrow from you.

You have heard that it was said, 'Love your neighbour and hate your enemy.' But I tell you, love your enemies and pray for those who persecute you, that you may be children of your Father in heaven. He causes his sun to rise on the evil and the good, and sends rain on the righteous and the unrighteous. If you love those who love you, what reward will you get? Are not even the tax collectors doing that? And if you greet only your own people, what are you doing more than others? Do not even pagans do that? Be perfect, therefore, as your heavenly Father is perfect.

Matthew 5:38-48

If I'd known that Jesus was going to choose the top of the steepest hill in the whole of Galilee to do his teaching, I might well have had second thoughts about setting out. The paths were littered with stones and I kept stumbling as my legs got tired but I could see the crowds up on the ridge and to be honest, it was the thought that Esther might be among them that kept me going even more than any vague hopes I had about Jesus.

I was only halfway to the top when I was forced to stop. My lungs felt as if they might burst at any moment, my calves throbbed and the glare of the sun was giving me a headache. Stupidly I had brought no water with me and my tongue felt twice its normal size.

I leaned against a rock and gazed out at the heat haze shimmering over the valley. It was on days like these that I felt like a small kid, with tears lumping together and clogging up my throat. I guess it was all down to the memories – memories of those first weeks after I found myself lost and abandoned by my father. It was hot then and I hadn't as yet learned the skills of stealing and begging – all I recall of that time is thirst and hunger and tears, the taunts of other kids and – just occasionally – the kindness of a stranger, usually a woman, with a cooling draught of water or a plate of food – or even a cast-off garment from one of her own family. But no one ever asked me to stay.

I shook myself to rid my mind of such useless thoughts and was about to scramble to my feet and set off up the hill again, when I realised that the crowd was dispersing, and clusters of people were walking towards me, clearly heading back to the villages. This was good; with a bit of luck I would find Esther without having to tackle the rest of the hill.

'Such nonsense!' A broad shouldered man who was in the front of the line of followers strode past me, his staff thudding on the ground in time with his words. 'He's talking rubbish . . .'

'Asking the impossible . . .' another agreed.

'All that stuff about not looking at a woman with lustful longing . . .'

'Yeah, well we know you couldn't stick to that one, eh David?' his companion teased. 'What did he say you had to do? Gouge your eye out or be chucked on the rubbish pile of humanity?'

'And what about cutting off your hand if you find yourself raising it in anger?' another, older man grunted. 'With servants like mine, a quick show of force is the only way.'

'Well, speaking for myself,' the first man declared, 'I'm heading back to the real world. There's only so much fantasy one can stomach!'

I wondered what on earth Jesus could have been saying about self-mutilation – and instead of putting me off, it made me want to find out more. I climbed onto a rock to get a better view, and spotted a group of women standing way back near the top of the hill. I kept my eyes firmly on them, praying that Esther was among them; but after a few minutes I realised the group weren't moving down the hill with the rest of the crowd.

There was nothing for it: I'd have to finish the climb. There was no way I could stick to the path; too many people were threading their way down and I knew from experience that I'd be jostled and pushed out of the way. Instead I headed up through a patch of scrub, the thorn bushes scratching my feet and ankles. I kept my eyes fixed on the ground; this was perfect territory for snakes and scorpions and my sandals had more holes than hide.

'Reuben!'

A hand grabbed my shoulder and I nearly leapt out of my skin.

'Hey, this is amazing!'

I wheeled round and found myself face to face with Caleb. Relief flooded me – there's only so long you can kid yourself that being alone is the best way to be.

'We were talking about you just a few minutes ago,' Caleb said. 'Me and Esther. What are you doing here?'

I gestured that I was looking for them, and he laughed.

'Come on, I'll take you to Esther – she's up there with Susanna. She's fallen on her feet – that woman is seriously well off. But nice with it.' He beckoned me to follow him. 'And hey, listen – you won't believe this, but things are looking up for me too. I'm going to be one of Jesus' disciples.'

I gave him a sideways glance and raised an eyebrow at him.

'No truly,' Caleb gabbled. 'I found out just now that he's up for it – teaching people how to drive out demons and stuff like that! Just imagine – I could end up famous like him.'

I tapped my forehead and pointed to him to indicate that he had, in my opinion, taken leave of his senses.

'It's true,' he insisted. 'I heard him tell Peter and Andrew and a whole lot of others that he was sending them out to do just that. If they can learn, so can I. Look – there's Esther!'

I was glad for a change of subject and looked towards the clump of straggly trees at which he was pointing. Jesus was sitting on a rock, and Andrew and Peter were sprawled on the grass at his feet. A small crowd – not more than fifty people – were scattered around and a group of women were unpacking food, while listening intently to Jesus. And then I saw her. Esther. She was motionless, a loaf of bread in her hand, and her head cocked to one side, like a dog listening for the sound of his master's return.

'Yes, I know that the law says "an eye for an eye and a tooth for a tooth",' Jesus was saying. 'But what I'm saying you should do is this. If someone punches you on the right cheek, turn and offer him the left as well.'

The man's mad, I thought. I mean, the healing was wonderful – miraculous even – but if he was going to go around spouting rubbish like that, people would soon label him insane.

'And if someone is suing you and asks for your tunic, give it to him – but throw in your cloak as well,' Jesus added. 'And if someone forces you to go one mile, go two.'

I sighed, nudged Caleb and raised my eyes heavenwards.

'You did that though,' he said thoughtfully.

I frowned. What was he on about?

'You did – Esther told me. She asked for somewhere to sleep and you did more; you fed her, found me, and then helped both of us get to Jesus. You went the extra mile. And you didn't have to.'

There was so much I wanted to say – that it was the fact that Esther hadn't recoiled from me that made me want to help; it was because I wanted to be seen walking through the streets with a pretty girl that I had agreed to go to the temple. But without words, it was too much to explain.

'Hey, come on,' Caleb urged. 'They're eating!'

He ran the last few yards, with me trailing along behind. Jesus had stopped speaking and was tucking into his food enthusiastically. I kept my eyes firmly on the ground, trying to look invisible. I had a horrible feeling that Andrew would not be best pleased to see me here instead of back at Bethsaida.

'Welcome!'

So much for keeping a low profile. Jesus had raised a hand and was beaming at us as if greeting long lost friends. Esther had jumped to her feet and was running over to us, and Susanna was already clearing a space for us to sit.

'Reuben – is something wrong? Is it Ruth – the family . . . ?'

Peter was at my side in an instant. I shook my head and clapped my hands to suggest that everyone was just fine.

'Then what are you doing here?' he asked. 'You're supposed to be . . .'

'Peter.' Jesus mouthed the word so softly that I don't think Caleb heard him and then he turned and looked at me full in the face. 'Reuben, Caleb, welcome. Join us please.'

My heart was thumping so fast that it felt as if it would burst out of my ribcage. Jesus had looked at me. He'd seen my disfigured face and stunted limbs. And he'd smiled. Could it be that he was getting ready to work his magic on me? To make me whole? And how come he knew my name?

'Come and sit with us,' Susanna was saying. 'There's plenty of food.'

'No, we must feed you!' someone else shouted.

'Come here, young fellow – I'll share whatever I have with you. It's my duty to care for people like you who are . . .'

Luckily, the last speaker let the sentence hang in the air. I'd never had such attention, or so many offers of food and hospitality. It was cool. But Jesus clearly didn't think so.

'Stop!' he demanded. 'What's with this sudden outpouring of generosity? It's no good thinking that you can earn good-behaviour points with your heavenly Father by parading your good deeds in front of me and your friends. No way!'

Hang on, I thought. Don't put them off – the food smelt delicious and I was up for grabbing as much of it as I could. It felt odd to suddenly be the centre of kind attention; I was used to the other sort but this was a bit overwhelming.

'When you do something kind for someone,' Jesus went on, 'don't make a show of it – there are enough people around in the streets and synagogues who do that on a regular basis. And they get their buzz from showing off about it. But you . . .' He made a sweeping gesture with his arm that included everyone, even those at the back who were whispering among themselves.

'You need to keep these good deeds secret. It's not the good opinion of men you should be looking for but God. And believe me, your heavenly Father will see these things that you do quietly and without show, and he will reward you for them.'

He turned again and looked at me and Caleb. 'Now eat!' he laughed.

> Jesus said 'Do not store up for yourselves treasures on earth, where moth and rust destroy, and where thieves break in and steal. But store up for yourselves treasures in heaven, where moth and rust do not destroy and where thieves do not break in and steal. For where your treasure is, there your heart will be also.'
>
> *Matthew 6:19-22*

I waited all day. At first I thought that Jesus would heal me when everyone had finished eating – he kept looking in my direction and I guessed he was working out how to do his magic, or which bit of me to work on first. Esther was obviously thinking the same thing.

'Jesus can cure anything, Reuben,' she had whispered to me within seconds of my sitting down. 'Go and ask him to make you better.'

Well, I could hardly do that – not while he was in full flood talking about money being unimportant and how people shouldn't worry where their next meal was coming from or what they were going to wear. I figured that this guy had never had to buy his own food, or worry about keeping warm when the rain came.

'Look at the birds,' he said, pointing to a flock of stonechats flying above our heads. 'They don't store up food or fret about what tomorrow might bring, yet God your Father cares for them. And look at those scarlet anemones growing over there; not even Solomon in his most opulent robes was as splendid as one of those flowers.' He opened his arms, palms upturned.

'So – if God cares for birds and plants in this way – how much more is he going to look after you? Your faith is so wobbly, isn't it? Don't worry about tomorrow; just concentrate on the needs of the present moment and know deep down in the depths of your being that God can and will take care of the rest.'

He looked round at the crowd – hundreds of faces fixed on his.

'I tell you, when you ask, you will receive, and when you truly seek, you will find what you are looking for. Knock, and the door will open to you. Everyone who asks, receives . . .'

Again he looked in my direction and began heading my way; my heart rate quickened and I glanced round to see just how many people were watching out for this miracle that was going to take place. It was obvious that was what he was leading up to – the healing of me. And then Thomas stepped right in front of him and stopped him in his tracks.

'Master,' he said, 'Andrew says that John taught his disciples to pray – but I for one don't know how we are meant to do it? What are we supposed to say?'

Jesus smiled. 'Well, the first thing to remember is that prayer is a private thing. Don't stand on street corners where everyone can see you, and don't babble on and on – it's not the number of words that matter, it's the sincerity and longing for God that counts. God knows what you need long before you've opened your mouth to ask him for anything!'

'Yes,' Thomas said, a mite impatiently I thought, 'but how do we speak to Yahweh?'

'This,' said Jesus, 'is what you say:

'Our Father in heaven, may we always keep your name special and holy. May your kingdom come on earth, and may what you want be done by us every day, just as it is done in heaven. Give us the food we need each day and forgive us for all the things that we do wrong, just as we forgive people who wrong us. Please don't let us be tempted to do bad things; save us from the mischief of the devil.'

For a moment he looked thoughtful. Then he took a deep breath. 'You see, if you forgive people when they hurt you or do you wrong, God your Father will forgive you too. But if you can't find it in your hearts to forgive . . .'

For a moment he stumbled over the words.

'If you can't do that – well, then God won't forgive you.'

Suddenly there was a lot of shuffling of bottoms, and clearing of throats and packing up of baskets among the crowd. I don't know what they were feeling but if it was anything like what was going through my mind, it was pretty unnerving. Was Jesus really saying that everyone deserved to be forgiven? Even people like my father who'd flung me out and walked away without a backwards glance? Even those boys who had stoned poor Aaron to death – would God forgive them? Would he forgive me – not just for the stealing but for the cutting too? Would he?

But to be forgiven, Jesus had just said I had to forgive. Not just forgive my father, which was nigh on impossible, but forgive all the people who had called me cretin and imbecile? How could I do that? Just thinking about them made me want to bang my fists into my head.

'It all comes back to the same thing in the end. The fact is, it's easy to love people who are your friends, people who show you kindness and help you along the way – it's far more difficult to love those that curse and harm you. When you love those that hate you, and when you give freely, not expecting to get anything back, that's when my Father's heart rejoices because that's what he does – he gives to the ungrateful again and again.'

Clouds were rolling in from the east and there was a rumble of thunder in the distance. A breeze picked up, rustling the leaves of the trees. Jesus glanced round the crowd and smiled. 'And now, go in peace before we all get drenched,' he said.

Most of the crowd scuttled off down the hill as the first drops of rain fell but Susanna and Esther, seeing that neither Caleb nor I had moved an inch, paused.

'You have somewhere to go?' Susanna asked us anxiously. 'My home is always open to you – there's always work to be found and . . .'

'Thank you but no,' Caleb interrupted hastily. 'I'm going to be a disciple.'

Susanna smiled.

'Really? Well, that's marvellous. And you Reuben?'

I gestured towards Peter and Andrew and indicated that I would be with them that night. Of course, once I was healed, I'd be off to make a new life but there was no way I could explain that with signs and miming.

'Well,' she said, 'I am sure we shall be seeing a lot more of one another. Come along, Esther we must hurry back. Remember I told you about my cousin Mary, the one from Magdala; she is coming to visit and I have a feeling you will want to hear her story.'

'Don't disappear, will you?' Esther said, although I wasn't sure whether she was talking to me or Caleb. 'Don't go away without telling me.' And then she waved and followed Susanna down the hill.

'This is it,' Caleb whispered to me. 'I'm going to tell Jesus what I want to do.'

Jesus was already setting off down the hill, deep in conversation with Peter, James and John, but as he drew level with us, he paused.

'It's Caleb, isn't it? The one who wanted to understand?'

'That's right, Master,' Caleb replied eagerly. 'I want to be just like you and do everything you do and . . .'

'You presumptuous little upstart!' one of the disciples shouted. 'How dare you speak to the Master in that way. As if you . . .'

'Wait,' Jesus said sternly. 'Who are you to judge him? It's very easy to find fault with other people but more important to take a long hard look at yourself. When you've got rid of all your faults and failings – then you can start thinking about those of other people.'

'I . . .' Caleb began again, but a guy dressed in black from head to toe interrupted.

'You are so right, Master – we must not judge. I, for instance, a humble man – I intend to follow you wherever you go, no matter what, because I am a . . .'

'Before you start making wild promises,' Jesus said, 'you have to realise that those birds flying in the sky up there – they have nests to go back to. The foxes that prowl round the rubbish dumps at night

– they have holes where they can keep dry and warm. But the Son of Man has no place to lay his head.' He smiled at Caleb. 'That's something you need to realise too,' he said.

'Master, I don't care,' Caleb insisted. 'I can sleep anywhere, I can . . .'

'And you must enter through the narrow gate,' Jesus added.

Caleb frowned. 'Enter where? What gate? Is it in Jerusalem? I can go there – I can go . . . what do you mean?'

'What I mean is this – there's no easy way to reach God. It's not a part-time hobby and everything isn't just going to fall into your lap. Wanting to understand is the first step – but it's a long journey and it will take your full-time commitment, every second of every hour of every day.'

'Yes I know – but you'll teach me? I mean, I'll do whatever you say . . .'

'You will? Then what I say is this: follow me by all means. But first, open your heart, open your ears, open your mind.' He smiled at Caleb, and then turned to me. This is it, I thought.

'You too, little one.' He leaned forward, ruffled my hair, chuckled and then set off down the hill, all but Andrew following him.

For a moment I stood motionless, holding my breath. I hardly dared look. He'd touched me and that meant – surely it meant that he'd healed me. I glanced at my legs. They bowed inwards just as before. My arms were as short as ever. My hand was still a claw.

But perhaps that was just too difficult to remedy, even for Jesus. Surely, though, someone who could cleanse a man of leprosy could sort out my face?

Slowly I raised a hand to my lip, my fingers trembling as I touched the corner of my mouth.

It was still distorted, hooked up at one side to my left nostril. Nothing had changed. That was that then. I was a hopeless case – too much even for this supposed Messiah man.

'Come on,' Caleb was urging. 'It's going to pour any minute.'

Let it, I thought miserably. What do I care? I've been soaked to the skin enough times for it not to bother me. We hopeless cases are just garbage, after all. And yet. And yet, Jesus had bothered to stop, to speak to me. What was it he had said? 'You too little one . . .'

Normally I detested it when people called me little but somehow the way he said it had been like a pet name, an endearment – just as the way he'd ruffled my hair was exactly what I'd seen fathers and mothers do in the marketplace to their little children. So why hadn't he done something? It wasn't fair.

'You too little one.' He'd said that after telling Caleb to – what was it? Open his heart, his mind and his ears? Well, that made sense for Caleb – if he was going to be a disciple, he'd have to pay attention, memorise the rules, learn all the tricks of the trade. But me? Did he mean I should hang around, follow him with the others? I could – except that how would I eat? If I wasn't down at Bethsaida helping out, I'd have to scrounge food wherever I could. Not that it was a problem, I'd done it for years; but somehow I guessed stealing from market stalls wasn't on Jesus' list of things it was OK to do.

'Why do you worry about what you will eat?' His words rang in my ears as loudly as if he were still standing beside me.

'Reuben! Are you coming or not?' Caleb grabbed my arm.

I nodded. Why not? Let's put all this to the test I thought, conscious that I was fighting not to scrape my palms with my fingernails. I'll give him the benefit of the doubt this once; maybe it's slow magic, maybe I'll wake up tomorrow and something will have changed. Maybe every time I'm hungry, food will magically appear at my feet. Maybe. Or not.

So what has that got to do with me?

1. The law 'an eye for an eye and a tooth for a tooth' was given to help judges make the punishment fit the crime. It was *not* an excuse for revenge but that's what some people took it to mean. Are we ever tempted to say 'I was just doing to her what she did to me?'

2. These remarks would have offended the Jews because they wanted a strong military leader who would overcome the Romans, not someone who would turn the other cheek to them. But Jesus taught that giving mercy and justice was more important than receiving it. How does that affect our thinking about punishment and justice today?

3. Why did Jesus say that if someone asks for a tunic, we should give them a cloak as well? What about going the extra mile for someone? That has become a well-known phrase in our time. What do you think it means in practical terms? Reuben gave an example. Can you add to that through your own experience of someone going the extra mile for you? Or you for them?

4. Jesus made it clear that God isn't impressed with show-offs! He doesn't want us to give great displays of piety and then treat our neighbours like dirt; he doesn't want us only to be generous when lots of people are looking. God knows our innermost thoughts – there's no need to 'go public' in order to gain Brownie points. OK, but it's hard isn't it? When we do something kind, or give generously, it gives us a warm feeling – but the feeling is even warmer when someone tells us how good we are being! But we are not doing it for our own benefit but because God wants us to. His love and pleasure is ample for our warmth!

5. Take no thought for tomorrow? That's hard when all around us we are being told to revise for exams, to plan for our future career, to save for our retirement, to take out insurance policies to protect our houses, cars, travel plans . . . so what is Jesus talking about? Was this just an instruction for people in rural Galilee 2000 years ago, an instruction that has no bearing on our life today?

What do you think Jesus means by it? What happens when we spend a lot of time *thinking* about what might happen tomorrow? Worrying about failing an exam instead of getting on revising for it? Take no thought probably means do not dwell on these things; give it your best shot but set worry aside. Discuss how that suggestion makes you feel.

6. 'When you ask you will receive.' Have you ever asked God for something and not received it? For one thing, we need to ask in faith and more importantly, we need to note that Jesus didn't say 'you will receive it at once'. There is a difference between asking for what we need, and begging him for what we *want*. Discuss the difference between need and want in areas such as money, possessions, friendship, relationships and status.

7. How often do we tell God what we want? Expect him to fit in with our plans for our life? Notice Jesus' response to Caleb.

8. The Lord's Prayer: What does it really mean? When we look at it line by line, rather than chanting it without thinking, we realise that it is full of the most amazing statements and promises.

   Our Father: Jesus is telling us that God is not just his father, but ours too. We need to always acknowledge first and foremost who we are talking to. He is the only true God who created all things in this universe, including ourselves. He loves us and we need to show our love for him.
   Who art in heaven: Heaven refers to God's kingdom, but in the view of many clever scholars it also means 'harmony'. Therefore Jesus is saying that when we connect with God, we have a sense of harmony and peace in our life. This is an inward peace that never leaves us, even in the middle of storms and crises.
   Hallowed be thy name: God is to be honoured, adored and respected – we should never take his name in vain or use his name as a swear word.
   Thy kingdom come: This means may your plans for your world come to fruition soon.
   Thy will be done on earth as it is in heaven: Help us to know and understand your purposes for us and to realise that God is in charge in every part of our lives, however challenging and difficult they may be.

Give us this day our daily bread: We are asking God to provide our bodily needs but also need to remember that bread signifies the word of God too. Jesus is encouraging us to let the word of God be the first thing we digest every day.
And forgive us our sins and we forgive those who sin against us: Forgiveness is God's great gift to us; unless we forgive others, we have no right to expect forgiveness ourselves.
And lead us not into temptation, but deliver us from evil: God would never lead us into temptation. Jesus may well have meant 'do not allow us to be led into temptation (by others). We pray that when evil lurks, God will open our eyes to see it, and give us the strength to turn away from it.
For thine is the kingdom, the power and the glory, forever and ever: God is supreme, God is over all; he is life, truth, love – over all people. He is the All in All. Always. Forever. No matter what.

9. Jesus wants us to love the people who hate us – is this possible? How do we even begin to manage it? Talk in your group about what you mean by 'hate' – it's a far more vicious word than we sometimes imagine. What does hatred do to communities? To nations? How does one small act of hatred grow? Remember that to love the people who hate us does *not* mean that you have to like what they do.

10. Full-time commitments can sound off-putting. But if we never take the first step, we will never discover what a joy it can be to commit to Christ. What commitments do you have in your life that make you scared of using that word in relation to your journey with Jesus?

CHAPTER TWENTY

The gentlest touch

Esther

It was horrible. Up on the hill, listening to Jesus and seeing Reuben again, I'd felt happier than I had in ages. Being with Susanna made me feel safe – and that was a new sensation. But then, within hours, everything was turned on its head.

As we got to the bottom of the Hill of Hattin, where the path forks, we found a group of men waiting for us. And I mean us. They fixed their eyes on Susanna, Joanna and me and then as one, moved towards us, elbowing us out of the way and spitting at our feet. They pushed Joanna so hard that she fell to the ground, and as Susanna and I went to help her, one of the Pharisees stuck out his foot so that I too tripped and gashed my knee on a sharp stone. Blood began pumping out and running down my leg and I clenched my teeth together to stop myself from crying.

'Slut!' One of the men leaned right over me, so close that I could smell the stale sweat and the sour odour of his breath. My whole body was shaking, and I wriggled backwards to get away.

'Leave her!' It was James, John's brother, who shouted at the man, but all he did was laugh, before moving with the others a little further down the path to where Jesus had paused to take a drink of water.

'Lord, oh Lord,' one of them began in a sneering, mocking tone. 'Do you . . . ?'

'Hold it right there!' Jesus shouted, tossing the goatskin at Philip. 'You don't fool me with your "Lord, Lord". What's the point of calling me that and then going against everything I teach? Treating people the way you do?'

'We know the law,' one began puffing out his chest and eyeballing Jesus. 'And we know that rabbis of any standing at all don't go around with . . . with people like that!' He jerked his head in our direction.

'Tell me,' Jesus said quietly. 'You have a home?'

'Of course,' said the Pharisee, frowning at the sudden change of subject.

'And it is built on the beach?'

'Don't be ridiculous,' the man laughed. 'What kind of fool do you take me for? It's in the centre of town, near the top of the hill. It's a very fine . . .'

'And yet you behave like a man who would build his house on sand,' Jesus shrugged.

'What are you talking about?'

I must admit I had been wondering the same thing myself as I sat there mopping up the blood with the hem of my robe. Susanna was caring for Joanna who was sitting, head between her knees, as white as a sheet. John was squatting beside them, offering sips of water and ignoring the sneers of the Pharisees.

'People who hear what I say and then don't put it into practice in their lives are just like someone who blithely goes ahead and builds a house on sand. The moment the rains come, or the river bursts its bank, what happens? The house is so flimsy it collapses and the man is homeless.' He paused. 'What I'm looking for is people who listen to what I have to say and then go out and live by it! They are like people who dig deep and put solid foundations on rock before they start to build their house. For them, the storms and the rains and the gales won't be a threat because their house will withstand anything.'

The Pharisee sniffed. 'We didn't come for a lesson in building techniques,' he muttered.

'You didn't come to learn at all,' Jesus commented. 'But think about what I've said. Build your life on flimsy foundations and at the first sign of difficulties or problems, you will be all at sea. Build your life on what I teach and . . .'

'Our lives are built on the laws of our ancestors!' one of the other men shouted. 'We don't need to stand and take this from some wandering preacher who hangs out with – with them!' He wheeled round and jabbed a finger towards us.

'These friends listen to my words and they care for my needs,' Jesus said softly, but the man had already turned on his heel and was striding along the path, the others close behind. Jesus came over to us and laid a hand on Joanna's shoulder. 'Sadly this is the sort of thing that will happen to those who follow me,' he sighed. 'If you want to . . .'

'Master, all I want is to be with you,' Joanna smiled.

'And me,' Susanna said.

'Then go home now, rest a while and we shall meet again soon,' Jesus said. 'And thank you for your care – the food was delicious!'

He was about to go when he paused and looked at me. 'Don't be afraid,' he said gently. 'As long as you never let yourself be led astray by what people say, you'll be OK. Judge people by how they treat you and others. After all, those delicious grapes we had earlier didn't come from a thorn bush, did they? The figs weren't picked from the thistles by the path? Eh? Were they?'

Despite the pain, I couldn't help laughing. 'No, sir, of course not,' I murmured.

'So just you remember that,' he smiled. 'And now go home with your mistress and sleep well,' he said stretching out his hand to help me to my feet.

It was only after he and the disciples had headed off down the road to Capernaum that I realised that my knee had stopped bleeding. And there wasn't a single mark to show where the cut had been.

'You make me laugh,' Susanna said the following morning as I was chopping vegetables in preparation for the visit of her friend Mary. 'You keep peering down at your knee as if you expect it to suddenly hurt again.'

'It was Jesus, wasn't it?' I asked for the third time. 'It was him who healed it?'

'What do you think? How else could it have happened?'

'But why me? And it was after all a very little thing really – why would he . . . ?'

Susanna paused on her way out of the door. 'Perhaps,' she said gently, 'he knew that you had suffered enough pain these last few months. Or perhaps . . .'

'Yes?'

'Perhaps he has work for you to do,' she murmured. 'But for now, I need you! You're a great help to me but I have to say you are one of the slowest onion peelers I know!'

With a visitor in the house, I kept discreetly in the background, taking care of the food preparation and making sure that the floors were well swept and the oil lamps kept primed. Susanna was clearly very fond of Mary, who was everything I would have liked to be; tall, willowy, with huge grey-green eyes and thick, onyx black hair. She was nothing like Joanna, Susanna's other close friend; Mary was softly spoken and had an air of fragility about her, as if she expected something terrible to happen any moment.

It was one evening, towards the end of their meal, when Susanna called me to her. 'This,' she said turning to Mary, 'is Esther.'

I bowed my head and dipped respectfully.

'Esther, Mary has a story to tell which I think you will want to hear,' she said. 'It's about Jesus. Come, sit down.'

I didn't know what to expect. Mary didn't meet my gaze but just took a deep breath, pressed the palms of her hands together and sighed deeply.

'It is hard to know where to begin. Until a few months ago, I was a very bad woman . . .'

'No, no Mary,' Susanna interrupted. 'Not bad. You were just sick, that's all.'

Mary smiled wanly. 'Let me put it another way,' she said. 'I was like two separate people; the nice Mary and the mad Mary.'

Mad Mary! At her words the conversation I had overheard in Capernaum came flooding back to me. But this elegant lady couldn't be the same one, surely? I kept quiet, eyes averted, the very model of the quiet well behaved listener.

'I was born in Magdala,' she went on. 'My father had a salting business there; we were comfortably off. My father didn't like me. I wasn't a boy and I was – different.' She paused. 'I couldn't bear to be in the house, doing all the things good little girls were supposed to do,' she said. 'Cooking, making bread, learning to handle the loom or sew neatly. I would have days – weeks, even – of feeling angry, so, so angry. I remember throwing things, tipping over the table in my mother's kitchen, smashing pots and then running. Running and running and running.'

'I . . .' I couldn't believe that I had almost spoken. That would have been the height of rudeness; I knew my place. I also knew what it was like to want to run and run till no one could find you.

'My father always caught me,' she went on as if reading my thoughts. 'He or one of the men in the town would seize me and take me home and then my father would hit me – he said it would knock the badness out of me. He was wrong; it never did.'

For a moment I thought she was going to cry, but Susanna squeezed her hand, and she took a deep breath and continued. 'I wasn't always like that – other times, I wouldn't speak for days, not because I wanted to be naughty but because I felt as though something was stuck in my throat and that if I tried to speak I would choke. Those times, I didn't eat and all I wanted to do was sleep. Father didn't like that either.'

She pursed her lips together. 'Susanna was the only person who seemed to like me whatever mood I was in,' she whispered. 'We're only distant cousins but her family used to come to Magdala to visit and to do business and she and I would spend time together. But then I ruined that too.'

'No Mary . . .'

'Yes, I have to tell it all, otherwise everything that has happened will be for nothing,' she insisted. 'One day, the black demons that by then I knew lived deep inside my gut spewed out. Such a little thing that made them do it. A kiss.'

She must have seen the puzzled look on my face, because she laughed briefly.

'Don't get the wrong idea,' she said. 'I saw Susanna's father kiss her, give her a hug and call her – what was it now? – his precious little lamb. My father had never, ever done anything like that with me.' She took another deep breath. 'The demons inside burst out of me – I grabbed Susanna, I pulled her hair, I kicked her, spat at her, smashed a water jar at her feet, and then I ran. And you know the most amazing thing?'

She clearly expected an answer, and although I had an idea what she might be about to say, I feigned ignorance. 'No Madam.'

'Susanna came after me,' Mary said. 'She sat with me for hours while I ranted and raved and cried and beat my fists against my head and used words that I guess she'd never heard in her entire life – and then when I was calm, she hugged me and said it would all be alright.'

'That's when you came to stay with us for a while,' Susanna interjected.

'That's right – your mother was so kind,' Mary acknowledged.

She turned back to me. 'I never went back. My parents died that winter, and Susanna's mother the year after – and Susanna offered me a home.'

'So why . . . ?' I began and then remembered who I was.

'Why don't I still live here?' Mary asked. 'I'll tell you.'

She took a long draught of wine and broke a piece of cheese from the wooden platter in the middle of the table. 'When you are as I was, tormented, scared of yourself, you don't think rationally,' she explained. 'One day, just a year or so ago, when I was having a really bad episode, crying and saying I wanted to die, Susanna tried to calm me by suggesting a walk. She took my arm and led me outside, but I was having none of it. I shoved her away, screaming at the top of my voice. She fell and hit her head on the corner of a cart in the yard outside. She was dazed, there was blood on her head and she kept shouting "Mary, go . . . go Mary . . . go!"'

'I was trying to tell her to go and get Ziva,' Susanna explained.

At that name I gasped, my mouth open to ask a multitude of questions but Susanna held her hand up and gestured for me to wait.

'I ran and ran,' Mary said, 'all along the coast path towards Bethsaida, tears pouring down my face. Then it came to me – all I had to do to end this misery was run straight into the lake and keep going. It would all be over in moments – and I'd be at peace.'

I didn't know where to look. I felt my eyes fill with tears at the thought of what she must have been going through – or was it the name of my sister that had made my emotions so raw?

'I ran across the beach, blinded by tears – and ran straight into . . .'

'Jesus!' Susanna couldn't hold back her excitement. 'Tell Esther, Mary, tell her . . .'

'I was about to,' Mary teased. 'Jesus – who of course at that time was just another man as far as I was concerned – was standing at the water's edge a few yards from where I was splashing my way into the lake. He came over to me, put a hand on each shoulder and stopped me dead in my tracks. I shouted, screamed – I thought he was going to – well, I didn't know what I thought. And then he spoke.'

I held my breath.

'He said, "Mary, Mary," and looked deep into my eyes. Then he shouted "Be gone out of her – be gone. Now!"'

'What happened then?'

'I felt my legs give way beneath me, my chest tightened as though my lungs were about to burst through my skin, and I retched and retched as if some terrible sickness had got me in its grip. I was terrified: I thought I was dying.' She paused and took a deep breath. 'And then, just seconds later, I felt this indescribable peace. The sort you feel just before you drift off to sleep on a summer's night.'

She closed her eyes for a moment, a faint smile on her lips. 'He looked at me, stretched out his hand and helped me to my feet,' she whispered. 'You are well – that's what he said to me. And I knew. I knew that the black demons were gone for good. I don't know how I knew, but every fibre of my being told me it was true.'

A tear trickled down my face. 'So he can do it,' I said. 'He could cure Ziva if only I could find her.'

'You will find her,' Mary said calmly. 'When the time is right. Right for her, not you. You will find her.'

She reached for the water jar and I realised it was empty. 'Forgive me, Madam,' I said hastily. 'I will . . .'

'One moment,' Susanna said. 'Mary, just finish your story and then we must retire for the night. Esther looks exhausted.'

'I went back to Magdala,' Mary said. 'To my parents' house which was still mine even though it had fallen into disrepair. I sorted it out, trying to ignore the looks of amazement on the faces of neighbours who expected me to go manic any second – and I sold it.'

'So you will live . . . ?'

'I will follow Jesus,' she smiled. 'I have money, I can support myself – and I can, like Susanna, provide help for him and for his disciples. What else would I do with the rest of my life but serve the one person who made me whole again?'

So what has that got to do with me?

1. Esther has her first experience of the price of following Jesus. It is hard for us today to understand just how radical Jesus' attitude to women actually was. We are used to women being accepted as equals in most ways that we don't really grasp what an enormous change it was for Jesus to speak to women, to spend time with women, to notice women even, in a society that really relegated women to a position not much higher than the furniture. What areas of society today do you think would equate to the women who followed Jesus? Is any group scorned or marginalised or is everyone regarded equally? What challenges faced the women disciples? What challenges face us as disciples of Christ today?

2. The parable of the man who built his house on rock and the one who built on sand is very familiar to most of us from primary school! The house, of course, represents our life. What do you build your life on? How can we make sure that the foundation of our life is built on something solid? Is it possible for someone who has no faith of any sort to have a solid foundation for life? What would that be? Even rocks can be split open by earthquakes; what happens to us when something threatens to 'shake us to our foundations'? Where do we turn?

3. What effect does Mary Magdalene's story have on you? Why do you think the author wanted to explore fictitiously what might have happened in her life? What elements of her friendship with Susanna strike you as being (a) unusual and (b) an example to us?

4. When Jesus met Mary and prevented her from committing suicide, she describes the feeling that gripped her. It was not without pain; the pain came first, the peace second. Often Christ comes to us and heals us in ways that make us face our darkest side first. But he always does it in love.

5. Mary says that she wants to spend her time and money supporting Jesus. 'What else would I do with the rest of my life but serve the one person who made me whole again?' Jesus is not on earth any more: how can we support him today? Is it all about money in the church collection and quoting the Scriptures? Or is there much more to 'supporting' him than that? How would you best be able to support his ministry wherever you are today?

CHAPTER TWENTY-ONE

Falling out – and falling in

Reuben

I was hurting all over. Head throbbing, heart aching, lungs like bands round my chest. Every time I opened my eyes the trees, the sky and the sun seemed to be spinning out of control all round me. I wanted to throw up but it seemed as if my body was too exhausted even to make the effort to do that. I curled myself into a ball and prayed that sleep would come. It didn't. All that happened was that the events of the past week swirled round and round in my head until in the end I gave way and let the tears fall. And once they started, I simply couldn't stop.

I was alone. Not just in that moment, but always. And all I wanted was something that would fill the gaping hole inside me. I wanted someone to hold me, to take care of me, to worry about me. I wanted that even more than I craved the power of speech or a strong pair of legs. If the stories I had heard over the past few days were true, if this new kingdom Jesus was going to set up was a place where everyone mattered, no matter who they were or what they looked like, then there was only one thing to do. I had to find him and this time, I had to do whatever it took to make him agree to let me be a part of it.

In the end, I must have fallen asleep – a restless, muddled sleep in which my dreams were full of the events that had led me to this barren hillside in the middle of nowhere.

That day, coming down from Hattin Hill, I had made my mind up to go back to Peter and Andrew's place, ask for work and wait for an opportunity to confront Jesus in full view of other people so that he would have a good audience for the healing. I figured he couldn't refuse me, not if the moment was public enough to put his reputation on the line.

> When Jesus had entered Capernaum, a centurion came to him, asking for help. 'Lord,' he said, 'my servant lies at home paralyzed, suffering terribly.'
>
> Jesus said to him, 'I will come and heal him.'
>
> *Matthew 8:5-7*

I had been following Jesus and the gang on the lake-shore path to Bethsaida, with Caleb tagging along and talking non-stop about how he was going be Jesus' top apprentice, and a few stragglers walking three abreast deep in conversation, when there was a commotion behind me.

'Let me through, please – you have to let me through!'

I turned. It was a Roman centurion, a broad-shouldered, stocky guy with that beaky kind of nose that so many of them seem to have. His suntanned face was creased in a frown and beaded with sweat, which wasn't surprising considering all those clothes they have to wear.

'Let me through!' His voice was deep and throaty and his Aramaic pronunciation was all wrong.

'We're not causing any trouble,' someone protested as he elbowed them out of the way.

'We're just going home,' another insisted. 'Minding our own business.'

'I'm not here to make trouble for you,' the centurion said, pushing past Caleb and me until he was only a few feet from Jesus. 'Lord, Lord – please – just a moment of your time!'

Jesus turned and looked at him inquiringly.

'Lord, my servant – my most faithful, long-serving servant – is ill,' the centurion panted. 'He has some kind of paralysis and is in dreadful pain.'

Jesus nodded thoughtfully. 'I will come and heal him,' he said.

He looked so tired that I doubted he could walk another furlong but already he was moving towards the centurion as if to ask the way.

'Oh no, Master, I don't deserve to have you coming all the way to my house. All I ask is that you just say the word and then I know my servant will get better.'

'You believe that?' Jesus looked gobsmacked.

'Of course I do,' the centurion replied. 'In my job, I am in charge of a hundred men. If I say to one of them "Go there," he goes; if I order another to come, he comes. What I say goes. How much more then will what you say carry authority?'

Jesus shook his head as if he couldn't believe what he was hearing. Then he turned to Andrew, Peter, James and John who were standing the closest to him. 'You know, I haven't found this kind of simple trust in the whole of Israel, among people who are supposed to know all about God and the way he works.'

He turned and beckoned to Thomas, Philip and believe it or not, to me and Caleb too. 'This man is the first of many people who will come from all over the place – from east and west to join the feast in God's kingdom, along with the prophets of old. Believe me, people who like to say they have grown up "in the faith" but who in fact have no real, vibrant, living faith – they'll be cast aside and left to wonder just what it was that had happened to them.'

Jesus turned to the centurion. 'Go home,' he said. 'What you believed would happen really has happened.'

'Master!' The centurion dropped onto one knee, raised his eyes to Jesus and mouthed his thanks. Then he turned and strode away.

'Wow!' Caleb breathed, nudging me. 'Did you see that? He didn't even go there, he didn't even have to touch the servant. How does he do that?'

He didn't expect an answer but what I would have liked to say was this. If it was so damn easy to heal a man he couldn't even see, then surely it would take him ten seconds to do something for me? He'd seen me, he'd even spoken to me back on the hill – and all he could manage was 'You too little one'. Well, I'd stick to my plan; I would give him the benefit of the doubt. After all, he was tired and maybe he wanted to make sure I'd hang around until he decided the moment was right.

I'd give him a couple of days. And if he still did nothing, I would know. I would know that I was just too difficult a case even for the man they were all calling the Messiah.

It was a good plan I thought. Trouble was Jesus had a different one. The next morning he was gone.

I had left my sleeping place in the outhouse and ventured into the courtyard in the hope of getting some breakfast. Peter's wife was in the doorway of the house, furiously shaking a mat, her face scarlet.

'Looking for Peter and Andrew, are you?' she called. 'Don't bother – they've gone. With him. When will they be back? Don't ask me, I'm just the wife.'

She stomped back into the house, reappearing almost instantly with another mat on which to take out her anger. 'You want work?'

I nodded.

'Well, you best go and see Zebedee – doubtless James and John will have dropped him in it again. What is with this Jesus? I mean . . .' She dropped the mat and sighed.

'He's a great healer, I know that more than most after what he did for Mother but – Peter and Andrew are great fishermen. That's their job. That's what they do. What I don't get is how come Jesus thinks he can just whisk them away and leave that lot . . .' she jerked her head in the direction of the hired hands who were mending nets down by the water, '. . . leave that lot to run the show,' she finished.

She glanced at me. 'Hey, I'm sorry, it's not your fault and here I am taking it out on you. Go to the kitchen – there's some bread and fruit on the table. Take what you need.'

After I'd eaten, I made my way along the shore to Zebedee's boats. Sure enough, it soon became clear that James and John, along with the rest of the twelve that Jesus had picked on Hattin Hill, had left as well.

'James says they are doing the work of the kingdom,' Zebedee sniffed. 'They've always been impetuous those two but this is going a bit too far.'

I gestured that I could help and he nodded, tossed some cork floats at me and intimated that I should get on with it.

'We need all the help we can get,' he said. That's when I thought of Caleb. I figured he could do with a job and besides, I wanted some company my own age. So I ran to the back of the outhouse but he wasn't there, even though I'd shown him a good place to bed down.

'Are you looking for that mate of yours?' Zebedee asked when I returned to the boat. 'Don't waste your time – he went off with Jesus too.'

A lump swelled up in my throat. He hadn't even bothered to say goodbye.

'John said they were heading off for a trip round Galilee,' Zebedee sighed. 'I don't know what to make of it all. Now are you going to deal with those floats or not?'

I did try, I really did. I focused on the jobs Zebedee gave me to do, I ate the food Peter's wife left for me, and I kept telling myself how lucky I was. But it didn't work. All I could think about was the fact that Caleb was off getting in with Jesus' gang, and that meant in all probability that he had met up with Esther again. I'd heard Susanna tell Philip that she would make sure that the twelve never went hungry or short of money – and to do that she would have to go to them wherever they were.

And my bet was Esther would go with her. Caleb and Esther, Caleb and Esther. Images of them together, sharing food, laughing, listening to Jesus kept me awake at night. The more I thought about it, the more I realised that Caleb had everything going for him – strong muscles, good looks, and the power of speech – everything to make someone like Esther want to be with him, whereas I – well, I was just the kid she was nice to because she felt she ought to be.

At first it was just scratches – and careful ones at that. High on my thighs, under my tunic; under my hair where it hurt like hell but didn't show and on the soles of my feet so that every time I walked the pain acted like a kind of release. That might have been enough had it not been for the arrival of Samuel, Zebedee's cousin. He had been expected for several days; Zebedee's wife, Salome, was in a state worrying about wasted food. When Samuel finally arrived, Zebedee was so relieved that he was angry!

'And where have you been?' he demanded. 'Three days we've been prepared for you – what kept you?'

'Cousin, such goings on you won't believe,' Samuel replied. 'Just wait till I tell you.'

I wouldn't have heard Samuel's news in the ordinary way of things – but the kitchen girl was ill with a fever and Zebedee's wife had roped me in to help out.

'Firstly, I was delayed at Nain by the crowds following this Nazarene – what's his name – Jesus?' Samuel began, heaving his not inconsiderable weight onto the bench. 'Scores of them, I'm not exaggerating. Sounded like they were having a party, laughing, joking . . .'

I took my time arranging the food on a serving platter, straining my ears to hear more while trying to blot out the image of Caleb and Esther having fun together.

'Anyway, I was just stopping off to get my cartwheel fixed when – well, I hardly know where to start.'

'The beginning?' Zebedee suggested.

As Jesus approached the town gate, a dead person was being carried out – the only son of his mother, and she was a widow. And a large crowd from the town was with her.

Luke 7:11, 12

'The crowd suddenly went quiet,' Samuel went on, 'and as soon as they did I realised why. A funeral procession was heading through the gate. I could hear the flute players and the wailing of the mourners, even though at first I couldn't see very well because of the throng of people.'

A shiver ran down my spine. I've always had a fear of death. I put the platter on the table and went back to the kitchen for pitchers of wine and water. Samuel had a loud voice and I could hear most of what he was saying as I filled the jars.

'The wheelwright left one of his apprentices to mend the wheel and invited me up on to the roof of his house out of the scrum – I've known him for years and we enjoy a catch up whenever I'm passing that way. His house is just inside the town gate.'

I placed the pitchers on the table and he took a long draught of wine and wiped his mouth on the back of his hand.

'He told me that the dead man – well, little more than a boy really – was the only son of a widow, a friend of his wife who had struggled to make a living ever since her husband died the year before. From his roof we had a good view of the procession – and of what happened next.'

'Which was?' Zebedee urged. 'Reuben, the figs and olives!'

I had deliberately left them in the kitchen so that I had an excuse to take my time fetching them while eavesdropping on their conversation. As I entered, Salome jumped back from the doorway – she too had clearly been eavesdropping. 'Sssh,' she hissed putting her finger to her lips.

'This Jesus was a few feet from the gateway as the funeral pyre passed,' Samuel was saying. 'Poor Reuma, the boy's mother, was in a state of collapse, howling with grief and hardly able to stand. Jesus went right up to her and told her not to cry. And then he touched the coffin.'

'No!' Zebedee gasped, spewing crumbs all over the table in his amazement. 'But that would make him unclean . . .'

'Wait, you haven't heard anything yet,' Samuel interrupted. 'You know what he said next?'

Salome nudged me and gestured to me to take the dish of fruit to the men. I nodded and ambled back to the table.

'He looked at the body and he said, "Young man, I say to you, get up!"' Samuel paused for the full effect of such a statement to sink in. 'And he did!' he concluded triumphantly.

My dish of fruit crashed to the ground, pomegranates, figs and grapes rolling under the table. Despite the crash Zebedee hardly flinched.

'He – raised – a – dead – man?' Zebedee articulated each word as if speaking to a very small and gullible child. 'You are telling me that you saw a dead man come back to life?'

'I know it sounds incredible, but it's true,' Samuel insisted. 'There were at least a hundred witnesses and you should have heard them – shouting, crying, praising God, dancing – and Reuma hugging her son and falling to her knees and kissing Jesus' feet.' He sniffed. 'I have to tell you, Zebedee, it brings tears to my eyes, just remembering it all. I think that what I heard people saying must be right.'

By then I was under the table, picking up the shards of pottery and scattered fruit.

'And what exactly are they saying?'

'That a great prophet has come in the form of this Jesus – that God has sent him to help us at last. Mind you, if what I hear on the streets is true, he's making a lot of enemies among the Pharisees and teachers of the law. Apparently some of the things he says are totally subversive.'

Zebedee rubbed his chin and pulled at his beard. 'My boys,' he murmured. 'They are with him. I worry about them.'

I was scrabbling out from under the table, my hand full of pottery pieces when I stood up too soon and cracked my head on one of the struts.

Zebedee exploded with anger.

'Reuben, enough! Haven't you got jobs to do down at the boats? Let's hope you do them better than you cope waiting at table or you'll be out of a job.'

I flinched. He was usually gentle and forgiving – all the hired hands said he was the easiest taskmaster in the whole of Galilee.

I gestured apologies.

'I said scram!' Zebedee shouted. 'Just get out of here!'

I skulked back into the kitchen. Salome was at the bread oven with her back to me and I knew that the sight of the broken dish would set her off on one of her tirades about money being scarce, so I grabbed a piece of bread and some figs while she wasn't looking and stomped down to the beach. The hired hands, along with Peter's young son and a couple of Zebedee's cousins were making the boats ready to go for the night's fishing. I walked along the beach and sat on a rock. OK, so I'd smashed a pot – big deal. What about all the good things I'd done? And I'd like to see Zebedee carry pots and platters with one hand. I was still clutching one of the pottery shards in my hand. I sliced it hard across my thigh.

It hurt like hell. Good. The worse the pain the quicker the demons go.

I hurled it away and watched the blood ooze down my leg, thinking all the time about what Samuel had said. Frankly, it didn't make sense. Dead people are dead. Their hearts stop beating, they stop breathing in and out – they grow stiff and cold. So how could anyone, even the most talented healer on earth, bring them back to life?

God decided when people died, I knew that. 'It was God's will' was what people said when they stood around the tombs. In that case, surely only God could bring someone back to life? Instantly my stomach lurched, my heart raced and I felt so lightheaded that I thought I might pass out there and then. Was Jesus a God? What was it John the Baptist had said that day down by the Jordan? 'Behold the Lamb of God!'

The Lamb of God. What did that mean? Somewhere from the recesses of my mind, I remembered a woman's voice. 'Who's my precious lamb then?' There had been a baby on her knee and I remember hating the kid because she was loved and fondled and sung to and I wasn't.

'Behold the Lamb of God!'

Was Jesus someone God really adored? Another god come down from heaven to . . . ? To do what? It was too much. I couldn't get my head around it. I don't know how long I sat there thinking – I do know the boats left, darkness fell and I was beginning to feel chilly when I heard footsteps behind me. It was Zebedee. I jumped to my feet, dropping the food that lay uneaten in my lap onto the sand.

'I'm sorry.' Zebedee's voice was gentle and he sounded troubled. 'I shouldn't have spoken to you the way I did.'

I made crossing gestures with my hands to say it didn't matter even though it had.

'It was Samuel's story that made me edgy,' he admitted. 'If Jesus can bring people back to life then he must be a really great prophet – one like Elijah, who brought a widow's son back to life in the same way. And I've been grumbling and muttering curses about James and John leaving me in the lurch, when all the time I should have been rejoicing that Jesus wanted to have them as disciples.'

He sighed. 'Even so I confess I miss them,' he murmured. 'I know my days are numbered and . . .'

I shook my head vigorously although deep down I had been thinking for some time that Zebedee was growing more frail and more weary as every day passed.

'It's true, Reuben – but I just want to see James and John again before – well, while there's still time to put things right,' he murmured. 'I would go and find them, but who knows where they are by now? From what I hear, Jesus goes wherever the mood takes him.'

He picked up a stone and began idly tossing it from one hand to the other.

'At the synagogue last week I bumped into a friend of James, a guy who is still a staunch supporter of John the Baptist. He told me that they had visited John in prison, and he'd sent them to find Jesus and to ask him straight: "Are you the expected Messiah?"'

He paused, put his hand into the pocket of his robe and tossed me a fig. 'Apparently John is really disheartened, full of doubts about why he is shut up there in prison while Jesus walks free.'

He stared out to the darkening sea on which his boats were drifting gently, their lamps flickering. 'Jesus told him to go back to the prison and tell John just what he had seen for himself – lepers being cleansed, the lame walking, the blind able to see again. And he said something else – something that I guess applies to me too. He said that even when you're unsure or full of doubt you should cling to the one who comes to tell the truth.'

He rested a hand lightly on my shoulder.

'If you were norm— If you were up to it, Reuben I could send you out to look for my boys and tell them I need to see them. But I guess I'll have to wait till the morning and then get one of the village lads to go. Assuming I can find one I can trust.'

He patted me on the head. 'Goodnight, Reuben,' he said. 'And once again, I'm sorry.'

I nodded curtly, and turned away. Sorry he might be but he still wasn't thinking before he opened his mouth. 'If you were normal.' That was what he'd been about to say, and the words cut into me as sharply as if they'd been carved into my skin with a knife. What was normal? Why would he think I wasn't up to it? I had a brain – a better one in many ways than most of the boys my age. I felt things just like other people and I had guts – oh yes, I had guts in good supply. I could go and find James and John as easily as anyone else; OK, it might take a bit longer than someone with long legs and an even gait might need, but I could do it.

In that moment, I made up my mind. I'd go – and I would leave straight away before he had the chance to search the village for someone 'normal' in the morning. And if he found himself short-handed without me, well tough. He could call on all the 'normal' kids to help out, couldn't he?

I left at once, anger and determination driving me on. As the first fingers of dawn light rose over the lake I reached Capernaum. Instinctively I headed for the old shack, knowing that it was too early for Mordecai and Hillel to have left for their pitches near the synagogue.

Mordecai jumped as I drew back the shredded piece of sacking hung across the doorway. The place had the same dilapidated air about it, the same smell of rancid food, urine and other unspeakables and it suddenly hit me that I had been really lucky – living down by the shore, fed, and with a roof that didn't leak to sleep under at night. It also occurred to me that I had hardly spared a thought for my old friends since that day when Peter's mother-in-law was healed.

'What on earth are you doing back here?' Mordecai grunted.

'Who is it?' Hillel asked anxiously.

'It's Reuben,' Mordecai said, grinning at me. 'Well, well, I guess you've come to your senses at last. Realised that the Jesus guy was just one more pretender, a sham Messiah, a fake . . .'

I shook my head vigorously.

'You're a hopeless case,' he sighed. 'Mind you, there seem to be a lot of people as crazy as you are. I've even heard stories about him raising the dead – talk about delusions . . .'

I grabbed his arm, stamped my foot and gestured that I'd heard the story too and I believed it.

'Oh get real,' Mordecai said. 'Shall I tell you what I think?'

I shook my head again, pointed to his eyes and wrote 'Jesus' in the dirt and drew an eye beside it.

'Me? I haven't *seen* him – and it's my bet he won't be back this way in a long time. He'll be looking for somewhere new, some other poor souls to con and . . .'

I shoved past him and out through the doorway. How dare he speak like that about Jesus? Didn't he realise that he was slagging off someone who was – who was what? I didn't know exactly but one thing I knew because I felt it in my heart. Jesus was special and he didn't lie.

'Hey, come back, what's got in to you?' I heard Mordecai quite clearly but ignored him. I guess with the wisdom of hindsight I should have gone back to thank him. It was his denial of Jesus that made me certain that he really was who he said he was.

I went on, through the town, up a hillside, down again – and found not a trace of Jesus. By mid-afternoon I must have travelled eight miles and I was hungry – I hadn't eaten the evening before having forgotten in my anger all about the food dropped from my lap when Zebedee caught up with me. I approached a few people in the little hamlets I passed through, but all I got was a tirade of abuse, a few jeers and a nip on the ankle from a dog sent to chase me away. And then someone threw a stone.

I didn't see it coming; it hit me on the side of my forehead and within seconds blood was dripping into my left eye. Panic enveloped me; I turned and began hobbling back along the twisting path that I had been following minutes before. After hours of walking my legs were so tired that even my version of running sent hot needles of pain through my body. Behind me I could hear laughter and the rattle of stones that fell short of me, their obvious target. As I ran, my breath coming in short painful rasps, all I could think was that this was what it had been like for Aaron. And I was terrified. Blood was blinding my left eye and I couldn't see the path clearly, which meant I stumbled on every loose stone or slippery stretch of mud. It was odd, I thought, that I welcomed pain when I had inflicted it on myself but pain that came from elsewhere just scared me.

Eventually, just as I thought my lungs would burst, I realised the jeering had stopped but it wasn't until I had rounded a bend in the path and veered off up a slope covered with grazing sheep, that I dared to turn round. There was no sign of anyone. I slumped to my knees, and crawled the last few yards to hide behind an outcrop of rock. Higher up the hill, I could see the shepherd; I figured that the thugs would hardly come and hunt me down here.

I was spent, my energy drained. The wound above my eye was throbbing relentlessly and as I touched my eyebrow gingerly, my finger was coated with congealing blood. I tried to spit into my hand to clean the blood but my mouth was so parched that there was no saliva there. I thought about trying to reach the shepherd boy – he would be sure to have water – but when I moved, the ground seemed to spin away from me and I fell back again, nauseated and dizzy. And that's when finally I fell asleep.

I dreamt I was in a torrential rainstorm. Water poured over me, icy cold and from somewhere far away a voice kept shouting something unintelligible. The ground shook under me – and suddenly I was awake. I found myself staring into the anxious face of a young boy. It wasn't raining – the boy was frantically splashing my face with water from a goatskin pouch. I could see at once that he was wealthy – his ketonet was spotless, right down to the edge of his sleeves and his sandals were of the softest leather. I struggled to get up, afraid that I had somehow strayed onto private land, but the moment I moved I felt sick.

'You're alive!' the boy cried. 'Thanks be to the great Yahweh! I thought you'd copped it. You look a terrible mess. What happened?'

He had the clipped, cultured voice of a posh person and his accent was certainly not from round Capernaum way, but he seemed genuinely concerned, so I went through the usual palaver – pointing to my mouth, shaking my head – and he got it at once.

'You're dumb? Tough call. I've got a cousin whose small with legs like yours but she can talk – oh, boy can she talk! And she doesn't have your . . .' He hesitated. 'I mean, her face is OK, and everything.' He eyed me with what seemed to be genuine sympathy. 'I'm Seth, by the way.'

I wrote Reuben in the dirt, the letters even more crude than usual as my hand was trembling.

'Hey, Reuben, you should get to see that Jesus guy – he'd sort you out.'

I heaved myself into a sitting position leaning on one arm in an attempt to deal with the dizziness. I put my free hand over my eyes, and mimed a search of the horizon.

'You're looking for him?' Seth was clearly quick on the uptake. 'He's been in Nain – and you will never guess . . .'

I made it clear I'd heard the story already.

'Thing is,' he said, sitting down on the grass beside me, 'well I probably shouldn't say this to anyone but it's not like you're about to tell, is it?'

He didn't wait for an answer, but I saw by the way he glanced at my bow legs and the twisted hand that he didn't see me as any kind of threat. I also saw that the leather pouch slung on a strap over his shoulder was bulging with what I hoped might be food. The nausea of earlier had eased, but judging by the noises emanating from my distended stomach, my gut needed pacifying big time. I took a chance, tried my crooked smile and pointed to his bag.

'What? Oh – you hungry?'

I nodded.

'Here – it's not much 'cos I've eaten most of what I had. Trouble is, my father's steward seems to think that whenever my father and I go off anywhere, we're going to starve to death. Still, if my leftovers will help . . .' He tossed a wedge of bread, some curd cheese, two barley cakes and a ball of almond paste onto my lap. Leftovers? Until I'd fallen in with Andrew, they would have amounted to at least two days' supply of food.

For a moment I was too intent on stuffing food into my mouth to wonder what he had been about to tell me. I needn't have worried; the guy might not be suffering from hunger but he sure did have a severe case of verbal diarrhoea.

'I've seen this Jesus,' he said eagerly. 'My father is – well, let's just say he's keeping a close eye on him. He's really important you know – my father I mean, not Jesus.'

I would have tried to put him straight but I was too busy demolishing the second barley cake to bother.

'See, some of my father's friends want to get some real hard evidence – you know, about Jesus and what he's doing. I mean, he's saying some pretty way out things. Like when he healed the crazy dumb man and . . .'

I choked on the cake and looked at him wide-eyed.

'And then he said . . .'

I grabbed his arm and pointed to my mouth, opening and shutting it with my thumb and forefinger to imitate someone talking.

'Sure,' Seth nodded. 'That's what I mean – he could do you too. In fact, you'd be easy – this other guy was possessed. You seem quite normal.'

I could have hugged the guy.

'Only you might want to avoid the fallout afterwards!' he added.

I frowned and held my hands out, palm upwards, to let him know I didn't get what he was talking about.

'Jesus got really angry,' he said. 'One of my father's friends said that he reckoned the only reason Jesus could get rid of demons was because . . .' He paused and I waved my hand at him to urge him on.

'Because he is in the pay of the devil!'

He looked at the ball of almond paste in my lap and I could see he was regretting being quite so generous. I tossed it back to him and he grinned.

'Thanks.' He bit into it with relish. 'So, like I said, Jesus got pretty mad. He said that if he really was the devil and he cast out devils, then devils would be no more. At least, I think that's what he said.'

Jesus said to the Pharisees 'If Satan drives out Satan, he is divided against himself. How then can his kingdom stand? And if I drive out demons by Beelzebub, by whom do your people drive them out? So then, they will be your judges. But if I drive out demons by the Spirit of God, then the Kingdom of God has come upon you.'

Matthew 12:26-28

Seth sighed. 'My father did explain what everyone was getting so het up about; I had my bar mitzvah last year and I am supposed to pay attention to all that theological stuff; but when it gets too involved, I switch off.' He grinned. 'Anyway after that it all got a bit personal. Jesus said that if someone isn't on his side, then they're against him,' he went on. 'No half measures, that was his take on it. He said they could say what they liked about him, and in the end they'd get forgiven but if they said a single word against the Holy Spirit they would never, ever be forgiven. I reckon he should have left it there and maybe my father and his friends would have given up and gone home. But he really blew it for himself.'

I frowned. I'd finished my food and all I really wanted now was to know where I could find Jesus, but Seth had only paused to take a swig of water.

'You know what he called them? I mean, these are really important men – high up Pharisees . . .'

That took me aback. Seth seemed a nice kid – yet his dad was a Pharisee. My experience of Pharisees didn't exactly make me feel warm towards them.

'. . . and Jesus should have shown some respect,' Seth went on. 'But you know what he called them? A brood of vipers! And he added that what they said carried no weight because their hearts were wicked!'

I couldn't help thinking that whatever else Jesus was, tact and discretion were not his strong points.

'I guess I should stop talking so much,' Seth grinned. 'Call it a dry run for being quizzed by my father on what he's been teaching me. If I hadn't managed to get away for a bit, I'd have gone stir crazy. Lessons, lessons and more lessons – and that's even when we're supposed to be on holiday.'

He pulled at a few tufts of straggly grass and glanced up at the sky. The sun was sinking in the west and there would only be a couple more hours of daylight left. I scrambled to my feet, dusting off the grass and flakes of dried mud from my tunic and gestured that I needed to get going.

'Me too,' Seth nodded. 'Glad you're OK; hey, do you reckon I saved your life?'

I wasn't sure that I would go that far but he looked so eager that I nodded.

'Great, because I want to be a physician,' he told me. 'And I haven't ever found anyone to practise on till I saw your legs sticking out from those rocks.'

He grinned. 'Maybe I'll see you around. My father's in a meeting with a lawyer friend of his – I guess now that Jesus is in Capernaum, they'll be discussing what to do next.'

Capernaum? Jesus had been in Capernaum all the time? And I'd been chasing all over the countryside getting battered by stones and drenched in water all for nothing?

'Which way are you going?' Seth asked.

I pointed in the direction of Capernaum.

'Really? That's so cool,' Seth replied. 'We can go together. I like to have someone to talk to.'

It felt good to be wanted and it felt good to have company. But the best bit of all was that Seth didn't see the irony in his last remark. He saw me as someone he could have a chat with. It struck me that he might be rich, but perhaps deep down he was just as lonely as I was.

So what has that got to do with me?

1. The centurion showed great faith; firstly faith that, even though he was not a Jew, Jesus would listen to him, and secondly faith that Jesus could heal wherever he was. But there is something else to notice: what was it in his own life that made him relate to what Jesus could do? Read the conversation carefully again!

2. 'It was a good plan I thought. Trouble was Jesus had a different one.' How do we feel when our plans don't work out, even when we believed they were for the best? Do we really believe God has a hand in it all, or is it all just down to 'bad luck' or 'fate'?

3. For many of us, the idea of someone being physically raised from the dead is hard to get our heads around. We assume it doesn't happen today, but perhaps we need to think hard about that. When surgeons bring people back from the brink of death, do we stop to think who has given them that skill? How often do you hear of doctors saying that they are mystified about the disappearance of tumours, or the rapid recovery of someone for whom they had almost given up hope? Is this purely down to scientific and medical know-how, or does God intervene?

4. Reuben says that he can't get his head around the words of John the Baptist about Jesus being 'the Lamb of God'. The great thing here is not that he doesn't understand but that he keeps turning it over in his mind. What are the big Don't Get-It's in scripture for you? Do you dismiss them as too complicated or do you try to get your head around it and if so how? What is the most comfortable way to do this? By going online? By asking friends or teachers? By round the table discussions with family? Or is it easier simply to forget it and get on with something else? Does the church make it easy for you to find out stuff that puzzles you? How could it be made easier?

5. It wasn't until Mordecai began slagging Jesus off that Reuben realised that he was someone special. He still didn't understand fully but he knew what his heart told him. How often do we listen to our hearts even when our head says something isn't possible?

6. When Seth tells Reuben what Jesus has been saying, Reuben comments that Jesus isn't a model of tact and discretion. When is it right to be outspoken and when is tact more important? Is there any issue that would cause you to 'say it like it is', regardless of who you were speaking to? When does being outspoken work for us? And when does it work against us? What do you think Jesus used as a guideline?

CHAPTER TWENTY-TWO

Sowing the seed

Esther

'You're very quiet, Esther,' Susanna said to me early one morning as, along with Mary from Magdala, we packed up baskets with food for Jesus and the disciples. 'What's wrong?'

'Nothing,' I replied. 'It's just that – well, I was thinking about what happened yesterday and I don't get why Jesus would behave like that. Why didn't he just do what those people wanted?'

> Some Pharisees said to him, 'Teacher we want to see your credentials. Give us some hard evidence that God is in this. How about a miracle?' Jesus said, 'You're looking for proof but you're looking for the wrong kind. All you want is something to titillate your curiosity, satisfy your lust for miracles. The only proof you're going to get is what looks like the absence of proof: Jonah evidence. Like Jonah, three days and nights in the fish's belly, the Son of Man will be gone three days and nights in a deep grave.'
>
> *Matthew 12:38-40, The Message*

'You mean, do another miracle just to shut those Pharisees up?' Susanna asked, shaking her head. 'Hardly.'

'But why – I don't get it,' I persisted.

'Esther, how many miracles has he done already? If they don't believe in him now, then they never will.'

'But he talked in riddles,' I said (a bit petulantly I admit – when I don't understand something, I like to think it's because the other person is being difficult, not that I'm missing the point). 'All that stuff about Jonah . . .'

'You don't know the story?' Susanna asked. 'How Jonah disobeyed God's plan for him and ran off in the opposite direction to the one he was meant to go? He got swallowed by a whale and was in its belly for three days and three nights – and after he was spewed out on the beach . . .'

'Yuk!' I shuddered.

'He got the message, and went back to Ninevah and changed people's lives by preaching God's truth.' She paused. 'But I'll be honest – I didn't understand what the Master meant when he said he was going to be in the grave for three days and three nights. Once you're dead, you're dead and that's that. Not that I want to think about him dying.'

Mary laid a cloth over the basket she was packing and turned to me. 'The thing I remember about what he said was the bit about the rubbish,' she smiled.

I frowned. I didn't remember anything about that.

'He said that we all think we've cleared all the junk and unimportant stuff from our lives and are good and ready for heaven, but if we don't accept his message, all we've done is make space for the demons to come right back in again.' She shuddered. 'I know what it's like to have demons take over your life,' she murmured. 'That's why I reckon there is only one place to be – and that's as close to Jesus as it's possible to get.'

I don't know why I was feeling stroppy that day – maybe it was because my monthly time would soon be due, but I couldn't help voicing out loud what I was thinking. 'Well, he didn't seem to want his own mother and brothers to get close to him, did he? He says we should love everyone and take care of them and then he goes and ignores his family when they come visiting.'

> While Jesus was still talking to the crowd, his mother and brothers stood outside, wanting to speak to him. Someone told him, 'Your mother and brothers are standing outside wanting to speak to you.' He replied to him, 'Who is my mother and who are my brothers?' Pointing to his disciples he said, 'Here are my mother and my brothers. For whoever does the will of my Father in heaven is my brother and sister and mother.'
>
> *Matthew 12:46-50*

Susanna laughed. 'He didn't ignore them,' she assured me. 'He was over the moon to see them – I saw him later hugging Mary his mother and teasing his brothers. All he was saying was that everyone – you, me, Mary, the disciples – anyone who loves him and believes in him are all one family, not just those with a blood tie to him.' She smiled. 'Did you see the man with the white beard who was there?'

I nodded.

'That's Cleopas, Jesus' uncle. His father Joseph's brother. He brought sad news: Joseph died last week. That's why they are all here.' She gestured to me to check on the bread oven. 'Oh, and that reminds me, Mary – his mother, I mean – will be staying around here for a few days. You must meet her – she is a very special person.'

'I . . .' I paused. Perhaps it was best not to mention that I'd met her before. 'I'd like that.'

Susanna glanced out of the doorway. 'My goodness,' she cried. 'Look at the crowds!'

I followed her gaze. The sun was hardly up, yet the lake shore was thick with people, and the noise of chattering, of braying donkeys, rickety cartwheels and food sellers seizing the opportunity to make a bit of extra money carried on the breeze right to our doorway.

'Come on,' Mary Magdalene said eagerly. 'If we want to get near enough to hear Jesus talk, then we'd better get a move on.' She turned and touched me gently on the shoulder. 'Don't worry,

Esther,' she said softly. 'It doesn't matter that you don't understand it all. Neither do I. I think all that really matters is that we want to understand.'

Although the lake shore was thronging with people, we managed to make our way to the front, partly because many of the regulars recognised Susanna, and partly because for once there didn't appear to be too many hecklers or self-important Pharisees barging their way up to Jesus and shouting the odds.

I saw him before he spotted me and my bad mood fell away like the skin peeling off an over-ripe fig.

'Caleb!' I shouted but my voice was lost in the babble of the crowd. 'Caleb!'

'It's alright, Esther,' Susanna said. 'You go and join your friend for a while. But make sure you stay near enough to Jesus to hear what he has to say.'

I thanked her and scurried away, dodging in and out of the crowd, my eyes fixed on Caleb. He was standing on a rock near the edge of the lake, talking to another boy of about the same age. It wasn't until I was a few yards away from them that Caleb shifted his position, and I saw a third person sitting on the ground a little way apart from them. It was Reuben.

I couldn't believe my luck – to find both of them in the same place at the same time! It was then that I realised what my problem had been. I had been missing them – missing being with people my own age, missing the chance to be me. Susanna was wonderfully kind and generous but she was still my employer and my social superior by a long way and although we had great conversations and she taught me a lot, it wasn't the same as speaking my mind with mates who knew what it was to feel half a person most of the time.

'Hey, you guys, over here and give us hand, will you?'

I had been about to grab Caleb's arm when two men, one of whom I recognised as Peter, strode over, their arms full of fishing nets.

'There's no way Jesus can make himself heard standing on the beach,' Peter said. 'He'll have to get in my boat – we're just going to dump these back at the house to make some space. If you guys can push the boat out, we'll be in business.'

All three of them headed towards the boat, but it was Caleb and the other guy who got there first and, shoulders to the prow, pushed it out into the water, as Jesus, hitching up his mantle to avoid the waves, climbed aboard. The expression on Reuben's face as he turned and plodded back up the beach almost broke my heart.

'Reuben!' I called and he turned, his mouth dropping open in surprise as he caught sight of me. 'It's so good to see you!' He gestured to me that he felt the same about meeting me and then beckoned me to follow him. Gesturing to a small boat that didn't look in the least bit seaworthy, he motioned me to climb in after him.

It didn't take me long to see why. The boat was leaky and some of the planks were rotting but it was moored on a level with the boat that Jesus was in and we could see him clearly without having to peer over the heads of the crowd or put up with being elbowed out of the way by people who thought they had more right to be there than we did. Some of the disciples were standing knee deep in the water close to Jesus' boat; others were hovering on the shoreline.

Reuben stood up and beckoned to Caleb and the other guy, and they splashed through the water, and heaved themselves into the boat beside us.

'Are you OK, Esther?' Caleb asked. 'I've been thinking about you – are you still with that woman? Susanna, isn't it?'

I nodded, conscious that the other guy's eyes were boring into me.

'Hello, I'm Seth,' the guy said and I could tell from his accent that he wasn't from round these parts. 'My father wanted to hear this preacher guy but he's with his oh-so-boring friends so I thought I'd stick around with Reuben for a bit.'

The way he was dressed suggested that he had never had to climb into a boat or handle smelly fish in his life. 'Where are you from?' I ventured.

'Jerusalem,' he said. 'We're heading back there tomorrow. My father . . .'

Just then Jesus stood up in the other boat.

'I want to tell you a story,' he began, and although I had a dozen questions that I wanted to ask, there was something so compelling about his voice that I said nothing. The crowd fell silent; the only sound was the lapping of the waves against the boat, and the distant wailing of a baby.

'There was a farmer who went out to sow his seed,' Jesus began. 'As he was scattering it, some of it was blown by the wind and fell on the path. You can imagine how that pleased the birds! They swooped down and ate it up within seconds. The farmer carried on scattering the seed, and some of it fell on gravel; it sprouted fast enough but it couldn't put down roots so as soon as the sun came up it withered and died.'

It occurred to me that this farmer was pretty stupid not to have cleared his ground before he started. I remembered my grandmother's little patch of land at the back of her house in Nazareth; I could see her in my mind's eye, collecting stones for hours before sowing her vegetable seeds. She could have taught this farmer a thing or two.

'Yet more of the seed fell into the weeds . . .'

Weeding had been my job when I visited her. She used to say that some weeds were tasty and could be cooked. 'Better in the pot than in the ground,' was one of her favourite sayings.

'. . . and the weeds grew up and choked the plants so they too died before their time,' Jesus went on. 'But—' He paused. 'Some seed fell on good ground and flourished, producing a harvest beyond the farmer's wildest dreams.'

A murmur ran through the crowd, but it was one of puzzlement, irritation even.

'What's he getting at?' one man said.

'What's with all this talk about farming?' muttered another.

'Are you listening to me!' Jesus shouted. 'Are you really listening? Taking on board what I'm trying to tell you?'

One of the disciples, a guy I didn't recognise, stepped forward and looked up at Jesus. 'Master,' he said in a deep gravelly voice, 'why exactly are you telling this lot stories? Wouldn't you be better just . . .'

'Thomas, listen,' Jesus replied. 'What you need to realise is that you twelve are the lucky ones; you've been with me for some time now, and you've got a bit of a feel for what God's kingdom is all about. But these people aren't in that position and they need stories to help them understand.' He sighed and mopped the sweat off his brow – the day was hot and humid and any breeze there had been had dropped.

'Although some of them won't get it no matter how many stories I tell,' he added sadly.

He turned, raised his voice and spoke to the crowd. 'Let me explain,' he began. 'The seed represents God's word, his truth. The seeds that fell on the path represent the people who hear God's word, but the devil jumps in, fills them with unbelief – and they lose their chance of being saved.'

A murmur rippled through the crowd, but this time it was more subdued.

'Then the seed that fell on the gravel – that's those who are over the moon and bursting with excitement when they hear the Word, but who have no staying power at all. For them, it's just a passing fad and the moment life gets tricky, they forget it all.'

I glanced at Reuben and Caleb. I had never seen either of them so enthralled. Seth on the other hand was scowling and biting his thumbnail. He glanced at me and the scowl turned to a grin. That was the moment when my heart decided to leave its usual place in my chest and lurch into my throat; my blood rushed to my face and for some reason, my mouth dried up and my hands shook.

I turned away and concentrated on Jesus. Or at least, I tried to.

'As for the seed that fell among the weeds,' he was saying, 'they are the people who indeed hear the Good News, but think that other things like making money, accumulating possessions, being seen to be one of the in-crowd and having fun are much more important.'

He turned and for a moment it seemed as though he was looking directly into our boat – at the four of us.

'But,' he went on, 'the seed that fell on the good soil represents all those people who hear the Word, absorb it, and hang on to it, no matter what happens. They are the ones who will reap the harvest of my kingdom.'

'But what is this kingdom? I don't see anything changing!' someone shouted from the crowd.

'That guy is always having a dig,' Caleb muttered. 'We disciples get so fed up with him.'

Reuben made a spluttering noise into his hand and I could see he was struggling to contain himself.

'You're a disciple of Jesus? Really?' Seth gasped, edging a little closer to him.

'I hang out with them,' Caleb replied. 'Kinda.'

'Go on tell us,' the man in the crowd shouted again. 'What is this kingdom?'

Jesus smiled. 'I'll tell you,' he nodded. 'It's like a mustard seed planted in a field. Now you know that the seed of the black mustard tree is the tiniest of all the seeds we have but when it grows, it gets to be nine feet tall, so large that birds nest in its branches.'

He turned and gestured towards a group of women, Susanna, Mary and Joanna among them, who were sitting close by. 'Another example that you'll understand in an instant,' he said. 'You know what it's like to work yeast into your dough to make barley bread loaves? You have to wait, don't you? Wait till the dough rises. But without that yeast, there's no way it will ever rise.'

Suddenly he laughed. 'And now, with all this talk of bread – let's take a break! Eat, drink – and ponder in your hearts on everything I have said.'

'It's alright, Esther,' Susanna smiled as I hurried back to her to help her distribute the food she had brought. 'Just share out these rolls and the cheese among the disciples and then take some for yourself and your friends.'

She peered into the baskets. 'On second thoughts,' she said, 'there may not be enough. Here!' She handed me a pile of leptons. 'Zebedee's wife is selling smoked fish over there,' she remarked, pointing along the shoreline, 'and I'm sure you'll find fruit sellers too.'

When I had taken the food to Thomas, Bartholomew and Philip, I hurried back to the others, eager to tell them that we could all eat well that day.

'But how come you're hanging out with the disciples?' Seth was asking Caleb. 'You're way younger than them and . . .'

'I'm fifteen next month,' Caleb retorted. 'And anyway, Jesus says everyone is welcome – so it doesn't matter how old you are, does it?'

'I guess not,' Seth said. 'And you?' He turned to face me. 'Sorry, I don't know your name.'

'Esther,' I replied. Or rather squeaked. What was it about this guy that reduced me to a gibbering idiot?

'Are you a follower?'

'I – er – um – I work for Susanna,' I gabbled. 'She gives money and food and stuff to the disciples. And what's more she's given me . . .'

'Yes, but do you believe? I mean, do you think he's the Messiah? The Promised One?'

No one had ever asked me my opinion about anything other than the availability of goats' milk or the best recipe for corn cakes. I stared at him, but there was no trace of teasing on his face. 'I don't know,' I admitted, 'but I've seen him do things that seem impossible. Like cleansing a leper and making paralysed people walk again.'

Seth nodded. 'Some people think he's dangerous,' he murmured.

'Dangerous?' I gasped. 'That's ridiculous – how can making people better be dangerous?'

'It's not just the healing,' Seth said, in the kind of way that made me think he was reciting something he'd been taught. 'My father is a very important man – a member of the Sanhedrin.'

I didn't have a clue what the Sanhedrin was but no way was I going to look ignorant in front of this fit guy.

'Really? How interesting!' I muttered.

'They don't like the way Jesus keeps breaking the law, time and again, and then telling other people to do the same! You have to admit, it's just not on. He even ignores the rules about the Sabbath!'

'You don't know what you're talking about!' Caleb burst out. 'Jesus told me – well, I heard him telling Philip and Nathaniel – that God's work was for all times and all places and if he says that . . .'

'Well, my father knows the law better than anyone,' Seth parried. 'Jesus lets his disciples work on the Sabbath, pick grain on the Sabbath . . .'

'Aha! Well, that's not a sin, because . . .'

'Because what?' Seth demanded.

'I'm trying to remember,' Caleb admitted. 'I know – you can pick corn with your fingers if you're out for a walk and find some, but you can't cut it with a knife on the Sabbath because that's harvesting. My old master told me that.'

It all sounded pretty petty to me, but I said nothing. Just then, Seth jumped to his feet and pointed along the beach. 'That's my father,' he said. 'Over there with that tall guy. I must go – he won't be best pleased if he finds me lolling around here chatting with a bunch of no-hopers.'

'With *what?*' Caleb shouted.

'Sorry, I didn't mean that – it's just what he would say, you know about people like you three. I don't agree but . . .'

'So why say it if you don't think it's right?' Caleb snapped. 'Daddy's boy, are you? Just go – we wouldn't want to tarnish your precious reputation!'

'Please, I'm sorry . . .'

'Goodbye!' Caleb made a big thing of turning his back on Seth. I turned to smile at him – but he'd already set off to join his dad. And he didn't look back.

So what has that got to do with me?

1. How often do we say that if only we could witness a miracle we would believe in God? And yet there are miracles all around us! What springs to your mind when we speak of modern-day miracles? Do you think God is at work in them, or is it just chance?

2. Jesus wasn't denying his responsibility to his earthly family. Remember he made sure his mother would be cared for even when he was hanging on the cross. What he was saying was that spiritual relationships are as important as blood relationships; and that his believers should all be one loyal, interdependent, supportive family.

3. Thinking about the parable of the sower and the seed, and applying it to our lives today, what do you think 'the weeds' that choked the good seed would be? What would be the ways in which our growth gets 'choked' so we cannot flourish?

4. Jesus said he told stories to help people understand. If he was here today, in your home town, or school, college or family, and he had all the modern-day techniques at his disposal, what might he use to explain his truths? Apps on an iPhone? Daily text messages? Videos on YouTube? Websites with stories and prayers? Well, actually, all those are available to us! The important thing is not *how* we read and hear God's word but that we *do* read and hear it.

CHAPTER TWENTY-THREE

Storms and swine

Reuben

Till that remark of Seth's, I'd been feeling pretty pleased with myself. I'd found James and John – who were in the middle of a heated argument – and after a lot of patient miming and mouthing, got them to understand that their father needed them right away. OK, so maybe I exaggerated somewhat – I was particularly pleased with my theatrical representation of him clutching at his chest and falling to his knees, face first in the dirt. That was what had them running full tilt for their house shouting his name at the tops of their voices.

I'd been pretty gobsmacked when Seth decided to hang around after Jesus pitched up at the lake shore. From his continual chattering, I'd learned that he and his father – who I discovered was called Nicodemus – had been in Capernaum for a wedding. His father had been ill and was taking time out from his duties to regain his strength. Very soon, they'd be heading back to Jerusalem where they lived.

At first I had been sad that I wouldn't see him again. That changed pretty quickly after he had called us all 'no-hopers'. OK, so he'd back-tracked and tried to say he didn't mean it and that he was only quoting his father, but it didn't cut any ice with us. Puzzled me a bit though; he'd seemed just a friendly chatterbox kind of guy – so how come the sudden change when his father was around? Then again, I thought, maybe I wasn't the only one who did whatever it took to stay on the right side of my father. Not that in my case it had made a blind bit of difference. And my mood wasn't helped by Esther's reaction to what had just gone on.

'That guy is so up himself,' Caleb had snorted as Seth walked off with his father and his cronies. 'Typical spoiled rich kid.'

'He's didn't mean it!' Esther burst out. 'He seemed really nice. You shouldn't have yelled at him the way you did.'

'And whose side are you on?' Caleb demanded. 'The only reason a boy like him would even speak to people like us would be to put us down.'

'Well, I think you're wrong,' she muttered. 'Like you've never said anything stupid.'

And without even a backward glance at either of us, she stomped off to where Susanna and her friends were sitting. I had never seen her like that and I thought it was odd that she'd fight the corner of someone she'd only spoken half a dozen words to. As it happened, neither Caleb nor I had time to brood. No sooner had Esther stomped off than Andrew came over to us, with Philip, Bartholomew and Thomas trailing behind.

'Jesus wants to go over to the other side of the lake,' he said. 'Peter's getting our boat ready but we'll need Zebedee's boat as well, and I can't find James or John anywhere.'

I gestured that I knew where they might be.

'Can you tell them . . . oh! I mean, Caleb, can you go with Reuben and tell them to follow us over?'

I didn't hear what else he said. I'd set off as fast as I could knowing full well that I was perfectly capable of making myself understood. I noticed that Caleb didn't make any attempt to follow me. When I arrived at Zebedee's house, a lot of hugging and back-slapping was going on. I waved my arms at them and James turned round.

'Reuben!' Zebedee cried before James could open his mouth. 'My sons are here! Thank you!'

I pointed to the shore, imitating rowing a boat, and then ran on the spot to indicate the need for speed.

'Jesus wants us?' John asked. 'To row him? So early in the day?'

I nodded. I reckoned the detail of who went in what boat wasn't up to me.

'We must go,' James said to his father. 'But we'll be . . .'

'I'm coming too,' Zebedee told them. 'I'll bring my boat – I want to find out more about this guy who has turned your heads so!' He wagged a finger at them but I could tell by the way he was smiling that any disagreement between them had been sorted out.

By the time I'd got back to the beach, Peter was pushing his boat out from the shore. It was hot and humid, without a breath of air, and I could see Jesus lying back on a cushion in the prow of the boat, looking totally wiped out. Several of the disciples were with him, shoving and pushing to make space on the bench.

As James and John climbed into their boat, along with Judas and Thaddeus, I saw Caleb further down the beach, hurling some nets into a fishing boat and climbing in along with Zebedee. That's when I made up my mind. If he was going, so was I. I grabbed James' sleeve and gestured that I wanted to go with them. He laughed.

'Don't be silly, Reuben,' he said. 'We could be gone for days – with Jesus, you never know.'

I nodded frantically, and pressed my palms together in a pleading gesture.

'Oh, let him come,' John said. 'But I'm telling you Reuben, when we get to the other side you're on your own, OK? You find your own way back – or wherever you want to go. Get it?'

I nodded obediently and began struggling to climb into the boat. James hooked his hands under my armpits and lifted me the rest of the way. I sat on the bench that straddled the middle of the boat, my short legs sticking out in front of me, and pretended I was a rich person being carried to a foreign shore by my trusted slaves. I tipped my face up to catch the breeze and feel the spray against my cheeks. This, I thought, is the life.

It came from nowhere. One minute I was sitting with my eyes shut listening to the swishing of the oars and the banter between James and John; the next my body was hurled to the floor as the boat began pitching and tossing. Great clouds had blown in from the west, and rain began beating down like torrents of sharp needles.

Clutching onto the side of the boat I peered through the gloom. The boat carrying Jesus was only a couple of boat lengths ahead of us, but I kept losing sight of it as larger and larger waves swamped the deck.

I was screaming – silently of course, pleading with Yahweh to save us. Why had I begged to come when all that was going to happen was that I would be drowned and lie forever at the bottom of the lake? James and John were swearing, grappling with the oars but having no effect whatsoever on controlling the boat. We rolled from side to side, then pitched over the crest of a wave before dipping down, down, till I was sure we would hit the lake floor.

I wasn't the first to vomit. Judas threw up over the side seconds before me.

'We're going to die, I know we're going to die,' he cried as our boat leaned precariously to the left and water poured into the hull. 'Do something . . .'

His words gave way to another bout of violent retching, and that set me off again. By now we were almost level with the boat carrying Jesus, and I could hear the shouts of Peter and Andrew above the roaring of the wind.

'Master, Master, we're going to drown!' I heard Peter cry.

Wiping the vomit from my mouth, and clutching onto the gunwale with my good hand I peered at the other boat. And blinked. And peered again.

Jesus was stretched out at the front of the boat and for a moment I thought he was dead. His eyes were closed, his body limp and relaxed.

'Wake up, Master, we're sinking!' Andrew yelled.

He was asleep? How could anyone sleep through this terror? With that, Jesus stirred. Slowly he raised himself to a sitting position and looked around him.

'Master, save us!' Peter shouted.

Jesus stood up in the prow and opened his arms wide. 'Quiet! Be still!' he shouted.

And just like that the wind dropped. I don't mean it eased bit by bit. It just stopped blowing. The waves ceased, the boat righted itself, and apart from our drenched skin and ashen faces you wouldn't have known anything had been wrong.

'Oh my friends, why were you so afraid?' Jesus cried.

Because we were an inch from death perhaps? Because our stomachs were lying somewhere on the lake bed?

'Why is it that you still have so little faith!' Jesus cried.

Like me, James, John, Judas and Thaddeus were all shaking from head to foot. It wasn't just the cold – speaking for myself I was scared witless. Who was this man?

James put it in a nutshell. 'My God,' he said. 'Who is he really? Even the wind and waves do as he says.'

For the rest of the way across the lake, no one spoke. Gradually the sound of chattering teeth diminished and the smell of sick faded. I glanced across at the other boats on the lake. In each one, people were standing, clutching onto one another and staring at Jesus' boat. Jesus meanwhile had sat down and gone back to sleep.

I'd never been to Gerasene country before and within ten minutes of landing on the shore, I wished I hadn't bothered. Everyone was looking pretty shaken up after the storm, and the funny thing was that, rather than crowding round Jesus and thanking him for saving their lives, several of them seemed to be keeping their distance, backing off in little groups and murmuring to one another while casting puzzled glances over their shoulders at Jesus. He, of course, seemed to be totally unfazed by it all.

> They sailed to the region of the Gerasenes, which is across the lake from Galilee. When Jesus stepped ashore, he was met by a demon possessed man from the town.
>
> *Luke 8:26, 27*

I was just wondering what I should do next when the peace was shattered by the most unearthly howling that I have ever heard in my life. Worse than the sound of the slaughterhouse, it literally made my blood run cold and judging by the reaction of everyone else around, it had the same effect on them.

If the sound was bad, the sight that met our eyes as we all looked up the limestone cliff behind us was even worse. A wild thing – I can hardly use the word man to describe him – stark naked, with long matted hair, and limbs scarred with a hundred scabby cuts and bruises, was running towards Jesus, wild-eyed and gabbling incoherently.

Jesus raised a hand towards him and the man fell at his feet screeching and spitting.

'What do you want with me, eh?' he bellowed. 'You're Jesus, I know that – Jesus, Son of the Most High God!'

Jesus raised his hand higher and the man howled like a dog being beaten with a pronged stick. 'Don't hurt me, don't torture me!'

Suddenly the man's whole body arched in a convulsion, he rolled over on the ground, foaming at the mouth and biting the soil like some possessed animal.

'What is your name?' Jesus asked. This, I thought to myself, backing off as fast as I could, is hardly the time for social niceties.

'Legion,' the man wailed. 'Because there are so very many of us.'

More like him? I glanced around fearfully but the surrounding countryside was free of lunatics. Then Jesus raised his hand even higher and for a moment I thought he was going to strike the guy – not that I could have blamed him.

'Please, don't send us to the deep dark pit, please not the pit, not the pit . . .'

'He's demon-possessed,' I heard John say to Andrew. 'This must be the man I've heard about – the one who even when they chain him up, breaks free and escapes.'

'Son of the Most High God, not the pit!' the man screamed. 'See the pigs! Send us to the swine, not to the pit!'

Jesus turned his head and looked up the hillside. This being Gentile country, there was a large herd of pigs rooting about, their noses to the ground.

'You devils, come out of this man!' Jesus shouted. 'And go – go to them!' Jesus made a sweeping gesture with his arm towards the herd.

The man's body jerked and thrashed and then became still, lifeless as if he had died. His shrieking and moaning ceased but in its place was another sound – the trampling of feet, snorting and grunting.

'Stand back!' someone shouted. The entire herd of pigs was careering down the hillside towards the lake, several dozen of them, pursued by the swineherds crying out to them to stop. It was a terrifying sight. As they neared the bottom of the hill, they seemed to gather speed; the crowd scattered and I saw that a couple of unlucky people were knocked off their feet in the stampede.

The swineherds were screaming and shouting and waving their staffs, but to no avail. As one body, the pigs rushed, grunting and snorting, into the lake. They thrashed about, colliding into one another in their panic wallowing and struggling further and further from the shore. Within minutes, every one of them had drowned, their great swollen corpses rolling on the surface of the lake.

The swineherds were not best pleased at the loss of their pigs, I can tell you; they stormed round the village shouting about what had happened, with the result that dozens of people from the surrounding houses came to peer at the once-mad man and mutter among themselves. I guess you could understand the pig keepers being put out but you would have thought that the local townsfolk would have been in awe of Jesus. I mean, that mad guy had been a pain in their community for ages and within minutes of Jesus driving out his demons, he came up to him, wrapped decently in a cloak Thaddeus had handed him, asking if he might listen to his teaching.

I thought they would all be doing what everyone always did – dashing off to bring out their sick and diseased friends and relatives, but instead a group of village elders approached Jesus.

'We want you to leave,' they said. 'What you're doing – we can't cope with it, it's not natural – we just . . .'

'I will go.' Jesus didn't argue with them, he didn't even look offended. He simply turned to his disciples, smiled and asked them to turn around and go back to Capernaum.

'May I come too?' the now-sane man pleaded. 'Please. I want to stay with you.'

'No,' Jesus said, kindly but firmly. 'Go back to your home and tell everyone just what a wonderful thing God has done for you. Tell everyone how the Lord has worked to restore you.' With that, Jesus hitched up his mantle and calmly climbed back into Peter's boat. The other disciples followed him; I was about to go with James and John, but John stopped me.

'We are going in Peter's boat,' he said. 'You must – as I told you – find your own way home.' He touched my shoulder. 'Don't look so worried,' he smiled. 'I am sure my father will take you. And I'd be glad if you would keep an eye on him till we get back – help him all you can. Will you do that?'

I nodded, albeit reluctantly. It seemed I was going to have to wait yet again for Jesus to do something for me.

Just then, a group of men, dusty and bedraggled, appeared round a bend in the road. 'Master! Wait!' one of them cried, breaking into a run.

'Not more interruptions,' John sighed. 'Jesus is exhausted – we all are. Can't people just leave him alone for a bit?'

I glanced up at Jesus. He certainly looked drawn and tired but he stood up as the leader of the group reached his boat.

'Master, terrible news . . .' he began.

John nudged me and glanced along the shore.

'Reuben, you'd better hurry,' he said. 'My father is casting off!'

I wanted to stay and hear the terrible news but reckoned it was probably another person in need of Jesus to heal a friend. I broke into a run, as John called out to Zebedee to wait.

As I reached the boat, I heard a loud cry from behind me. Turning, I saw Jesus sitting in the boat with his head in his hands, his shoulders shaking. I couldn't imagine what had happened, but had no time to think about it because as Zebedee hoisted me into the boat I realised that I wasn't the only passenger.

Lying in the stern with his eyes closed was Caleb – and he didn't look well.

So what has that got to do with me?

1. Faith is tested when we experience situations that terrify us; illness for ourselves or loved ones, loss of home, bereavement, natural disasters. When we watch television coverage of earthquakes or tsunamis, or read about genocide in Africa, or the cruelty of despotic regimes we are tempted to ask: 'Where is God in all that?' Where do you think he is?

2. If you had been in that boat in the storm, and seen Jesus sleeping, what would your first reaction have been?

3. Jesus ordered the storm to cease and *then* asked the disciples why they had so little faith. What strikes you about the order of those two events?

4. Jesus often told people he had healed *not* to mention it to anyone. Why did he ask the demoniac to speak out? For one thing, this was Gentile country and Jesus wanted his mission to be known among and for the Gentiles; secondly the Gentiles didn't have any preconceptions about a coming Messiah and so wouldn't try to make him king or a political leader but would take him at face value. When God touches our lives, we should share the Good News with our family and friends. How easy is this? If it is difficult, what makes it so hard?

5. Jews did not keep pigs: Gentiles did. The swineherds made their living out of looking after them and it is understandable that they were upset at the loss of the animals. But the people of the village who had been disturbed by the demon-possessed man for years asked Jesus to leave. Why do you think that was? Do you ever wish Jesus and his teaching would just 'go away'?

CHAPTER TWENTY-FOUR

A new life

Esther

'We have come to a decision.'

Susanna had called me in from the courtyard where I was washing the linens and she looked anxious.

'It's not enough to do what we've been doing,' she began. 'Mary and I – well, the thing is we are going to follow Jesus.'

I frowned. 'But you've been a follower ever since I met you,' I said.

'But now,' Mary interjected, 'we are going to be with him. All the time, wherever he goes.

'And me?' My voice cracked. I knew I was being selfish, but if they went, what would happen to me?

Susanna smiled. 'Only you can decide that, Esther,' she said. 'I can't tell you what to do. But if you want to come with us, then we'd be happy to have you. If you don't, then you can stay in my house for as long as you like.'

Stay in this beautiful house forever? With no worries about finding work or earning money? It was like a dream come true. Day after day, warm, dry, food to eat. Day after day, alone and nowhere near Jesus . . . 'I want to be with you,' I said firmly. Houses were great; security was amazing. But I had grown to love Susanna and without her, what would be the point? And Jesus – there was something about him; I had to find out more.

'Are you sure?' Susanna asked. 'You have to understand, Esther, that not everyone thinks Jesus is the best. Not everyone is going to listen to his teaching and do what he says – already we've heard a lot of people in positions of power saying that something has to be done to get rid of Jesus, to shut him up and stop him drawing the crowds.'

'Which means there might be angry scenes, even times when people close to him get yelled at and abused,' Mary added.

'Remember how it was when we came down from Hattin Hill that day,' Susanna went on. 'It could get a lot worse than that. We're women and we don't have husbands.'

She hesitated and Mary cut in, 'Some of us have done things in the past that people don't want to forget . . .'

Susanna touched my arm, 'Esther, you have to realise the risks.'

'I'm coming with you,' I repeated. 'Please.'

Susanna nodded. 'Then go and prepare my things – just the bare minimum,' she instructed. 'And . . .' She paused as the latch on the wooden door rattled. 'Come in!'

The door opened and a woman, panting for breath, stood there, her eyes shining.

'Susanna, forgive me, but I had to come,' she began. 'Am I intruding?'

'Hannah, no of course not,' Susanna said, beckoning her to a stool. 'Mary, this is Hannah, who used to be my neighbour.' Susanna poured a glass of wine and handed it to her visitor. 'Is it – I mean, are you worse? Is the – the affliction troubling you?'

'No, no, no!' Hannah cried. 'That is why I have come. He stopped it – he stopped the bleeding. Twelve whole years of haemorrhaging and one touch . . .' At this she burst into tears.

'I can't tell you, I don't know how to put it into words,' she sobbed. 'Me – a useless, shunned, hated woman and he knew. He knew when I touched him.'

'Tell us,' Mary said eagerly. 'Tell it all.'

'I don't know where to start,' Hannah began. 'I was at my wits' end. The bleeding was non-stop, I had no energy and I just wanted to die. There was no money left for doctors – all that went years ago and for what?' She sighed. 'I had heard about Jesus healing people of all manner of illnesses but what could I do? I couldn't go into a public place because . . .'

She didn't need to finish her sentence. Any woman with that kind of problem was unclean and to go near men – well, it was unthinkable.

'Then a couple of days ago, I was coming back from the well, and I heard these two men talking. I think they were disciples of Jesus because I saw them again later, but at the time I hadn't a clue who they were. They were talking about Jesus and saying how he seemed to be turning all the rules upside down – turning on its head everything that society said was right!'

'That's exactly what he's doing,' Susanna nodded.

'These men said he was taking an awful risk,' Hannah went on. 'And you know what? Something in my head said "Why don't I take a risk too?"'

Mary nodded and leaned forward in her seat.

'Go on.'

'Yesterday, I saw Jesus. Well, I saw a huge crowd coming along the main street, and I guessed that Jesus must be the cause of it. So I went out. As luck would have it . . .'

'Luck?' Susanna whispered, but it seemed Hannah didn't hear.

'. . . Jesus was just passing the junction with the path from my house and the main street,' she said. 'I knew I couldn't speak to him but I felt such a tug, such a powerful urge to be close to him. You won't believe what I did? I touched his robe.' Her voice trembled and she put her hands to her face for a moment. 'And Susanna – it stopped. The bleeding, that dreadful ache in my loins, the dreaded gushing from my body, it all stopped in an instant.'

'God be praised!' Susanna breathed.

'But just then, Jesus stopped dead in his tracks,' Hannah went on.

'And he spoke to you?' Mary urged.

'Not to start with,' Hannah said. 'He just looked at the crowd and said "Who touched me?"'

She took a sip of wine.

'One of his disciples pointed out that with the crowd the way it was, a dozen elbows could have been nudging him. But all Jesus did was shake his head and wave the guy away. He said that he knew someone had touched him and that power had gone out from him.'

'What did you do?' I asked, and then rapidly apologised for not knowing my place.

'This is my friend Esther,' Susanna told her and I glowed inside. She called me friend and not servant.

Hannah smiled. 'What did I do?' she repeated. 'I nearly passed out with terror! It seemed as if the people immediately around Jesus had just melted away and there he was in front of me and I knew I had no escape. So I knelt down in front of him and admitted it was me. And told him that I was cured.'

'And?' Three of us spoke in unison.

'He spoke to me,' she said, tears welling up in her eyes. 'Such gentle words.'

She closed her eyes.

'He said daughter – yes, he called me, Hannah, daughter, can you imagine that? He said, "Daughter, the faith and the courage that brought you to me have given you healing and health. Go now, and live in peace."'

Susanna sprang up and hugged her friend. 'That is so wonderful, my dear,' she exclaimed. 'To think that after all this time, he has made you well.'

'And you know what?' Hannah replied. 'He treated me as though I was worth something – he never once said that I shouldn't have touched him. It was as though I was more important than the rules.'

For a moment, no one spoke.

It was Mary who broke the silence. 'The men you overheard on your way home from the well were right,' she murmured. 'Jesus is turning the world upside down.'

I had been sent to the basket maker to buy another carrier for the food we would take with us when I heard someone call my name. I turned – and there, running along the path towards me, was Seth.

'I thought you were going back to Jerusalem,' I cried, trying not to look too thrilled to see him.

'We were supposed to,' he panted, stopping and bending forward to catch his breath. 'But after everything that happened the other day . . .'

'The storm you mean? And Jesus . . .'

'Storm? No – the little girl being healed. Haven't you heard about it?'

I shook my head.

'OK, so I'll tell you but first – I'm really sorry. About what I said yesterday.'

'It's alright . . .'

'No it's not alright,' Seth sighed. 'It was a horrible thing to say. My father calls people who don't have – well, you know – money, jobs, position – he calls them no-hopers and tells me I shouldn't hang around anyone who can't help me up the ladder to success and position.' He sighed. 'But you know what? One of my best mates back home is a slave boy who works in my uncle's house. He's nicer than all the boys I meet at synagogue.'

I smiled and decided to change the subject. 'So what about the girl who was healed?'

'Oh yes, right,' he said. 'Well, this kid's father, Jairus, is a friend of a friend of my father. He's really well off – Jairus, I mean, and my dad's got a lot of time for him. He's in charge of arranging the services at the synagogue – he knows a whole load of stuff about the Scripture, even more than my father, I reckon.'

He flopped down on the ground and gestured to me to do the same.

'Anyway, when we got to his house to pay our respects before going home, he wasn't there, and his wife was in the most terrible state. Their little girl, Chanina, was seriously ill and Jairus had gone to find Jesus, to beg him to come and make her better.'

'And did he?' I gasped.

'Hang on, I'm getting to that bit,' he snapped. 'We were about to leave them in peace when there was the sound of wailing from a room at the back. Chanina was dead.'

By the expression on his face, I guessed what he was about to tell me but I said nothing.

'Her mother sent the servants to tell Jesus that it was too late . . .'

'But it wasn't, was it?' I burst out before I could stop myself.

'How did you know?'

'Because Jesus keeps doing things that seem impossible,' I stammered. 'But go on – tell me what happened.'

'You're right,' he admitted. 'Jesus came and he walked into the room and we heard him say "*Little girl, get up!*" And she did – she got up. Not only that but she just walked out of her room and around the house as though she'd never had anything the matter with her in the first place. And do you know what Jesus said? This is the bit I don't get.'

I shook my head.

'He told everyone there not to say a word about it,' Seth declared. 'Why would he do that? If I'd just brought someone back to life, I'd be shouting it from the rooftops, but Jesus was more concerned with ordering a good meal for Chanina.'

'Susanna reckons that Jesus doesn't want people following him around just to see miracles happen. He wants them to come because they're interested in his teaching about . . .'

'This kingdom he keeps on about?' Seth interrupted. 'It's a load of revolutionary, subversive nonsense that can't possibly work – that's what my uncle says.'

'But why?'

'Oh come on, the first thing he'd have to do to set up his own kingdom is get rid of the Romans, and oust Herod, and no way is anyone going to let that happen!'

He stood up and dusted himself down.

'Anyway, I've got to go,' he said. 'My father has to be back in Jerusalem for a meeting of the Sanhedrin. But . . .' He smiled shyly. 'Thanks for forgiving me for being such a jerk! See you again maybe?'

Maybe I was just kidding myself but he sounded as if he really wanted that to happen. Not that it would. No way would I ever get to see Jerusalem, not in hundred years.

> When Jesus had called the Twelve together, he gave them power and authority to drive out all demons and to cure diseases, and he sent them out to preach the kingdom of God and to heal the sick. He told them 'Take nothing for the journey – no staff, no bag, no bread, no money, no extra tunic. Whatever house you enter, stay there until you leave that town. If people do not welcome you, shake the dust off your feet when you leave their town, as a testimony against them.' So they set out and went from village to village, preaching the gospel and healing people everywhere.
>
> *Luke 9:1-6*

'I'm not sure Jesus would approve of all this,' Mary sighed, glancing at the loaded baskets and scrips we had prepared.

'Why not? It's for him and the disciples,' I said.

'I know and I guess that makes it alright,' she nodded. 'It's just that when he told the twelve senior disciples that he was giving them new powers to go out and drive out demons and heal people, he said that they weren't to take anything with them.'

'What? Nothing?' Susanna asked.

'Nothing at all,' Mary repeated. 'No staff, no bag, no food, no money – not even a change of clothes.'

Yuk, I thought – they would be rancid within days.

'He said they should only stay where they were welcomed; if people weren't interested, they weren't to make a scene but just move on somewhere else. I suppose . . .'

Before she could finish what she was saying, the door burst open.

'Susanna, Mary, forgive me!'

It was Joanna, the friend of Susanna who had been with us when the Pharisees were so hateful to us. She had left the day after to return home to her husband, Chuza, who was steward to Herod Antipas.

'I had to come – there's news and it's not good.'

Susanna took her arm and sat her at the table, gesturing to me to fetch water to wash her feet.

'What is it?' I heard Mary ask.

At that time Herod the tetrarch heard the reports about Jesus, and he said to his attendants, 'This is John the Baptist; he has risen from the dead! That is why miraculous powers are at work in him.'

Now Herod had arrested John and bound him and put him in prison because of Herodias, his brother Philip's wife, for John had been saying to him: 'It is not lawful for you to have her.' Herod wanted to kill John, but he was afraid of the people, because they considered John a prophet.

On Herod's birthday the daughter of Herodias danced for the guests and pleased Herod so much that he promised with an oath to give her whatever she asked. Prompted by her mother, she said, 'Give me here on a platter the head of John the Baptist.' The king was distressed, but because of his oaths and his dinner guests, he ordered that her request be granted and had John beheaded in the prison. His head was brought in on a platter and given to the girl, who carried it to her mother. John's disciples came and took his body and buried it. Then they went and told Jesus.

Matthew 14:1-12

'Herod has had John the Baptist killed!'

'No!' Susanna gasped, her face turning pale. 'Why? How could . . . ?'

Joanna sighed. 'That's what I asked Chuza,' she replied. 'Of course, he had to be careful what he said – walls have ears – but when we were alone, he told me what he had hinted at before. It all stems from the fact that Herod married his brother's wife, Herodias.'

'Yes, but John always said that was wrong . . .'

'Precisely,' Joanna nodded. 'Chuza says that Herod wanted to kill the Baptist there and then but he was scared because he knew the people revered him as a prophet.'

'So what made him do it now?'

'You won't believe it, but it's true,' Joanna declared. 'Herod threw the usual birthday celebration for himself and he asked Herodias' daughter to dance for the guests. Herod had drunk – well, let's just say he hadn't held back – and at the end of the dance he said that Salome had performed so wonderfully that he would give her whatever she wanted.'

Susanna thumped her fist on the table. 'That's ridiculous!' she cried. 'What did the girl ask for?'

'Chuza reckons that she didn't ask for anything – it was her mother who manipulated her. She sent her to Herod to say that the only thing she wanted was John the Baptist's head on a platter.'

'Surely he refused?' Mary breathed, turning pale and clutching the table edge.

Joanna shook her head. 'Chuza says he wanted to – but he'd made an oath, in front of all those oh-so-important guests – people who he needed to support him and his administration – so he agreed.'

'Dear God!' Susanna murmured, a sob in her voice.

'John's disciples are bereft,' Joanna went on. 'They've buried John's body and a group of them have gone to find Jesus and tell him what's happened.'

'It will devastate him,' Mary breathed.

'I came straight away; Chuza is a good, good man, and he believes in Jesus; but he has to be so careful. He was glad for me to come and spend some time listening to the Messiah, as long as the story is that I'm visiting you; but he says that we should stay alert and more importantly, make sure Jesus realises the danger he is in.'

'You are sure, aren't you, that he is the Anointed One?'

'I have never,' said Joanna, 'been so sure of anything in my whole life.'

So what has that got to do with me?

1. When we decide to follow Jesus, we take risks too. What sort of risks are involved today?
2. Hannah thought it was 'luck' that Jesus was passing when she most needed him. Do you see that as merely a coincidence? Does Jesus draw near to us when we most need to sense his presence? How does he make his presence felt?
3. Do you think that Jesus is still turning the world upside down? If so, in what ways? If not, what makes you believe that?
4. If your faith is wavering, what would you need to see Jesus do to restore it? Something for the world? Or something for you? Is it easier to believe in his Word when he does something specifically for us? Would Jairus and his family, or Hannah and her neighbours, have believed in Jesus without seeing these miraculous signs worked on their loved ones?
5. Jesus told the seventy he sent out to take nothing with them. Was this practical? What harm would there have been in them taking a change of clothes, a bag of food for emergencies, or some money? What message do you think Jesus was trying to get across to them about the nature of their new ministry? How much time do people today spend preparing for 'what might happen'? How often are our thought patterns along the lines of 'What if?'

CHAPTER TWENTY-FIVE

Dark memories

Caleb

That day – the day of the storm and the pigs – was one of the worst of my entire life. Not the worst, obviously, but a pretty close second. When Reuben had climbed into Zebedee's boat and asked me what was wrong, I had simply waved him away and curled up in a ball and let Zebedee do the explaining. It satisfied Reuben but of course, it was only half the story.

'He's been horribly seasick,' Zebedee chuckled, though why he should find violent vomiting, not just during the storm but for half an hour afterwards, a source of amusement, I couldn't work out. At least he had the good grace to be a bit more serious about the other business.

'And then he got knocked over by a rampant pig!'

OK, I suppose it sounds funny but believe me it wasn't. It wasn't just the pain of being trampled over by an enormous hog; it was the agony of the memories that welled up inside my head – memories about which Zebedee, of course, knew nothing.

I'd never seen a pig before and I don't ever want to see one again. We don't have them where I come from – dirty things, and no one in their right mind would contemplate eating their meat because it's forbidden in the law. I guess those Gentiles don't know any better. The sight of several dozen of the hateful things careering down the hillside towards you is the stuff of nightmares; I tried to dodge out of the way but there was nowhere to go – the herd were spread out and if I avoided one, another one was in my path. I was thrown to the ground and this huge brute ran right over me, its hooves bruising my ribs and almost taking my breath away.

I cried. I'm not proud of it, but I lay there, hands over my head, and I cried. It wasn't the pain – that was bad, but I'm gutsy and even when I almost chopped a finger in half working back in Cana, I didn't cry. It was the memory that did it.

As that pig trampled me, all I could see in my mind's eye was my little sister Kizia. I saw the expression on her face as I yelled at her and told her to get out of my sight and go and play; I saw her, head bowed, trotting obediently outside and I saw myself slipping out of the door of our house and down the street to see my friend Joshua.

I heard again the distant scream – 'Caleb! Caleb!' – remembered how I told myself she was just having one of her not infrequent temper tantrums. And as I saw yet another pig dash past me, its muzzle only inches from my face, I saw the sight that will haunt me for the rest of my life. The sight of that rabid dog dragging my little sister through the dirt as if she was just a piece of torn rag.

That's why I couldn't speak to Reuben. That's why I let Zebedee give the only version of the day's events that he knew. The fact that I had sent my own sister to her death was something I couldn't share with anyone. Ever.

From the middle of the lake we could see a huge black shadow moving along the shore a couple of miles to the south. It wasn't until we were nearer the shore that I realised that it wasn't a shadow at all; it was swarms of people moving like a great wave.

'That'll be where Jesus is, then,' Zebedee remarked. 'They were heading south of the village – James told me they wanted some peace and quiet. Doesn't look as if that plan worked, does it?'

I shook my head but didn't speak. I was bone weary. All I wanted to do was sleep.

'You look done in,' Zebedee said as he beached the boat. 'Reuben, see that he gets some food and a decent place to sleep. You can go to my place and . . .'

Reuben shook his head and gestured towards the south.

'Reuben, no!' Zebedee said. 'Caleb is in no fit state to go anywhere. Now get going and ask my wife for some bread and olives,' Zebedee winked. 'It's baking day today. And tell her I'll be back when I have attended to the boat.'

Then he turned to me, 'If you're not better in the morning . . .' He hesitated. 'Well, then maybe you should go and speak with Jesus.'

Reuben nodded furiously and scrambled out of the boat. I followed him wearily, catching my breath as the cuts on my legs hit the cold water of the lake.

I'll say one thing for Reuben. He may be small, he may be a bit ugly looking, but when he gets an idea in his head, there is no stopping him. He did everything Zebedee had told him to do; took me to Salome, did a pretty passable mime of a galloping pig and a vomiting idiot, which Salome clearly didn't understand at all, pointed to the freshly baked barley bread cooling on the table – and then turned to leave.

'Wait!' I cried.

He paused, giving me a quizzical look.

'Where are you going?'

He pointed in the direction we had seen the crowds massing.

'What – now?'

'Reuben, stay,' Salome urged. 'I have lentil stew and there's plenty to go round.'

For a moment I could see him waver. He ran his tongue along his twisted lip and glanced from Salome to the fire in the courtyard, over which an iron pot was steaming. Then he shook his head, inclined his head to one side and looked questioningly at me.

'Your friend is staying right here,' Salome declared, in the tone of voice that brooked no argument. 'There'll be plenty of time for him to go gallivanting off with you when he's rested.'

Reuben turned to go.

'Wait!' Salome cried. 'If my husband said I was to feed you, then feed you I shall, whether you are here or not.'

She picked up a couple of musht fish, and a few barley loaves and put them in Reuben's bag, along with some olives and dates.

'Go safely,' she said. 'And don't worry about this lad – I'll make sure he's taken care of.'

And she smiled at me. 'You young people,' she sighed. 'You do go getting yourselves into trouble, don't you?'

You don't, I thought, know the half of it. I just smiled and allowed myself to enjoy the novelty of being looked after.

So what has that got to do with me?

1. At this point in his life, Caleb felt he couldn't share what had happened in his past with anyone. Have you ever felt like that? Do you believe that you can share everything – good, bad and ugly – with Jesus, or does that just sound like some myth preached in church on a Sunday? Do you feel that it would be all well and good if Jesus was sitting beside you but since he's invisible, it's not really helpful? Do you think that God can put people in our path who can help us or do you think it's always a case of going it alone?

CHAPTER TWENTY-SIX

Speak up, eat up!

Reuben

By this time it was late in the day, so Jesus' disciples came to him. 'This is a remote place,' they said, 'and it's already very late. Send the people away so that they can go to the surrounding countryside and villages and buy themselves something to eat.' But he answered 'You give them something to eat.'

Mark 6:35-37

It took me a long while to reach the normally deserted area of scrubland where the crowds were. I'd never seen so many people in one place; thousands of them, stretching along the shoreline, up the hillside, perching in the branches of the few trees that clung to the rocky soil and yet others standing on rocks with children perched on their shoulders.

I couldn't see a thing. I pushed and shoved my way through the crowd and then I heard a familiar voice.

'It's ridiculous – why can't they just go and get their own food?' It was James – he was a few feet away from me, talking to Andrew and Philip.

'To feed this lot would take – what? Eight months' wages at the very least! Like we have that kind of money!' Philip agreed.

'Well, at least we ought to do what Jesus said,' Andrew urged them. 'See if anyone around here has some food.'

I pushed my way past a couple of large men and tugged on Andrew's sleeve.

'What! Reuben – what are you doing here?'

I opened the bag slung over my shoulder, took out the two fish that Zebedee's wife had given me, and the five barley rolls and shoved them into his hand.

'I see you have food, Andrew!' Jesus emerged from the crowd with a broad smile on his face.

'Well, Master – Reuben here has just given us these two fish and this bread but frankly, that's a drop in the ocean among all these people!'

Jesus smiled. 'I'll tell you what – give me the food and you go and spread the word that everyone should sit down just where they are.'

'But Master . . .' Philip stammered.

'Just do it,' Jesus replied.

Like a wave, people began dropping down on the ground as the message was passed from group to group.

'Sit down!'

'He says we must sit!'

'Make room, sit down . . .'

Jesus turned to me. 'Thank you,' he said. He broke the small loaves in half and lifted them up. '*Ha-motzi lechem min hashamayim . . .*' he intoned, blessing the bread. He beckoned the disciples, and gave them each some bread to distribute. Then he blessed the fish and handed one of them to me.

'Take this and offer it around,' he said. I couldn't believe it; he'd spoken to me. I was doing something for him. I was like one of his crowd! I turned to a group of people sitting nearby. They had three children with them, as well as an elderly man and several women. The fish I had would just about go round if no one was greedy.

'Thank you, thank you,' they said as I broke off pieces of the fish.

That fish never got smaller. Well, it did – I mean, gradually its backbone appeared and I flipped it over and broke off pieces from the other side but then I noticed bits of flesh I'd missed from the first side. I moved from group to group, and still there was more flesh on the fish. I don't know how long it would have lasted because suddenly Peter was at my side.

'Jesus wants you,' he said. 'Give that to me – I'll carry on handing it out.'

I turned and went back to where Jesus was standing, my heart thumping. This was it – I had to make him understand what I wanted. I might never have another opportunity.

Jesus looked straight into my eyes. 'Thank you for giving up your food,' he said.

I pointed to my lips, went down on my knees, looked up at him and pointed to my mouth again.

Jesus reached out his hand and raised me to my feet. 'Tell me what you want,' he said.

A red hot shaft of anger shot through my chest. He should have known; if he really was this prophet, this magician, this person who knew everything, he wouldn't have asked me to do something I couldn't do. That was just downright cruel. I shook my head furiously, pointed to my lips and shook my head.

'I don't speak, Master . . .'

My throat vibrated, my mouth felt as if someone had sliced it at the corners, and sounds – real sounds came out. 'I don't . . .'

But I was! I was speaking! The words were distorted, my throat felt like a thousand splinters of pottery were lodged in its skin, but I made sounds.

'You do speak now, Reuben,' Jesus said gently. 'And in days to come you must speak of me to those who do not know. Now go in peace.'

And he turned and disappeared into the crowd.

I don't know how long I stood there. My whole body was trembling, my throat felt as if it was on fire and my sight was blurred with tears. I had spoken.

Tentatively I tried again. 'I . . . can . . . speak!' I uttered the words softly at first and then louder. 'I can speak!'

I touched my mouth. My lip was no longer hooked to my nose. I ran my tongue over my palate. It was whole; no cleft, no division. I glanced down. My arms were still short, my hand twisted, my legs crooked. But I had a voice.

In the distance I saw Andrew and Nathaniel, each carrying a basket laden with food. Stepping between the groups of picnickers, I limped over to them as fast as I could. Out of habit, I tugged on Andrew's sleeve and then realised that I didn't have to do that any more.

'An . . . der . . . oo! And-roo!'

Andrew dropped the basket he was carrying and stared at me. 'Reuben – you can talk?'

'Jesus did it,' I said. 'He – glaf – gave me a ice – no, a voice.'

There were tears in Andrew's eyes and I realised that I, too, was crying. Andrew dumped his basket on the ground, squatted down and enveloped me in a bear-like hug.

'This is wonderful,' he cried. 'What a day! Two miracles in as many hours!'

'Two?'

'You see this crowd? How many people do you reckon are here?'

I shrugged. 'Thousands,' I said.

'At least five thousand and that's not counting the women and children,' Nathaniel butted in. 'And they've all been fed.'

'So you found enough?' I asked, and then suddenly had a thought. I began miming – and again, realised that all that was behind me now. 'Was it Soo – Susanna, and Mary and the other women? Did they bring perslies – sorry, supplies?'

Nathaniel shook his head. 'These people were all fed from the food you handed to Jesus,' he said. 'Every one of them.'

'That's imp— imp— impossible!' I stammered. I was still getting used to hearing my own voice.

'As impossible as you regaining the power of speech?' Andrew queried solemnly. 'With Jesus, Reuben, it seems that nothing is impossible.'

After Jesus had dismissed the crowd, I set off for home, desperate to find Esther and Caleb and surprise them with my new powers of speech. Just as I was leaving, Peter came over to me with a broad grin on his face.

'So you can speak now, little man?'

'Yes,' I said. 'Jesus did it.'

'Well, you can put that voice to good use for me,' Peter said. 'When you get back to the village, go to see my wife, and ask her to speak to the hired hands and keep them on for another month. Can you do that?'

I nodded.

'Pardon?' Peter teased.

'Yes, I can do that,' I said. My voice seemed to be high and squeaky one minute and low and throaty the next, but what did I care?

'I'll be home soon, I'm sure, but there's no way Andrew and I can run the business and do the work Jesus wants us to do.'

'We're ready, Peter!' Andrew called, and I saw that nearly all the disciples were already aboard the boat.

Peter slapped me on the back. 'See you around,' he said.

'But where's Jesus?' I asked, noticing that he wasn't in the boat. It had suddenly struck me that I hadn't thanked him properly for what he'd done for me.

'He's gone away on his own to pray,' Peter said and sighed deeply. 'He says that the people have got the wrong idea about what he's come here to do. He says he needs time with the Father and he will catch up with us later.'

'But you will be coming back? Tomorrow?'

'We'll be back when Jesus decides we'll be back.' Peter replied.

'I need to see him,' I stammered.

'In which case,' Peter smiled, 'you'll find a way, won't you?'

It was dark by the time I got back to the village and too late to risk disturbing Susanna and Mary. As I passed Zebedee's house, I hesitated and then, taking a deep breath, I knocked on the door.

'Who is it?' Salome called.

'Reuben!'

There was a pause. 'Zebedee!' Salome called. 'Come here, quickly!'

I could hear huffing and puffing and the sound of a chair being scraped on the floor.

'Someone's out there up to no good,' I heard Salome mutter.

'What do you mean?' Zebedee asked.

'They say they're Reuben – which of course they're not, because he can't say anything! It's a trick!'

A minute later, the door opened a fraction and Zebedee peered through the gap.

'Hello, Zebedee, hello Salome, how are you? I've come to say thank you.'

If I live to be as old as Zebedee, I will never forget the expression on his face.

'Reuben . . . Reuben, you're speaking!'

Salome was staring at me wide-eyed.

'It *is* you,' she gasped.

'Jesus gave me back my voice,' I cried. 'Just a few hours ago; and if it wasn't for you it wouldn't have happened.'

Salome had sunk onto a stool and was still staring at me open-mouthed.

'What did I have to do with the Lord's miracle?' she asked.

'You gave me two fish, remember? And bread . . .' And I proceeded to tell them how I had given the food to Jesus and how he'd made me speak and then fed thousands of people.

'Just who is this Jesus?' Salome asked. 'There's never been anyone who can do the things he does.'

'He is the Lamb of God,' I heard myself say. 'I mean that's what John the Baptist said about him, not that I know what that means but he's going to set up a kingdom and . . .' It was as though all the thoughts and questions and muddles that had been swirling round in my mind all these months were now suddenly pouring out of my mouth unbidden.

'How's Caleb?' I said hastily, opting for a safer subject.

'Sleeping,' Salome said. 'And you look as if you could do with a rest too. Why don't you join him in the outhouse? But please, promise me one thing?'

'What?'

'Don't give him the scare you gave me,' she smiled. 'Make sure he's properly awake before you start chatting.'

I couldn't sleep. Every time I closed my eyes, I relived the moment when Jesus had taken the food from me and asked me what I wanted. And I kept hearing him say, 'You speak now, and you will speak of me.' Beside me, Caleb slept, snoring softly and occasionally crying out in his sleep. I couldn't make out what he was saying; it was just babble, except for one word repeated over and over. 'Kizia! Kizia!'

Although it was hard, I resisted the urge to shake him awake and tell him what had happened. Instead, I lay on my back, listening to the wind rattling the door hinge and thought about how having a voice might change my life.

I could get a job as a servant. Or better still, maybe I could work on a market stall, because now I could shout out my wares with the best of them. If only he'd made me tall and lengthened my arms, I could do almost anything. Why had he just stopped with my voice, I wondered. Straightening legs wouldn't be too much for the man who made a paralytic walk, surely? Why hadn't he done the whole job?

The more I thought about what I might do in the future, the more I realised that I needed more healing. There was nothing for it; I'd have to find Jesus and explain the situation to him. I was pretty sure he'd see what needed to be done, just as soon as I'd told him my plans.

'This is so cool!' Caleb cried the following morning after he had recovered from the shock of hearing me announce that it was windy but the sun was shining. 'You talking – life's going to be a whole heap easier!'

'How come?'

'No more guessing what you mean when you mime – we can actually have some two-way conversations now! And I've had this brilliant idea – I was going to tell Benjamin, one of the hired hands about it but now you're . . .'

I leapt to my feet.

'What is it?' Caleb asked.

'I forgot – I have to see Peter's wife,' I said. 'And then I'm going to surprise Esther!'

'Wait for me,' he cried, scrambling to his feet and then clutching his chest. 'Ouch!' He sank back down. 'Maybe I'll catch up with you later,' he said. 'I need to find Jesus – do you know where he is?'

I shook my head.

'Having some downtime, the last I heard,' I said. 'I'll be back – then we'll go together, OK?'

'Sure,' he said. 'And hey – it's good to hear you speaking, it really is.'

Peter's wife wasn't quite so thrilled to hear the sound of my voice. Well, she was happy for me, but decidedly unhappy with my message.

'Hired hands are all very well, but they don't have the commitment,' she said. 'Did Peter say when he would be back?'

'Soon,' I said.

'Yes, well that can mean anything' she said. 'Are you hungry?'

I nodded, and then remembered I didn't need to. 'Yes, I am,' I replied. Actually, I wasn't that hungry but years of not knowing where my next meal was coming from had taught me never to refuse food.

She pushed a bowl of curds across the table to me and tore off a strip of dried fish. 'Take these out back and watch Ruth and the baby for me,' she asked. 'I have to go across to my neighbour and I don't want to wake the little one. I will only be gone a short while.'

I wanted to say that I couldn't stop, that I had to find Esther and share my good news but then I remembered how good her family had been to me, and decided that it was the least I could do. As it turned out, hanging around was the best thing I could have done.

Ruth was amusing herself by teaching me to sing all the songs she knew, one by one, laughing when my voice squeaked and clapping excitedly when I managed to copy her, when I heard the door of the house bang.

'Mummy, Mummy!' Ruth cried running into the house. 'Daddy! Uncle Andrew!'

They were here after all. Checking that the baby was still fast asleep in the hammock, I hurried after Ruth. There was no sign of Salome, but Peter and Andrew were standing in the doorway, kicking off their sandals.

> Jesus made the disciples get into the boat and go on ahead of him to the other side, while he dismissed the crowd. After he had dismissed them, he went up on a mountainside by himself to pray. When evening came, he was there alone, but the boat was already a considerable distance from land, buffeted by the waves because the wind was against it. During the fourth watch of the night Jesus went out to them, walking on the lake. When the disciples saw him walking on the lake, they were terrified. 'It's a ghost,' they said and cried out in fear. But Jesus immediately said to them, 'Take courage! It is I. Don't be afraid.' 'Lord if it is you,' Peter replied, 'tell me to come to you on the water.' 'Come,' he said. Then Peter got out of the boat, walked on the water and came towards Jesus. But when he saw the wind, he was afraid, and beginning to sink, cried out 'Lord, save me!' Immediately Jesus reached out his hand and caught him. 'You of little faith,' he said, 'why did you doubt?'
>
> *Matthew 14:22-31*

'Peter, stop beating yourself up about it,' Andrew was saying. 'You had courage – which is more than can be said for the rest of us.'

'I so wanted to be able to do it,' Peter sighed. 'To walk on the water like the Lord.'

'Walk on water?' I had spoken before I realised it. That was something I was discovering about not being mute any longer. Thoughts often came out of my mouth before I knew what was happening.

Peter turned, clearly surprised to see me. 'Your wife is visiting a neighbour,' I said in answer to his questioning look. 'She asked me to watch the children.'

He smiled weakly. 'I still can't get used to hearing you speak,' he said. 'But thank you.'

'Daddy, Daddy, play with me,' Ruth begged.

Peter smiled at her. 'Sweetheart, why don't you go next door and find Rebecca to play with? Just for a moment until Daddy has had a rest and then we'll go on an adventure together.'

'Promise?'

'Promise.'

Satisfied, Ruth skipped out of the house, much to my relief.

'Excuse me for asking, but did you say Jesus can walk on water?' I asked before the subject could be changed.

Peter slumped down onto the nearby bench without replying. Andrew poured two flagons of water from the pitcher by the door and passed one to his brother.

'We were out on the lake last night,' he began. 'There was a stiff wind and we were having to row pretty hard to battle against it. We were a good three miles from the shore, when we saw him.'

'Jesus!' Peter burst out. 'Walking towards us on top of the water.'

'Only we didn't realise it was him,' Andrew added. 'To be honest, I was so frightened, I screamed. I thought it was a ghost.'

'We all did at first,' Peter admitted. 'Thaddeus clutched my arm, Judas and Philip cowered in the corner – and that was when Jesus spoke.'

'He told us not be afraid – that it was him, that everything was OK,' Andrew went on. 'That's when Peter said that . . .'

'I said, "If it is you, Lord, tell me to come to you on the water,"' Peter mumbled. 'And he did. He said, "Come."'

He rubbed his hands wearily across his eyes.

'And I messed up.'

'Peter, don't,' Andrew said gently, touching his brother on the shoulder. 'You got out of that boat and you walked. I saw you with my own eyes. You walked.'

'That's amazing – you did that?' I couldn't get my head around what I was hearing.

'Oh sure I did, for a couple of seconds,' Peter grunted. 'Then there was that sudden gust of wind and the waves were all round me and I suddenly realised that people don't walk on water – and I was sinking, and all I could think about was that I was going to drown. I just cried out to Jesus to save me.'

'And he did,' Andrew added.

'Yes, and what did he say to me?' Peter said with a catch in his voice. '"*You of little faith, why did you doubt?*" I felt so ashamed.'

'No, Peter, you mustn't feel like that,' Andrew assured him. 'Remember too what we all said, each one of us, after you were both back in the boat.'

Peter frowned. 'What?'

'We all said that we really got it – we really knew then that Jesus is the Son of God. If you hadn't tried, we might still have gone on with doubts lurking in the back of our minds.'

Peter nodded. 'I guess I just wanted to show off – to prove I could be like him,' he sighed. 'Or maybe I was just testing him one last time. But now—' He paused, shaking his head. 'Now, all I want to do is get out there and tell the whole world that Jesus is Lord of all. I want to share everything with everyone.'

He turned to me.

'I guess you feel like that right now, Reuben,' he smiled. 'Now that you've got the power of speech, I bet there will be no stopping you spreading the Good News.'

I looked at him and swallowed hard, a stabbing pain which felt a lot like guilt making me catch my breath. What had I been doing all this time? Working out how to get more from Jesus, making plans for my own security and future, that's what. In an instant, I knew what I had to do.

'You're right,' I said to Peter. 'I have to go. I have something really important to do.'

I found them in the usual spot. Mordecai was on the bottom step with his begging bowl, and Hillel was beside him, the strains of his lute almost blotted out in the bustle of the street.

'Oh it's you,' grunted Mordecai, as I tossed a lepton into his bowl. 'Never mind the lavish generosity – where's the apology for dashing off like that just because I disagreed with you?'

'I really am very sorry, Mordecai,' I intoned as loudly as I could. 'It was rude of me.'

Mordecai dropped the bowl and it rolled a few feet away. 'You— you— you spoke!' he gasped. 'Hillel, Reuben spoke!'

'Is it really him?' Hillel gasped.

'Yes, it's me,' I replied. 'Jesus gave me back my voice. And what's more, I'm taking you to him right now, whether you like it or not. If he can do it for me, he can do it for you.'

Hillel was on his feet, his lute tucked under his arm, before the words were out of my mouth. Mordecai, however, frowned, sniffed and stared at me.

'And you really were dumb? I mean, all this time I've known you – you weren't pretending not to speak?'

I sighed. 'Mordecai, I haven't time to argue. I was mute – now I have a voice. Hillel is blind – and if we get a move on, he will see and your useless arm will be restored. Get it?'

I knew when he got to his feet without bothering to pick up the begging bowl that at last I had got through to him.

'Master, this is my friend Hillel,' I stammered. 'He cannot see. But you can give him sight, I know you can, just like you gave me speech.'

Jesus looked at me long and hard and then turned to Hillel and took him gently by the hand.

'We will go a little further along the path,' he said to him.

As usual, there was quite a crowd around him, but he had eyes only for Hillel. When we reached the outskirts of the village, he suddenly spat straight onto Hillel's sightless eyes. There was a loud gasp from the onlookers.

'What's he doing?'

'That's disgusting?'

'Can he see?'

Jesus cupped Hillel's face in his hands. 'Can you see anything?' he asked gently.

'I— I can see people,' Hillel cried. 'But they look like trees walking around.'

Jesus covered Hillel's eyes with his hands for a minute.

When he removed them, I cried out in joy.

'Look! Look at his eyes!'

Gone was the vacant, sightless stare. Hillel's eyes were shining, his pupils darting from left to right.

'I can see, I can see!' he shouted. 'People, houses, Reuben, boats – oh Master, Master, thank you!'

The crowd cheered and clapped, and even Mordecai had a grin on his face like a huge slice of watermelon.

'Go home,' Jesus said.

'Master,' I ventured hurriedly. 'Mordecai – my other friend – his arm is . . .'

'What about his arm?' Jesus asked with a smile. 'There's nothing wrong with his arm.'

I turned to beckon Mordecai over. He was standing staring at his arm, flexing his fingers, opening and shutting his fist, raising it gingerly up and down.

'Oh!' I couldn't believe it; Jesus hadn't even touched the guy.

'My arm!' Mordecai cried. 'My arm – it's healed!' He looked up and I saw tears pouring down his weathered cheeks.

'Master, I was wrong. So wrong. You are the Promised One.'

So what has that got to do with me?

1. Do you ever feel that God asks things of you that you cannot possibly do? Reuben discovers that Jesus knows best! But often we don't get instant proof that he is enabling us to meet our challenges – or do we? What examples can you think of that move you on in a difficult situation? Does God ever use other people to empower us and in what way?

2. 'Having a voice' goes far beyond the ability to speak. Can you think of examples of places in the world where people don't have a voice? Do you ever think you are not heard, either in your family or in the wider society? As Christians, does 'having a voice' demand action? If so, in what way?

3. Reuben wonders why Jesus didn't 'do the whole job'? What do you think about the healing he gave to Reuben? Should he have completed the job and made him completely whole? Why do you think he concentrated on his voice and cleft palate?

4. Salome couldn't understand it when Reuben told her that without her the miracle couldn't have happened. He explained that it was she who gave him the food in the first place and then Jesus worked his miracle. Sometimes we just don't know where our acts of kindness may lead. Do you believe that miracles still happen today? More importantly, do you believe God could use you when he works his wonders?

5. Peter felt a failure because his determination to walk on the water turned to fear as he saw the waves. Was he really a failure? What was the effect of his telling the story? On Reuben? On the other disciples?

6. Why did it take two attempts for Jesus to restore Hillel's sight? Maybe because Jesus wanted to show that sometimes healing is gradual not instantaneous. Or maybe to illustrate that at first we don't see the spiritual truths clearly (Hillel saw people who looked like trees) – it can take time to see things as they really are.

CHAPTER TWENTY-SEVEN

A secret shared

Seth

I've always been close to my father. I'm an only child – my mother has been ill for many years, not just physically but in her mind as well. She has times when she is too fearful to leave her bed, and others when she will neither eat nor drink. We never discuss anything controversial or worrying in her presence, which is, I guess, why my father has always talked to me as though I were a grown-up – even when I was a four year old.

I'm proud of Dad – he's a member of the Sanhedrin, the ruling council of elders and high priests, and everyone respects him. He's one of those guys who rarely gets ruffled or annoyed and he always looks at both sides of any argument. But those last few days in Galilee, he seemed to be more and more troubled. We were riding on a cart, just the two of us, home to Jerusalem, when suddenly out of the blue he began to talk.

'I tell you the truth, I tell you the truth,' he muttered.

'Pardon? The truth about what?'

He turned and looked at me and sighed deeply. 'That's what Jesus said, over and over again, when I went to see him.'

There was a man named Nicodemus, a Jewish religious leader who was a Pharisee. After dark one evening, he came to speak with Jesus. 'Rabbi,' he said, 'we all know that God has sent you to teach us. Your miraculous signs are evidence that God is with you.'

Jesus replied, 'I tell you the truth, unless you are born again, you cannot see the Kingdom of God.'

'What do you mean?' exclaimed Nicodemus. 'How can an old man go back into his mother's womb and be born again?'

Jesus replied, 'I assure you, no one can enter the Kingdom of God without being born of water and the Spirit. Humans can reproduce only human life, but the Holy Spirit gives birth to spiritual life. So don't be surprised when I say, "You must be born again." The wind blows wherever it wants. Just as you can hear the wind but can't tell where it comes from or where it is going, so you can't explain how people are born of the Spirit.'

'How are these things possible?' Nicodemus asked.

Jesus replied, 'You are a respected Jewish teacher, and yet you don't understand these things? I assure you, we tell you what we know and have seen, and yet you won't believe our testimony. But if you don't believe me when I tell you about earthly things, how can you possibly believe if I tell you about heavenly things? No one has ever gone to heaven and returned. But the Son of Man has come down from heaven. And as Moses lifted up the bronze snake on a pole in the wilderness, so the Son of Man must be lifted up, so that everyone who believes in him will have eternal life.

'For God loved the world so much that he gave his one and only Son, so that everyone who believes in him will not perish but have eternal life. God sent his Son into the world not to judge the world, but to save the world through him.'

John 3:1-17

'You spoke with Jesus? When?'

'A year ago,' my father said. 'At Passover time.'

'You never told me . . .'

'No,' my father agreed. 'It seemed best to keep it quiet. I was taking a risk and . . .' He paused and sighed. 'I went to him one night after I'd been to a meeting. Everyone had been saying that Jesus was trouble, that his teaching was false – and something inside me kept nagging at me, that we were all missing the point.'

He shifted his position. 'And I'll be honest – I wanted to go to him when the others weren't around,' he admitted. 'I guess I was keeping all my options open; speaking to Jesus and yet still keeping the respect of the other council members.'

He turned to me. 'None of them know I went, and I'm trusting you . . .'

'I won't say a word,' I assured him. 'What did Jesus talk about?'

'He said that no one can see the kingdom of God unless he is born again.'

'What on earth does that mean?' I asked. 'Once you're born, you're born – you can't do it twice.'

My father smiled. 'That's exactly what I said to Jesus,' he replied.

'And?'

'He said that a human person gives birth to a flesh and blood baby you can touch and see and cuddle; but inside, the essence of the person is formed by something you can't see – the Spirit. He said we have to be born from above, as well as from our mother's womb.'

He glanced at me as if he regretted touching on such an intimate matter.

'So what is this Spirit?' I asked. 'How do you get it?'

'Jesus said it was like the wind – you hear it, you see it rustling the leaves on the trees, you see the waves being whipped up but you've no idea where it comes from. I was struggling to get my head around what he was saying and he got quite irritated with me.'

'With you? How dare he – you're one of the best teachers in the whole of Jerusalem!' I exclaimed.

'I have a lot to learn, I know that now,' he sighed. 'At the time I wanted to sit on the fence, to play it safe. But now . . .' He paused, turned and gripped me by the shoulders. 'I keep remembering what he said. And you must remember it to – because although I don't understand, not fully, I know that this is something more important than anything I have ever believed or taught in my life.'

'Go on.'

'Jesus said, "*For God so loved the world that he gave his one and only Son that whoever believes in him shall not perish but have eternal life.*"'

He closed his eyes and breathed deeply.

'Seth, I cannot get those words out of my mind and I keep turning everything over and over in my head. I've seen what he does – the miracles, the healings – but more, much more than that I have heard him speak and his words touch my heart in a way that nothing has ever done before.'

He dropped his voice and chewed his lip. 'I don't know how to say this without sounding foolish,' he said. 'But this business about being born again – I keep remembering you as a baby. One day, you were staring around the room with that unfocused, newborn look, and the next you had this wide-eyed look of amazement on your face! You were actually focusing and seeing things properly for the first time. That's how I feel now, about Jesus.'

I was gobsmacked.

'I'm seeing what he's doing. He is shining a light into the dark places of our world and it scares me.'

'You're not scared of anything!' I retorted.

'Sometimes, Seth, the things we understand, no matter how bad they are, don't frighten us. It's the things that we don't understand, the things that show up all our faults and prejudices and bigotry and seem to ask of us more than we can give that terrify us.'

For a while he said no more. I sat in the cart, listening to the clip clop of the mules' feet and then suddenly, had a brilliant idea. 'You know Jesus is going to set up this amazing new kingdom, where everyone will be equal? Well you could be his right-hand man, his adviser and . . .'

'Seth!' my father burst out. 'Watch your tongue!'

I flinched. 'What do you mean? I only said . . .'

'I know, I'm sorry,' my father replied more gently. 'But you have to understand this. Whatever you think, you do not want people – especially our sort of people – to associate our name with Jesus. Do you understand?'

He jerked his head in the direction of the carter who was idly flicking the mules with his whip.

'No, I don't,' I admitted.

'There are things brewing, Seth, that could bring trouble to anyone who openly supports this man,' he sighed. 'Think what you like about him – but keep those thoughts to yourself. That's what I'm doing. At least for the time being.'

We had travelled on in silence for some time, until the carter stopped to water the mules and we went into the caravanserai to eat.

Beckoning me to a quiet corner, my father took a long draught of water and began to speak without making eye contact with me. 'You know I spent yesterday talking with Simon, my old friend?'

I nodded.

'He told me the most extraordinary story,' my father went on. 'It's not exactly what I would normally discuss with a boy your age but it says a lot about Jesus and it might help you to understand my confusion.'

'Please tell me,' I urged.

'Simon invited Jesus for a meal,' my father explained. 'They were stretched out at the table talking about all manner of things and enjoying the food, when a woman rushed in.'

My father cleared his throat and sniffed, a sure sign that he was uncomfortable with what he was about to say. 'This woman – she was, let's say, of ill repute . . .'

'A prostitute, you mean?' Honestly there are times when my father acts as if I were six years old.

'Yes,' he said curtly. 'Well, of course, as Simon told me, he didn't know where to put himself, he was so mortified. Before he could take action, the woman had rushed up to Jesus, knelt at his feet and began sobbing her heart out.'

'Why? Was she ill?' I asked. 'Did she want him to heal her?'

'She was clutching an alabaster jar of perfume, and crying so much that her tears actually dropped onto his feet,' my father muttered, as if saying the words quickly would diminish the shame of uttering them. 'This harlot then broke the neck of the jar, tipped the perfume over his feet, mixed it with her tears, unbound her hair, let it fall all over her face and then leaned forward and wiped Jesus' feet with it.' He was cringing by the end of the sentence, such was his embarrassment.

'She anointed his feet?' I gasped. 'That's a slave's job. What did Jesus do?' I gasped.

'Well,' my father said, 'what Simon tells me is that just as he was thinking that Jesus was a fake, because any prophet worth his salt would have known in an instant that the woman was a whore, and thrown her out without more ado, Jesus seemed to read his mind.'

'So he told him not to be embarrassed, did he?' I suggested.

'Huh,' my father grunted. 'That's not Jesus' style. No – he told a story. And far from making Simon feel better, it made things a whole lot worse.'

He leaned back and tipped his face up towards the sun. 'Two men,' he said, 'owed money to a moneylender. One owed him five hundred denarii, the other just fifty. Neither of them had any hope of repaying the money, so the moneylender cancelled the debts of both men.'

'Like that would ever happen!' I laughed.

'So Jesus asked Simon which of the two men would love him the most for what he'd done and Simon said . . .'

'Well, it's obvious,' I butted in. 'The one who had owed the most.'

My father nodded. 'That's right – and Simon got it right too,' my father said. 'But did Jesus leave it at that? Oh no – he went right on and rubbed Simon's nose in it.'

'What do you mean?'

'He said that when he'd arrived Simon hadn't had the good manners to offer him water to wash the dust of the road from his feet, but that the woman had washed his feet with her tears and dried them with her hair. And what's more, he said Simon didn't greet him with a kiss but the woman not only kissed his feet but poured perfume on them. Because of that love, he said, her sins, which he agreed were many, would be forgiven. Then he touched the woman and said, out loud so that everyone in the room, and probably half the street, could hear, "Your sins are forgiven you!"'

My father looked me full in the face for the first time since he had started speaking. 'You must guess the effect all that had on the other guests,' he sighed. 'Every time Jesus forgives sins, he puts himself in the place of God – and by doing so, he's just stacking trouble for himself. Simon won't forget it – and he wields a lot of authority in the Sanhedrin.'

'But,' I ventured cautiously, 'Simon was a bit rude wasn't he? I mean not to do all the polite things like providing water, and olive oil to anoint his head. You told me that we should welcome all guests that way, no matter who they were.'

'We should, and Simon was very discourteous,' my father agreed. 'The problem is, he is now one very angry, and very powerful man. Not the sort of guy you want to argue with.'

'But I thought you believed that Jesus . . .'

'I believe what I believe,' he nodded slowly. 'I just choose to keep it to myself. And you will do the same.'

It wasn't a question. It was an order.

So what has that got to do with me?

1. Nicodemus went to see Jesus at night. Why? Was he afraid of his peers or was there a deeper reason? What normally happened during daylight confrontations between Jesus and Pharisees? Who are the people in your life who might sneer or question your commitment to find out more about Jesus? Why do you think they do that?

2. Read John Chapter 1 verses 4 and 5. What contrast do you see here between the description of Jesus and the way that Nicodemus sought him out?

3. When someone is baptised into the Christian faith, both water and the Spirit are involved. How?

4. Who is the Holy Spirit? God is three in one – God the Father, God the Son and God the Holy Spirit. God became a man in Jesus, so that he could die for our sins. Jesus rose from the dead and when he ascended into heaven, he promised to send the Holy Spirit so that his spiritual presence would remain with all believers for ever. Do you find the Holy Spirit harder or easier to understand than God the Father, or God the Son? How do you think the Holy Spirit affects your life? Have you ever had an experience in which you felt the Holy Spirit was playing a big part?

5. Do you ever feel tempted to keep quiet about the fact that you are a churchgoer, or interested in finding out more about Jesus? Do you think it is harder for Christians than for young people of other faiths and if so, why?

6. Jesus said: 'For God so loved the world that he gave his one and only Son that whoever believes in him shall not perish but have eternal life.' The whole of the Good News of Christ is summed up in this verse. Here is the example of true love – when you love someone dearly you are willing to give to the point of self-sacrifice. God gave up his Son and Jesus, who was totally innocent and free from sin, took the punishment and paid the price for our sins – and then gave us new life. It is such a huge, amazing gift that we find it hard to understand but when we believe in Jesus we trust in

his power and his love, even though intellectually we can't possibly grasp the enormity of it.

7. The woman was able to 'gatecrash' the party because in Jesus' time meals of that sort were not private affairs; anyone could walk into the house and watch the diners. In the same way today, anyone – absolutely anyone – is welcome in God's house, the church. Does the church always make people feel that way? Does your local church feel like 'open house' to you? If not, in what ways would you like it to be different?

CHAPTER TWENTY-EIGHT

The rock

Caleb

When Jesus and the disciples set off for Caesarea Philippi, we all went with them. No one actually invited me along – it just seemed to be taken for granted that where Reuben and Esther went, I'd tag along too, and to be honest, although I was feeling a whole heap better, I didn't want to be alone. Every night since the incident with the pigs, I had dreamed of Kizia; I saw her face, I heard her voice, I felt that limp, lifeless body in my arms and when I woke, the stab of guilt and grief in my chest was like a knife being plunged between my ribs. It was only when I was with my friends that I could shove the memory to one side, box it up and play-act at being the cool, laid-back guy.

It was a long day's walk from Capernaum to Caesarea Philippi, about twenty-five miles, and as we drew near the outskirts of the city, Jesus stopped and made no attempt to enter the gates.

'It's a pagan place,' Joanna explained. 'The people worship all manner of idols. They have the strangest ideas about their gods – and no idea about the true God.'

At this Jesus who had been speaking to Peter and James, turned and beckoned to us all to gather closer. 'Tell me,' he said. 'Who do people say that I am?'

'Some say John the Baptist,' Philip replied.

'I've heard that people reckon you are Elijah the prophet,' Thaddeus commented.

'Or Jeremiah!' said Thomas.

'In fact, a lot of people just list the ancient prophets and say that you are one of those,' interjected Judas.

Reuben nudged me. 'There are those who call him a lot worse names than that,' he whispered.

'And how about all of you? Who do you say that I am?' Jesus demanded.

There was a long pause. Jesus looked at Andrew and Philip, then James and John and Judas. None of them met his gaze. Then Peter spoke.

'You are the Christ, the Son of the Living God,' he declared.

Jesus' face shone. 'God bless you, Simon son of Jonah! You didn't come to that realisation through book learning or your own cleverness – God my Father has made you aware of the reality of who I am.'

He stretched out his hand and rested it lightly on Peter's head.

'And now I can tell you who you are – your true identity. You are Peter – the rock. And you will be the foundation for my community of people – a church so bursting with vibrancy and energy and love and commitment that nothing – not even the gates of hell itself will be able to suppress it.'

Everyone was motionless. You could almost hear hearts beating. I stared at Peter. He was just an ordinary looking, regular sort of man, no different from any of the other disciples and yet he was clearly the apple of Jesus' eye. Lucky thing.

'And that's not all,' Jesus said. 'I am giving you the keys to the kingdom.'

'Master?'

Peter was clearly as puzzled as I was.

'Whatever you embrace down here on earth, will be embraced in heaven. And whatever you shun and recoil from here will be shunned in heaven. But one thing you must all understand. You must tell no one that I am the Christ.'

Now this just didn't make sense.

'But Lord, why . . .'

'But Master, surely we should proclaim . . .'

'Listen!' Jesus cut in, and there was a deep weariness and sadness about him. 'Soon I must go to Jerusalem and it won't be pretty. I will suffer – deeply. The Pharisees and teachers of the law have got it in for me. There is only one thing they want and they will get it.'

'What? What do they want?' Matthew asked.

'They will kill me,' Jesus said. At that chaos broke out. Mary cried out and gripped Susanna's arm, Joanna looked as if she might faint, the disciples shouted in protest and Esther snatched my hand.

'They can't – they wouldn't . . .'

'We won't let them lay a finger on you!'

'They will kill me,' Jesus repeated. 'But after three days . . .'

'Master, no!' Peter shouted grabbing his arm. 'Never, never, never – this won't happen! Say it won't happen!'

'Peter, stop! What is this? Satan has got into you! He is trying to get you to think in the narrow human way – not in the way of God! I won't tolerate it!'

He sat down wearily on the grass and put his head in his hands. Mary went over to him and began gently massaging his neck.

'Master,' she ventured. 'Surely if people want to harm you, then you must stay out of their way.'

At that, Jesus got to his feet.

'You are all following me,' he said. 'Some of you have been with me a long while, others have only just seen the light. But this you must know. If you want to be a true follower, then you have to set your own wishes and ideas to one side and go where I lead. And it won't be easy. You won't find yourself – your true self – by thinking about what *you* want or who *you* want to become. When you decide to lose all that ego and just let God direct your life, that's when you will truly live.'

'I don't get it,' someone murmured.

'You could gain all manner of earthly possessions, but if you give up your soul, the very essence of yourself, in order to do that – well, you'll gain nothing. Before long the Son of Man will come with crowds of angels and you will be rewarded. Some of you . . .' He made a sweeping gesture round the crowd. 'Some of you will see the Son of Man in all his glory.'

As he moved away with the inner clique, I hung back.

'Did you understand any of that?' I asked Reuben and Esther.

'I sort of switched off when he spoke about dying,' Esther admitted. 'They won't do that, will they? They won't kill him?'

'You can't trust Pharisees,' I blurted out, because this talk of murder was too near the mark. 'They'd do anything they wanted to.'

'But,' Reuben said thoughtfully, 'what I don't get is this. Jesus can work miracles, right? We've all seen it. So surely, when push comes to shove, he'll be able to save himself.'

'Of course!' Esther murmured. 'Even if they hurt him, he'd heal himself at once.'

'If that's the case,' I argued, 'why did he talk about dying as if it were a done deal? As if he knew it was going to happen, no matter what.'

Neither of them answered. In fact, we said very little to one another for the rest of day. And judging by the unfamiliar silence among the crowd, we weren't the only ones shaken to our foundations.

After six days Jesus took with him Peter, James and John the brother of James, and led them up a high mountain by themselves. There he was transfigured before them. His face shone like the sun, and his clothes became as white as the light. Just then there appeared before them Moses and Elijah, talking with Jesus.

Peter said to Jesus, 'Lord, it is good for us to be here. If you wish, I will put up three shelters – one for you, one for Moses and one for Elijah.'

While he was still speaking, a bright cloud covered them, and a voice from the cloud said, 'This is my Son, whom I love; with him I am well pleased. Listen to him!'

When the disciples heard this, they fell face down to the ground, terrified. But Jesus came and touched them. 'Get up,' he said. 'Don't be afraid.' When they looked up, they saw no one except Jesus.

As they were coming down the mountain, Jesus instructed them, 'Don't tell anyone what you have seen, until the Son of Man has been raised from the dead.'

Matthew 17:1-9

'So how come they get to go off with him, and we don't?'

'If you ask me, those three are getting a bit up themselves . . .'

'It's not their fault Jesus wanted them to go . . .'

'But why always them?' That was Judas. 'What's so special about Peter and James and John? Except that they make more noise than the rest of us put together?'

The disciples had been muttering among themselves all morning, ever since Jesus had set off up Mount Tabor with Peter, James and John. The rest of them had tried to follow but Jesus was having none of it and they were pretty miffed, I can tell you. I could see their point. Those three were always the ones closest to Jesus, the ones who sat next to him at meals, who debated and discussed and hung on his every word. Even Andrew – who, let's face it, was Peter's brother and who had acted as host to Jesus on dozens of occasions – was something of an outsider, not that he seemed to mind. Actually, I'd always thought Andrew was a bit too accommodating; his brother hogged the limelight but it was Andrew who always thought about the consequences of leaving the fishing boats, Andrew who arranged for cover, Andrew who took time to check on the stragglers in the crowd and help anyone who had a problem.

We were all hanging around, wondering how long Jesus would be up the mountain, when a man came up to Philip and Thaddeus.

'You work with Jesus, right?' he asked.

'We do,' Thaddeus said.

'And you can work miracles too?'

'We have been given the power to heal,' Philip said, and there was a note of pride in his voice.

'Then I beg you, cure my little boy,' the man said, gesturing to a lad of about eight years old who was clinging onto his hand. 'He has seizures, terrible ones – sometimes when my wife is cooking, he falls into the fire, so wild are his convulsions. And once, he nearly drowned by falling out of my boat into the lake. We are at our wits' end. Please, heal him.'

Philip walked up to the boy and touched his head. 'You are healed,' he said, and glanced at Thaddeus. 'You will be well.'

At that moment the boy fell to the ground, foaming at the mouth, choking on his own tongue, his limbs thrashing uncontrollably.

'Come out of him!' Thaddeus shouted.

But nothing happened. The boy's body continued to jerk and twitch, blood pouring from his bitten tongue.

'You can't do it, can you?' his father shouted. 'You— you . . .'

'What is going on?' Jesus, along with the three oh-so-special disciples, appeared at Philip's side.

'Master,' cried the boy's father. 'It's my boy – I thought your disciples could heal him, but you know what, they haven't a clue!'

Jesus turned and looked at Philip and Thaddeus.

'You still haven't quite got it, have you?' he remarked.

Then he turned to the boy who was still in the grip of the convulsion.

'Come out!'

The boy's body relaxed, his eyes opened and he stood up.

'Daddy?' he said. 'Daddy, I'm better – I feel different!'

The boy's father gripped Jesus' hand, stumbling over his words as he poured out his thanks. After he had left, Philip expressed what we were all thinking.

'Why couldn't we do it? Why couldn't we heal him?'

'Because deep down, you didn't believe that God would give you the power; you didn't open yourselves to let God's Spirit enter you and carry out his work.'

He smiled. 'In the years to come, remember this: faith is the key. When you face a problem, don't look at the problem, look at God and know, know deep in your heart, that he will give you the power to move mountains. Nothing will be too hard for you if you remember that.'

When Jesus decided to head back to Capernaum, Esther and the other women went ahead to prepare to receive him. Reuben and I hung back, keeping as close to Jesus and the inner set as we could. Ever since Reuben had found his voice, he had been putting it to good use, but even I was surprised when he suddenly quickened his pace, caught up with John and asked him what he and the others had been doing up the mountain with Jesus.

'Nothing,' John said and turned away.

'Peter?' Reuben persisted.

'Just . . . talking with Jesus,' he shrugged.

'That's right,' James added. 'Just chatting.'

But the look that passed between the three of them made it perfectly clear that they were lying through their back teeth.

During the long walk back to Capernaum, you could sense a shift in the atmosphere. Peter, James and John were in a huddle together the whole way, which didn't go down well with the rest of the crew. Jesus was silent, walking at a distance from the rest of us and somehow making it clear without saying a word that he needed to be left alone for a bit.

Reuben and I were fairly subdued too. To be honest, my mind was in turmoil. I'd set out to find Jesus after that wedding in Cana simply because I wanted to learn to do what he did. That was back in the days when I thought he was some high-class magician who would pass on the tricks of his trade to an eager apprentice. But now, all this talk of being the Christ, the Son of God, of being hunted down and killed – it didn't sit comfortably. In fact, it terrified me. I was beginning to wonder whether being with Jesus was such a good idea after all.

It wasn't until we were on the outskirts of Capernaum that Jesus rejoined the disciples. By then, Reuben and I were right up there with them, mainly because Andrew had been talking to Reuben about the need for a few days of hard work on the boats before they left again.

Jesus paused at the point where the path divides and held up his hand.

'I have something to say which you must take to heart,' he began. 'The Son of Man is going to be betrayed by people who do not understand the ways of God. He will be slaughtered and after three days will be raised to life.' Then he turned and continued walking.

'He's said it again,' Reuben exclaimed. 'He says he will come back to life.'

'Now that would be some miracle – maybe, maybe that's why he's going to let them kill him. So he can magic himself back to life?'

Reuben looked at me as if I had taken leave of my senses.

'If he's dead, he can't do anything, can he?' he reasoned. 'Once you're dead, you're cold, stiff, senseless . . .'

'Shut up!' I screamed.

The look on Reuben's face brought me back to my senses.

'I'm sorry, really,' I stammered. 'I've never been much good talking about death.'

'It's OK,' Reuben replied generously. 'Anyway, I guess Jesus is just going through a bad patch – imagining the worst. It'll be fine – no one would dare lay a finger on him. Not after all the amazing things he's done.'

I smiled and nodded, but my mind raced on. If it really was true that the authorities were set on getting rid of Jesus, they'd find a way; and it was my bet that they wouldn't exactly make life easy for the people close to him. Hanging out with him had seemed like such a great idea but was I really any better off now than I had been back in the days at Cana? Reuben had got his voice back, Esther had found a decent job, but me? Had following Jesus done anything for me? The short answer was no.

It was some time later, after Reuben had fallen behind (something he often did when his legs were paining him), that I felt a hand on my shoulder.

'Hey, what's with the long face?'

It was Judas. I hadn't spoken with him a great deal, but because he was the one in charge of the money, I had sometimes gone to him with one of the pieces I'd found – OK, pinched – and he'd given me cash for food.

'It's just all this talk of death,' I muttered. 'If everyone's turning against Jesus . . .'

'They wouldn't if they really knew him,' Judas said. 'Trouble is, he's a great guy but he doesn't have a clue about dealing with the people that really matter. In this world you have to know how to play things to your own advantage. Maybe if . . .'

'If what?'

'Nothing,' Judas said. 'I've just had a thought. Leave it with me.'

So what has that got to do with me?

1. 'Who do *you* say that I am?' Jesus asks Peter. He asks us the same question: it is our relationship with him that matters. We will all meet people who misinterpret who Jesus is, just as we meet people who get the wrong end of the stick about friends we hang out with, or the kind of people we ourselves are. Who do you say that Jesus is?

2. Peter said, 'You are the Christ, the Son of the Living God.' Right answer – but this knowledge didn't turn him into a saint overnight as we shall see. We can know things in our head and our heart but still mess up when it comes to living that truth in our lives. God understands that; what he longs for is our honesty, our willingness to call on him when we struggle.

3. How do you think the disciples reacted when Jesus said he was giving Peter the 'keys to the kingdom'? What did he mean by that?

4. Poor Peter! No sooner has Jesus elevated him to a great position of responsibility than he's ticking him off big time for saying that he won't let Jesus' prophesy about his future come true! Was Jesus being fair – or was he too harsh? Why do you think he said that Satan was manipulating Peter? How do you think Peter felt during this exchange? And how do you imagine the other disciples reacted?

5. Is it realistic of Jesus to ask us to set all our own wishes to one side when we follow him? We need to remember that God wants what is best for us – and sometimes what we want doesn't lead us down the right path. We need to put God first in everything and *it's not easy*! What might help us to do this? What prevents us? Do you ever feel angry with Jesus when you read his demands – of which there are many? It's OK to be angry: God can take it. He would far rather you were honest and angry than that you pretended to be holier than thou and never got close enough to him to tell him how you really feel.

6. 'In the years to come, remember this: faith is the key. When you face a problem, don't look at the problem, look at God and know, know deep in your heart, that he will give you the power to move mountains. Nothing will be too hard for you if you remember that.' Wishful thinking? Something that only archbishops achieve? Impossible? What is your immediate reaction to those words? Does Jesus say that faith will mean we never have a problem? Or that the problem won't overwhelm us?

CHAPTER TWENTY-NINE

Too hard to handle

Esther

I had got to know Mary from Magdala a lot more during our time away from Capernaum. Whenever she caught me looking sad, she would come and sit with me and she knew without asking that I was thinking about Ziva, my sister. I think she suspected that I had memories that were too painful to share but she always seemed to say the right thing.

'Stay close to Jesus and the way will open up to you, I know it will,' she said one day.

'If only I knew where Ziva was I could bring her to him,' I sighed. 'How can someone disappear from a town like Capernaum?'

I had asked around about the 'crazy woman' every time we had been to the town – but all I heard was that she hadn't been seen for weeks. This information was, more often than not, followed by comments such as 'Thanks be to God!' or 'Good riddance!'.

'I just don't get it,' I repeated.

'Anyone who doesn't want to be found can stay lost,' Mary replied gently. 'But the time will come and then you'll understand why we all had to wait. At least, that's how it seems to me.'

I didn't think that made much sense but she was so kind and easy to be with that I simply nodded and smiled and said that I was sure she was right.

It was on our second day home that Jesus and the twelve disciples came to eat at Susanna's house. Andrew, Peter, James and John had all been fishing the night before and the catch was a good one; we had spent the day baking bread, making barley cakes and stuffing dates with honey. Mary was singing at the top of her voice all day and for a moment that made me cry because it reminded me yet again of Ziva.

When the time came to eat, the place was overflowing. Peter had brought Abigail, his wife, along with his little girl and baby son; most of the other disciples had elderly parents or wives and children with them and the mood in the courtyard was lively, with people telling jokes, Jesus congratulating us on the food and wine and the children bubbling with excitement at the unexpected treat. I was busy serving and clearing platters, Reuben was fetching and carrying from the kitchen and Caleb was refilling wine jars from the store at the back of the house.

It was after the last crumbs had been eaten and Susanna had gestured to the three of us to join the gathering, that James, draining the dregs of his third goblet of wine, lent back on his elbows and cleared his voice.

'Master,' he said. 'Can you tell us who gets to be the most important person in God's kingdom?'

'Trust him to ask that,' someone muttered. 'He's already lining himself up as number one in heaven!'

Jesus laughed and glanced round the room. Seeing little Ruth playing a game of jacks with Tobias, Philip's nephew, he called her over to him.

'OK, so you want the truth?' he said. 'Unless you go back to being just like this little child, you won't have a chance of even entering the kingdom, never mind being important!'

James frowned. 'What do you mean?' he asked.

'You need the open mind, the joy in life, the willingness to discover the new in everything you see – do that and you will be great in the kingdom. Because when you respond to a child with love, it's as if you are responding directly to me.' He ruffled Ruth's hair and she giggled.

'Go back to your game, little one,' he smiled, and then turned back to James. 'But one more thing,' he went on. 'If anyone leads a child, or someone with a childlike mind, into sin or if they bully and manipulate them because they are so innocent – well, it would be better for that person to be drowned in the depths of the sea.'

He glanced across the room at the children. 'Those children have guardian angels who work for my Father in heaven – so don't any of you ever look down on or despise a child. Ever.'

There was a silence in the room. I thought about my father, the way he'd used me and abused me; I thought of Nathan, the steward in Cana; and I remembered what Reuben had told me about his dad – and then I thought how wonderful it would be to have Jesus as a father; how you would be so safe with him, and how great life would be. OK, he'd be strict, I was sure of that, and I reckoned you wouldn't get away with misbehaving but that would be fine because everything he said made sense and somehow you would know that no matter what, he loved you just because you were you.

'Not all kids are good though, are they Master?' Bartholomew remarked. 'Some are little thugs and you wouldn't want people like that, would you?'

'Bartholomew my dear friend,' Jesus interrupted. 'Let me ask you a question. If a man has a hundred sheep and one of them wanders off, what does he do? He leaves the flock and goes off in search of the one that is lost. And when he finds it, he is ecstatic! Happier about that one silly sheep than about the ninety-nine others that never dreamt of moving an inch.'

He took a long draught of wine.

'And that's exactly how your Father in heaven is – he cannot bear for one of his little ones to be lost – whatever their age.'

Reuben lent towards me. 'Wouldn't it be great if life was really the way Jesus says it should be?' he whispered. 'But it's not going to be, is it? God may worry about people who are lost but the rest of the world sure as hell doesn't!'

'Lots of people care . . .' But before I could finish my sentence, he had stood up and stomped out of the room.

I didn't wait and I didn't ask permission. I just got up and followed him.

'Just leave me alone,' Reuben snapped, sitting on his hands and rocking gently back and forward. 'I'm a waste of space and you should be back in there, soaking up every word of this fantasy Jesus is spreading!'

For a moment, I couldn't speak. This wasn't Reuben – not the Reuben I knew anyway. He didn't say things like that . . . and then I realised. It was only during the past couple of weeks that I'd heard him speak. All the rest of the time I'd known him I hadn't a clue what was actually going on inside his head. I knew nothing of his past – other than what he mimed, which suggested that he was on his own and had no family.

'Go on, go back in the house,' he grunted. He was standing now, one hand gripping the other, his teeth clenched as if against some awful pain.

'No.'

'Then I'll go,' he snapped and turning, he broke into a run, through the back alley that ran alongside the outhouses and up on to the hillside path. His gait was more stumbling than ever and twice I thought he was going to fall flat on his face. I glanced back at the house, knowing that very soon the guests would be leaving and Susanna and Mary might need me. But right now there was someone who I reckoned needed me more.

I didn't call out to him; I simply followed, keeping my distance but always near enough to keep him in sight. After a few minutes, his pace slowed; another five and he stopped stock still, leaning against the trunk of a cypress tree, head bowed and shoulders shaking.

I moved silently nearer and then I too stopped dead. He had turned; he was banging his head backwards and forwards against the tree trunk, faster and faster and then, just as suddenly, he stopped, stooped down, picked something up from the ground and slammed it into his arm.

'Reuben, no!'

I forgot all about discretion and delicacy and tore up the path, jumping over scrub to reach the tree.

'Stop it!'

If he had seen me coming I wouldn't have had a chance, but as it was I was able to grab the shard of broken pottery from his hand, slicing open my own finger as I did so.

'Reuben, Reuben, what are you doing? What is it? What's wrong?'

He stared at me through tear-filled eyes, huge red weals appearing on his forehead.

'I – told – you – to – go – away!' he sobbed. 'You shouldn't have stopped me!'

'But Reuben, you were hurting yourself . . .'

'No you don't get it, I was making the pain go away!'

He turned and slammed his fist into the tree trunk and I gasped as if the agony was mine and not his.

'Reuben, whatever is wrong, tell me. This isn't like you, this is . . .'

'This is the real me!' he shouted. 'And now everything is ten times worse than before.'

'Why?'

'Oh, stop pretending,' he shouted. 'Now you've seen me like this, that'll be it, won't it? You won't want me as a friend, you'll go and tell Caleb and everyone that I'm possessed and . . .'

'Reuben, stop it right now! Let's get one thing clear: you are my friend. You always will be my friend. Get it? My friend. Not just when you're feeling upbeat – all the time. Now please, please, tell me what's wrong. What can I do to help?'

It was as if all the energy had left him and he sank down onto the ground and shivered. I squatted down beside him, using the sleeve of my robe in a futile attempt to mop up the blood on his arm.

'It was him that set me off,' Reuben sobbed. 'Jesus. It was when he started talking about God loving it when someone who is lost gets found.'

Tears streamed down his face.

'When I got my voice back, I thought everything would be amazing from that moment on,' he wept. 'But it isn't, and that makes me feel wicked because I should be so grateful – well, I am grateful but . . .'

'But?'

'I'm still ugly, I'm still a dwarf and I'm fifteen – with no life ahead of me other than to either be jeered at or pitied and I don't want either. I want a life and . . . I'm just so angry. Why couldn't Jesus straighten my legs? Give me normal arms? Or at least make someone love me?'

I was struggling to hold back my own tears. 'I don't know the answer to the question,' I whispered, wrapping my arms round him. 'But one thing has happened even without Jesus doing it.'

'Oh yeah? What?'

'You've got someone who loves you,' I murmured. 'Right here. Now. Me.'

It took me a very long time to persuade Reuben to come back to the house with me. It was only when I agreed that he would hide in the outhouse and that I wouldn't tell anyone about what had happened, that he finally relented. I was worried; the cut on his arm had stopped bleeding but it was dirty and I could see (though I didn't make any comment) that there were several other livid scars on his arms and shoulder. The weals on his face were turning purple and there was a lump under his hairline that I could swear had doubled in size on the walk home.

When I crept back into the house, most of the guests had left but Jesus, Peter, James and John were still sitting with Susanna, Mary and Joanna and a couple of the other disciples. Susanna looked up as I tried to slip unseen into the kitchen. My heart sank as she beckoned me over.

'I am sorry, really I am,' I began, 'but Reuben . . .' I stopped. No way could I risk telling her the whole story now in case she insisted on knowing where he was. I couldn't risk breaking his trust.

'It's alright, Esther,' she smiled. 'But please, you two shouldn't just disappear like that; it's not polite and – well, to be truthful, I was worried about what was going on.'

'I'm really sorry,' I murmured, as humbly as I could. 'Please forgive me.'

'Of course,' she smiled. 'And where's Reuben?'

My heart sank. I couldn't lie but then again, telling the truth would be a total betrayal. Luckily, Peter came to my rescue.

'Speaking of forgiveness,' he said, turning to Jesus, 'how many times should I forgive my brother or sister when they do me wrong? Seven?'

'Seven? Make it seventy-seven times and you'd be nearer the mark!'

Peter looked gobsmacked.

'I'll tell you a story,' Jesus said, 'about what the kingdom of heaven is really like.' At once everyone wriggled nearer and focused on his face. Susanna beckoned to me to sit down, and even though I really wanted to slip away and check on Reuben, the thought of one of Jesus' stories was enough to keep me there.

'There was once a king,' Jesus began, 'who decided it was time to collect in all the money that his servants owed him. Now there was one chap who owed him a huge sum, thousands of talents. This man had no way of repaying the money to his master. "In which case," the king said, "there is only one thing to be done. Everything you own must be sold – and that includes your wife and children."'

At this we all gasped.

'Well, of course, the servant was devastated, at his wits' end. He fell to his knees, tears in his eyes. "My Lord, please be patient with me and I promise I will pay you everything I owe you."'

Jesus took a sip of water – he was good at building tension in his storytelling, and he waited for a minute while we all held our breath.

'The king felt sorry for the servant and told him that the debt was written off. Finished, gone, as if it had never been there!'

'Wow!' John breathed. 'Pretty rare kind of king, that one.'

'That's a great story,' James added.

'Ah, but it's only half the story,' Jesus told him. 'The servant was free and off he went. A couple of weeks later, this servant realised that one of the other servants in the household – a young chap at a lower level in the hierarchy – owed him a small amount, just a few denarii. He was incensed! He grabbed the poor guy, gripped him by the throat and ordered him to pay the debt there and then.'

'Can you guess what's coming?' Mary whispered to me.

'This lad fell to his feet and begged for mercy,' Jesus continued. 'But the servant – the one who had so very recently been freed of all debt by the king – refused to listen. He went straight to the authorities and had the boy thrown into prison, with orders that he should languish there until he could pay what he owed.'

'That's not fair!' I burst out, and everyone turned to stare at me. I felt the colour flood my cheeks, bit my lip. 'Sorry . . .'

'Esther speaks the truth,' Jesus said calmly. 'And the other servants in the household felt exactly the same. They went to the king and told him the whole story.'

He looked round at the group and his expression became serious.

'The king was incensed,' he said. 'He called the servant to him and really let rip. He demanded to know how it was that someone who had been treated so generously could go away and treat someone else so spitefully when what he should have done was show the same love and kindness as the king had shown to him.'

'So what happened?' someone asked.

'The king did exactly what my heavenly Father would do – he put the servant in prison until he could pay what he owed. God wants you – each and every one of you – to forgive your brothers and sisters in the same loving way that God has forgiven you.'

'Esther, you're as jumpy as frog in spring!' Susanna said after everyone had left. 'What's got into you?'

'Nothing, I'm fine,' I said. 'Are you going to bed now?'

'You're very eager to get rid of me,' she smiled. 'This wouldn't have something to do with what happened earlier, would it? Reuben?'

'I – promised – I can't say anything,' I stammered.

'Then I won't ask, but just tell me this,' she said. 'Is he in trouble? Does he need help?'

For a moment I didn't know how to reply. 'I think he just needs – us,' I murmured. 'He hasn't got anyone else. I guess he just feels lonely sometimes.'

'Then we must make sure that he knows he will never be alone for as long as we have anything to do with it,' Susanna smiled. 'Now I suggest that you go to the outhouse and tell him that.'

'You knew?' The words were out before I could feign ignorance.

'Esther, you've been shooting glances at that tumbledown building every five minutes since you got back,' she laughed. 'I'm not stupid. Now go – feed the guy and then get some sleep.'

She kissed my cheek. 'You are a dear, loving girl,' she said. 'Don't ever change.'

So what has that got to do with me?

1. Think of all the 'lost' people you know or have read about in newspapers or seen in television news or documentary programmes. What groups of people would you include as 'lost'? Do you think some of them want to be that way? What keeps people from wanting to be 'found'?

2. It is not until Reuben regains his voice that Esther realises that she doesn't know his whole story. Has anyone ever jumped to conclusions about you, or someone close to you – simply because they assume they know a lot more than they do? How does that make you feel? Have you ever made assumptions about someone's lifestyle or behaviour without knowing what led them to that place? How do you think a Christian should behave? Do you make assumptions about that too?

3. Reuben is afraid that Esther will tell 'everyone' that he is 'possessed'. Is his fear of people knowing how he is feeling and behaving worse than the actual self-harming? Is the damage that he imagines will be done to his reputation more frightening to him than his outbursts of frustration and pain? What would Jesus' response have been to him had he been with Esther?

4. The parable of the ungrateful servant has an interesting half-hidden question for us. Jesus says the king threw the ungrateful man into prison. Of course, this would have been a jail; but what other sorts of prison can people find themselves in as a result of their behaviour towards others? Or as a result of their unwillingness to stand up and be counted?

CHAPTER THIRTY

Could this be he?

Seth

'He's here. He's in Jerusalem.'

I didn't need to ask who my father was talking about. The expression on his face was enough. But out of politeness and to show that I was paying attention – something he frequently reprimanded me for not doing – I decided to speak.

'You mean – Jesus?'

My father nodded.

'I thought he would stay away,' he mused. 'In fact, his brothers were seen in town a few days ago but there was no sign of Jesus – not even when certain people made it their business to search him out.' He sighed. 'But now we hear that he is here – he has been spotted twice – and with the festival in full swing . . .' His voice trailed off, his face etched with concern.

It was the Feast of the Tabernacles, when we build booths with plaited branches and little thatched roofs. They can be seen everywhere; on the streets, in the squares, even on the roofs of some of the houses. We go to the Temple and offer sacrifices to give thanks for the autumn harvest and remember our ancestors' deliverance from Egypt. I love Tabernacles, and usually my father was in high spirits too, even in years when my mother's health has been particularly bad. Not this time; for several weeks he had been distracted and pensive, returning home from meetings of the Sanhedrin and shutting himself away with the Torah for hours on end. Sometimes his friend Archelaus would come with him and I would hear the low mutterings of conversation and then sudden shrill outbursts as my father protested at something Archelaus had said.

'I want you to come to the Temple with me today,' my father said briskly. 'You are old enough to attend more regularly and I want you to begin to listen to the discourses among my colleagues. You are born to a status and you must learn to grow into it.'

I sighed. All I wanted to be when I was old enough was a physician, a healer – someone who could make life better for those afflicted with disease and disability. I'd wanted it for as long as I could remember; I guess when I was little, I imagined being the person who would make my mother healthy again.

Perhaps the dream hadn't quite gone away.

When we reached the Temple, trumpets echoing over the street and the smell of bullocks' blood heavy in the air, it was clear that something unusual was going on, and before we had entered the inner court, Archelaus came hurrying towards us.

'He's there,' he declared. 'Jesus – teaching the people. And he's got them in the palm of his hand.'

'Then we must go and listen,' my father replied calmly.

As we pressed through the crush, Jesus' words rang out over the heads of the crowd.

'You wonder where I learned what I teach?' he asked. 'Let me tell you – none of it, not one single word, comes from me. It all springs from the One who sent me – my Father in heaven.'

At this a murmur rippled through the congregation and it wasn't all friendly.

'If you do the things I teach you to do, you will know intuitively that they are the truth,' he went on. 'Some people tailor their teaching to make themselves look good but that's not what I'm doing. I'm here to honour the one who sent me.'

'But the law . . .' someone began.

'Moses gave you God's law, right?' he shouted. 'And are you living it out in your lives? No way! Why are you trying to kill me? Is that in keeping with the law?'

'For goodness sake, the man's mad!' someone with a strange accent cried. 'Who's trying to kill him? It's ridiculous.'

At this point my father leaned towards me and spoke softly in my ear.

'It's all very well for visitors from miles away to say that, when they don't know the half of what's going on behind the scenes,' he whispered. 'But in truth, he's pretty near the mark. There is trouble brewing – serious trouble. If only Jesus would just back off, keep his own counsel – but I fear that's not the way he is.'

'We keep to the law of Moses,' Archelaus said, raising his hand to attract Jesus' attention. 'It is our life commitment to do so.'

Jesus sighed. 'Listen,' he said. 'You're all still in a stew because a few months ago I did something that you call miraculous on the Sabbath. Is that right?'

Archelaus nodded.

'But this is strange,' Jesus went on, 'coming from people who will circumcise a baby on the Sabbath because you say it is in keeping with the law of Moses . . .'

'It is,' Archelaus agreed.

'But circumcision involves just one part of the body,' Jesus argued. 'And yet you don't like it if I heal a man's whole body on the Sabbath! That makes no sense – because all you're doing is nitpicking. Try using your head and your heart to realise what is the right and God-given thing to do.'

Archelaus said nothing but turned and walked over to where we were leaning on a column. He shook his head and sighed.

'Nicodemus, we need to talk,' he urged, and taking my father's arm moved towards the doorway. My father nodded to me to follow them.

'I don't understand what's going on,' Archelaus began. 'I happen to know that there are people who want to be rid of Jesus – he was right about that. But he's here, out in the open, spouting a lot of contentious stuff – and where are they? Nowhere to be seen. And that must mean . . .' He shook his head as if in disbelief at his own thoughts. 'They must think that he really is the Messiah,' he sighed. 'And if they think that they are crazy – because we all know who Jesus is. Son of a builder from a one horse town. When the Messiah comes, no one will know him at all.'

My father was about to speak when Jesus' voice rang out loud and clear.

'There are those among you who think you know me, think you know where I come from, but you are so, so wrong!' he shouted.

Archelaus blanched and turned, gripping a balustrade as if to keep himself upright.

'I'm not my own boss, I don't decide what I teach and where I go and what I do,' Jesus went on. 'All that is the concern of my Father who sent me. You don't know him; I do because I come from him.'

At that a few people in the Temple surged forward towards Jesus, some touching his robe, others declaring that they believed in him.

'No Messiah could be more convincing or do more amazing things than you have done . . .'

'I believe, Master . . .'

At the outpourings from those who had been swayed by his teaching, my father and Archelaus exchanged worried glances.

'At least the majority are showing sense,' Archelaus said, inclining his head towards the clusters of Pharisees and lawyers who were gathering in corners and muttering among themselves. One of them broke away and came over to my father.

'We must meet,' he said. 'All of us and quickly. And we must get the chief priests to consult with us. This man is dangerous.'

'Don't you think that perhaps . . . ?' my father began tentatively.

'I think – as any sane person would – that this Jesus is a deceiver, a man set on taking advantage of the ignorant masses. Well, he has reckoned without us; we are far too on the ball to be deluded by some itinerant preacher!'

He glared at my father. 'We need to act now. This man must be stopped!'

The following day was the culmination of the Festival. My father and I were at the Temple early and had a good position to watch as the priests processed, waving the lulaws made from palm branches and willows tied with golden thread and carrying the etrog, the big yellow fruit that symbolised the fruit of the Promised Land. This being the seventh day of the festival, the procession circled the altar seven times, praying the *Hoshanos,* the prayer for God's blessing and that was when I spotted Jesus, and a group of his disciples, watching intently and reverently from one side.

We had just reached the point in the worship where one of the priests carried a vessel of water from the pool of Sloam up to the altar and poured it into the special basin containing wine. The water and wine flowed down a pipe which carried it to the Brook of Kidron by the eastern wall.

'And what does this symbolise?' my father murmured in my ear.

'Our prayer for the fall rains and our longing for the coming of the Messiah and his kingdom,' I recited dutifully – and that was when the sanctity of the moment was shattered.

'If anyone is thirsty, come to me!' Jesus cried out in a loud voice. 'Anyone who believes in me and acknowledges who I am will have streams of life-giving water flowing through him and spilling out of him – the Spirit of God in and through him, sustaining, empowering . . .'

I could feel my father stiffen at my side, as if he was expecting something terrible to happen.

'A man filled with this living water, this Spirit, is a blessing to the world.'

'He is the One, isn't he?' a man to our left muttered to himself. 'The Messiah – he has to be.'

'That's ridiculous,' his companion retorted. 'We all know that Christ will come from David's family, from Bethlehem where our ancestor David lived.'

By now the priests were looking far from priest-like – some of them had faces like thunder, others seemed incandescent that the attention of the congregation had moved from them to Jesus. One of the priests gestured to the Temple guards who were stationed all around the perimeter and one or two of them moved towards Jesus and then paused. He wasn't speaking now, but standing with his disciples, his eyes half closed in an expression of prayer and meditation. The guards turned, and one of them gestured to those nearby. Within moments they had marched out of the Temple.

'Phew!' I whispered to my father. 'I thought they were going to arrest him.

My father turned and gave me a long, hard stare. 'Seth,' he said, 'this is only the beginning. I want you to pray for me.'

'Why? I mean, of course I will but what do you mean?'

'I feel torn in two,' my father replied. 'I have known what I've worked for all my life – respect, position, a comfortable life. And I'm frightened of losing it all.'

'Why would you?' I asked in alarm. 'You haven't lost money, have you? Not like your cousin in Sepphoris?' That had been so shameful and if we were going to be reduced to begging charity from our relations . . .

'No, of course not!'

'Then what?'

'My whole life has been built on certainties,' he said. 'I have been certain of my role in society, certain of the wisdom of the Torah, certain that we – the Pharisees – were God's gift to our nation, the ones who knew how life should be conducted. But now . . .' He closed his eyes and sighed. 'I shouldn't be saying all this to you,' he went on. 'But you are my one and only son and you are now a young adult. I must speak to you as if you were older than your years.'

My chest swelled with pride. 'Go on,' I said. 'Tell me what I need to know.'

'It is hard for me to admit this,' he replied. 'But when I hear my colleagues talking about the trouble Jesus is causing, and how we have to take action very soon – I find myself wanting to stand up and shout at them to stop and think and listen!'

'So why don't you?'

'Because,' he said with a catch in his voice, 'your father is a coward.'

My father sent me home after that with instructions to tell the steward that he would be out all day and late into the night. I tried hard to remain awake until he returned but sleep overcame me and when I did wake up it was almost dawn.

Despite the early hour I could hear voices from my father's room. I slipped past my mother's room where she was still sleeping, and crept closer so that I could hear what was going on. I soon realised that there were several people in the room. I recognised my father's voice, of course, and Archelaus was there but the others were unknown to me.

'The guards will have their pay docked,' said one. 'They were supposed to bring Jesus to us and they failed!'

'He deluded them, just as he deludes everyone,' said another.

'It's clear that we are the ones who must act!' That was Archelaus, his voice shaking with anger. 'We can see things as they really are and it's our duty to deal with the man once and for all!'

I heard my father clear his throat. 'Hang on a minute,' he said. 'You know full well that our law – the law we represent and uphold – doesn't condemn a man without first hearing his side of the story?'

'For pity's sake man!' Archelaus stormed. 'Don't tell me he's turned your mind too? Surely you don't believe all this nonsense. Are you from Galilee too – are you as gullible as that rabble?'

I strained to hear my father's reply. He said nothing.

'Look at the facts,' Archelaus barked at him. 'Tell me this – does any prophet ever come from Galilee?'

'I think . . .' my father began.

'Think what you like!' one of the others shouted. 'We are leaving – and we will make sure that this matter is dealt with in the proper fashion – and fast. Thank you for your hospitality.'

This last remark was curt and sounded as if gratitude was the last thing the speaker felt. I ran quickly back into my room and feigned sleep. I was shaking with fury – how dare they speak to my father that way! I listened as the men left, and when I was sure that my father would be alone, I went to his room.

But he wasn't there. In fact he was nowhere in the house. Just then my mother awoke and called me and I had no choice but to go to her. All day I worried about what my father was doing and, ashamed as I am to admit it now, I took comfort from the fact that he had said he was a coward. I didn't believe it but if it meant he wouldn't get involved in arguments or get thrown out of the Sanhedrin, then I was glad.

All I wanted was for everything to carry on as it always had. For some reason, as the hours dragged by that day, I found myself thinking more and more of Esther and that little guy, Reuben. Esther had told me that the woman she worked for was totally devoted to following Jesus and I knew Reuben hung out with a couple of guys who seemed to be disciples. If Archelaus was right, and it was only ignorant uneducated people who believed what Jesus said, then how come the rich lady – Susanna, I think Esther called her – how come she was following him around the countryside instead of staying at home enjoying the comfortable lifestyle? It was easy to guess why Reuben was there; poor guy needed people to look out for him and besides perhaps he imagined Jesus would heal him, but rich women with servants and all the comforts they could possibly want had no need of a scruffy preacher with way-out ideas. Yet Esther said that Susanna thought his teaching would change the world.

All these thoughts were going round and round in my head the next time we went to the Temple. We were just outside when my father spotted Jesus sitting in the outer court, a group of disciples and townspeople gathered round him.

'I want to go and listen to what . . .' my father began, but his words were lost in a stream of cursing and shouting.

The teachers of the law and the Pharisees brought in a woman caught in adultery. They made her stand before the group and said to Jesus, 'Teacher, this woman was caught in the act of adultery. In the Law Moses commanded us to stone such women. Now what do you say?' They were using this question as a trap in order to have a basis for accusing him.

John 8:3-6

'Leave me alone, get off me!'

A group of Pharisees were manhandling a thin, raven-haired woman who was kicking and screaming like a banshee. Dragging her along in the dirt, they took her right up to where Jesus was sitting and flung her to the ground at his feet.

'This slut has been caught in the act of adultery,' one of them said. 'The law of Moses orders us to stone people like her. So tell us; what do you say about it?'

'What's adultery?' I asked my father.

'She's been with a man who is not her husband, a man who is already pledged to another,' he said abruptly. 'A sin indeed, a heinous sin! But where's the man – the law is that the man should be stoned too.' He paused. 'I have a horrible feeling my colleagues want to trap Jesus into saying something that will land him in deep trouble,' he sighed.

'So – what do you say?' one of the Pharisees repeated when Jesus didn't reply.

Jesus bent down and began writing in the dust with his finger.

'What's he writing?' I asked my father.

He shrugged. 'I don't know,' he said, 'but I'll tell you one thing. If he says the woman shouldn't be stoned, they'll have him for going against the law.'

At that moment, Jesus straightened up and looked at the woman. But still he didn't speak.

'Sir – what is your reply?' one of the older Pharisees, a man I'd seen many times at my father's house, demanded.

'If any one of you is completely without sin, then let him be the one to throw the first stone at her,' he declared, and then stooped down and continued scribbling in the dust. The woman tensed, her shoulders caving in, her head bowed and her hand clasped round her body in preparation for the first blow.

For a long moment, no one moved; it seemed as if the entire crowd was holding its breath. Then a couple of the older Pharisees shuffled off, then three more. Archelaus, who had arrived just after us, sniffed and turned, plodding slowly through the colonnade and out of sight. The younger men glanced at one another, and followed.

'Well, now,' Jesus said to the woman. 'What is your name?'

'Ziva,' she whispered.

'So Ziva, has no one condemned you?'

The woman, trembling from head to foot, swallowed a sob.

'No one, Master,' she stammered.

'Then neither do I,' he smiled. 'Go to your home – and remember, from now on, no more sinning.' He touched her on the shoulder and she looked up into his face. Then she knelt down and kissed his feet.

For some reason I wanted to cry.

After that I had to go to the rabbi for instruction on the Torah and when the lesson was over, all I wanted to do was get home and spend time with my friends. My father walked with me; since his illness his pace had been slower, and while I wanted to dash on ahead, I knew he took strength from having me at his side.

'An interesting morning,' he said as we made our way down the street away from the Temple. 'He called himself the light of the world.'

'What does that mean?'

'He says that we're all stumbling along in the dark and if we follow him, we'll see the light,' my father sighed. 'And you know what? He said something that makes me wonder if he isn't planning on . . . on . . .'

'On what?'

'On killing himself!'

'No! Why would he do that? He's a healer, he's . . .'

'He said he was going away – and believe me, in many ways, it would be good for everyone if he did. But then he said, that where he was going, none of us could follow.'

'That could just mean he was going to some foreign country . . .'

'No, I don't think so,' my father insisted. 'He said some really peculiar things. He said he wasn't of this world and told us that if we didn't believe that he is the person he claims to be, we would all die in sin.'

'But he can't talk to people like you, to members of the Sanhedrin, in that way!' I exploded. 'You're an upright citizen – no way are you sinful!'

My father paused, rubbing his side.

'Are you ill?'

'No, no, just a stitch,' he murmured. 'Let's sit for a moment.'

I sighed inwardly. At this rate, my friends would be off enjoying themselves before I was even halfway home.

'I didn't tell you this but the other day, Archelaus and some of the others asked me to sort out a problem,' he said. 'They brought a man to see me – he'd been blind since birth and now he can see, and he says it was Jesus who gave him back his sight.'

'Wow!' I gasped. 'How does he do those things?'

'Well in this case apparently he put mud on the man's eyes, and then washed it off and he could see. The guy swears that Jesus is a prophet; but some of my colleagues don't believe it. They said he was never blind in the first place. So I came up with an idea.'

'What was it?' The sooner my father got on with the story the sooner I could get home.

'I called in his parents and asked them what had happened. They were clearly terrified of being punished if they said the wrong thing so all they were prepared to say was that he was blind until now. As to how he got his sight back – they just told me to ask him.'

'Stalemate then?'

'Well, we got the guy back in front of us and Archelaus said that he should thank God and not Jesus because Jesus was an imposter. To which the man replied that he didn't know anything about who or what he was; all he knew was that he'd made him see again.'

My father rubbed his chin.

'I asked yet again, how did he do it? And oh my, did that guy let rip! He was clearly fed up with all our cross-questioning and he actually suggested that we were so keen to get the facts because we wanted to qualify to be Jesus' disciples! Well, you can imagine how that went down with some of them – they ranted and raved and said they were disciples of Moses and hadn't a clue about where Jesus had sprung from.'

'And what did you say?'

Suddenly my father looked shamefaced. 'Not a lot,' he admitted. 'The guy was in full flood by then, saying that if Jesus hadn't come from God he wouldn't be able to do the things he does. I'm ashamed to say that Archelaus and Simon and some of the others threw him out of the door – spat on him even.'

'And you?'

'Me? I did nothing,' he sighed. 'But I thought a lot. I keep remembering that night I went to find Jesus. He said so much that evening but it's that one sentence that keeps reverberating round and round in my head.'

'What? What was it he said?'

'Seth – I told you what it was, I told you to memorise it. Now think.

I struggled to remember all our conversations. 'Was it something about God loving the world and . . . I'm sorry, I can't remember.'

'He said, "*God so loved the world that he gave his one and only son, that whoever believes in him shall not perish but have eternal life.*" And when we get home I want you to write that down on your tablet and memorise it because . . .'

He shook his head thoughtfully.

'Because, do you know what? At the time, it was the thought of anyone giving up their only son that did it for me. You – my precious, wonderful boy – how could I ever sacrifice you? That story we hear of Abraham taking Isaac and doing what God said, offering him up to death – it's a story I've grappled with all my life. And now – I just wonder, I can't stop wondering.'

'Wondering?'

'Yes,' my father nodded. 'Wondering whether it can possibly be true. Whether Jesus truly is the Son of God.'

He looked at me, his eyes moist.

'After all, our whole faith is founded on the belief that the Messiah will come,' he said. 'So why are we all finding it so hard to believe that he might just come in our own time?'

So what has that got to do with me?

1. Why did the Pharisees only bring the woman caught in adultery to Jesus? Why not the man too?
2. Put yourself in the scene; what do you think Jesus might have written in the dust? Or did he draw something?
3. What does the fact that Jesus did not speak at once, or make a snap judgement, tell you about the way we should behave?
4. Would you have been able to cast the first stone? Do you know anyone who is without sin?
5. Seth's father admits he is a coward. Why was that a brave thing to do?

CHAPTER THIRTY-ONE

Now do you see?

Esther

'My dear Joanna – this is a surprise!'

Susanna embraced her friend and led her to a bench near the courtyard fire.

'But what are you doing here? You sent no word that you were coming.'

'I heard that you were ill,' Joanna said, 'and there was no way I was going to let you suffer without your friend at your side.'

'Ill?' Susanna frowned. 'I have admittedly had my usual seasonal joint pains but . . .'

'And of course,' Joanna interrupted, 'Chuza said that I must come to you at once. No one could question my presence here under the circumstances!'

'But my dear . . . oh! I see – you mean that . . .'

'I wanted to come – I'll tell you why in a minute – but I couldn't put Chuza in a risky position with Herod. At first it didn't seem to matter; Chuza was quite laid back about my following Jesus – indeed he expressed a lot of interest himself – but now . . .'

'Things are worse?'

Joanna rubbed the back of her neck wearily and took the flagon of wine I offered her.

'You know Jesus has been in Jerusalem?' she asked.

'Yes indeed, for the Feast,' Susanna nodded.

'The authorities are getting very edgy. So much has happened – I must tell you from the beginning.'

Susanna turned to me. 'Esther, go and prepare us some food, and call Mary,' she said.

Reluctantly I left the room, found Mary on the roof praying and then went to the kitchen. I strained my ears to catch the conversation from the inner room but could grasp only snatches; something about a blind man being made to see. That was nothing new, but I could tell from the urgency in Joanna's voice that there was more to come.

As I entered the room with a platter of honey-soaked pastries and a bowl of fruit, Joanna had clearly just delivered the punchline.

They brought to the Pharisees the man who had been blind. Now the day on which Jesus had made the mud and opened the man's eyes was a Sabbath. Therefore the Pharisees also asked him how he had received his sight. 'He put mud on my eyes,' the man replied, 'and I washed, and now I see.'

Some of the Pharisees said, 'This man is not from God, for he does not keep the Sabbath.'

But others asked, 'How can a sinner perform such signs?' So they were divided.

Then they turned again to the blind man, 'What have you to say about him? It was your eyes he opened.'

The man replied, 'He is a prophet.'

They still did not believe that he had been blind and had received his sight until they sent for the man's parents. 'Is this your son?' they asked. 'Is this the one you say was born blind? How is it that now he can see?'

'We know he is our son,' the parents answered, 'and we know he was born blind. But how he can see now, or who opened his eyes, we don't know. Ask him. He is of age; he will speak for himself.' His parents said this because they were afraid of the Jewish leaders, who already had decided that anyone who acknowledged that Jesus was the Messiah would be put out of the synagogue. That was why his parents said, 'He is of age; ask him.'

A second time they summoned the man who had been blind. 'Give glory to God by telling the truth,' they said. 'We know this man is a sinner.'

He replied, 'Whether he is a sinner or not, I don't know. One thing I do know. I was blind but now I see!'

Then they asked him, 'What did he do to you? How did he open your eyes?'

He answered, 'I have told you already and you did not listen. Why do you want to hear it again? Do you want to become his disciples too?'

Then they hurled insults at him and said, 'You are this fellow's disciple! We are disciples of Moses! We know that God spoke to Moses, but as for this fellow, we don't even know where he comes from.'

The man answered, 'Now that is remarkable! You don't know where he comes from, yet he opened my eyes. We know that God does not listen to sinners. He listens to the godly person who does his will. Nobody has ever heard of opening the eyes of a man born blind. If this man were not from God, he could do nothing.'

To this they replied, 'You were steeped in sin at birth; how dare you lecture us!' And they threw him out.

John 9:13-34

'No!' Susanna gasped.

'That's outrageous,' Mary cried.

'But it's true,' Joanna insisted. 'Those Pharisees threw that man out of the door because he would not deny that Jesus had restored his sight. But . . .'

She stretched out a hand and took one of the pastries. Joanna had a very sweet tooth and her size reflected her fondness for pastries.

'Apparently, word got back to Jesus that the Pharisees had behaved in that way, and he went and found the blind man. Well, not blind any more . . .'

'And what happened?' Mary asked.

'I wasn't there, and I've only heard this from my friend Veronica, but according to her Jesus asked the man whether he believed in the Son of Man?' She bit hungrily into her pastry. 'Well, of course, the poor man was at a loss,' she went on. 'He asked who the Son of Man was. That's when Jesus said "*you are speaking to him*". At that the guy knelt down and said that he believed. Veronica says that the look on his face was one of pure adoration.'

For a moment no one spoke, and then Mary broke the silence.

'Just imagine, he had never seen a living thing, and then he finds himself looking up into the face of the Messiah!'

'I sense there's more to your story,' Susanna said, touching Joanna's hand.

'There is,' Joanna sighed. 'Jesus was explaining that his purpose in coming into the world was to give sight to people who had been blind and to expose those who pretend to see the truth in everything as being in fact more blind that the sightless . . . Trouble is, he said it within earshot of a group of Pharisees – bigshots from the Sanhedrin.'

'And?' Mary asked.

'They were incandescent, as you might expect, demanding to know if Jesus was implying that they were blind. He said that if they were blind, it would be unfortunate but no fault of their own; but in reality because they went around claiming to see the truth so well, they would be held accountable for every failure in their lives.' Then she sighed again. 'I fear that from now on, the authorities won't rest until they have silenced Jesus.'

'That's ridiculous!' Mary stormed. 'That wonderful, loving, lovable man – how can anyone do anything other than want to spend the rest of their days hanging on his every word, attending to his every need, being his . . . companion, his helper . . .'

She jumped to her feet, knocking over her cup of wine and ran from the room.

Joanna and Susanna exchanged anxious glances. 'Best leave her for a while,' Susanna murmured as I hurried to get rags to clean up the mess. 'Jesus changed her life and she cannot bear to think of anyone harming a hair on his head.'

'Then before she comes back, I must tell you this,' Joanna said hastily. 'You know what Jesus is calling himself these days? The Good Shepherd. Of course, he wrapped it all up in one of his wonderful stories . . .'

'Tell us!' I had spoken before I realised it, but instead of looking annoyed, Susanna burst out laughing.

'Esther loves stories,' she explained to Joanna. 'She knows her Scriptures well, but she always adds little touches that I am sure come straight from that fertile imagination of hers!'

It was true. I always wanted to know the things that the clever prophets and storytellers didn't write down; what food did Deborah like, what jewellery did my namesake Esther wear and did Jael feel squeamish when she slammed the tent peg into Sisera?

'Sit down, Esther,' Susanna suggested, and turned to her friend. 'Go on, tell us the story.'

'Jesus told them to imagine a sheep pen,' Joanna began, 'and to visualise a man climbing over the fence instead of going through the gate. What kind of man would that be, he asked them.' She paused, looking at me.

'A sheep rustler, I guess,' I murmured, hoping it was the right answer.

'Exactly,' she replied. 'Jesus said that a real shepherd goes straight up to the gate, opens it and calls to the sheep, who recognise his voice at once. He knows every sheep by name, and they follow him to whatever pasture he leads them because they know his voice and trust him.'

'Just like we know Jesus and we go with him because we trust him,' Susanna commented.

'Got it in one!' Joanna smiled. 'Which is more than the Pharisees did. So he had to spell it out for them. First of all he said that he was the gate to the sheepfold; that anyone who goes through him to God will be cared for and cherished and find rich pasture. Those sheep rustlers are like people who are only interested in destruction – whereas he has come to give people real, empowering everlasting life.'

'Everlasting? Like – never dying?' I breathed.

'I think he means the life in heaven,' Joanna said. 'Although to be honest I'm not sure – I've so much still to learn.'

'Haven't we all?' Susanna said, and turned at the sound of a latch behind her. 'Mary! Come and join us – Joanna is telling us something of what Jesus was teaching.'

Mary slipped into the room and sat beside Susanna, glancing anxiously at the three of us.

'I'm sorry about . . .'

'There is nothing to be sorry for,' Susanna assured her. 'Joanna, go on, please.'

'Well, then Jesus said that he was the Good Shepherd, and not some hired hand who's in it for the money, and who would run a mile at the first sign of a wolf or some other predator threatening the sheep. The Good Shepherd, he said, knows the sheep individually and they know him. And then he said something that made my blood run cold.'

She glanced anxiously at Mary and then at Susanna.

'Go on,' Mary said softly but decisively. 'I need to hear whatever you have to say.'

'He said that he will always put his sheep first even if it means sacrificing his life,' she said. 'He said there were many sheep – by which I guess he meant people – not just the ones he's talking to these days. He wants to gather them to him so that there will be one huge flock, and one Shepherd – him.'

'But he doesn't need to put himself at risk to do that, does he?' There was a pleading tone to Mary's question.

Joanna bit her lip.

'He said it more than once – he said God loves him because he is so willing to sacrifice his life,' she murmured. 'But he said he also had the right to take up his life again – and to be honest, I don't know what he meant by that.'

Mary frowned. 'I don't get it,' she began.

'Neither did the people listening, if what Veronica says is true,' Joanna commented. 'In fact the crowd were split – half of them saying that Jesus was stir crazy and a maniac, and the other half saying that he sounded perfectly sane and besides, maniacs aren't in the habit of restoring sight to the blind.'

'He can do more than restore sight,' Mary asserted. 'He can make mad women sane, he can forgive sins that the priests say are unforgivable . . .'

'You're right,' Joanna said. 'That reminds me of something Chuza told me, something he'd heard from one of his cronies. There was a woman called Ziva . . .'

'Ziva! You know about Ziva!' I forgot everything I had ever been taught about etiquette and grabbed Joanna's hand. 'Tell me, tell me about her . . .'

The look on Joanna's face was one of pure horror. She swallowed hard, looked at Susanna, and grabbed another pastry as if desperate to put off the moment when she would be forced to speak.

'Esther has a sister called Ziva, and she has been searching for her for a long while,' Susanna explained. 'If you know anything . . .'

'Well, actually no, not much, in fact very little at all, just that – er – um . . .'

'Please, whatever it is, Madam, tell me, I beg of you!' I choked back the tears that were rising in my throat.

'Well, it might not be your sister, Ziva is a beautiful name, it could be anyone . . .'

'Just tell Esther what you know,' Susanna urged.

'Chuza told me that a woman who had, well, sinned was brought before Jesus and he said that anyone in the crowd who hadn't sinned once in their lives could be the first to throw a stone . . .'

I closed my eyes and held my breath. I knew the sins that demanded stoning. Not Ziva – not my big, beautiful sister . . .

'No one picked up a stone,' Joanna went on. 'They all drifted away and Jesus told her that he wouldn't judge her either. He just told her to go and never do it again.'

'And – where – did – she – go?' The words came out as sobs.

'My dear, I don't know,' Joanna said. 'Chuza just told me about it because he was amazed at the power that Jesus had to make that crowd search their own consciences. But I'll tell you what: when I go back to Jerusalem, I will ask if he knows more. Would that help you?'

I nodded. 'Thank you,' I whispered. 'Anything he knows, anything at all – please tell me.'

'I will, I promise,' she said.

'And now,' Susanna yawned, 'it is time for sleep. Now that the Feast is over, Jesus may well come back to us and we must be ready – ready to do whatever he asks of us. We can't do that if we're half asleep!'

'I – well, I'm not sure that he'll be back this way, at least not yet,' Joanna ventured.

Mary frowned. 'What aren't you telling us? What do you know?'

'This is just between us,' Joanna cautioned. 'From what I hear Jesus chose seventy of the guys who had been following him these last few months and sent them out into Judea. Cleopas was among them – you remember, Jesus' uncle? Their job is to prepare the way for him.'

After this the Lord appointed seventy-two others and sent them two by two ahead of him to every town and place where he was about to go. He told them, 'The harvest is plentiful, but the workers are few. Ask the Lord of the harvest, therefore, to send out workers into his harvest field. Go! I am sending you out like lambs among wolves. Do not take a purse or bag or sandals; and do not greet anyone on the road.

'When you enter a house, first say, "Peace to this house." If someone who promotes peace is there, your peace will rest on them; if not, it will return to you. Stay there, eating and drinking whatever they give you, for the worker deserves his wages. Do not move around from house to house.

'When you enter a town and are welcomed, eat what is offered to you. Heal the sick who are there and tell them, "The kingdom of God has come near to you." But when you enter a town and are not welcomed, go into its streets and say, "Even the dust of your town we wipe from our feet as a warning to you. Yet be sure of this: The kingdom of God has come near." I tell you, it will be more bearable on that day for Sodom than for that town.'

Luke 10:1-12

'They're going to Judea?' Susanna repeated. 'But . . .'

'I have a nephew,' Joanna confided. 'He's been following Jesus too – and he's one that has been chosen. But please, keep that to yourself.'

'Of course,' Susanna murmured.

'Jesus thinks that time is running out,' Joanna went on. 'He says there is a huge harvest of souls to be reaped but not enough people to do the harvesting. Uriah, my nephew, has been teamed up with a guy called Jacob; I offered to fund them for the trip, but Uriah refused. He said that Jesus told them they were to take nothing with them.'

'Nothing at all?' Mary gasped.

Joanna shook her head. 'Not even a spare pair of sandals.' Suddenly she laughed. 'I confess I am finding it hard to imagine Uriah in that kind of situation – especially as Jesus was quite firm about how they were to behave. They were to eat everything they were offered, whether it was kosher or not – and my nephew is the most finicky eater I've ever met!'

'And what are they to do in Judea?' Susanna asked.

'Heal the sick and teach about the kingdom of God,' Joanna said, her face clouding. 'I fear for them – I fear for Jesus. I believe he is who he says he is – but I also believe that he's heading for serious trouble.'

'God will protect him,' Mary declared. 'He won't let any harm come to him.'

'I hope you're right,' Joanna sighed.

'We must go,' Susanna said suddenly. 'First thing tomorrow. We must travel to Judea and join up with Jesus. If things are as you say, he's going to need all the support he can get.'

I was up the following morning before dawn. I did my chores as fast as I could and then sped down the lake shore path to the fishing area. Just as I had hoped, Reuben was there watching as the fleet came back with the night's catch.

'We're going away,' I gabbled. 'To Judea – and I don't want to go!'

'Judea? Why would you go there?'

'That's where Jesus is heading,' I told him. 'Joanna said so – and she said that people were out to get him, and that means anything could happen and Susanna's adamant we have to help him but I . . .'

'Hey, slow down!' Reuben said. 'So are you saying Andrew and Peter and the others won't be coming back to Capernaum?'

'I guess not,' I replied. 'Where Jesus goes, they go, right?'

'True,' he nodded. 'And I want to be where they are. I haven't finished with Jesus yet – there's so much more . . . anyway, do you reckon Susanna would let me tag along with her?'

'Yes, yes, I'm sure she would – oh Reuben, I'm so pleased you're going to come too!' I squeezed his hand but to my surprise, he pulled away and wandered to the water's edge, ready to help beach the incoming boats. I followed him.

'Reuben? What's the matter?'

'So what about Caleb? Have you managed to get him to change his mind? Is he coming along too?'

'I don't know,' I shrugged. 'I haven't seen him for a couple of days.'

'You haven't?' Reuben sounded genuinely surprised. 'But he said . . .' he checked himself.

'And change his mind about what?' I demanded. 'What are you on about?'

'He's been in the weirdest mood,' Reuben admitted. 'A couple of days ago he said that he reckoned he's grown out of this following Jesus nonsense – his words, not mine – and he was all for going off to Sepphoris and getting a job on one of the building sites there.'

'You think he's gone?' I burst out. 'That's terrible.'

'Would it worry you if he had?' Reuben retorted.

'Of course it would,' I confessed. 'He's one of us, he . . .'

'What you mean is you fancy him!'

I took a step back, aghast. 'Reuben, that is so not true!' I exclaimed. 'How dare you suggest such a thing?'

'But I thought . . .'

'No you didn't, you didn't think at all!' I stormed. 'Caleb's just a friend, the guy who helped me get away from . . . from my job!'

'And you're really not keen on him?'

'How many more times?' I shouted. 'If I'm keen on anyone – and I'm not saying I am – it's certainly not him!'

Reuben dropped his eyes to the floor and kicked the dirt with the toe of his sandal.

'Sorry,' he muttered. 'I thought – well, I assumed that if he went off to Sepphoris, you'd go with him.'

'Then you don't know me at all,' I retorted grumpily. 'Do you imagine I'd leave Susanna after all she's done for me? Give up the chance of sticking close to Jesus?'

'I guess not,' Reuben admitted. 'But then again, I never thought Caleb would either.'

He looked so downcast that I couldn't stay angry with him.

'You're an idiot,' I grinned. 'And I'll tell you something – if Caleb has left for Sepphoris, my guess is he'll soon get tired of being on his own. He'll want to come back and join the gang. After all, everyone wants to belong somewhere, don't they?'

As I spoke, an image of Ziva running down that alleyway in Capernaum flashed into my mind.

'Joanna's heard news of my sister,' I blurted out, and told Reuben everything she had said. 'I wish I could find her.'

Reuben grinned. 'Well, my guess is your chances have just soared,' he said.

'How come?'

'Esther, think about it,' he urged. 'Jesus forgave her for whatever it was she'd done, right?'

I nodded.

'She escaped stoning, yeah?'

I nodded again.

'If you were in her shoes, having gone through all that, what would you do?'

'Stick as close to Jesus as I possibly could,' I said and suddenly I got what he was trying to say.

'You mean, she might even now be wherever he is,' I gasped. 'And we're going to meet him and . . .' I grabbed Reuben and hugged him which wasn't polite but right then I didn't care.

'Oh Reuben,' I cried. 'I might find her. I might find Ziva. Do you think she'll recognise me? No, of course she won't because she hasn't seen me since I was four years old. What if she doesn't want to know me? What if . . . ?'

'Esther, stop!' Reuben laughed. 'Let's just find her first and worry about the rest of it later. My bet is that she'll be over the moon to see you. Like you said, everyone wants someone to belong to.'

So what has that got to do with me?

1. What qualifications did the seventy sent out by Jesus possess? University degrees? Teaching experience? Debating skills? What sort of people does Jesus want to work for him? What qualities do you value most in a teacher or youth leader?
2. Why didn't Jesus want his disciples to 'greet' people along the road? Was he being unfriendly?
3. Why do you think he ordered them not to take spare clothing or possessions with them?
4. 'Everyone wants to belong somewhere.' What does belonging to a church family give you? If you don't belong to one as yet, what do you imagine it would be like? What encourages you to find out more? What puts you off and why?

CHAPTER THIRTY-TWO

Telling it like it is

Reuben

I didn't think much of Judea. It was a rocky, barren sort of place, not nearly as lush or fertile as Galilee. The local people didn't seem particularly friendly either but being back with Andrew, Philip and the others made up for it. Peter was bursting to have news of his wife and daughter and there were tears in his eyes when I told him that little Ruth could now recite several of the psalms and knew her numbers and letters better than some of the village children twice her age.

'And our father?' James asked. 'Is Zebedee coping?'

'He misses you,' I said. 'But your nephews are working on the boats now and Salome's cousin is helping out. And I said you would be bound to be home soon.'

The brothers exchanged glances.

'Maybe,' John murmured. He might as well have denied it outright.

The first day we were back with Jesus something happened that turned out to be extremely embarrassing for me.

We were near to Bethany, a small village on the edge of the bleak Judean desert, close to the Mount of Olives, and the crowd had split into groups, clustering round fires, cooking food and sharing stories. I didn't want to move far away from Andrew, and Esther, who had spent all day searching the crowd for Ziva, was looking tired and despondent so I suggested that we should find a place on the edge of a group of about 200 people, some of them familiar to me but many of them strangers. Susanna had given Esther food and drink, which she shared with me, and gradually the colour came back into her cheeks and she relaxed. I couldn't help thinking that if only I had a decent body and arms long enough to hug her . . . but there was no point in thinking of her that way.

Among them was a group of scholarly looking men who had spent some time whispering among themselves. Suddenly one of them, who was dressed like a lawyer, stood up and approached Jesus.

'Teacher,' he said, 'tell me what I have to do to achieve this eternal life you speak of?'

His companions sniggered under their breath.

'Now you tell me,' Jesus replied. 'What does the law tell you to do?'

'Love the Lord your God with all your heart and with all your soul and with all your strength and with all your mind,' the man chanted in a somewhat bored voice. 'And love your neighbour as yourself.'

'Exactly,' Jesus nodded. 'Do all that and you will have eternal life.'

'That's all very well,' the man persisted. 'But who is my neighbour?'

Jesus smiled, took a swig of wine, wiped the remains of the stew from his mouth and leaned back against a rock.

'OK, I'll tell you a story.'

At that everyone shuffled closer, and some of the nearby groups abandoned their places and came over to listen.

'There was man who was making the journey from Jerusalem to Jericho when he was attacked by robbers. They tore his clothes off his back, beat him senseless and left him there, half dead.'

My mind flashed back to a little boy, abandoned by the roadside in the dark, sobbing with fear.

'A bit later,' Jesus went on, 'a priest came along and when he saw the man lying there, covered in blood and motionless, he crossed to the furthest side of the path and went on his way.'

'How could someone do that?'Esther whispered in my ear.

'Quite easily,' I replied bitterly, remembering all those people who must have heard my cries and taken no notice.

'Then a Levite priest came along,' Jesus continued, 'and he too took one look at the prostrate man and went on his way without even checking to see whether he was still alive. But then, just before dusk, a Samaritan turned up on the scene.'

At that, the crowd began muttering, some making lewd gestures with their hands and others using words that even I hadn't heard before. Samaritans, as we all knew, hated us Jews as much as we loathed and despised them – it had been that way since forever. Jesus held up his hand and the crowd fell silent.

'This man from Samaria went up to the man and knelt down beside him. When he saw how badly injured he was, he was overcome with pity for him. He took oil and wine from his saddlebag and cleansed the man's wounds, bandaging them up as best he could. Then he lifted the man onto his own donkey, and led him along the road to the nearest inn.'

I could feel my throat tightening, and tears filling my eyes. Suddenly I was that wounded man – I could feel the pain of the injuries, sense the fear coursing through his body, almost smell the drying blood oozing from his open wounds. I saw myself, that little boy alone, hurting, bleeding, scared of dying, but terrified of even trying to find his way home.

'This Samaritan stayed with the man all night, and the following morning he gave the innkeeper a sizeable amount of money with the instruction to take care of the wounded man. He promised that if the money ran out, the innkeeper would be reimbursed as soon as the man from Samaria came back on his return journey.'

'Reuben?' Esther touched my hand as tears coursed down my face. 'Reuben, it's OK . . .'

I turned away, rubbing my hand across my face. Jesus took another sip of wine, and looked at the man who had asked the question.

'So come on, tell me,' he challenged. 'Which of the three men that came down that road was a true neighbour to the guy who had been mugged?'

The lawyer paused. 'The one who treated him with kindness,' he replied.

Jesus nodded. 'Now you go and do the same,' he said.

He turned to take a barley cake from the basket at his side and as he did so his eyes met mine. His outline was blurred through the mist of my tears, but I could see that slowly, very slowly, he nodded. And I knew that he understood.

'Master, may I ask you something?'

Where I found the courage from, I don't know, but I hadn't slept all night and I knew that I had to find an answer to the things that were troubling me.

'Of course, Reuben,' he said. 'What is it?'

'You taught us all how to pray, but it doesn't work,' I gabbled. 'I mean, I'm really grateful, I can speak and that's down to you, but there are so many things I want and . . .'

'Stop right there, Reuben,' he laughed. 'Listen to me. Imagine for a moment that you had a friend and he came to you in the middle of the night asking you to lend him some food because one of his mates had turned up at his house and there was nothing for him to eat. And suppose you said that you couldn't be bothered because it was late, and everyone was asleep – what do you think might happen?'

I frowned. 'If this pretend friend was anything like the people I know, he'd batter the door down until I gave in.'

Jesus nodded. 'Exactly!' he said punching the air. 'You've got it in one. He'd get up and give the man what he wanted.'

'So do you mean . . . ?'

'What I mean is this,' Jesus said gently. 'Never give up on talking to my Father – and when you do, get straight to the point. Don't beat about the bush – ask for what you need and it will be given to you.'

I wanted to tell him that it sounded great but that in practice life didn't quite work out that way.

'Reuben, everybody who asks for God to fill their lives, will receive his Spirit; everyone who seeks the truth, will be given the insight to understand it. They will have what they need.'

'What they need,' I heard myself repeat. Need, not want, I thought.

Jesus smiled as though he could read my mind.

'You're getting there,' he said. 'Tell me, if Peter's little girl asked him for a plate of fish, do you think he'd serve up a snake?'

'Of course not,' I exclaimed.

'If a kid from your village asked you for an egg, would you stuff a spider in her mouth? Of course you wouldn't! So don't you think that if people who are human, with faults and failings, treat their own with love and care, God will do even more?'

I took a deep breath.

'I want to trust, Master, I really do,' I admitted. 'It's just that sometimes – with these legs and being so small and the twisted feet . . .'

'Reuben, you have your voice,' Jesus said gently. 'It is my gift to you. Stay close to me, listen, remember – and then use that voice in my service and you will receive more than you could ever dream of. Trust me.'

And with that, he walked away.

'I saw you talking to the Master earlier,' Andrew said to me as darkness fell. 'What was he saying?'

I repeated our conversation word for word; I had been thinking of little else all day.

'Use your voice to serve him – that's so right,' Andrew burst out. 'You're such a shining example of what he's teaching and it's only just registered with me that you're the very sort of person that can make people see the truth.'

I stared at him gobsmacked. 'Andrew, have you been drinking?' I asked. 'You know how people are with me – they even assume my brain is as twisted as my body!'

'Oh forget all that!' he interrupted. It was easy for him to say; he didn't have to live in my body.

'Think about it,' Andrew said, staring into my eyes, an earnest expression on his face. 'How long is it since you cut yourself?'

I felt as if I had been hit by a boulder. The shock of his words, exposing what I had believed to be a secret from the whole world except for Esther, made me physically jump backwards.

'Hey, it's OK,' Andrew said. 'I'm not judging you. I just . . .'

'How did you know?' For the first time in days my voice was a croak, just as it had been when it first returned.

'I saw the scars, I noticed blood on your clothes whenever you'd disappeared for a while and I'm not stupid,' he replied. 'The first time I ever met you I saw the pain in your eyes. I guess that's why I wanted to make sure you came to Bethsaida and hung around. So I could try to make things easier for you.'

'You did – you have,' I stammered. 'And I haven't cut myself for a long time, not since . . .' I paused, '. . . I guess not since I really got in with this crowd,' I finished. I didn't mention the one lapse – I just wanted to forget that.

'It's not getting in with the crowd that does it,' Andrew smiled. 'It's being close to Jesus, listening to him, learning, trying to understand. That's what has made all the difference to me.'

'But you've been sure of everything from the beginning,' I ventured.

'Oh, I've been sure that Jesus is the Messiah, but no way have I been sure of anything else,' he confessed. 'Least of all where I slot in to his mission.'

'But you're a disciple, one of the original ones,' I protested. 'You're with him 24/7, you're in on everything and . . .'

'Not everything,' he smiled. 'The thing is, I'm not like my brother, or like those sons of thunder James and John. They are up front and ready for anything. Peter's been bouncing with confidence ever since he was a kid; whereas me, I am more cautious, afraid of messing up and getting things wrong. My mother always says that I am the watcher and the waiter, and Peter's the one who rushes ahead without a backward glance.'

He chuckled.

'But we're not meant to be talking about me,' he remarked. 'Don't you get it? Jesus is changing you bit by bit and when he does that, he does it for a reason.' He held my gaze. 'Reuben, I reckon Jesus has work for you to do,' he said. 'Work that only you can do. And before you say another word, it has nothing to do with being clever or handsome or athletic. It's about sharing what you know in your heart with people who haven't been lucky enough to get the message yet. That's what keeps me going.'

He rested a hand on my shoulder. 'Why do you think he chose to restore your voice?' he asked. 'Why not your legs? Your arms?'

'I don't know, but I want to ask him to . . .' but before I could finish the sentence, he gripped my arm.

'I'll tell you why – it's so you could speak out to people just like you; people who've known pain and hurt and isolation. People who think they don't matter, who imagine God hasn't got time for them and their lives. You know what it's like not to know Jesus and you know what it's like to have found him. Isn't that something worth sharing – whatever it takes?'

Instinctively I looked at my hands. The palms were free of scratches. Slowly I lifted my sleeves. Old scars were visible, yes – but no new livid cuts, no crusting blood, no deep nail prints in the skin. That last time I had banged my head and injured my body seemed like another lifetime.

In that moment I knew that for as long as Jesus was near, I would be safe. He had given me my voice and now, without my even realising it, he had taken away my demons.

'How will I know who to talk to about what he's done?' I asked Andrew.

'You'll know,' he assured me. 'The Spirit – God's Holy Spirit – will show you.'

For the next few days, I kept as close to Jesus as I could. There was an enormous crowd following him, but he seemed more keen on talking to the inner set of disciples; and Andrew made sure I was with him all the time.

The amazing thing was that Jesus didn't seem to mind one little bit.

'I want to talk you as dear friends,' Jesus said one morning. 'There are a lot of religious bullies about and it's important that you don't keep silent through fear of them – or indeed, be tempted to speak in half-truths to avoid confrontation. It's true they may want to kill you . . .'

At that my stomach lurched. He said it in such a matter of fact way as if he was speaking about a temporary hiccup.

'. . . but what else can they do? Your soul, the very essence of you, they cannot touch. Just focus on God because it is he who holds your life here and now, and your life in the future, firmly in his hands.' He caught sight of me and smiled. 'What do people pay for five sparrows? A couple of pennies, no more – yet God doesn't overlook one of them. Each one of you is worth far more than sparrows, and your Father in heaven knows every hair on your head.'

'Or in the case of Thaddeus all the bald patches,' someone joked.

'It's hard, Lord,' one of the newer disciples said. 'These Pharisees and lawyers can be pretty intimidating; you never know how to respond to them. Sometimes it's easier to say nothing.'

Jesus smiled. 'If you stand up for me among all the people you come across every day, the Son of Man will stand up for you in the presence of God's angels. But if you pretend that you don't know me, then how can you expect me to defend you? Saying things against me simply because you lack understanding is something that can be forgiven; but attacking God's Holy Spirit won't be tolerated.'

'But the Pharisees . . .' the man urged.

'Don't worry about how you're going to defend yourselves in front of the authorities,' Jesus urged. 'When the time comes for you to speak up, the Holy Spirit will put the right words into your mouth.'

'I need help with words, Master,' someone else called out. 'My brother has been left some property and no matter how much I argue with him, he wants it all for himself. Will you tell him to split it with me, because he won't listen to me? I'm not an articulate man and . . .'

Jesus sighed and shook his head. 'I'm not here to act as judge over property issues,' he retorted. 'Besides, there are more important things in life to concern yourselves with than material possessions. Did I ever tell you the story of the rich farmer?'

'No, master – tell us!'

'This man owned some highly fertile land that produced an excellent crop. In fact the yield was so great that the man's barns weren't big enough to store the harvest. So he came up with what he thought was a great idea. He decided to pull down the barns that he did have and build bigger and better ones, so that he could stash away not only the crops but everything he owned, everything new that he purchased, and keep it all safe.'

'Sensible,' someone muttered.

'You think so?' Jesus challenged him. 'That's certainly what the farmer thought. He assumed that with so many good things stored up he could sit back, take life easy – eat, drink and be merry. In short, he thought he was in charge of his whole life! But . . .'

He paused and glanced round at his audience. I'd noticed it before – the way he made people wait for the punchline.

'But God had other ideas,' he finished. 'That very night the man would die – and then what good would all his earthly wealth be to him? Let that be a lesson to any of you who are more keen to store up possession for yourselves rather than concentrate on the inner riches that please God.'

'That's all very well,' I heard someone say, 'but is he telling us to be foolhardy? To spend everything we have and not bother to plan for our futures?'

'I've told you before not to worry about what you're going to eat or how many clothes you have to wear,' Jesus said. 'But I'll say one thing more; God knows your everyday needs and he will supply them. Your needs, remember; not every last trivial thing that takes your fancy.'

He cleared his throat.

'What you should do is sell all the surplus – all that dross you weigh yourselves down with but don't really need – and give the money you raise to those who have nothing. That way you will gain something that will never wear out, run out or break down – a place for yourselves in heaven.'

'That's all very well for rich guys,' I muttered to Andrew, 'but I haven't got any surplus – everything I earn goes on food and . . .'

'Well, that just emphasises what I was saying earlier, doesn't it?' Andrew chuckled. 'Your gift to people will be speaking out about your journey. It's no good, Reuben, you can't avoid it – that's what you have to do!'

So I did. Or at least, I tried. Whenever I saw someone staring at me – and believe me, that happened at least ten times a day – I would go up to them and smile. 'I am pretty odd looking, aren't I?' That was my opening gambit and it always took them by surprise.

Nine times out of ten, they would stammer or blush or simply turn away. 'Don't worry,' I would continue, still smiling. 'I'm used to being stared at but at least now I can tell you what it's like to be me. Until I met Jesus, I was dumb. Mute. Totally without speech.' That usually got a response.

'Jesus worked a miracle on you? What did it feel like? Did it hurt?'

Quite often, there would be the other unspoken question, the one you could read in the way their eyes scanned my body.

'Yes, he gave me my voice and no, he hasn't made me tall, or given me a straight pair of legs,' I would say. 'But he's . . .' And this is the bit I had to work on, because to begin with I usually felt like crying when I even thought the words, let alone spoke them.

'But he's sorted out my heart,' I would say softly. 'He's driven out the darkness that was always there and now I feel like a regular boy even if I don't look like one.'

It took a whole week of speaking to people like that before I could finish our chats the way I wanted to. 'Now I know, I really do, that Jesus is the Messiah, the Son of God.'

So what has that got to do with me?

1. Jesus told the lawyer to love his neighbour as himself. What does that really mean? What would you always do for yourself without a second thought? Are you prepared to do the same for your neighbour? Do you ever 'beat yourself up' over your shortcomings? How do you view the shortcomings and mistakes of your friends?

2. In the time of Jesus, the road from Jerusalem to Jericho was notorious for its danger and difficulty and was known as the 'Way of the Blood' because of the blood that was often shed on it as a result of muggings by robbers. What would be a parallel place in your city or town today? What protection do we have that first-century Jews couldn't benefit from?

3. What sacrifices might we have to make in order to love the Lord our God with all our hearts and minds and souls?

4. What is 'the truth'? How can we find out the truth amidst all the lies, and spin, and jargon that is part of modern life today? Do you think we know the truth through our brains or our hearts or both? Do you always believe people who are in positions of authority because of what they say? Or because of the way they act?

5. The author imagines Jesus telling Reuben to trust him. It's not always easy to trust God especially when our prayers seem to go unanswered or when things turn out the complete opposite of what we planned and hoped for. How do you think you could be helped to trust in God? And when we really feel that we can't trust him or anyone else, what should we do?

6. Andrew didn't tell Reuben that he knew he self-harmed for a long time. Why do you think that was? What did Andrew do that was a lot more helpful than confronting him? Why do you think Andrew admitted it to Reuben now? What can that teach us about helping friends in need?

7. Andrew says he is sure that Jesus is the Messiah, but he's not sure where he 'slots in' to his mission. Knowing and admitting that Jesus is Lord is what matters: he'll show you what to do when the time is right. How might he show you or any of your friends the plan he has for you?
8. Not everyone feels comfortable talking out loud about what Jesus has done for them. In what other ways can you bear witness to his effect on your life?

CHAPTER THIRTY-THREE

Going back, going forward

Caleb

When I left the others, I didn't do what I told Reuben I planned to do. I didn't go to Sepphoris. I went back to my childhood home. I went back to Bethany.

It took several days, partly because I didn't hurry; I was far too nervous about actually arriving there for that. Sometimes I walked, occasionally I hitched a lift on a cart. And all the time I asked myself just what I thought I was doing. I had always vowed that I would never return, that I would put those awful memories behind me and get on with making something of my life. And if it hadn't been for Jesus, that's what I would have done.

By now I could have risen to under steward in the household at Cana, or perhaps found work in a larger establishment. I'd left all that in order to learn to be like Jesus and that hadn't happened. Oh, he was a great guy; his miracles were amazing for those who were healed – but what of people like me? I didn't have a withered limb or ugly sores; he couldn't see the pain inside me that never went away, no matter how hard I pretended to be a cool, in charge kind of guy. Or maybe he could – maybe he saw the anger and the guilt; maybe he knew that I'd killed someone and that was why he didn't take me on as a disciple. Whatever. The only way I was going to get any peace was to go back to Bethany and face my father.

Just thinking of him made my heart race. The more kindly of our neighbours used to say that his rages were due to his poor health, to some sickness of his mind; and certainly after my mother died giving birth to Kizia, his bouts of illness and his violent temper became more frequent. I knew that when I saw him, he would probably hit me, hurl abuse at me and curse me to hell and back; but he wasn't the only one who was angry. I needed to tell him that I had done my best – day after day, week after week, when he'd left me to care for Kizia, to buy, or more often steal, food, or beg a few leptons from kindly passers by. I needed him to know that the reason I went in search of my mate Joshua that day was because Kizia and I hadn't eaten for three days and Josh's grandmother always took pity on us, even though she just about scraped a living from her scrubby patch of land herself and had to care for Josh and his brother Saul who lay day after day on his mat, as helpless as a newborn baby despite his six years.

I needed to let him know that it had been the sound of Kizia's wailing that had made me snap and call her a crybaby, but it wasn't really directed at her. It was aimed at him, my father, the man who should have been providing for us and keeping us safe. When he was in a good mood, he would sing to Kizia, cuddle her and tell her she looked just like our mum. Me he just ignored, but that was OK. It was better than the alternative.

Maybe if I could get him to see that I'd done my best, he would forgive me. And if he forgave me, perhaps the nightmares would stop and then the pain inside would go away. Maybe.

My heart began pounding as I approached our house – and then I stopped dead in my tracks. It had been falling down when I lived there, but now it was almost a ruin. It stood on the outskirts of the village, a half furlong from the nearest neighbour. Tall grasses choked what had once been the outside cooking area; the walls were crumbling and the roof had caved in. I ventured closer; there was no furniture inside, although in truth there had been precious little in the past. Two chickens were clucking in what had once been the sleeping area and the carcass of a dead bird lay in the doorway. There was no sign of a fire, just a few twigs burnt to charcoal in one corner. The place looked as if no one had lived there for months.

'Hello?'

I wheeled round, heart in my mouth at the sound of a deep male voice – and just as quickly, relaxed. It was Lazarus, one of the most popular men in the village who used to teach us children our letters.

'Lazarus, sir,' I began. 'You won't remember me but . . .'

'Is it – are you little Caleb? Well, not so little now but . . .'

'Yes, it's me,' I nodded, holding my breath.

Lazarus clasped my hand and pumped it up and down. 'So you have come home at last? May the good Lord be praised!' Then he glanced round at the ruin. 'I'm sorry – this place, it's not as it was . . .'

'My father – is he . . . ?'

'Dead? Yes,' he said. 'Last year.'

To my horror, I broke into sobs.

'Dear boy, I put that so badly – I should have been more sensitive. To lose a parent . . .'

'No, no, it's not that, I'm pleased he's dead,' I wept. 'Except that now I can't tell him what it was like, I can't get him to see that I never meant to be a murderer and that means I won't get forgiven and I can't go back to Jesus and . . .'

'Jesus? You've been with the Messiah?'

His words stopped the flow of my tears.

'You know about him?' I asked.

'Know about him? He's a dear friend,' Lazarus laughed. 'But come, first things first. You must be weary and hungry no doubt. My sisters – you remember them? Mary and Martha?'

I nodded. 'They gave me cake sometimes,' I smiled.

'Well, no doubt there will be cake today,' he replied. 'And I know they will be delighted to see you. Now come.'

'Now tell us,' Martha urged, after I had eaten my fill of goat meat stew and fig pastries, 'where have you been all these years? What have you been doing? Who has cared for you?'

'My brother tells us you have spent time with Jesus,' Mary broke in. 'He was here just a few days ago, you know.'

As Jesus and his disciples were on their way, he came to a village where a woman named Martha opened her home to him. She had a sister called Mary, who sat at the Lord's feet, listening to what he said. But Martha was distracted by the all the preparations that had to be made. She came to him and asked 'Lord, don't you care that my sister has left me to do the work by myself? Tell her to help me!' 'Martha, Martha,' the Lord answered, 'you are worried and upset about many things, but only one thing is needed. Mary has chosen what is better, and it will not be taken away from her.'

Luke 10:38-42

'Jesus was here? In Bethany?' I spluttered.

'He ate with us, and talked with us,' Mary said.

'He ate and talked with *you*,' Martha butted in. 'And he wouldn't have eaten at all if I hadn't been slaving away in the kitchen.'

'Now, now,' Lazarus interrupted. 'Remember what Jesus said; listening to him was the most important thing that day . . .'

'Huh!' Martha muttered. 'That's as may be but I didn't see him refusing the lentil stew and it doesn't cook itself, you know.' Suddenly she broke into a broad grin. 'But I guess he's right,' she admitted. 'I do get myself in a fluster when guests come. I just like everything to be perfect. Now come on, Caleb, tell us what has been happening.'

I told them about my time in Cana, about leaving the job to follow Jesus and about meeting Esther.

'Esther, eh?' Lazarus said with a twinkle in his eye. 'You blushed when you mentioned her name.'

'No way!' I retorted. 'She's just – a girl. Besides, she fancies this idiot called Seth . . .'

'Ah, so I am right,' Lazarus laughed. 'You do like her. Anyway, carry on.'

'And then there's this guy, Reuben,' I began, and told them the whole story from the very first day in Capernaum, right up to Reuben getting his voice back, and me being trampled by the pig.

'So what brings you back here?' Martha asked in between darting back and forth to the kitchen to replenish the water pitcher or check on the bread oven. 'Why have you left Jesus and your friends?'

'Because Jesus doesn't want me,' I began. 'You can't blame him, I'm wicked.'

'What are you talking about?' Lazarus burst out. 'Jesus wants everyone – and to say you're wicked is ridiculous!'

'It's not,' I retorted. 'I murdered my sister and Jesus says that if you even think badly of someone, that's evil, never mind killing them. If he knew . . .'

'Stop right there!' Mary cried. 'Caleb, you've got it all wrong. For one thing, you're not a murderer – whatever gave you that idea?'

'My father said I had as good as murdered Kizia,' I stammered. 'He said I was meant to watch her and . . . I didn't mean for that dog to get her, I was just so hungry and she was crying and Josh's gran . . .'

Martha put her arm round my shoulder and Mary pulled her stool closer.

'You were a little boy of eight,' she said softly. 'Your father was – well, he was a troubled and disturbed man who didn't – couldn't – care for you. Everyone in the village used to say how amazing you were, the way you looked after Kizia.'

'I didn't do it well enough though, did I?'

'Can I tell you something?' Lazarus interrupted. 'We've heard what Jesus has been doing, how he drives out demons and restores sanity to those with problems of the mind. I believe if he had been here when your father was alive, he would have touched him and healed him.'

'And that would have allowed your father to see the reality of what had happened,' Mary insisted. 'That a rabid dog snatched your sister and that would have happened even if you had been right beside her. It wasn't your fault, Caleb.'

'And,' Lazarus added, 'had your father been there, I doubt he could have done anything either.'

I swallowed hard as the tears threatened to spill over once more.

'I shouted at her, I called her names,' I murmured. 'Those were the last words I ever said to her. I can't forgive myself for that.'

'But Jesus can,' Lazarus said. 'Go back to him. Tell him of your pain. Let him give you the gift that your father isn't around to receive.'

'I don't know where Jesus is,' I ventured.

'Ask anyone on the road,' Martha suggested. 'Such a huge crowd there was following him when he left, I guess you'd see them a mile off!'

'But for tonight, you must stay here,' Mary declared. 'You look worn out. Martha, make a mat ready for Caleb in the back room.'

'Oh me again doing all the work, is it?' Martha retorted. 'Who do you think I am? You can't just . . .'

'Sorry, sorry, sorry,' Mary laughed. 'I'll do it. You rest your weary legs, Martha.'

'Huh,' said Martha. 'I'd better sort it. I'm better at that kind of stuff than you are.'

'I can't win,' smiled Mary winking at me. 'Sleep well, Caleb. Tomorrow is another day.'

I wasn't at all sure about the idea of going back to find Jesus, but the sisters and Lazarus kept telling me that it was the only way to find peace and forgiveness.

'Just tell Jesus everything,' Mary said. 'That's all you have to do.'

'Come and see us again,' Lazarus added. 'We'll be praying for you.'

Martha was right. Within two hours of leaving Bethany, my cloth bag weighed down with food from their kitchen, I began to see groups of people, all walking purposefully in one direction.

'Were you there yesterday when he healed that bent old woman?'

On a Sabbath Jesus was teaching in one of the synagogues and a woman was there who had been crippled by a spirit for eighteen years. She was bent over and could not straighten up at all. When

> Jesus saw her, he called her forward and said to her, 'Woman you are set free from your infirmity.' Then he put his hands on her and immediately she straightened up and praised God.
>
> *Luke 13:11-13*

It was obvious who they were talking about. As far as my eyes could see, there were lines of people heading north. I hurried on, determined not to stop until I had found Jesus. My days of hovering on the edge of the crowd were over; now I wanted to come face to face with Jesus and tell him everything. If it worked that would be wonderful; if not, at least I would know that I faced the future alone.

It was about midday, the sun blazing from a cloudless blue sky when I heard a cry behind me and someone grabbed hold of the back of my tunic. I wheeled round, ready to fight off the mugger – and saw a dark-haired girl sprawled at my feet, arms splayed out and her chin bleeding.

'Forgive me,' she stammered, struggling to get up. 'I tripped – I didn't mean to grab hold of you.'

'It's OK,' I assured her, stooping to help her up. I realised she was older than me, and very beautiful. Suddenly I felt clumsy and gauche.

'Are you alright?'

She rubbed her chin. 'Yes, I'm fine,' she said. 'I'm used to falling flat on my face.'

She smiled at me, the corners of her eyes crinkling.

'Thank you for your help,' she murmured and then paused, her head to one side. 'Excuse me for asking, but haven't I seen you somewhere before?'

'I don't think so,' I said eager to get on my way. 'Unless you've seen me in the crowd with Jesus?'

'You're a disciple of his?' she gasped. 'How long have you been with him? Is it true he's only a couple of miles away? I have to see him again . . .'

'Again? So you've seen him before?'

'Seen him? He saved my life!'

She brushed the dirt from her skirt and mopped the blood on her chin with the back of her hand.

'I would walk with you and tell you all about it but I had better not,' she sighed.

'Why not?'

She glanced over her shoulder. 'I have a reputation,' she said abruptly. 'Or rather, I had one. There are still people who would think badly of you simply for speaking to me.'

'Well, stuff them!' I replied. 'We're both going to find Jesus so we might as well walk together.'

That was better. Now I sounded more like a man and less like a tongue-tied kid. She smiled at me gratefully which had an extraordinary effect on my knees and we set off. It took me only a few seconds to realise that whatever else Jesus had done for her, he hadn't finished the job. As she walked, her right leg dragged behind her, the foot turning in almost at right angles to her shin. I'd heard about people like her, although I couldn't quite remember where.

'Tell me about Jesus saving your life,' I encouraged as she didn't speak. 'What happened?'

'It's difficult to talk about,' she admitted. 'I mean, I've only just met you and I don't even know your name.'

'Caleb,' I said. 'And you?'

'Ziva,' she replied.

'I've heard that name somewhere before,' I mused.

'Really? It's not a very common name – my mother chose it. My father never liked it much.' She faltered.

'So are you going to Jesus to get him to mend your leg?' I asked.

She turned and looked at me full in the face.

'I am going because I want to repay him in some way for what he did for me,' she said. 'I don't know how I can but I'm sure that if I just turn up, he'll give me something to do.'

She took a deep breath. 'I was living a terrible life,' she began, dropping her voice as a group of men and young boys strode past us. 'I had a good job and I blew it because of the awful black rages that used to swallow me up. I ran away, I lived rough, I stole – and . . .' she paused, '. . . and then one day I met a man.'

'You're married?'

She laughed curtly. 'The man I met was married and he and I . . . we spent our nights together,' she murmured.

'You did *what?* Are you mad?'

'I was mad, yes,' she nodded. 'All my life I've been running – running away from the past and running to find something, someone that would make me feel safe and loved and wanted. I thought that man was the one. I didn't know he was married until it was too late.'

'You got found out?'

She nodded. 'They dragged me to Jesus,' she said. 'And he saved me from being stoned to death. He told the people that if they knew, without a single shadow of a doubt, that they had never done anything wrong in their whole lives they could hurl the first stone. No one did.'

There were tears in her eyes and she stumbled as the path got more rocky.

'When they had all gone, he took my hand, and helped me to stand. Then he said that he wouldn't judge me either. I was forgiven. Then he said "Ziva go and don't sin any more." I felt as if . . .'

'Ziva! Of course!' I burst out. 'Oh my God, Ziva! It's you!'

She looked alarmed.

'Don't tell me you've heard about me? Surely people aren't still talking? Will I never escape the past?'

'No, no, nothing like that,' I gabbled. 'You've got a sister, right?'

Her face clouded and she turned away. 'A long time ago . . .'

'No, now, right now! She's been looking for you – she saw you in Capernaum . . .'

Ziva turned and stared at me. 'It's not possible,' she said slowly. 'What would my sister be doing in Capernaum? She lives in Aaenon . . .'

'No, she doesn't, not any more. She got a job in Cana, that's where I met her and . . .'

'So what's her name, this girl you think is my sister?' she asked curtly. Her eyes had clouded and she had turned her face away.

I took a deep breath. 'Esther,' I said. I thought that Ziva was going to faint. She staggered back, her hand clasped to her mouth.

'She— Is it— Could it be?' she stammered.

'We'll find her,' I assured her. 'She's working for a lady called Susanna.'

For the next hour as we walked I told Ziva everything that had happened in the past two-and-a-half years – well, almost everything. I didn't talk about my sister. I wasn't going to talk about her to anyone until I had seen Jesus. Ziva was laughing, then crying, then telling me she didn't dare believe me, then insisting that I must be right because yes, Esther's grandmother had lived in Nazareth, and yes there was a neighbour called Judith.

'God is good, God is good,' she kept saying. 'He brought you to that place on this very path at just the right moment and if I hadn't fallen over I might never have known that Esther was nearby. Isn't God amazing?'

I didn't reply. I had never thought of things like that before. One thing did occur to me though. Esther was going to be over the moon to see Ziva, and she'd be pretty chuffed with me for being the one to find her. It might even make her love me.

The thought was such a shock that I didn't speak for the rest of the journey.

So what has that got to do with me?

1. Why do you think Jesus told Martha that her sister Mary had chosen the better way to be that day? Are you ever so busy *doing* things for Jesus that you don't have time to spend *with* him? Doing might get us noticed by other people but being quiet with Jesus is essential if we are to grow in relationship with him.
2. How and where can you best be 'quiet with Jesus'? For some it may be in church, for others sitting on a beach or walking their dog in the countryside. For some, listening to music and for others rock climbing, open air swimming, painting or cooking. There is no right or wrong way; Jesus meets us in the silence wherever we are.
3. Ziva believed that God had intervened to make her fall over right beside Caleb. Do you believe that 'accidents' and 'coincidences' are a sign of God at work in our lives?

CHAPTER THIRTY-FOUR

Reunited

Esther

My head throbbed, my throat was burning and every bone in my body ached. I had been walking all day, searching the thousands of faces in the crowd on the hillside, desperate to find my sister. She had to be here, surely; if what Joanna had said was true, then I knew Ziva would follow Jesus. But now I was on the edge of the huge circle of people who were listening to Jesus and there was no sign of her.

On the far side of the crowd, I could just make out Susanna and Mary, along with some of the other younger women; I knew they would be looking for me as the light was dimming, but the thought of walking another step was just too much. The sound of Jesus' voice, telling another of his stories, was soothing and familiar; I slid to the ground, resting my back against the trunk of a sycamore tree and closed my eyes. If I just rested for a moment or two, I would be fine.

Jesus said, 'The kingdom of heaven is like a net that was let down into the lake and caught all kinds of fish. When it was full the fishermen pulled it up on the shore. Then they sat down and collected the good fish in baskets but threw the bad away. This is how it will be at the end of the age. The angels will come and separate the wicked from the righteous and throw them into the fiery furnace where there will be weeping and gnashing of teeth.'

Matthew 13:47-50

'The kingdom of heaven is like a net that was let down in a lake and caught all kinds of fish . . .' Jesus' voice wafted over to me. In my mind's eye I was back on the lake shore at Bethsaida with Reuben and Caleb – and Seth. The boats were bobbing on the waves, and the sun was glinting on the surface of the water.

'When it was full, the fishermen pulled it up on the shore.'

I could almost smell the fish as they were tossed onto the mats, their beady eyes glinting and making my head hurt even more.

'Then they sat down and collected the good fish in baskets, but threw the bad away. That is how it will be at the end of the age; the angels will come and separate the wicked people from the good ones, and hurl them into the fiery furnace . . .'

They were red and black with fangs and teeth, and the flames were hot – hotter and hotter, burning my skin and searing my throat. Nathan was in the flames snatching at my hand; my stepmother was there, screeching at me that I was a liar and a no-good troublemaker, and brandishing her broom ready to strike me over the head. I opened my mouth to scream for help but no sound came out. The flames began licking round my feet, crawling up my legs – and then the earthquake came. I was shaken like a rag doll, tossed, thrown, nearer and nearer the flames.

'Esther, Esther . . .' The voice was familiar but I couldn't remember where it came from. The earthquake was getting more violent, the shaking rattling my teeth in my skull.

'Esther, wake up!'

I opened my eyes. The earthquake stopped.

Two dark eyes filled with tears stared into mine, a hand gently stroked my hair.

'Esther, Esther, is it really you?

'Ziva?' I whispered.

I rubbed my eyes. Was this still part of the dream?

'It was me that found her!'

I turned my head wincing slightly at the pain over my eyes. Caleb was kneeling at the side of me, a broad grin on his face.

'I found your sister!'

'Ziva – is it a dream? Are you real?'

'Yes, silly, it's me! Oh Esther, Esther – I'm so sorry, so, so sorry!'

She wrapped her arms round me, and I could feel the dampness of her tears on my neck.

'I'm sorry I never came back – I wanted to but . . .' She choked back her sobs. 'I am never, ever going to let you out of my sight again,' she sobbed.

'Are you – are you OK?' I asked. 'When I saw you in Capernaum . . .'

'I'm fine,' she said, pulling back and kissing the top of my head. 'I'll tell you everything, but first we need to see Jesus. You have a fever and he can drive it away.'

But Jesus had disappeared. There was no sign of him, or the main group of disciples. The crowd was dispersing, threading their way back down the path like a long dark snake.

'He has left for Jerusalem,' one of the newer followers remarked. 'It is the Feast of Dedication soon.'

'At least we can get back to our work for a while,' muttered another. 'My wife is not best pleased with me for spending so much time away from the fields.'

'From what I hear, you might have plenty more time to hoe and rake,' his friend replied. 'There's talk of a lot of hatred for Jesus in Jerusalem; why he's insisting on going I don't know.'

Ziva clutched my hand tightly. 'I wish he hadn't left,' she said. 'I would have begged him to make you well.'

'But I am well,' I said. 'I feel absolutely fine now. You're here.'

Ziva touched my forehead, felt my wrist, and insisted that I open my mouth.

'You're cooler,' she murmured. 'And your heart's not racing now. I've never seen a fever go that fast.'

Susanna cried when she saw Ziva, and Mary cried because Susanna was crying and Reuben and Caleb looked embarrassed and then we were all suddenly hugging and laughing and I was so happy that I thought my heart would burst right out of my chest.

We went back to Susanna's home in time for the Feast of Dedication; Reuben and Caleb stayed at Salome and Zebedee's house and Ziva and I spent the next few days getting to know one another again.

'Can you ever forgive me for leaving you with that brute?' she asked over and over again. 'Did he . . . ?'

'He tried,' I admitted, 'but God was good to me. I found out that when I eat pomegranates I get huge blisters on my skin and if I eat centaury I vomit. That kept him away!'

It hadn't been quite that easy, but the relief in Ziva's face was my reward for the white lie.

So what has that got to do with me?

1. Esther chose not to tell her sister the whole truth about her father's behaviour to her. Why? Is there ever a time when withholding the whole truth from someone is the right thing to do? When would it be the wrong thing? But it is important to remember that when someone tries to harm us, we need to tell a person we trust; we should never feel that we have to handle it all on our own. Esther had escaped from her threatening situation which was why she could afford to protect her sister's feelings.

CHAPTER THIRTY-FIVE

Confrontation

Seth

Then came the Festival of Dedication at Jerusalem. It was winter, and Jesus was in the temple courts walking in Solomon's Colonnade. The Jews who were there gathered around him, saying, 'How long will you keep us in suspense? If you are the Messiah, tell us plainly.'

Jesus answered, 'I did tell you, but you do not believe. The works I do in my Father's name testify about me, but you do not believe because you are not my sheep. My sheep listen to my voice; I know them, and they follow me. I give them eternal life, and they shall never perish; no one will snatch them out of my hand. My Father, who has given them to me, is greater than all; no one can snatch them out of my Father's hand. I and the Father are one.'

Again his Jewish opponents picked up stones to stone him, but Jesus said to them, 'I have shown you many good works from the Father. For which of these do you stone me?'

'We are not stoning you for any good work,' they replied, 'but for blasphemy, because you, a mere man, claim to be God.'

Jesus answered them, 'Is it not written in your Law, "I have said you are 'gods'"? If he called them "gods," to whom the word of God came – and Scripture cannot be set aside – what about the one whom the Father set apart as his very own and sent into the world? Why then do you accuse me of blasphemy because I said, "I am God's Son"? Do not believe me unless I do the works of my Father. But if I do them, even though you do not believe me, believe the works, that you may know and understand that the Father is in me, and I in the Father.' Again they tried to seize him, but he escaped their grasp.

John 10:22-39

It was the month of Kislev, the middle of winter and my father and I were at the Temple for the Feast of Dedication. My father was edgy – not that that was anything new. Even the name of Jesus agitated him these days; he couldn't stop talking about him and yet when the prophet was in Jerusalem, my father became anxious and irritable.

Today was no exception. We were at the Temple, walking through Solomon's Colonnade and we came upon Jesus surrounded by a group of rabbis and teachers. They were a vociferous bunch, and there was a lot of arm waving and shouting going on. Jesus and some of his disciples were standing in the middle of the group, the disciples looking anxious and Jesus, as usual, the picture of unruffled calm. I thought that I'd like to be like that when I'm a physician.

'How long are you going to go on like this?' one of the senior Jews shouted. 'If you are the Messiah, tell us straight.'

'You don't believe what I tell you, so why should I keep repeating it?' Jesus replied. 'What I do bears evidence to who I am and it's God who makes it all possible. Shall I tell you why you don't believe me?'

'Because we're not gullible,' someone muttered.

'Because you're not my sheep,' Jesus countered. 'You're not one of my flock. I can give the people who follow me and believe me the gift of real and eternal life. Nothing can separate us. My Father has given them to me and no one can take them away from my protection. That's what it means to be of my flock.'

'Oh dear God, what are they doing?' my father gasped.

Two of the men had stooped down and picked up large stones, which they were tossing in their hands.

'They're going to stone him!'

Jesus looked at the two of them. 'I've performed many miracles, through the power that my Father has given me,' he remarked calmly. 'Which one of these are you going to stone me for?'

'It's not the miracles that bother us,' snapped the older of the two men. 'It's the way you blaspheme – you who are a mere man, pretending to be God! It's outrageous!'

Jesus didn't flinch. You had to give him credit – he had guts.

'Now just hang on a minute,' he said. 'All I am doing is quoting Scriptures. Didn't God say, "*I tell you, you are 'gods'* "? If God called the leaders of the Israelites gods, because they did his will, then how can it be wrong to say that I, the one whom God sent to you now, is the Son of God?'

'This is despicable!'

'No, listen!' There was a fresh urgency in Jesus' voice. 'If I wasn't doing the things my Father does, then you'd be right to have a go at me. But forget about who I say I am and look at the evidence before your own eyes. You've seen what I do; you know what God does. Now do you get it?'

No one replied but no one threw a stone.

'God and I do the same things, God and I are the same. We are Father and Son. He is in me. I am in him.' With that he turned and walked away.

'Nicodemus!' One of my father's colleagues strode over to us. 'Did you see that? Did you hear it all?'

'I did,' my father replied a little nervously.

'When the Feast is over we shall have him,' Rabinth said. 'This has gone on long enough. He is undermining everything that is sacred, everything that we are here to uphold. Don't you agree?'

For a moment, my father didn't speak. 'It is,' he replied, 'a difficult situation. The man is . . .'

'The man is a blasphemer!' stormed Rabinth. 'Surely you can see that?'

'He does,' my father sighed, 'say some extraordinary things. But is he really doing any harm?'

'You call yourself a God-fearing Jew and you make a comment like that?' Rabinth shouted. 'He says he is equal to God – how much more harmful can you get than that? Dear God, man, you've taken leave of your senses!' He turned as if to walk away and then paused. 'And possibly taken leave of your right to sit in the Sanhedrin?' he remarked more quietly. 'Think about it, Nicodemus, my friend. Think about where your loyalties really lie.'

'He's slipped away,' my father announced a few days later, as I was grappling with a particularly tedious passage in the Torah. 'No one has seen him in the city for almost a week. Maybe now there'll be an end of it. If he just keeps away from Jerusalem, maintains a low profile, things might die down.'

He leaned back in his chair and it struck me that he was looking older, more weary and dispirited than I had ever seen him. He was rubbing his temples just as he had before his last illness hit him.

'Father, are you alright?' I asked.

'Yes, yes, it's just that I am not sleeping too well these days,' he replied. 'And this damp weather doesn't suit my old joints!'

'We could take a trip to see your cousin in Capernaum,' I suggested, trying desperately not to sound too eager. The truth was that I had been thinking more and more about Esther, not that it would do to let my father know that. She was clearly not one of our sort, to use his phrase; but even though I'd only been with her for a total of about three hours I couldn't get her out of my mind.

'No, no,' he replied. 'There's so much to be done here and your mother doesn't like it when I am away.'

It always puzzled me when my father spoke like that, since as far as I could tell my mother didn't realise whether he was there or not. I guess it made him feel better to imagine that she did. I was about to ask permission to go to my uncle's house when there was a hammering on the door. My father's steward appeared within seconds, looking more than a little flustered. Behind him, breathing heavily, stood Archelaus and another portly man with a long beard and thin, hard mouth.

'Gentlemen,' my father murmured, heaving himself out of his chair, 'you find me relaxing with my son.'

That was his polite way of telling them that they had no right bursting into his home before the steward had had the chance to check that it was convenient. If they were aware of the breach in etiquette, they certainly showed no signs of it.

'Nicodemus,' Archelaus panted. 'My friend Erez here has news of the upstart Jesus!'

My father sighed heavily. 'Jesus is no longer in Jerusalem,' he pointed out. 'He's not troubling us and . . .'

'That's what you think!' Erez retorted. 'Just listen to what I have to say.'

Reluctantly, my father gestured to them to sit down and sent me to order refreshments from the kitchen. I knew I shouldn't go back into the room, so I lingered outside, close enough to hear every word but out of sight.

'Jesus is only a few miles away in Peraea,' he said. 'Far too close for comfort – so a group of us told him to make a run for it because Herod was after his blood.'

'So you do want to keep him safe?' my father asked, his voice lifting.

'Don't be ridiculous,' Erez replied. 'We don't want him coming anywhere near Jerusalem, that's all – personally I couldn't give two hoots about his safety.'

'Tell Nicodemus what Jesus said,' Archelaus urged.

'He called Herod a fox and said that it wasn't right for any prophet to die except in Jerusalem!' Erez declared. 'And then he waxed all lyrical – I can't remember his exact words . . .'

> O Jerusalem, Jerusalem, you who kill the prophets and stone those sent to you, how often I have longed to gather your children together as a hen gathers her chicks under her wings, but you were not willing! Look, your house is left to you desolate. I tell you, you will not see me again until you say, 'Blessed is he who comes in the name of the Lord.'
>
> *Luke 13:34, 35*

'. . . but it was all about how he wanted to protect the people of Jerusalem and how it's too late now. He said we wouldn't see him again until the day when we all agree that he is blessed and comes in God's name.'

'As if,' Archelaus muttered.

'I don't see what you are getting so worked up about,' my father said.

At that moment, the steward came out of the kitchen with a tray of refreshments. I put my finger to my lips and he winked at me. He's a nice guy and his son is one of my best mates so I knew he wouldn't grass me up.

There was a short silence as drinks were poured and food served and then I heard Erez clear his throat.

'Last Sabbath Jesus had a meal at my brother-in-law's house . . .'

'He is a follower?'

'Of course he's not – it was a plant,' Archelaus interrupted. 'We need to keep a close watch on him and we'll use whatever means we can.'

'Anyway,' Erez went on, 'one of the guests was a man with swollen joints – terrible they were. Nice guy, but he could hardly move for the vastness of his limbs. Anyway, Jesus asked everyone whether they thought it was OK to heal on the Sabbath. No one said a word – and he went right ahead and healed him. The dropsy disappeared and the guy went on his way.'

'In the past, we've been very wary of allowing anything like that on the Sabbath,' my father muttered, and I couldn't help thinking that he was choosing his words carefully – sitting on the fence, one might say.

'Well, it's wrong, of course it is, but the time for debate is over,' Erez said. 'We need to accumulate as much evidence against him as we possibly can. Jesus of course, goes on and on about how we'd rescue a child that fell down a well on the Sabbath, and that's true, but . . .' He hesitated. 'Anyway, there's more.'

I wanted my father to stop him right there and point out that he had changed the subject and that he ought to admit that healing people was brilliant whatever day of the week it was, but sadly he didn't say a word.

'I told you it was my brother-in-law's house, right?' Erez said. 'He owes me a lot, you know – I was the one who argued his case when my father – God rest his soul – said that he wasn't good enough to marry my sister. So naturally, when it came time to eat, I sat at the top of the table in the VIP position.'

'Well, you would, of course,' my father agreed.

'Jesus – the wandering yokel preacher from God knows where – had the audacity to start moralising about table plans,' he stormed. 'Told us that we shouldn't choose the place of honour because someone better might come along and then we'd be asked to move which would be hugely embarrassing. Well, OK, that might happen if some shopkeeper sat at the top of the table, but me? Oh, yes, it was me he was addressing, never took his eyes off me . . .'

The memory was clearly more than he could cope with as with that he was gripped by a paroxysm of coughing and for some time little more was said. I was about to slip away when I heard my father's voice.

'Tell me, did Jesus make you move down the table?'

'I'd like to have seen him try!' Erez snapped. 'Oh sure, he said that everyone should be humble and sit at the lowest place, and then they might be invited to move up a few seats. He dared to suggest that some of us Pharisees were snobs, that we had high and mighty opinions of ourselves, which of course is nonsense. I mean, yes, we are high born, cleverer than most people and well respected but we are certainly most caring of those unfortunate enough to be born beneath us.'

'But everyone has their place,' Archelaus cut in. 'If Jesus had his way, every time we gave a dinner party, we'd not only invite our friends and relatives but – what was it he called them?'

'Misfits, outcasts and the rejected,' Erez spluttered. 'Then he embarked on one of his stories.'

There was once a man who threw a great dinner party and invited many. When it was time for dinner, he sent out his servant to the invited guests saying, 'Come on in, the food is on the table.' Then they all began to beg off, one after another making excuses. The first said, 'I bought a piece of property and need to look it over. Send my regrets.' Another said, 'I just bought five teams of oxen

> and I really need to check them out. Send my regrets.' And yet another said, 'I just got married and need to get home to my wife.' The servant went back and told the master what had happened. He was outraged and told the servant, 'Quickly, go out into the city streets and alleys. Collect all who look like they need a square meal, all the misfits and homeless and wretched you can lay your hands on, and bring them here.' The servant reported back, 'Master I did what you commanded – and there is still room.' The master said, 'Then go to the country roads. Whoever you find there, drag them in. I want my house full! Let me tell you, not one of those originally invited is going to get so much as a bite at my dinner party.'
>
> *Luke 14:16-24, The Message*

'So,' my father said, 'we're sitting here, eating and drinking – and if Jesus had his way, I'd be sending my son out into the street to bring in a few vagabonds and down and outs to join us?'

'Exactly!' Erez exclaimed. 'As if!'

'I'm not so sure . . .' My father's voice was suddenly firm and decisive. I heard him push back his chair and walk towards the door. I ran into my room just in time.

'Seth? Seth! Come here please!'

I sauntered out of the room as if I had been there for ages. 'Yes, Father?'

'I want you to do something,' he began, and then turned as Archelaus and Erez stood up.

'But surely – you're not leaving?' my father asked. 'I was about to send Seth here to bring in some strangers – we should after all put Jesus' teaching to the test, should we not?'

I have never seen two men leave our home so fast.

So what has that got to do with me?

The Feast of Dedication commemorated the rededication of the Temple in Jerusalem by Judas Maccabeus in 164 BC after its desecration by Antiochus IV. Kislev is the equivalent of our December.

1. In Jesus' day it was the custom to send two invitations to a party; the first announced the event and the second told the guests that everything was ready. The guests in Jesus' story insulted the host by making excuses when they got the second invitation, having accepted the first. God's first invitation came from Moses and the prophets and the second from Jesus, his Son. The religious leaders accepted the first and believed that God had called them to be his people; they then insulted God by refusing to accept his Son. What do you think the lesson for us might be in this?

2. The teaching of Jesus about bringing in the poor and dispossessed to share in the feast isn't just a nice story. It's what he wants – and expects – us as his followers to do. What does it really mean in practical terms today? How would it affect our day to day life if we took that message to heart? How can we make sure that everyone shares in the plenty we have? Do you think Jesus was speaking only of a regular meal round a dinner table or is there something more to his message?

3. When Jesus says, 'Didn't God say, "I tell you, you are 'gods'",' he is quoting Psalm 82 verse 6. His argument was that if God chose to call humans 'gods' (because they represented him in administering justice in Israel) why was it blasphemous for Jesus, the true Son of God, to say that he was equal with God? The problem was that his critics were focusing on laws and words and not on Jesus' actions. When someone says they are a Christian and try to prove it by quoting chunks of Scripture or telling you that they go to church twice every Sunday, look at what they do the rest of the week. That will be the way to discover whether they've 'got it' or not!

CHAPTER THIRTY-SIX

Telling it to the Lord

Caleb

For a few days, I felt deflated and let down. All the way from Bethany I had been psyching myself up to talk to Jesus face to face; and what had he done? Gone off to Jerusalem on the very day I arrived. I couldn't help thinking that was the story of my life.

Esther and Ziva had no time for anyone but each other which I guess was natural; but I had hoped to get Esther on her own and somehow move things on a bit between us. Now that Seth was out of the way, I did fancy my chances a bit – after all, we'd been through a lot together and if it hadn't been for me, Esther would never have got to Capernaum, met Susanna or found her sister. When we passed one another in the street, or I saw her returning from the well with Ziva, she always waved and said hello; but within seconds, she was chatting nineteen to the dozen and not giving me a backward glance.

To say I was miffed is the understatement of the year. Even the celebrations of the festival, the lighting of the nine branched menorah and the special foods like *livivot,* the delicious potato pancakes and the *sufganiyot* doughnuts did little to raise my spirits.

And then one afternoon, after Reuben had dragged me down to the water's edge to help him put fresh pitch on one of Zebedee's boats, we heard a commotion further along the beach. Ruth and a number of the other village children ran shrieking with delight towards a group of men who had just rounded the corner from the Capernaum road.

'Is it them? Are they back?' Reuben exclaimed.

I dropped my brush and ran towards the group. As I drew nearer, I recognised Andrew, Philip, James and John. Their mantles were dirty, the blue fringes covered in dust and I noticed that Andrew was limping slightly. What struck me most, however, was their air of urgency and anxiety. They hardly acknowledged our greeting; James and John went straight to their home and Andrew headed straight for Peter's house.

'Something's going on,' Reuben muttered to me. 'And it doesn't look good.'

It wasn't until the evening that things became clear. As usual, it was Andrew who came to find us, pressing a few coins into our hands, asking whether we were well and enquiring after Susanna and Mary.

'I must find them,' he said. 'But first, I need to know something. It's really important. You've been following Jesus on and off for – what – two-and-a-half years now, right?'

We nodded.

'So – are you true followers or part-timers?' he asked. 'I need to know because either you are committed to him one hundred per cent and will go wherever he goes, or you're just dipping a toe in the water, in which case I might as well employ you to stay here and keep an eye on things for Peter and me.'

I opened my mouth to reply but he held up his hand and carried on speaking rapidly, glancing over his shoulder from time to time.

'Things are hotting up and not for the better,' he said. 'Jesus is determined to go back to Jerusalem very soon and that can only mean – well, I don't even like to think what it might mean. Anyone who goes with him has to be in it for the long haul, and Peter and I, Philip – all of us twelve – have made that commitment. Not that our wives are exactly thrilled about it.'

He put a hand on each of our shoulders.

'So,' he sighed. 'I guess you'll be happy to stay here, earn a reliable wage, have lodging . . .'

'Hang on a minute, there's no way I'm doing that!' I burst out. 'I have to talk to Jesus, I have to see him and if that means going a hundred miles away, that's what I'm doing!'

Andrew stared at me long and hard and then nodded and turned to Reuben.

'And you? You've settled in well round here, people like you and you've made yourself very useful. I guess you'll be staying?'

Reuben looked distinctly uncomfortable.

'You've been really good to me,' he began, 'and I'm grateful, I really am, and I know your family will need help but – well, I can talk now because of Jesus and it was you who said I should talk about him to other people like me, so you can't really blame me for saying that I'm hanging out with him, not staying here.'

Andrew's face lit up with a broad grin. 'That's wonderful!' he cried. 'I had to give you the opportunity to change your mind; you can see that, can't you?' But his face clouded. 'It won't be easy,' he warned. 'Jesus says . . .' Suddenly his voice became choked. 'He says he's going to be killed.'

I touched Andrew's sleeve. 'He can save himself,' I stressed. 'He's the Messiah, after all.'

'He could,' Andrew whispered. 'But will he?'

Within forty-eight hours, we had joined Jesus in Peraea – not just Reuben and I, but Susanna, Mary, Esther, Ziva and several other people from the village. Salome, Zebedee's wife, came along; she said she wanted to meet Jesus face to face without spending her time darting to and from the kitchen. Susanna had received a message from Joanna, enquiring after her health and saying that she would be '*visiting a good friend who was in need of some support and funding*'.

'The message also says that her husband is tied up with business for Herod, who is worried about many developments in and around the city,' Susanna told us. 'I guess that's her way of telling us that he's on the warpath.'

As usual, there were crowds of people travelling with Jesus but this time I wasn't going to rest until I had spoken to him, and my chance came the very first evening. Susanna and Mary were preparing food for Jesus and the disciples and Andrew and some of the others were lighting a fire. No one had seen Jesus for a while – the rumour was that he had gone off by himself to pray.

Suddenly, I spotted him, emerging from a coppice of trees and making his way slowly down the hill towards the crowd. I knew I would never get another opportunity like this one and I broke into a run, heading up the stony path to meet him before my nerves could get the better of me.

'Master, may I speak with you?'

'It's Caleb, isn't it – the guy who wanted to understand?'

'You remembered?'

'Of course – and do you now begin to understand?'

I felt my lip tremble. 'I understand that I can never be what I wanted to be,' I whispered.

'And what was that?'

'I wanted to be like you,' I confessed. 'To be one of your inner circle, to learn to heal and . . .'

'Master, the food is ready!' Matthew's voice wafted up from the clearing below. 'Come and eat.'

'In a minute,' Jesus shouted back. 'You carry on.' He turned back to me. 'And now you don't want that?' Jesus asked gently.

'Of course I do!' I cried. 'But it's not like it was – I used to want to be famous and have people admire me for what I could do.'

'And now?'

'Now I want to be like the people you heal,' I admitted. 'I want to be better.' I bit my lip to stop it from trembling. 'I did a terrible thing and there's no way I can ever feel right again unless . . . unless you help me.'

Jesus smiled and touched my hand. 'Tell me,' he said, sitting down on a nearby rock and gesturing to me to do the same.

So I did. I told him all of it – not just about my father, and the way he neglected us; not just about the day Kizia died because I had turned my back on her or about the nightmares; but about how I'd stolen jewellery from guests at the house in Cana, how I had cheated on the master by pinching food and selling it in the village; about how all I had wanted was to be someone important and respected, whatever it took.

'And my sister – I called her names,' I stammered. 'You told us that even to think a bad thing about someone was evil, and I actually shouted it at her! And . . .' I took a deep breath, closed my eyes and said the words I hadn't breathed to anyone since that awful day.

'And when I saw the dog dragging her down the street, I was too scared to go and try to stop it!' Then the tears flowed. I felt a fool – a man of fifteen doesn't cry in public, but I couldn't help it.

'That's why you don't want me, isn't it? Because I'm not just a murderer, I'm a coward!'

Jesus took both my hands in his. They were large and warm, roughened by living in the open air but the gentlest hands I've ever held. Not that many people have wanted to hold my hand, come to think of it.

'Caleb, it is in the past, it is forgiven, it has gone,' he said softly. 'The sins of your father, the sins of neglect and abuse, they are forgiven too.'

He touched my shoulder.

'And you must understand one thing above all else: I do want you. I need you.'

I felt my shoulders drop and the tension drain from my body.

'You – need – me?'

'Listen,' he said. 'You must have seen shepherds on the hillsides when you were growing up?'

I nodded.

'If a shepherd loses a sheep, what does he do? He leaves the flock in the pen and goes out to find the one that's lost. And when he does find it, he's over the moon – so excited to have got it back, that he goes into the village and tells everyone to come and celebrate with him.'

I frowned. I couldn't quite see what sheep with a poor sense of direction had to do with anything.

'You know what, Caleb? There is more joy in heaven at this moment over one person – you – who has found his way again than over ninety-nine people who never lost it in the first place.'

'So – you weren't ignoring me because you hated me?'

'I hate no one,' Jesus replied. 'Sometimes it's necessary to wait until a person is ready to receive my teaching, to allow my Father into their heart.' He chuckled. 'Come and eat with us,' he offered. 'I can see my friends are impatient.'

'Me? Come and eat? With you?'

'Caleb, is that so hard to understand? Don't tell me you're not hungry?'

'I am,' I admitted. I realised that yes, my stomach was rumbling, but there were other things I was hungry for and I had an idea that I would get them from Jesus.

'So come,' he said.

We made our way down the path, Jesus humming softly to himself. He gestured to me to sit next to Andrew. None of the disciples seemed to mind, or even be surprised, that I was there. Susanna and Mary served the food, Ziva poured wine, and Esther topped it up with fresh water. I wanted to say something witty or clever but my mind was in such turmoil that I couldn't even look at her.

'You know,' Jesus said to them, 'talking to Caleb here has reminded me of something.' He took a chunk of bread and some curd cheese. 'My mother – where is she? Oh, over there chatting. Why am I not surprised?' He chuckled, took another bite, and carried on.

'She once lost a coin and she searched the house for hours, sweeping, moving furniture, lighting lamps, and she wouldn't let up till she'd found it. It was stuck in a dark corner under a piece of broken pottery! She was so thrilled when she found it that she rushed out and told all her neighbours and spent the rest of the evening gossiping with them and drinking pomegranate juice!'

He looked round at the group. 'That's how it is with God,' he said. 'Every time someone who has lost the way turns back to him, the whole of heaven bursts out laughing with joy!'

'But surely Master, there are some people who behave so badly that there's no turning back?' Judas asked.

'I've told you before, Judas, that's not how it works,' Jesus replied. 'I'll tell you a story about . . .'

He paused and looked over my shoulder. 'Well, well, look who's here!' he exclaimed.

I glanced up and saw Reuben hobbling towards us over the rough ground. I'm ashamed to say I was pretty annoyed; here I was for the very first time in the inner circle, and the last thing I wanted was to share the moment with anyone else.

'Forgive me, Master,' Reuben said, 'I wouldn't have come and interrupted you but then I saw Caleb was here and I thought that meant it was OK for just anyone to join in.'

'Absolutely!' Jesus exclaimed. 'And that's perfect timing because I was about to tell a story that is just the kind of thing I want you to hear.'

He broke off a piece of fish and bit into it.

'There was a man who had two sons. The younger one was an impetuous sort of boy, always looking for something new and exciting, and one day he said to his father, "Give me my share of the estate now – I don't want to wait till you die. I want it now."'

'A right little money grabbing upstart,' Judas muttered.

I said nothing. If my father had been wealthy I bet I'd have tried it on too.

'The father divided his property between the two sons,' Jesus continued, 'and within a few days, the younger one was off! He travelled far and wide, and spent the lot on wild partying, drinking, gambling and mixing with a crowd of very unsavoury people. He did whatever he wanted without a thought for the future.'

'Stupid,' Judas muttered.

'Now it happened that a severe famine hit that country,' Jesus went on. 'The harvest failed, heavy rains ruined the vegetables so that they rotted in the ground and within months, food was very scarce and what remained was sold at a premium. And remember, the boy had not a single lepton left.'

'What did he do?' Reuben asked.

'He went to one of the local farmers and offered himself as a hired hand,' Jesus smiled. 'The job he landed wasn't exactly what he had hoped for; he was sent to look after the pigs.'

‘Pigs!’ I gasped. If there was anything on earth that I wanted to avoid for evermore, it was pigs.

Jesus nodded. ‘He was so hungry that he would have eaten the pods that the swine were eating – but no one seemed to notice him at all, never mind give him a meal,’ he sighed. ‘After a week he came to his senses. He said to himself, “My father’s hired hands get a square meal every day and I’m stuck here, starving to death. I must be mad – I shall go back home to my father. I shall say to him that I know I have done wrong – to him, and to God; I’ll admit that I know I no longer deserve to be treated as a son, but I’ll plead with him to employ me as a hired hand.” And that’s what he did.’

‘I bet the father was furious,’ I murmured to Andrew. ‘Mine would have beaten the living daylights out of me.’

‘Somehow I don’t think that’s how this story will end,’ he whispered.

‘Now the boy was still quite a way off from his father’s house,’ Jesus went on, ‘when his father, who was up on the roof, spotted him stumbling and limping along the road. He left what he was doing, rushed down the road and threw his arms round the boy’s neck, tears coursing down his cheeks.’

Reuben sniffed, and I noticed that he had tears in his eyes.

‘The boy told his father that he realised that after his extravagant and irresponsible behaviour he was no longer fit to be treated like a son. But before he could ask him to give him a job as a servant, his father laid a finger on his lips to silence him and led him into the house. “Come quickly,” he shouted to the servants, “bring the plushest robe in the house, and new sandals, and fetch the ruby ring from my chest. And while you’re about it, kill the fatted calf – we’re going to celebrate!”’

‘That’s a great story,’ Thaddeus said, tearing off a piece of bread and passing the loaf to Jesus.

‘Oh, but it’s not finished yet,’ Jesus told him. ‘The servants were a bit taken aback because for weeks their master had been quiet and withdrawn and they asked what the celebration was for. “My son was dead to me, and now he’s alive,” their master cried. “He was lost and now he is found!”’

You could hear the sighs as the disciples leaned back assuming that now the story really was over.

'The noise of the rejoicing echoed into the fields behind the house,' Jesus went on. 'That's where the older son was working. He was puzzled and called one of the servants over to him and asked what was going on. When the servant told him the cause of the celebration, the brother was furious.'

Everyone became alert again, and a few looked confused.

'"Well, you can count me out!" he stormed, and refused to go into the house. When the servant told the boy's father what was going on, he went outside and pleaded with his elder son.

'"You just don't get it, do you?" the elder boy shouted. "For years, I have worked my fingers to the bone for you, obeyed every order you gave me and yet not once did you even give me a kid goat to roast and have a bit of a party with my mates. Yet my no-good brother – that waste of space who spent all your money – comes home and what happens? You throw the party to end all parties! It stinks!"'

Jesus was a good storyteller; he did all the different voices and even his facial expressions changed with each character.

'The father wrapped his arms round the elder son and hugged him. "Let me explain," he said. "You have been with me all along and everything I have is yours. The reason we are celebrating is because your brother was as good as dead to us and now he's alive to the reality of what he's done; he was a lost soul and now he's found new direction. Isn't that a cause for celebration?"'

Jesus glanced round the rapt faces.

'So I say again, that's how it is. Your Father in heaven never gives up yearning, and waiting and longing for those people who are lost to come back to him. When they do – well, his joy is beyond words.'

For a while no one spoke, and nothing could be heard but the sound of chewing and the song of the birds. Then Jesus beckoned to Reuben and me.

'Are you good at remembering things, you two?' he asked with a twinkle in his eye.

I nodded.

'I guess so,' Reuben said.

'Then remember these stories I've told you and all the ones I will go on telling until the day when I have to leave you,' he said.

'Leave us?' I spluttered. 'But . . .'

'Remember the stories,' he repeated, 'and tell them to others. Tell them to people your age and younger; tell them to the folk like you who have never had anyone at home who would teach them the truth of the kingdom of heaven.'

He took my hand and rested the other on Reuben's head.

'Caleb, you've always wanted to be a true disciple, haven't you?'

'Yes Master,' I cried.

'So do as I say – spread the Good News of God's kingdom in ways people can understand,' he said. 'And Reuben, you are small; you see the world from the perspective of little children and of those who struggle in a body that doesn't quite do what they wish it would. Don't spend too much time wishing things were different; use who you are in the service of the Father who created you and loves you.'

He moved his hands down to his side and smiled.

'So off you go – go and begin your ministry of witness to me.'

So what has that got to do with me?

1. Caleb realises that he cannot move on with his life unless Jesus helps him. He has discovered that he needs healing as much as those with physical or mental disabilities. In opening up to Jesus, what did he receive? Why does Jesus need to wait for us to go to him?

2. To a shepherd, every sheep is of great value, and if one is lost, the shepherd will spare nothing to find it. God's love for us is so enormous that he seeks us out and is overjoyed when we turn to him. Why do you think the shepherd left ninety-nine of these valuable animals to go and search for just one?

3. Caleb was a bit annoyed when Reuben joined the group. Are we ever so keen on being one of the 'in' crowd that we resent the arrival of others who need company, love and recognition as much as we do? How can we avoid this happening?

4. The younger son in Jesus' story wanted to live life his way, doing whatever he wanted; he had to hit rock bottom before he realised his mistake. Sometimes people have to go to the depths of misery before they are willing to turn to the only one who can help. What is the main difference between this story and the story of the lost sheep and the lost coin? What does the shepherd and the woman do that the father in the last story doesn't do? What does this tell us about God's gift to us?

5. When the elder brother sees the party being thrown for his previously wayward younger brother, he is furious, saying that he's been loyal and hardworking and never had a party given in his honour, but that his brother, who has broken all the rules, is the centre of attention. Are we ever resentful when people who in our view 'don't deserve it' are treated with care, compassion and love whilst we feel undervalued or ignored? Have we ever done anything stupid and been grateful for the forgiveness shown by our friends and family? Does the church ever behave like the elder brother?

6. The father forgave his son willingly and eagerly. How easy is it to forgive? Are there things we simply cannot manage to forgive and if so, how should we deal with that?
7. The author imagines Jesus telling Reuben and Caleb to go out and bear witness. How do we do that? Where can we start? Which of our God-given talents can we use to help spread the message in ways people who know nothing of Christ can understand?

CHAPTER THIRTY-SEVEN

From death into life

Reuben

'Where is he? I have to find him – time's running out! Where is Jesus?'

I was sitting with a group of little kids, telling them the story of how Jesus fed a vast crowd with two fish and five loaves when a thin, wiry man dashed past me and grabbed Philip by the arm.

'Please, tell me where I can find him – it's urgent!'

'Jesus is praying,' Philip replied. 'But please, wait with us and when he comes back . . .'

'There's no time to wait!' the man gabbled. 'Lazarus – his dear, dear friend – is seriously ill. His sisters are desperate for Jesus to go to him. Every minute counts!'

'What's the problem?' Peter, who had also been at prayer nearby with Matthew and Andrew, came over to Philip.

'One of Jesus' friends is sick,' Philip began.

'Near to death,' the messenger insisted. 'I have to find Jesus, prayer or no prayer!'

'Look – he's coming!' I jumped up and pointed across the clearing, and then hurried towards Jesus.

'Master,' I shouted when I was near enough for him to hear, 'there's a man saying that your friend Lazarus is dying and they need you to go to him right away.'

To my surprise, Jesus' pace didn't quicken – in fact if anything he seemed to be walking even more slowly than before. It seemed an age before he reached me and when he did I repeated what I'd said, even tugging on his sleeve to reassure myself that he wasn't still in some kind of prayerful trance.

'I heard you Reuben,' he said softly. 'Thank you for telling me.'

Shock, I thought to myself. If this Lazarus man is a close friend, it'll have hit him hard. Although I couldn't quite work out why because all he had to do was get a move on and go to him and make him better. What was the problem?

'Reuben, Reuben, you didn't finish the story!' One of the younger children was jumping up and down impatiently as Jesus and I reached the messenger.

'Just a minute,' I murmured.

'Thank God!' the messenger gasped. 'Rabbi, I come from Martha and Mary – from Bethany. Lazarus is very ill and they beg you to go to him.'

Jesus said nothing for a moment and then nodded. 'Don't worry,' he said calmly. 'This sickness he has isn't fatal. In fact, it will be an opportunity to show the power and glory of God through the work of his Son.'

You could see that the messenger didn't have the faintest idea what he was on about.

'So – he'll get better?'

Jesus smiled. 'Go back to Bethany,' he said. 'Tell the sisters what I have said. Go in peace.'

And with that he turned and walked over to where Mary and Susanna, along with a number of other women, were washing clothes in the stream. And he did absolutely nothing.

Two days later, Caleb and I were gathering firewood after breakfast when Mary hurried over to us.

'Leave that,' she said. 'We won't be needing it – Jesus is leaving and he's asked some of us to go with him.'

'Us too?' Caleb and I spoke in unison.

'Of course,' she said, beckoning us to follow her. 'We're a team, right? But . . .'

She hesitated, her face becoming serious again. 'The disciples aren't happy,' she sighed. 'He's going back to Judea.'

'But I thought Peter said that was the one place to avoid,' I queried. 'He said the authorities there were determined to kill him?'

Mary swallowed hard. 'I know,' she nodded. 'But Jesus says that we have to do God's will and that way things will work out as he intends. Sometimes he's so hard to understand.'

By the time we rejoined Susanna and Esther, Jesus and the twelve were ready to leave, staffs in hand.

'So where exactly are we going?' Peter asked. 'Please tell us you've reconsidered and that you'll give Judea a wide berth. In case you've forgotten, the last time you were there you only just escaped a stoning.'

'We're going to Bethany,' Jesus replied.

'Bethany?' Caleb almost jumped out of his skin.

Jesus nodded. 'Our brother Lazarus has fallen asleep and I'm going to wake him up,' he said, and picking up his staff he set off along the path.

'But Master, wait!' Bartholomew cried. 'If he's asleep, that's no problem. He'll wake up of his own accord.'

Jesus paused and turned to face us. 'He's dead.'

Everyone gasped and Bartholomew looked acutely embarrassed.

'No! Please say it's not true!' Caleb's face paled and for a moment I thought he was going to faint.

'It is,' Jesus nodded. 'And I am pleased he died when I wasn't there because now you will all have yet another opportunity to strengthen your belief in the works of my Father. Now – no more talk; let's get going.'

'Terrific!' Thomas blurted out. 'Oh well, let's go – let's march right into their hands! We might as well all die together!'

Caleb was very quiet on the way to Bethany. Esther and I tried to engage him in conversation but he answered us in monosyllables and even refused the honey-filled dates Esther offered us.

'Caleb, it'll be OK,' Esther said gently when we were just a mile or so from Bethany, 'Jesus said he would wake this man up – but tell us, why are you so upset about a stranger?'

'I need to tell you stuff,' he burst out. 'When I was a kid I lived in Bethany. Terrible things happened and Lazarus – he was one of the few people who was truly kind and . . .'

For the next twenty minutes, Caleb poured out his life story to us and to be honest, I was speechless. I'd thought that compared with me, he'd had it easy; he'd always seemed an in-control sort of guy and certainly I'd never imagined for one minute that he'd had his own demons to deal with.

'And you were there? Just a few weeks ago?' Esther asked. 'When you said you were going to Sepphoris?'

Caleb nodded. 'They were so kind to me,' he murmured. 'They didn't blame me for Kizia's death; they still said they'd be my friends.' Then he took a deep breath. 'What about you two?'

Esther gave him a hug and for once I was glad she did.

'You don't need to ask that, do you?' she pleaded. 'Not really?'

'We're your mates,' I said gruffly. 'Always will be, no matter what.'

'Thanks. That means a lot,' Caleb replied. 'I'm glad you know the truth.'

We walked for a little while in silence, and then Caleb spoke again.

'Do you really think Jesus will – but surely even he . . . ?'

'He said he'd wake him up,' I reminded him. 'And that can only mean one thing. Can't it?'

'Reuben, he'll have been buried by now,' Caleb persisted. 'What can Jesus do?'

'I guess,' said Esther, 'we're about to find out.'

As we reached the outskirts of the village, a well-built woman ran down the street towards us and fell at Jesus' feet.

'Why didn't you come?' she sobbed. 'If you'd done as we asked, my brother would still be alive. I don't get it! Why? Why?'

'That's Martha,' Caleb whispered. He moved towards her, but the woman was gazing up at Jesus.

'But Master, even after all that's happened, I know that God will give you anything you ask for. That's true, isn't it?'

Jesus touched her shoulder. 'Your brother will rise again,' he said gently.

'Yes, yes, I know the Scriptures,' she sobbed. 'I know he will be raised up in the resurrection at the end of time.'

Jesus stood stock still. 'You need not wait for the end of time, 'he said. 'Because I am here. Now.'

He raised his voice, so that everyone turned to look at him.

'I am the resurrection and the life,' he said. 'Everyone who believes in me will live, even though they die; and everyone who lives their earthly life believing in me will never die. Do you believe this, Martha?'

She bowed her head. 'I've never stopped believing that you are the Christ, the Son of God, the one promised to us,' she murmured.

'Go now, and bring your sister Mary to me,' he said.

Mary was as different from Martha as chalk from cheese. She was bowed with grief and had to be helped along by two of the Jews who were with her, wailing loudly. When she reached Jesus she fell into his arms, weeping bitterly.

'Oh Master, if only you had been here, my brother would not have died!'

Jesus cupped her face in his hands and looked around at the weeping crowd. For a moment, it looked as if he was struggling with a huge rage; his face burned and his teeth were clenched.

'Where have you put him?' he asked.

'Come and see, Master,' Martha and Mary replied at once.

As Jesus let go of Mary, I looked at him full in the face. He was weeping, his shoulders shaking and his features contorted with sorrow.

'There's no denying how much he must have loved him,' one of the mourners said.

'Tears are all very well now,' said another. 'But if he loved him that much, why didn't he do something sooner? I've heard them say he can restore sight – he could have prevented this death, surely?'

We followed Jesus to the cave tomb way up on the hillside. On the way we passed a ruined house.

'I lived there,' Caleb whispered. I'd never seen him so pent up, as if he was battling to keep control of his temper. As we reached the tomb, the crowd fell silent.

'Take the stone away from the entrance to the tomb,' Jesus ordered.

'Master, no!' Martha burst out. 'He's been dead for four whole days – the stench will be unbearable.'

'It's unthinkable,' someone called out.

Jesus turned and looked directly at Martha. 'Martha, what have I just said? I told you that if you believed you would see the glory of God.' Then he turned to four stalwart men standing nearby. 'Go on – roll the stone away.'

With a lot of heaving and puffing and panting, the men moved the massive stone from the white limestone cave. Jesus looked heavenwards, closed his eyes and raised his arms up high.

'Father,' he cried, 'thank you for listening to me. I know you always listen but I'm talking this way for the sake of these people so that they might really believe with all their hearts that you did send me.'

He dropped his hands and walked to the entrance of the tomb. I realised that I was holding my breath.

'Lazarus, come out!' he shouted. 'Come out now!'

For a moment nothing happened. The crowd stood motionless; the only sound was the faint rustling of the leaves and the distant sound of a bird calling to its mate. Then there was a rustling, a shuffling sound from inside the tomb.

And then a great gasp went up from the crowd as a figure appeared in the entrance; a human figure wrapped from head to toe in burial cloths with a veil over his face. Some people screamed; one woman fainted. Susanna grabbed hold of Mary's hand, Esther buried her face in Caleb's chest. I stood blinking, hardly able to comprehend what had happened.

'Unwrap the grave cloths and let him go,' Jesus said.

Then he bowed his head, pressed his hands together and stood stock still while the crowd around him erupted.

So what has that got to do with me?

1. We think we know what Jesus ought to do and why, and often we are way off the mark. Why didn't Jesus go at once to Bethany? Why did he leave his friends to wait alone at a time when they needed him the most?

2. Why did Jesus let Lazarus die?

3. In this story we see a different side to Martha from the bustling, busy woman of before. We see her deep faith. Can we say with Martha, 'I believe that you are the Christ, the Son of God?'

4. Jesus wept when he saw the grief of the sisters. He cares enough to weep for us when we are grieving too. Which of the emotions that we feel day by day – anger, frustration, joy, anticipation, sorrow, hope, disappointment – has Jesus not felt too?

5. Imagine you are witnessing the raising of Lazarus. What would be your reaction? Why did the chief priests and the Pharisees still want to be rid of Jesus?

6. Jesus didn't unbind Lazarus himself. He told the onlookers to unbind Lazarus and let him walk free. What message does that give to us?

CHAPTER THIRTY-EIGHT

So where do you stand?

Seth

'My dear Joseph, how wonderful to see you! I had no idea you were back from your trip – come in, come in!'

I was just as delighted as my father to see Joseph of Arimathea, and not only because ever since I was a small boy he always brought me a gift when he travelled away on business. He was a large, broad-shouldered guy with a deep gravelly voice and a way of looking on the bright side of everything – which meant that over the years, as my mother's health and ability to understand what was going on around her deteriorated, it was Joseph who kept my father's spirits up and arranged exciting trips for me.

'Where have you been?' I asked him eagerly. 'Far away?'

'Well, I was on business for the Romans – investigating the state of some tin mines overseas,' he said, 'but . . .' He hesitated, and glanced at my father. 'I suppose the boy is old enough now for me to speak freely,' he queried. 'After all, it's his generation who will be picking up the pieces if we get this wrong.'

My father indicated with a brief wave of the hand that I might stay.

'Get what wrong?' I asked.

'Seth, you may stay,' my father said sternly. 'I did not say you could interrupt.'

'Sorry,' I muttered.

After Joseph had been served with food and drink, he leaned back in his chair and folded his hands across his ample stomach.

'Have you heard of the goings on in Bethany?' he asked.

'Indeed we have,' my father replied. 'Or at least, we've heard what surely has to be an exaggerated account of the true events. I mean, a man four days dead, coming back to life – that's embellishment if ever I heard of it.'

'It is gospel truth,' Joseph asserted. 'I was there.'

'You were – but I thought . . .'

'The day after I returned from my trip, I heard of the death of Lazarus,' Joseph explained. 'I'd known the guy for years – he was a wonderful teacher and I often thought he'd missed his vocation as a rabbi. Anyway, the friend who alerted me to his passing was setting out for Bethany to pay his respects to the sisters and I went with him.'

'So you were there when Jesus arrived?'

Joseph nodded. 'It's all true, Nicodemus,' he said. 'Jesus brought Lazarus back from the dead.'

'What – you mean?' I blurted out.

One look from my father killed the question before I could finish.

'I mean,' Joseph said, giving me a kindly smile, 'that Lazarus walked out of that tomb, bound head to foot as you would imagine, and when they released the cloths, he was as alive and coherent as you and I are right now.'

He took a long draught of wine and shook his head.

'I don't blame you for being sceptical,' he said. 'If I hadn't seen it with my own eyes, I would have felt exactly as you did.'

My father fiddled with the fringe on his robe and then stood up and began pacing the room. 'Has this altered things?' he asked. 'Are people now beginning to see?'

Joseph sighed. 'There were a number of people who put their faith in Jesus that day,' he admitted. 'But I'm sad to say that several of our number – Pharisees of good family and reputation – are demanding an immediate meeting of the Sanhedrin.'

'To what purpose?' my father asked.

'To sort out what should be done to curb Jesus' popularity,' Joseph stressed. 'The thing is, Nicodemus, before I say any more, I need to know where you stand. We're old friends and we've never had secrets from one another.' He glanced round the room. 'Come on, tell me straight,' he urged. 'Are you for Jesus or against him?'

I was furious, so angry that I felt the blood pounding in my temples. To be sent out of the room as if I were some kid who hadn't had his bar mitzvah yet just wasn't fair. My father went on and on about the need for me to grow up and take an interest in political and religious debate; and then, when something really important was on the cards, he reverted to treating me like a child.

He and Joseph were talking in such low voices that even my eavesdropping skills were tested to the limit, but after a few minutes I heard the word 'Caiphas' and a great thud as one of them banged his fist on the table. After that, they raised their voices and I got to hear most of what they were saying.

'You must come to the meeting,' Joseph was saying. 'Caiphas is, I am sure, one of those in favour of getting rid of Jesus – in fact, he's said to one or two of my colleagues that he thinks it's far better for one man to die . . .'

'Die?' My father's voice cracked.

'Die,' repeated Joseph. 'Far better, in Caiphas' view, that one should die than that the whole political system should be brought to its knees.' He tugged at his beard. 'There is a feeling that if Jesus isn't stopped, the Romans will see him as leading yet another Jewish uprising. They will crush it – and us. Caiphas wants Jesus dead.'

'That's outrageous,' my father shouted.

'So you *are* for Jesus?' Joseph murmured.

I didn't hear my father reply but I guess he must have nodded, if Joseph's response was anything to go by.

'Good man,' he said. 'Speak to no one of it. You and I must watch and wait.'

'Is there nothing we can do?' my father asked.

'These are dangerous times and we must keep our own counsel for the time being,' Joseph replied. 'But when the time comes, we must use every resource we have to see that justice is upheld. For now, act as if you were at one with all the others.'

So what has that got to do with me?

1. The members of the council, the Sanhedrin, were frightened of what the Romans would do if Jesus was allowed to carry on his revolutionary ministry. They feared that they too would be crushed. To what extent in the world today do you think that political and personal interests influence the way governments act? Do you think that governments in Christian countries always act in Christ-like ways? In what ways do you think ordinary people can change things?

CHAPTER THIRTY-NINE

Suffer the little children

Reuben

It was finding Hadlai and his sister Eda that did it for me. They were huddled together in a tumbledown shed on the outskirts of a village on the borders of Samaria and if it hadn't been for the sudden rainstorm I might never have come across them. Well, the rainstorm and the fact that I had once again well and truly messed up.

I had tried so hard. I had done what Jesus said and talked to anyone who was interested about the difference he'd made in my life. I'd repeated the stories he told to all the kids who hung round the edges of the crowd and I put up with their remarks about my legs and my lips and tried to smile my way through it all.

But I was tired. So, so, tired. It wasn't fair; I wasn't even sixteen yet but my body behaved as if I was fifty. More and more these days the walking caused my hips to ache; I had shooting pains down my left leg and there were huge callouses on my deformed feet which meant that I had to walk on the sides of my feet and not the soles. Some nights the pain was so bad that it kept me awake and believe me, there's nothing worse than listening to the snores of those around you when you can't even manage an hour's oblivion.

And then we came across the lepers. Jesus was heading for Jerusalem for the Passover and the crowd, while still big, was smaller than it had been in recent weeks. I'd tended to keep myself to myself during the day; I knew I was in a dark place, fighting the pent up anger and pain, and it didn't seem right to inflict it on Susanna and Mary who were kindness itself. What could they do about my wretched body with its aches and pains? Nothing. There was only one person who could have done that and he'd chosen not to. The odd thing was, though, that not once did I attempt to hurt myself.

Anyway, we were on the outskirts of a village on the edge of Samaria when these ten lepers came out to meet Jesus. You could see the effect that had on the people with him; lepers were bad enough, but Samaritan lepers? The crowd slowed down and the lepers, to give them their due, kept a respectful distance; but they shouted out at the tops of their voices to Jesus.

'Jesus, Master, have mercy on us!'

Jesus didn't move from where he was. 'Go now, and show yourselves to the priests!' he called back.

They turned and began to walk away – and suddenly they burst out, shouting, crying, grabbing one another and staring at their arms and legs.

'I'm clean!'

'Me too – my sores, they're gone!'

'It's a miracle!'

They disappeared out of sight and we went on our way. It's odd but a year before everyone would have been talking nineteen to the dozen about the miracle; now it was as if we all expected it. It was almost commonplace.

I think that's when the anger inside me started growing fast. One word from Jesus and ten men with a lifelong disease were cleansed; I, who had spent two years or more doing my best to be what Jesus told us to be, was aching, and hurting and putting up with the same sidelong glances and muttered whispers as I always had. Sure, I had a voice and a less ugly face and I was grateful for that but to Jesus, that was nothing. It was as easy for him as braiding Esther's hair was for Susanna.

It was an hour or so later that one of the men whom Jesus had cleansed came running towards us. Jesus was walking with Peter, James and John (what a surprise) at that point and the ex-leper rushed up to him and threw himself on the ground at Jesus' feet.

'Thank you, thank you, Master!' he cried. 'I can't tell you how grateful I am. Praise be to God for what you have done!'

Jesus stretched out a hand and raised him to his feet.

'Didn't I cleanse ten men?' he asked.

'You did, Master,' the man replied.

'So tell me, where are the other nine? You are a Samaritan, aren't you?'

'I am.'

'And yet you, a foreigner, were the only one who bothered to come back and give thanks and praise to God? Well, get up and go home; it is your faith that has healed you.'

The black, slimy, vicious little demon that I thought Jesus had got rid of once and for all was there, in my throat, pounding in my head, twisting my gut for all he was worth.

'You had faith and did he heal you? Oh, sure a token gesture but why would he do more? You're not worth it!' It was as if the thing had a voice. My breathing started to come faster, I bit the inside of my cheek until I could taste the blood and then the twitching began in my fingers.

I had to get away. It was all coming back – the badness that I thought had been banished forever was inside me, as black and as powerful as ever. He hadn't got rid of it – not for long. I was back where I started from – nothing had changed. The outside was better, but the inside was as foul as it had always been. He'd let me down big time.

I turned and I ran. I ran through the pain in my legs and the ache in my feet. I ran with tears pouring down my cheeks. And then it began to rain and I saw the shed. It wasn't the shelter that appealed to me as much as the old nails lying scattered outside. I grabbed two huge, rusty nails and barged into the shed.

It was dark and the rain was beating on the leaking roof and running in rivulets down the inside of the walls. 'Worthless, useless boy!' I shouted as I tore one of the nails down my arm. The pain was excruciating – and then, the relief was exquisite. That was enough. I sank to my knees in the corner of the hut and wept. I wept because I'd failed; I wept because after all these weeks, I'd done it again. I wept because I was rubbish.

At first I thought the rustling sound coming from a pile of sacking in the far corner of the shed was made by rats. I threw the nails away, picked up a piece of wood and crept over, ready to chase the hateful things out. Then I saw the hand – a tiny hand clutching at a piece of blue cloth. Gingerly I tweaked back the sack and there they were.

'Go away – you touch my sister and I'll kill you!'

The boy couldn't have been more than six years old but he jumped up and stood in front of the little girl arms spread wide as if to repel any attack. At his feet, curled up with her back to me, was a tiny girl, probably not more than two years old.

'I am not going to hurt either of you,' I said, dropping the piece of wood.

'You shouted,' the boy said.

'I know but . . .'

'That's what happens,' he said. 'Shouting first, hitting next. But if you touch me . . .'

For a moment, I saw my six-year-old self standing in front of me. I saw the fear and I felt the dread. I wanted to cry but that wouldn't have helped this kid.

'I won't touch you, I promise – do you think arms like this can hit hard? And why would I want to hit you?'

He said nothing but his features relaxed just a little.

'What is your name?' I asked gently.

'What's it to you?'

'OK, but tell me, do you like figs?'

I put my hand into my bag and held out the fruit. He snatched it, and began stuffing the figs into his mouth and then stopped.

'Eda,' he whispered. 'Food.'

He broke the figs into tiny pieces and gently rolled his sister over to face him. He put them one by one into her mouth. At the sight of her my heart lurched; her hooked lip was like mine, but her whole mouth and tongue were distorted and she could barely chew.

'So I know your sister's name,' I said. 'And mine's Reuben. Couldn't you tell me yours?'

'Hadlai,' he muttered.

'Where do you come from?' I asked. 'Are you lost?'

He didn't answer but merely stared at me. 'Your face is like Eda's face,' he said eventually. 'But you can talk. How come?'

'Freely you have received, freely give.' Jesus' voice echoed in my head as I gazed at the children. They were both scrawny, undernourished and filthy; the little girl clutched her brother with one hand and the strip of dirty cloth with the other. Both pairs of eyes were filled with loss and longing.

'Come with me,' I said. 'There's someone I want you to meet.'

'Will there be more food?' the little boy asked. 'Enough for two?'

'There will,' I assured him. 'I promise.'

It took a long time. I started by carrying Eda but even though she was as light as a feather, she clearly wasn't at all sure that I was an OK person and so in the end it was Hadlai who staggered along clutching her to him, his face strained with the effort. When we finally approached the village, he stopped and stared at the crowd. It had grown in size and there were lots of women with babies in their arms, and children tugging at their skirts, all crowding round Jesus.

'Master, please, touch my son . . .'

'Master just touch my daughter and her life will be a good one . . .'

'I don't want to go there,' Hadlai stammered. 'Those people . . .'

'These people are my friends,' I said gently. 'I won't let anyone hurt you.'

From the look on his face, Hadlai very much doubted that it was in my power to protect them, but at that moment, Eda started crying, a thin, weak wail without tears.

'Come on,' I urged. 'It'll be fine.'

Being so small meant that once I had got closer to where Jesus was, I couldn't see over the heads of the people in front of me but I spotted James and John a few yards away, looking hot and bothered.

'Will you please all clear off now and leave Jesus in peace!' James shouted.

'Your children aren't ill – they don't need Jesus,' John insisted.

'Stop right there!' Jesus' voice rang out over the heads of the crowds.

'Let these little ones come to me,' he demanded. 'Don't ever stand in their way – it's children like these who are the pride and joy of the kingdom of heaven.'

James and John pulled back, looking embarrassed.

'And what's more,' Jesus added, 'unless you become like one of these children, you can forget everything about being part of the kingdom yourself.'

Just then, the crowd parted slightly and Jesus spotted me. He beckoned and I led Hadlai and Eda to him.

'Master, I found these . . .'

He put his finger to his lips and shook his head. His gaze was fixed on my arm.

I had forgotten about it. There was blood on my hand and the gash was turning a livid red. Hastily I adjusted my sleeve and dropped my eyes from Jesus' penetrating gaze.

'The children . . .' I stammered.

He closed his eyes and drew the two little ones closer to his side. At that moment, there was a commotion behind me, and I was almost knocked off my feet as a very large woman pushed past.

'Hadlai, Eda, is it – oh my darlings!'

Jesus raised his eyes.

'Master, forgive me, but these two – oh dear, oh my poor little ones!'

Hadlai turned and flung himself into the woman's arms.

'Nana, Nana . . . you came!'

The toddler wriggled out of Jesus' grasp and tottered over to the woman.

Her lip was as perfectly formed as Hadlai's and when I heard her cry 'Nana' I knew her healing was complete.

The woman gazed at her granddaughter and grabbed Jesus' hand.

'Thank you, thank you!' It was the children's grandmother. 'Her mouth – you've mended it!'

'She is healed, but it was Reuben who brought her here,' he said gently.

At that the woman turned to me. 'I'm so grateful,' she cried. 'My daughter – she does this, she runs off, she abandons them, but no more! Now they're here with me, and I'm not going to let them out of my sight ever again!' With Hadlai gripping her hand and the toddler in her arms, still hanging onto her piece of blue cloth, she disappeared into the crowd.

Jesus had his eyes fixed on my arm as if he could see through the fabric of my tunic. I knew what I had to do. Right there, ignoring the press of the throng trying to get his attention, I knelt before Jesus.

'I am so sorry, Master,' I whispered, forcing myself to look him full in the face. 'I was so angry.'

'With me.' It wasn't a question, it was a statement.

I wanted to deny it. I wanted to say that he wasn't the one I was furious with, it was myself. But that wouldn't have been true and he would have known I was lying.

'Forgive me Master. Please forgive me.'

Jesus leaned forward and touched my arm. 'Reuben, Reuben, you are beautiful in the eyes of God,' he murmured so softly that I doubt anyone else could hear. 'Now learn to love yourself as much as he loves you.' He smiled. 'Now go and find your friends – they love you too.'

On my way through the village, I lifted my sleeve intending to try to wipe away the blood. There wasn't a single mark left. Every scar of the bad times had gone.

So what has that got to do with me?

1. What do you think prevented the nine lepers from returning to Jesus to thank him for cleansing them?
2. Do you find it easier to ask God for something or to give thanks for what you already have?
3. For Reuben, the black cloud threatened to return big time. Sometimes our love of God and our acceptance of his healing power in our life is not, to begin with, enough to permanently get rid of whatever habit or behaviour is challenging us. When we imagine we are slipping back into our old ways, what should we do? What sometimes prevents us from turning again to Jesus?
4. Jesus knew Reuben was angry with him. He knew Reuben thought he'd let him down big time. What was healing about Reuben's response to him?
5. What was Jesus' gift to Reuben after this encounter?

CHAPTER FORTY

One day in Jericho

Esther

I was excited – I had never been to Jerusalem, and Jesus had told us once again that he was heading that way. I set off that morning with a spring in my step, and even the knowledge that we were on the borders of Samaria couldn't dampen my spirits. But the feeling of joy wasn't destined to last long.

From the moment we had left our lodgings, things felt different. The crowd following Jesus was smaller than usual; I guess quite a few of the regular followers weren't keen on venturing into Samaria and others were preparing to go to their own hometowns for the Passover which was only ten days away. Jesus was quiet and thoughtful, walking a good quarter of a mile ahead of the disciples, head bowed in thought. James and John were bickering among themselves about something or other, Thaddeus and Bartholomew were complaining of stomach cramps and Peter was edgy and uptight, constantly mumbling about the insanity of Jesus' chosen route. I was pleased to be walking with Reuben, who seemed in very high spirits, and Caleb who at one moment, I had thought, was going to hold my hand.

He didn't. But he kept looking at me out of the corner of his eye. Of course, I pretended not to notice but when I stumbled on a loose stone on the path, he grabbed my hand and held on to it for at least a minute after I had regained my balance. The only trouble was that I kept wondering whether Seth's hand would feel any different in mine. I knew it was a ridiculous waste of time; I was never going to see Seth again and even if I did, the son of a

Pharisee of high standing and a servant girl from Galilee . . . it was a non-starter.

'Wow, look at him!'

Caleb nudged me as a tall man of about eighteen strode past us at speed, heading for Jesus. He was really good-looking with lighter skin than most of the people I knew. His tunic was richly trimmed and his mantle was of the finest cloth without a speck of dirt on it. It only took a moment to see why – a bay stallion trotted past us led by a young servant boy and halted a few feet away. By the time we had caught up with Jesus, the young man had got his attention.

'Tell me, good teacher, what must I do to ensure that I gain eternal life?'

Jesus eyed him up and down from the top of his head to the feet shod in expensive leather sandals.

'Why are you calling me good?' Jesus queried. 'There is only one person who is good and that is God. Besides, you know the commandments surely? Do not murder, don't commit adultery, don't steal, don't tell lies, don't cheat anyone, and give your father and mother the respect due to them.'

'I have done all those things, ever since I was a small child,' the man said.

Caleb nudged me. 'I bet he hasn't,' he whispered. 'I mean, no one is that perfect, are they?'

I mentally ran Jesus' list through in my mind. I was OK on the murdering and adultery front but I had pinched food, told fibs and as for respecting my father . . . no way. Did Jesus really mean we had to respect our parents no matter what they did to us?

Jesus was looking at the young man full in the face, and it was a look of pure love, as if he was a member of his own family.

'Alright,' he said. 'So there is only one thing left to do.'

'Yes, teacher?' the man urged eagerly.

'Go and sell all you have and distribute it among the poor. That way, you will still have plenty of treasure, but it will be heavenly treasure. And when you have done that, come and follow me!'

The man's expression changed from one of smug self-righteousness to one of abject horror and disbelief. After a minute, he turned, beckoned to his servant, mounted his horse and rode away without a backward glance.

Jesus turned to the group of us standing nearby and sighed.

'It is so hard for people who have a great deal of material wealth to enter the kingdom of heaven,' he said. 'Indeed, it's easier for a camel to go through the eye of a needle than it is for the rich to gain entry to God's kingdom.'

'What chance is there for anyone then?' Caleb muttered.

Jesus heard him and turned round at once. 'There's no chance at all if you rely on your own wits – but every chance if you allow God to take control.'

At that, Peter, who had been standing with Andrew and Philip, butted in. 'Take our case, then, Master,' he said. 'We left absolutely everything we had to follow you.'

'I know that, Peter,' Jesus replied calmly. 'And believe me, no one who gives up the security of home, of family life, of farming the land or fishing the lake, because of me and my teaching will lose out because of taking that choice.'

'Yes, but tell that to the folks back home,' James murmured.

'You'll get everything back ten times over – but I have to tell you, it doesn't mean there won't be trouble for you as well. But the prize is not now, in this life; your reward will be eternal life. So many people who look like winners to you right now will end up as losers; and the losers, the ones who seem to have nothing that the world values, will gain the first prize!'

He hitched his mantle into his girdle and beckoned to Peter. 'Listen,' he said. 'The kingdom of heaven is like a vineyard owner. He goes out one morning at the crack of dawn to hire workers to pick the grapes. He agrees that he will pay them one denarius for a day's work. Later that morning, after he's completed other business, he spots some more men, idly killing time in the town square, so he offers them work and promises them a fair wage. He does the same thing at midday and at three in the afternoon, because he couldn't bear to see fit men hanging around with nothing to occupy them.'

Jesus glanced round at us with a wry smile on his face. 'Now when the day's work was done, the owner of the vineyard asked the foreman to call the workers in and pay them, starting with the ones that were hired late in the day and working his way through to those who had been there since dawn. And that's when the trouble started.'

'Wasn't the man good at arithmetic?' Thaddeus joked.

Jesus smiled. 'What happened was this,' he replied. 'He gave the men who were hired last of all one denarius. Of course, those who started work early had expected that they would be paid that amount but realising that they'd done at least eight hours more labour, they got very excited, thinking that they would receive at least double. But they were given just the same – one denarius. In fact every worker, no matter how long they had laboured, received the same.'

'But that's so unfair!' Caleb muttered in my ear. 'If I'd been in their shoes, I'd have kicked up a fuss, I can tell you.'

'What happened?' Peter asked. 'Knowing you, there has to be a twist in the tale!'

Jesus laughed. 'Well, one of the workers from the early morning crew spoke up. "Don't you realise that working in the heat of the day was a lot harder than doing a couple of hours picking in the cool of the evening?" he asked. "Why are you being so unfair?"'

Jesus paused.

'"I'm not being unfair," the owner replied. "I have paid you the wage we agreed. I also decided that I would pay everyone the same. It's my money and I can do with it whatever I like. You have received what you were promised and just because I'm generous, that's no reason for you to be mean and tight-fisted."'

Jesus rubbed the back of his neck as if weary with storytelling. 'So now, all of you, do you begin to get it? Do you begin to understand what I mean when I say that the kingdom of heaven turns everything upside down? That the first shall be last and the last shall be first?'

As we scrambled to our feet and resumed the journey, Reuben nudged me.

'Hey, if this first and last thing is true, we'll be up there with the best of them won't we? That is so cool.' He paused. 'Do you get all this stuff about the kingdom? I mean, what it will look like and where it is?'

I shook my head.

'Caleb?' Reuben persisted. 'Do you understand any of it?'

'I thought I did,' he admitted. 'I thought Jesus would overthrow the government, set himself up as king and everyone who followed him would be made for life. But now I'm not sure what he means. But one thing is certain.'

'What?' I asked.

'He's heading for Jerusalem and he's obviously got a plan,' Caleb stressed. 'And I for one want to be there when he sorts it all out.'

'Ziva, what's wrong? What are you crying for?'

It was early evening and Ziva had been with Susanna and Mary preparing food for Jesus and the twelve. Jesus had been quiet and thoughtful all afternoon and when we stopped for the night, he had called the twelve to him, along with Mary and Susanna and some of the other women, and taken them to one side. I had seen them deep in conversation and then suddenly, things had erupted. Peter jumped to his feet waving his arms in the air and arguing with Jesus; Bartholomew and Matthew sat with their heads in their hands and James stormed off and began punching a tree trunk with his fist.

That was when Ziva came rushing up to us, tears streaming down her face.

'What's going on?' Reuben cried.

'Jesus is going to Jerusalem and no one wants him to but he won't change his mind,' she cried. 'He says that when we get there he will be betrayed to the religious leaders. He says they will . . .' Her voice cracked. 'They will sentence him to death!'

'No!' Caleb and I cried out in unison.

'They can't do that,' Reuben cried. 'He's done nothing wrong!'

'He stopped those men from killing me' Ziva gulped. 'So surely . . .'

'Exactly!' Caleb said. 'He'd do the same for himself.'

'So why did he say he would die?' Ziva persisted. 'And he said something else. He said he would rise again in three days. I guess that's how long it takes to get to heaven.'

'He can't die,' Caleb declared. 'That would make a nonsense of everything. He said he has come to bring peace and justice so it's obvious – he's going to sort out the Romans. One day he'll die, sure – we all will. But it won't be yet. It can't be.'

A group of us women were sitting round the fire mending some clothes that evening. Mary, the mother of Jesus had joined us; she said very little, sitting quietly next to Susanna who was her friend and listening intently to all the conversations around her. Even though it was some time since Joseph, her husband, had died, there was still a deep sadness in Mary's eyes that never disappeared, even when she laughed.

Suddenly, without warning, Salome jumped to her feet.

'I've got to do it and I've got to do it now,' she declared. 'Look, he's coming over to us with my boys – I'm never going to get another opportunity like this.'

She tossed her mending to one side as Jesus approached, not only with James and John, but several of the other disciples.

'Peace, friends,' he said. 'We were just wondering whether there was any more of that wonderful fig pastry going begging?'

'I think we have some,' his mother began, but Salome interrupted.

'Master, there's something I need to say to you.'

'Go ahead,' Jesus replied, which was just as well because it was obvious that Salome had no intention of stopping.

'My husband Zebedee and I have given up our sons to you. And it's not been easy; we've had to do without their help for weeks at a time, for almost three years now. So – I want to ask something of you.'

'What is that?' Jesus said, biting hungrily into the pastry.

'Promise me that when you come to power, my boys will be there beside you, one on your right and one on your left.'

'For goodness sake . . .' Peter burst out.

'What's so special about those two?' Philip demanded.

Jesus held up his hand.

'Salome, you don't have the faintest idea what you are asking,' he said.

He turned to James and John. 'Are you capable of drinking from the cup that I'm about to drink?'

'Yes, we can do anything,' they replied. 'We're in for the long haul.'

Jesus sighed. 'Actually, you will drink it – but as for your position at my side, that's not up to me.'

'Did you put your mother up to this?' Bartholomew blurted out.

'Typical of you two,' Judas muttered.

'Stop it, all of you!' Jesus shouted. 'And listen to me – you've seen how Gentile rulers behave, lording it over their subjects and calling the shots to suit themselves. Well, that's not the way it's going to be with you.'

He rubbed his eyes wearily. 'How many more times must I tell you? Anyone who wants to become great must first become a servant. Whoever wants to take the prime position must become a slave first.'

'But . . .' Salome stammered.

'This is what the Son of Man has done,' he told her, fixing her with a steely gaze. 'The Son of Man came not to be served but to serve – and then to give his life away in order that others might have life in all its glorious, joyful abundance.'

He leaned over and took Salome's hand.

'Your love for your sons does you credit,' he said. 'But it is love for God that will give you peace. So now I have a question for you.'

'Master?'

'Will you follow me?'

'To Jerusalem?' Salome asked aghast.

'To Jerusalem and way beyond,' Jesus replied.

I knew what her answer would be. After all she had Zebedee to think of, and her daughters and grandchildren; she had the hired hands to keep an eye on, not to mention helping Peter's wife to care for her mother. It wasn't fair of Jesus to expect her to leave all that behind.

'Will you?' he repeated.

'Yes,' she replied, nodding slowly as if pondering a totally new piece of information. 'Yes, Lord, if you wish it, I will.'

Jesus lingered in and around Jericho for a few more days, long enough for Salome to return home with a few of the other followers from Capernaum and make arrangements for the care of Zebedee.

'My neighbours are good people, and they will cook for him,' she told Susanna before she left. 'And he will be content knowing I'm with my boys.'

'You were like a mountain lion defending her cubs,' Mary said dryly.

'I guess I was a bit over the top,' Salome sighed. 'I don't think I'd realised quite what an effect Jesus has had on the boys. Especially John. I feel in a way as if I don't know them any more.'

'What do you mean?' Susanna asked.

'It's John I notice the change in the most,' Salome explained. 'They were both boisterous, fun loving, mischievous lads but now John is so much more thoughtful and quiet and he comes out with the most amazing comments. I asked him if he could sum up in just a few words what it was about Jesus that made him and James happy to leave everything they'd ever known – home, family, security, the lot – and follow him to – well, who knows where?'

'What did he say?' Mary asked, looking intently at Salome.

'He said, "*In him is life and the life is the light of all people everywhere. The light shines in the darkness and the darkness will never, ever extinguish it.*"'

'The light of people everywhere,' the other Mary, Jesus' mother, repeated softly. 'Never to be extinguished.'

With that she bowed her head and walked unsteadily away from us into a coppice of olive trees.

'I'll go to her,' Mary Magdalene said, but Susanna shook her head.

'Leave her,' she murmured. 'There are times when a mother needs to be alone.'

So what has that got to do with me?

1. Does Jesus expect us to respect our parents regardless of how they treat us? What if they have been cruel or abusive towards us? What was the point you think he was making? Is it possible to forgive those who have failed in their parental duty? If not, is it OK to tell God you can't forgive? Remember that God through his Holy Spirit can work miracles. Sometimes we need to respect the fact that other people, including parents and carers, have their own demons to battle with and for those who do not know the redeeming love of Christ that can be really hard.
2. If you had been one of the vineyard workers who had slogged all day in the hot sun and been paid the same as a guy who turned up an hour before the shift ended, how would you have felt? Was the vineyard owner being fair? How would you feel if you'd been a member of a drama club for years, working backstage, having walk-on parts, painting scenery and then suddenly a newcomer got the leading part in a big production?
3. What do you think it means to have life 'in all its full abundance'? Does it mean having whatever you want in terms of possessions? If not, what does it refer to?
4. In what sort of situations today would Jesus' teaching that anyone who wants to be great must be a servant first apply? Is it true today?
5. 'In him is life and the life is the light of all people everywhere. The light shines in the darkness and the darkness will never, ever extinguish it.' If you were putting this message on an iPhone app, how would you do it?

CHAPTER FORTY-ONE

The man in the tree

Reuben

We were at Jericho when I saw him.

The crowd following Jesus was getting larger again; wherever we went people poured out of houses, taverns and outhouses to see him and I'd got used to keeping on the fringes in order to avoid being knocked over or, worse, spending all day gazing at people's backsides. The air was pungent with the smell of balsam; Susanna had told me that the oils produced in Jericho were valued throughout the world and made a lot of people very wealthy.

It was strange that it was the first day that I had ever gone on ahead of Jesus and the others; but Susanna had asked me to buy some supplies and I was only too aware of the weight of coins in the leather pouch she had entrusted me with. When you're carrying that amount of money it's sensible to steer clear of crowds, even those who are professing to be upright and law abiding.

I had just rounded a bend in the road and come to a stretch that was lined with sycamores when I spotted something in the branches of one of the trees a hundred yards ahead of me. At first I thought it might be a wild cat but as I drew near, the thing shifted position.

'Ouch!'

It was a man.

'Hey you!' he called down to me. 'Is this Jesus really coming this way?'

I stared at him. He was just like me. Well, no – that's not strictly true. His clothes probably cost more than I would earn in a year and his arms were longer. But his head was too big for his body and he was small. Even from where I was standing I could see that he was probably no more than a couple of inches bigger than me.

'Can you hear me?' he yelled. 'I said . . .'

'Yes, yes, he's only half a mile or so behind me,' I shouted back. 'Um – what are you doing up the tree?'

'Huh,' the man snorted. 'I'd have thought you of all people would work that out. I want to see this Jesus and the chances of that happening if I'm down on the ground are nil.' He shifted his position, hanging on for dear life to one of the sturdier branches. 'I hope it's going to be worth it,' he muttered. 'It's pretty uncomfortable up here. Are you hanging around to see him too? Because if you are you'd better shin up another tree pretty quick.'

'Oh no,' I replied and I confess there was a note of smugness in my voice, 'I'm actually one of Jesus' followers. I've been with him for ages and I know his disciples really well.'

'You? Been with Jesus? Really?'

'Really,' I said.

'So tell me, is he everything that people say he is? I hear he heals the sick and makes the blind see. Someone even said that he mixes with anyone, even people who – well, anyone.'

'He does,' I nodded. 'And I could tell you – listen! I can hear them coming.'

I pointed back down the road from where the sound of chattering intermingled with pipe playing drifted on the breeze. Within minutes, Jesus and some of the disciples came into view. I was relieved to see that Susanna wasn't with the leaders; I wasn't sure she would be best pleased to see me hanging around when I was supposed to be at the town market. I knew I ought to get going but I was enjoying being able to show off about my connection with Jesus and thought that once he'd passed by, I could do what Andrew said, and tell this guy what he'd done for me.

By now, Jesus was level with the tree. He stopped dead in his tracks and looked up at the rustling branches.

'Zaccheus,' he called, 'come down at once! I'd like to stay at your home today.'

Well, to say I was gobsmacked is an understatement. How did Jesus know this man's name when they'd never met? How come he suddenly decided to invite himself to stay with a total stranger?

What was even more surprising was the speed with which Zaccheus shinned down the tree trunk and dropped to the ground. I had been right; he was only a couple of inches taller than me and I noticed that one shoulder was higher than the other.

'Master, you want to come to my house?' he stammered.

'I do,' Jesus nodded.

'You are most welcome,' he said. 'I can't believe that you – that I – oh Master!'

'I can't believe it either,' a large man with a greying beard and very bad body odour sniffed, glancing down at me. 'He's a tax collector, you know – scum of the earth!'

'This Jesus certainly has a strange taste in friends,' remarked another younger man. 'I guess that everything he eats at the house of Zaccheus will have been bought out of the money he creams off the taxes we pay! Filth!' With that he spat onto the ground.

Zaccheus looked at him and then back at Jesus. 'Master, right now this very day I'm going to give half of my income to the poor of this town,' he declared. 'What's more, if ever again I am caught cheating anyone, I'll pay them back fourfold.'

Jesus clapped his hands and beamed at Zaccheus, who scurried off down the street to prepare to receive Jesus. Then Jesus turned to face the crowd, who were still muttering under their breath.

'Today salvation has come to Zaccheus and his household. He too is a son of your ancestor Abraham.'

He opened his arms wide, as if he wanted to embrace the entire crowd. 'Remember, the Son of Man came to find the lost and to bring them to the safety of the kingdom.'

'So Master, you really will be setting up your kingdom when we get to Jerusalem?' It was Bartholomew who had pushed forward to ask the question.

Jesus sighed deeply. 'You think that the kingdom is suddenly going to materialise within weeks,' he said. 'Let me try to explain.'

He sat down there and then at the side of the road, and, like a wave rippling out from him to the edge of the crowd, everyone dropped to the ground to listen.

'There was once a man, a prince of royal birth, who had to go on a long journey to pick up the papers that would authorise him to rule his country. Before he left, he called ten of his servants to him and gave each of them a sum of money. He told them they were to use the money to keep things going until he got back again.

'The people of his country hated him and they signed a petition to say that no way did they want him in charge. But despite that, he came back with the necessary authority to rule.'

The man next to me grunted. 'So much for the power of the people,' he said. 'Those with position and money always win out in the end.'

Jesus cleared his throat and continued. 'The king called the servants to him and asked them what they had done with the money he had left them. The first announced that he had invested the money and that it was now worth ten times what it had been when his master left. The king was delighted. He said that because he'd proved himself so efficient over a small task, he would make him governor of ten cities.'

'Wow!'

'Amazing!'

The crowd were clearly hooked into the story.

'Then the second servant came and said he'd managed to make five times what he was left and he was given governorship of five towns. But then another servant was questioned.'

I knew Jesus and his stories well enough by now to realise that when he used the word 'but' the punchline wasn't far off.

'This servant handed back the money that had been left. "I wrapped it in a piece of cloth," he admitted, "because you are a hard taskmaster and when people get things wrong you become angry."

'"You're so right," the king stormed. "And yet you've got things so wrong! Why didn't you at least invest the money in something safe so that on my return there would have been a little interest for me to collect? But no you did nothing – nothing at all with what I entrusted to you!"

'Then he ordered that the money should be taken away from him and given to the one who had made the most profit!'

'But he'd already been rewarded,' someone at the back of the crowd shouted.

'You're right,' Jesus replied. 'And listen carefully because what the king said to the servants is what I am saying to you. Take risks and you will get more than you imagined possible; sit on the fence and play it safe and in the end you will lose even the little you have.' With that he got up, dusted down his robe and set off down the street to Zaccheus' house.

'So Reuben, I don't see a bag of groceries anywhere!'

I jumped to my feet as Susanna tapped me on the shoulder.

'I'm so sorry, I'll go right way – it was the story and the man in the tree . . .'

'Reuben, I'm teasing you!' Susanna smiled. 'It's true isn't it, what Jesus was saying? You must realise that more than most of us.'

'How do you mean?'

'Well, you've risked a lot for him, haven't you? Andrew told me he offered you a secure job back in Capernaum and you turned it down to come with us and follow Jesus. It can't have been easy for someone like you – someone who's always had to fend for himself.'

'I'm happier now than I've ever been,' I told her. 'And you know what? I can't imagine a different way of living now. When Jesus has sorted everything out in Jerusalem, do you think he'd give me a job?'

It was so long before Susanna replied that I wondered if she had heard me.

'I think,' she said eventually, 'that you must just get on with the job he's already given you.'

'Oh sure, I'll tell people all about him but I meant, a proper job . . .'

'A paid job you mean?'

'Well . . .'

'Reuben, none of us know what lies ahead,' she murmured.'All we have is today. And I think what Jesus needs is our love, and our support – and our commitment to say it like it is. That won't be easy because when people don't want to hear the truth, they usually turn against the person telling it.'

She squeezed my arm. 'Just be you, tell your story – oh, and if you don't very much mind, go shopping! Jesus may have dinner sorted, but we all need to eat too!'

So what has that got to do with me?

1. Zaccheus thought he had come to find Jesus but in reality Jesus had come to find him. Jesus is always searching for us and asking us to come to him but he never forces our response. What situations in everyday life might be a call from Christ?
2. How do you think Zaccheus felt when Jesus said he would stay in his house? Why did Jesus do this rather than simply talking to him in the street?
3. Jesus told the parable of the king's servants to explain how people should live between his death and second coming. How can we use our gifts in ways that will further God's purpose and bring him joy? Do you imagine that you have to do amazing things that hit the headlines in order to please God? If so think again! Listening to a friend, praying for others, visiting a sick relative – all those things gladden God's heart and further his kingdom.
4. Zaccheus was a tax collector, shunned by society because despite being a Jew, he worked for the Romans and in all probability creamed off some of the taxes for himself. Despite this, Jesus loved him and that love changed Zaccheus just as Matthew, another tax collector, had had his life changed. Who are the people we might ignore, or shun, or openly criticise? How do you think Jesus would want us to treat them, and how could we set about it?
5. Zaccheus didn't just say he was going to change, he did something about it. Does your faith result in action?

CHAPTER FORTY-TWO

A den of thieves

Caleb

Six days before the Passover, Jesus arrived in Bethany, where Lazarus lived, whom Jesus had raised from the dead. Here a dinner was given in Jesus' honour. Martha served, while Lazarus was among those reclining at the table with him. Then Mary took about a pint of pure nard, an expensive perfume; she poured it on Jesus' feet and wiped his feet with her hair. And the house was filled with the fragrance of the perfume. But one of his disciples, Judas Iscariot, who was later to betray him, objected. 'Why wasn't this perfume sold and the money given to the poor? It was worth a year's wages.' He did not say this because he cared about the poor but because he was a thief; as keeper of the money bag, he used to help himself to what was put into it. 'Leave her alone,' Jesus replied. 'You will always have the poor among you but you will not always have me.'

John 12:1-8

It was no good. Despite everything that Jesus said, despite the kindness of Lazarus and his sisters a few months earlier, I wasn't comfortable in Bethany. Every street held a memory; every household knew something of my past.

And everywhere I looked I saw Kizia. Jesus said I was forgiven, that it was all in the past. So why was I still feeling so bad?

The day after our arrival, Lazarus gave a dinner in honour of Jesus who was staying at his house. The twelve disciples were at the meal, of course; the rest of us were scattered round the village, many sleeping in the open, others, like Susanna and Mary, lodging with friends. It was a warm evening with a gentle breeze, and yet I felt as if I was suffocating. I had to get the hell out of there.

'Where are you going?' Esther asked as I jumped up and hooked my tunic into my girdle.

'For a walk,' I said abruptly, 'and no – I don't want company.'

I hated myself for being so snappy but I craved space and silence and Esther was the kind of girl who made chatting into an art form. Without looking back, I set off up the Mount of Olives, grabbing a sturdy stick from beside the path, and smashing it into the scrubby bushes in an attempt to get rid of emotions that even I didn't understand. I felt angry, frightened and confused; angry because after all this time I was no nearer to knowing what the future held for me; frightened because whatever Jesus liked to say about not giving a thought for what I was going to eat, I only had one of my stolen pieces of jewellery left and once I'd traded that for money, where would I be without a paying job? And confused because for all the talk of a new kingdom on earth, and peace and justice, as far as I could see nothing had changed in three years. The Romans still barged through the towns and villages, demanding money, ordering people to wait on them hand and foot, taking crops that didn't belong to them; people with money still called the shots and those without scraped by on their wits and the kindness of their neighbours. I wanted more out of life than that. Much more.

I don't know how long I walked but as the temperature began to drop and the sun had finally disappeared beneath the horizon, I realised that I needed to get back to the village before dark. In daylight it was easy to keep a lookout for snakes lurking in the grass; but at night there would be wolves and wild cats to contend with and although I wouldn't have admitted it to anyone else, my experience with the pigs had left me somewhat nervous of stray animals.

I was walking back across the scrub when I heard a man's voice from inside a small coppice of trees to my right.

'Wanton waste! And then to speak to me as if I didn't know what I was talking about! He's losing the plot, there's no doubt about it.'

Out of the fading light, I could make out a familiar figure and within seconds my suspicions were confirmed. Striding from the thicket onto the path in front of me was Judas Iscariot and to my surprise, he was alone. He continued muttering to himself under his breath, stabbing his staff into the ground as he walked.

'Hi, Judas!'

He spun round, hand raised, and then on recognising me, dropped it and let out a sigh of relief.

'What are you doing up here?' he demanded.

'I could ask you the same,' I replied. 'I thought you were living it up at Lazarus' house.'

'Huh!' he grunted. 'Living it up is about right – but not in the way you think. I'm so angry – it makes a mockery of what he's been teaching.'

'Jesus?' I ventured. 'What do you mean?'

Judas looked at me long and hard. 'OK, let me run this past you,' he said, as I fell into step beside him. 'This woman Mary, right – she comes up to Jesus toward the end of the meal with a pot of pure nard. You know what nard is?'

'Perfume, isn't it?' I queried. 'But I thought it was only the nobility that could afford that kind of stuff.'

'Precisely!' Judas exclaimed. 'And what does Mary do? She empties the lot over Jesus' feet and then – the audacity of it! – she loosens her hair and wipes his feet with it!'

'Wow!' It occurred to me that Mary must love Jesus like crazy to be that generous.

'Never mind "wow"!' Judas snapped. 'Don't you realise that you could buy a whole heap of . . . well, you could feed the poor of ten villages for a year on what that cost. I said as much to Jesus.'

'I bet he agreed, right?' I knew how Jesus was always telling us to care for those who had nothing.

'You'd have thought so wouldn't you? But oh no! He turns to me and demands that I should leave her alone. He talked as though I was the one in the wrong, not her! And then he started talking in riddles, the way he so often does. He said that she was looking ahead to the day of his burial.'

He hit out at a small bush with the end of his staff. 'You will always have the poor with you but you won't always have me, that's what he said,' Judas muttered. 'As though that justified everything.'

He turned and stared hard at me. 'What do you think?'

I was pretty chuffed that one of the inner circle should care what I thought, and I was enjoying having an adult debate with Judas. The truth was, I didn't know what I thought so I did what I always did in such situations.

'You're a clever man,' I flattered. 'What do you think Jesus will do when we get to Jerusalem?'

He shot me a quizzical glance. 'I hope – I sincerely hope – he'll force the hand of the Romans and set up his own government,' he declared. 'But he won't have a hope in hell of doing that unless he gets on the right side of the authorities and the way he's carrying on these days, that's just not going to happen.'

Judas kicked a stone out of his path.

'He needs to focus on the real issue,' he said. 'Ingratiate himself with those in power, because if he doesn't change tactics soon . . .' He left the words hanging in the air as we drew near to the village and saw some of the other disciples lounging around outside Lazarus' house.

'You seem a bright lad,' Judas remarked as he acknowledged a wave from Matthew. 'I suggest you keep your ear to the ground, your eyes sharp and your thoughts to yourself. For the time being, watch and wait.' He nodded thoughtfully. 'And if you hear anything, any suggestion of discord or people turning against Jesus, keep me informed, yeah?'

'Of course!' At last, I thought, I had a purpose, a way to get into the inner circle. 'You can count on it!'

'Good man!' Judas said slapping me on the back. And with that, he strode off, the money bag that was permanently round his neck jangling as he walked.

The very next day, Jesus announced that we would be entering Jerusalem! You could feel the excitement and anticipation. It was the Sunday before Passover; Salome had returned from Capernaum, bringing fresh clothes for the women; Esther was hopping about unable to keep still for more than five minutes at a time, and a group of children were laughing and joking with Reuben, as they taught him their songs. Reuben could speak well these days but his singing – oh, boy, was it tuneless!

There was an air of eager expectancy as we set off – people were chatting, anticipating what Jesus would do and say when we arrived in the city. Even my bad mood lifted, caught up in the enthusiasm of those around me. The rains were over and at last the roads were less muddy which was just as well because the closer we got, the larger the crowd became; not just followers of Jesus, but groups of Pharisees and Saducees, merchants, pilgrims – all heading to Jerusalem for Passover. There were camels laden with goods, mules weighed down by loaded panniers, carts almost buckling under the weight of their passengers.

But Jesus walked slightly apart from the rest of us, calmly, steadily, but without saying much. I stayed close to Judas and the other disciples; Esther and the other women walked together chatting nineteen to the dozen. And then suddenly we came to a ridge near the village of Bethphage and there, in the distance, we could glimpse the city! Zion, City of our God. Jerusalem!

I couldn't believe it – I was here! I felt a lump in my throat; at last we were here, and I, Caleb barJonas, was going to be at the centre of the action. Just then Jesus beckoned to Judas.

'Take one of the others with you,' he said and go into the village.' He pointed to a cluster of small white houses half a mile away. 'As you enter the village, you'll see a colt tethered there – untie it and bring it to me. Be gentle with it – it hasn't been broken in yet. Oh, and if anyone questions you, tell them that the Lord needs it and will send it back safely very soon.'

'Yes, Master, of course,' he said and turned to beckon to one of the other disciples.

'I'll go with you!' I said hastily. 'I'd be pleased to help.'

'OK,' he said. 'Let's go.'

We found the colt just as Jesus had said. It was tethered to a post outside the first house in the village, and as I grappled to untie the knot, a man came up to us.

'What do you think you're doing?' he thundered.

'The Lord needs it,' Judas said.

'And he will have it returned very soon,' I added.

'Ah yes,' the man nodded. 'Jesus. Yes, yes, take it.'

I was astonished. I'd expected that we would have had to wrangle and argue but Judas tossed him a coin from the money bag, and gestured to me to lead the colt. I was a trifle nervous; Jesus said it had never been ridden and I imagined it might rear up or lash out with its hooves but it ambled along as docile as a lamb, just occasionally nuzzling me in search of a titbit.

As we approached Jesus, Judas strode ahead of me. 'We have the colt, Master – and it was just as you told us,' he said.

That's how it was that it was I who handed him the rope, his fingers touching mine as he took it firmly in his grasp. I shall remember that touch always.

'Master, you need something to sit on,' I heard myself saying. 'Take my mantle – it's a bit ragged but . . .'

'Thank you, Caleb, that will be a lot more comfortable,' Jesus smiled.

At that, several others offered him their cloaks and eventually we set off. Now there was a real air of festival about the long procession – some people were singing, others playing flutes or banging drums, full of joy at coming to the holy city. It was infectious; I spotted Esther whirling Reuben round and round and several of the women literally dancing along the path. Loads of people had cut branches from the trees and were waving them rhythmically in the air. Others threw their cloaks on the ground in front of him, just as if he was already a crowned king. I'd never felt so excited in my whole life.

When we reached the point where the road turned and ran down the Mount of Olives the view of the city was clear and unobstructed. Everyone fell silent; some dropped to their knees kissing the ground, others, including myself, just stood awestruck, and stared. The sun was glinting off the golden roof of the Temple and its walls were purest white; it was like something from a dream.

Then the silence was broken as someone began to chant a hymn of praise: *'Blessed is he who comes in the name of the Lord!'* Others picked up the song and soon the whole crowd were singing at the tops of their voices: *'Hosanna in the highest! Glory, glory to God on high!'*

For some reason, that didn't go down very well with a group of elderly Pharisees. They strode over to Jesus, their faces like thunder.

'Teacher, can't you control your disciples? Tell them to be quiet!'

Jesus shook his head. 'If I did, and if they kept quiet – well then, the very stones under your feet would shout out in their place, praising God!'

He dismounted from the donkey and walked to the edge of the ridge, overlooking the city. He stood there for a long while, and I could have sworn he was crying. His shoulders were shaking and from time to time he brushed his hand across his face.

> As he approached Jerusalem and saw the city, he wept over it and said, 'If you, even you, had only known on this day what would bring you peace – but now it is hidden from your eyes. The days will come upon you when your enemies will build an embankment against you and encircle you and hem you in on every side. They will dash you to the ground, you and the children within your walls. They will not leave one stone on another, because you did not recognise the time of God's coming among you.'
>
> *Luke 19:41-44*

Suddenly he raised his voice in a great cry, 'O Jerusalem, Jerusalem, it need not have been this way! You could have had peace but now you face only destruction! And why – because you didn't recognise the truth in front of your own eyes!' Then he turned, his eyes red, and remounted the donkey, kicking it onward down the path to Jerusalem.

The closer we got to the city gates, the denser the crowds became. There were sprawling lines of stalls and booths, with traders shouting out their wares at the tops of their voices. The noise was unbelievable; a dozen different accents and foreign languages all fighting to be heard.

The noise of our procession competed with the shouts of the sellers.

'Hosanna to the anointed one!'

'Jesus the Messiah is here!'

You couldn't help but get caught up in the excitement. I waved the palm I had picked up from the ground and shouted as loudly as anyone.

'Isn't this amazing?' Thaddeus laughed as he hurried past me. 'The whole city has turned out for Jesus! This is it – the moment we've been waiting for! He'll set up his kingdom and . . .'

I didn't catch the rest of what he said because the cheers rose to a crescendo as more and more palm branches were thrown in front of Jesus' donkey and people poured out of houses and workshops dancing, blowing flutes and waving their arms in the air. Some had climbed walls to get a better view, others were running alongside the procession calling to their friends to come and see the Messiah.

'Can I stick with you?'

I felt someone grab my arm as four Roman soldiers walked right in front of us and began breaking up a disturbance by one of the stalls. It was Reuben, looking hot, dishevelled and very panicky. I hadn't seen him for several hours and was surprised at how pleased I was that he'd caught up with me. Judas had got into deep conversation with some of the other disciples and although I had tried to get involved, it went way over my head; all about politics and the division of power – boring stuff like that.

'If you don't mind, that is,' Reuben added. It wasn't like him to be so passive and subdued.

'Sure,' I said and then the strangest thing happened. I looked down at him – he only comes up to my thigh – and it was as though just for a brief moment, I was seeing things through his eyes. A mass of legs, the tips of the soldiers' swords swinging at eye level, the wheels of passing carts brushing past his shoulders. I realised that while I could see Jesus ahead astride the donkey, all Reuben would be able to see was the animal's hooves; while I could brandish my palm branch with little effort, it was in fact the same length as Reuben's whole body. I guess that was the first time I had really taken on board what Reuben's life, minute by minute, was like.

'If I get lost here, I'll never . . .' he began.

'No way will I let you get lost, mate,' I assured him. 'We'll just follow where Jesus goes, OK? Together.'

He beamed and nodded. 'Everything's so big,' he gasped as we went through one of the city gates built into the vast defensive walls. 'I mean, it's always big to me but this is just something else.'

'Tell me about it,' I replied, grabbing Reuben's arm as an aggressive looking beggar thrust himself in front of us. 'Where's Esther? We need to keep an eye on her too.'

'You do, you mean,' Reuben teased and I was pleased to see he was looking a little more relaxed. 'She's back setting up camp with the other women. Ziva's here somewhere though; she seems to . . .' he hesitated.

'What?' I asked, trying not to salivate as the smell of roasting figs assailed my nostrils.

'I don't know,' he admitted. 'She's not like Esther and she's certainly not – oh, I don't know. Maybe I'm just being silly but I saw her flirting like crazy with someone in the crowd.'

'One of our lot?'

'Oh no,' Reuben said. 'He looked foreign – and rich!' He shrugged. 'Anyway, enough about her. We need to keep up with – oh! Look! Is that . . . ?'

'The Temple,' I breathed. 'It must be. I never thought it would be so . . . so . . .'

'Magnificent?' Reuben suggested. 'Is that real gold on the walls?'

'That's what I've heard,' I nodded. 'Come on – there's Jesus – he's going in! Can you run? I want to catch up, I want to see for myself . . .'

Reuben was already hobbling ahead of me. Together we dodged the throng, never once taking our eyes off the great white building.

The Temple was nothing like the synagogue back at Capernaum, nothing like the one that I'd visited at Cana. In the colonnades there were lines of tables where people queued and pushed and shoved to change their money into temple coins; opposite were stalls where doves, caged in wicker baskets, were being offered for sale. There were clusters of men, with lambs over their shoulders, waiting to hand them over for sacrifice. The air was full of smells; incense and oils mixed with the odour of terrified birds and animals. Mingled with the cries of the traders and the clinking of coins came the sound of voices lifted in prayer from deeper inside the Temple; snatches of psalms being chanted by unseen worshippers and the occasional striking of a cymbal.

When Reuben and I caught up with the disciples, Jesus was standing stock still staring ahead of him at the rows of money changers weighing coins in their metal scales.

'No!' he shouted. 'No! No!'

With that he strode up to the nearest table, and with a sweep of his arm tipped it over sending coins rolling in all directions. He did the same with the next and the next, while all the time the money changers were crawling on their hands and knees to retrieve their money, shouting abuse at him, while others stood wide-eyed in astonishment.

'What's he doing?' Reuben gasped. 'What's got into him?'

'I won't stand for this,' Jesus thundered. 'The Scriptures declare, "My Temple will be called a house of prayer," but you have turned it into a den of thieves!'

He flung another table to the floor, before turning and striding between the columns and wrenching the lid off one of the wicker baskets, letting the doves fly free into the air.

'And what's more, it is written that God wants mercy, not sacrifice,' he shouted, pulling the lids off of basket after basket, releasing a whole cloud of fluttering birds and causing people to duck to avoid them. 'Knowledge of God is what's needed, not a lot of burnt offerings!'

I moved nearer to where Judas and the other disciples were standing, frozen to the spot, their eyes full of fear.

'He's gone too far this time,' I heard Judas mutter to Matthew. 'They won't stand for this.'

By now several of the temple priests and guards, alerted by the uproar, had pushed their way through and were trying to stop Jesus. But he was on a mission; he snatched up a length of rope and began lashing out at the traders.

'Don't you remember what God said to the prophet Isaiah?' he ranted. 'He said "*I have no pleasure in the blood of bulls and lambs and goats. When you come to appear before me, who has asked this of you, this trampling of my courts? Stop bringing meaningless offerings!*"'

He lashed out with the rope once more.

'And yet you pay no attention! You who profess to know the Scriptures! Now get out, all of you and stop defiling this holy place!' With that he stormed out into the courtyard the disciples scurrying behind like anxious hens.

'This could turn nasty,' I muttered to Reuben as we hurried after them. 'We need to get out of here and fast.'

I'd already noticed clusters of Pharisees, priests and lawyers huddled together in corners, casting disparaging glances in Jesus' direction.

'Keep moving, Master,' Peter urged. 'We need to leave – like now!'

Jesus, however, didn't seem to feel the urgency. When a group of Pharisees approached him, he stopped and greeted them courteously.

Their manners were not as good.

'What do you think gives you the authority to behave the way you do? To teach the things you teach? Go on – tell us!'

Jesus looked thoughtful. 'I am going to ask you a question,' he said. 'Give me a straight answer and then I will tell you what gives me the authority to act as I do.'

'So what's the question?' one of the Pharisees demanded.

'Think about John's baptism – who authorised that? Heaven? Or human beings? Tell me that.'

For a few minutes they muttered among themselves. Then the leader of the group turned back to Jesus. 'We don't know the answer to that,' he admitted.

'Right,' Jesus said. 'Then I won't answer your questions either.'

You would have thought that when he saw those same Pharisees scuttling off muttering under their breath, Jesus would have realised that it was time to beat a hasty retreat. But no – despite there being at least a dozen more high ranking officials lurking about in the courtyard, Jesus stood in the middle of the crowd and began teaching as though this was just a normal day in Galilee.

'There was once a man who planted a vineyard,' he began. 'He built a wall round it, dug a winepress and built a watchtower. Then he leased it to some tenant growers and went off on a trip. When the time came for the harvest, he sent one of his servants to the tenants to collect some of the fruit; but they seized the servant, beat him and sent him back empty-handed.'

He looked directly at the group of Pharisees and they glowered back at him.

'He sent another servant, and they beat him up too; he sent a third and they killed him.'

The crowd gasped but Jesus went straight on.

'So then he sent his only son, whom he loved dearly. He believed that whatever else these people had done, they would at least respect his son. But he was wrong.' Again he fixed his gaze on the Pharisees. 'These tenants got together and decided that if they killed the son and heir to the vineyard, then everything would be theirs. So that's what they did; they slaughtered him. What do you think the vineyard owner would do?' He paused, his eyes scanning the crowd.

'I'll tell you,' he shouted. 'He'll get rid of those tenants once and for all and give the vineyard to others. And you—'

He stared at the Pharisees. 'You of all people should understand!' He was shouting now. 'You who know the Scriptures so well – haven't you read the words of the psalmist? *"The stone the builders rejected has become the cornerstone – it is the work of God and it is wonderful to see"?'*

At that every one of the Pharisees turned on their heels and strode out of the temple courtyard.

'I'm hungry, I muttered to Reuben a few minutes after we'd left. 'Do you think those stalls back by the gate . . . ?'

'I haven't any money,' Reuben sighed.

'I wasn't thinking of using money,' I winked. 'I mean, it's very crowded and things get knocked over and . . .'

'I haven't done anything like that since Jesus . . .'

'Me neither,' I admitted. 'But it is tempting, and I am hungry . . .'

'I don't know,' Reuben hesitated, and that's when I had my great idea. I broke into a run and caught up with Judas.

'My friend Reuben – the one Jesus gave a voice to,' I began (after all, bringing Jesus into the conversation could only work in my favour), 'he's starving and I wonder, just perhaps if you could give us enough for a loaf or . . .'

Judas paused, stepped away from his companions and opened his money bag.

'You're doing what I asked?' he queried. 'Keeping an ear to the ground?'

'Oh sure,' I said. 'That tall Pharisee – the one with the scar on his forehead – he said time is running out for Jesus and anyone else who doesn't start toeing the line. He said it would be as well to shut the mouth of this . . .' I hesitated, trying to remember what I had overheard, '. . . this upstart and do the same to his followers.'

Judas looked alarmed. 'He said that? The tall one?' he murmured. 'Good lad. Always good to know who one's enemies are. Here, take this and get a good meal.' With that he hurried after the other disciples.

'Look!' I opened my palm and Reuben gasped at the number of coins Judas had given me.

'How did you persuade him to do that?' he asked as we hurried towards the food sellers' stalls.

'We're good mates,' I bragged. 'I scratch his back, he scratches mine.'

I felt so good saying it, like I'd finally arrived. I waited for Reuben to congratulate me but he didn't say a word. He was too busy salivating over some roasting lamb on a nearby spit.

So what has that got to do with me?

1. Jesus has forgiven Caleb yet he still feels 'so bad'? Why do we find it so hard to accept that we are forgiven? Why are we tempted to hang on to our guilt and to past hurts? And if we do accept that we are forgiven, does it make it easier for us to forgive others?
2. Jesus wept over Jerusalem because its leaders had rejected God's offer of salvation and he knew that their nation would suffer. God offers salvation to everyone; it is up to us to accept him into our lives and let him direct and guide us. All of which sounds terrific – but why are we still tempted to do things 'our way', to cherry-pick the bits of Christ's teaching that sit comfortably with us, and ignore those bits that are more challenging? Is it through fear? Stubborness? Peer pressure?
3. Jesus' predictions about the ruin of Jerusalem came true forty years later. In AD 66 the Jews revolted against Roman rule and in AD 69 Titus, the son of the Emperor Vespasian, was sent to crush the rebels. In AD 70 they burned the city and 600,000 Jews were killed. Jesus was no cheapskate astrologer; his words and his predictions are truth.
4. Are you surprised that Jesus showed such intense anger? We often think of the children's hymn about 'gentle Jesus meek and mild' but here we see his righteous anger over the misuse of a holy place. What is righteous anger? Under what circumstances is it right for Christians to express anger, and when is it not appropriate?
5. In the story of the vineyard, the man who planted it is God, the vineyard is the nation of Israel, the tenants are the religious leaders, the servants are the prophets and priests who are faithful to God, the son is Jesus and the others are Gentiles. Does this explain the anger of the Pharisees when they heard the story?

CHAPTER FORTY-THREE

Temple truths

Seth

'This is getting out of control!'

'All that palm waving and cheering and singing – didn't they realise it would just make things worse?'

'He's just inflaming the situation – if he would tone it down . . .' My father sounded stressed and anxious. He and Joseph of Arimathea had returned from the latest meeting of the high council and were closeted in my father's room.

'Tone it down?' Joseph exclaimed. 'Come off it – you and I and at least three others have complained for years that the money changers were taking over the temple precincts. It was just that he had the guts to do something about it.'

'True, but it was the way he went about it,' my father sighed.

'A bit over the top possibly,' Joseph admitted. 'But then it seems the Nazarene does nothing by halves!'

'Joseph, are you deliberately ignoring what Ezechiel said at the meeting last night?' my father sighed.

'About Jesus doing far more than ridding the Temple of commerce and bartering, you mean?' Joseph asked.

'Exactly,' my father nodded. 'He maintains that what Jesus was really doing was taking a swipe – a death blow, you might call it – at the whole foundation of Temple worship. Ezechiel reckons he released all the birds, not just because he resented money changing hands, but because he wants an end to sacrificial worship.'

For a moment, there was silence. Then Joseph cleared his throat and I could hear his chair scraping against the floor. 'I don't know about that,' he declared, 'because he doesn't seem to want to change everything we do. I mean you have to admit that what he said about giving Caesar his due was dead clever. Who could argue with that?'

Loitering outside my father's room I decided that the time had come to put him to the test. If he thought I was old enough to study all the boring stuff he gave me day after day, then I was old enough to be in on this discussion. I pushed aside the curtain dividing my father's room from the passage and stepped inside.

'Father, forgive me for interrupting but may I join in? I want to learn about . . .' I hesitated. The truth was that I wanted to know as much as possible about the man that Esther and the others had been so sure was going to turn the world upside down.

'. . . about any threats to our nation,' I finished. I knew I sounded like a stuck-up little prig but sometimes the end justifies the means – or so I've been taught.

'Stay,' my father nodded. 'In fact, let me run this past you. Some of our members went to see Jesus earlier. They told him that they respected him because he taught God's truth . . .'

'That was a lie for a start!' Joseph blurted out. 'They don't respect him! It was a set-up.'

'If I might finish,' my father said politely, turning back to me. 'They asked him whether it was right to pay taxes to Caesar or not? So Seth, what would you have said?'

'Me?' I gasped. 'I – er – well, I guess it's the law. You don't pay, you get thrown into prison. So I suppose he said it was right to pay them.'

'Jesus,' my father smiled, 'is cleverer than you.'

'Be fair on the lad,' Joseph added. 'Jesus is wiser than all of us.'

He beckoned me to his side. 'He got them to produce a denarius and then asked them whose head was on it,' he went on. 'Of course, they said it was Caesar's head. And you know what he said then?'

He didn't wait for me to guess which was just as well because I hadn't a clue.

'He said, "So give to Caesar the things that are rightfully his, and give to God the things that belong to him."' He clasped his hands together. 'That shut them up,' he sighed. 'But it also made them a whole heap more angry than they were to start with.'

My father nodded.

'The mood at the meeting today was ugly,' he said. 'Caiphas has ordered spies to go out in the streets and report back every word that Jesus speaks.'

'And the fact that King Herod is in Jerusalem means there are twice as many Roman soldiers patrolling the streets than usual,' my father added. 'This crowd that follows Jesus everywhere seem oblivious to the risks they're taking – I know they're only Galileans but honestly, if they had any sense . . .'

'People have come all the way from Galilee?' I burst out. 'Just his disciples you mean?'

'I wish,' my father muttered. 'But no, there are hundreds, if not thousands of them. A scruffy lot for the most part but surprisingly a number of women, well off, educated women by all accounts who by rights should be at home caring for their menfolk and not . . .'

'Really? Are you sure?'

My father glared at me and I prayed that I hadn't gone too far.

'Of course I'm sure,' he murmured. 'I don't just sit in the council, you know. I do go and see for myself. Joseph too – we don't just follow the herd.'

Joseph nodded.

'This Nazarene seems to have the power to attract people to him like – like bees to honeycomb. And to be honest, much of what he says makes sense. He opens up so many questions, so many possibilities . . . and I confess he's forced me to look at the whole way we do things in a different light.'

'He's one of the people and yet he's one on his own,' my father sighed. 'Do you think . . .'

I wasn't listening any more. I was planning. If Susanna and Mary were in Jerusalem, then Esther would be too. Of that I was certain. And if she was in the city, I was going to get out there and do my very best to find her.

'This is a time for great caution,' Joseph said, as if he had been reading my mind. 'We don't know who can be trusted and who cannot.'

'We can't just sit around and do nothing,' my father ventured.

'Indeed not,' Joseph agreed. 'But for now, we'll have the most chance of influencing the outcome if we attend the meetings and try to calm things down.'

'For Jesus?' my father asked.

'For Jesus,' Joseph replied. 'I fear that we only have a short time in which to make sure that sanity prevails.'

And I only had a short time in which to find Esther. Once Passover was over, Jesus would go back to Judea or Galilee and that would be that. Time was running out.

I went out early the following morning. My father had already left to do some business on the other side of the city; my mother – well, she was having a bad day; she didn't know who I was, never mind care where I was going, and the servants were easily persuaded that I was off to see my uncle.

The city was throbbing with life, even at that early hour. I went straight to the Temple; I realised later that it was a stupid thing to do but at the time, I imagined Jesus would be there, and if he was there, the disciples wouldn't be far off.

I made my way straight to the Court of the Women; if Susanna and Mary were with Jesus, that's where they would be; they had no choice as they weren't allowed to go any further And my luck was in: Jesus was there with a crowd of his disciples. The problem was that at least four of my father's cronies from the Sanhedrin were there too – any of whom would have recognised me in an instant. Jesus was already in full flood and everyone's eyes were fixed on him so luckily I was able to sneak round the back of the crowd and kneel down behind one of the white marble pillars; if anyone came near I would close my eyes and pretend to be deep in prayer.

'The teachers of religion and the Pharisees are good at getting across to you the law of Moses,' Jesus was saying. 'So listen to them.'

Well, I thought, that's a change – maybe Jesus had decided that, after all, the time had come to backtrack and appease the leaders.

'Yes, listen to what they *say* when they teach you the law of Moses,' he said, 'but don't be tempted to do what they do! They tell a good story, but they don't live out their teaching.'

Then again, I thought, perhaps backtracking wasn't his style.

'They don't teach God's law the way they should – as something you can feed on and be nourished by and gain joy from. No, they just wrap it all up in a whole heap of their own rules and regulations, burdening you with stuff you can't possibly carry. And don't they love it!'

A couple of Pharisees, one of whom was Rabinth, my father's friend, were moving silently round the crowd, drawing nearer to where I was hiding. I dropped my head to the floor, laid my palms on the cold stone, and hoped against hope that I looked the picture of passive devotion.

'The thing about the Pharisees,' Jesus went on, his voice echoing around the colonnade, 'is that they love to show off – they want their phylacteries to be wider and their tassels longer than anyone else's; they grab the best seats in the synagogues and preen themselves when people call them "rabbi".'

I opened one eye, took in the look of fury on Rabinth's face and shut it again.

'The plain fact is this: you shouldn't call anyone rabbi because you only have one master and you are all brothers and sisters. And you shouldn't call anyone on earth "father" because you have only one Father – your Father in heaven. As for calling anyone teacher – don't do it! The only teacher you have is the Christ.'

At that, a babble broke out among the crowd, not all of it friendly.

'Let me tell you this,' Jesus went on. 'Whoever puffs himself up and tries to make himself important, will be brought to his knees, and everyone who denies themselves and acts humbly will be given a far higher position.'

It was at that moment that I realised that my hiding place was actually not hidden at all. If I'd had half a grain of common sense, I would have noticed the eleven trumpets – the money chests – lined up against the wall, waiting for worshippers to drop in their offerings. In my head, I could hear my rabbi intoning the lesson I'd had to learn as a small boy: 'Trumpet one and trumpet two for the half shekel temple tribute, trumpet three for the turtle dove money, trumpet four for the pigeons . . .'

I pulled my head covering down over my forehead and kept my head bowed as several of the Pharisees, including Archelaus and Rabinth, made their way to the chests and began taking money from their girdle pouches and dropping the coins noisily into various chests.

'I'm giving rather more than usual this week – for incense, you know – so important . . .' Rabinth shouted across to Archelaus.

'I'm contributing not only to incense but to new vessels for our worship – I know I'm criticised for being too generous but I can't help being abundant in my giving,' Archelaus replied even more loudly.

Jesus strode over and stood between the two of them. 'Look at this!' he shouted, turning to face his disciples. I shrank back behind my pillar. 'This proves my point,' he declared. 'These two men are being generous indeed – and don't they make sure we all know it! But look over there.' He pointed to the far end of the Court of the Women. A bent old lady was standing by one of the money trumpets; slowly she counted out first one, then two leptons.

'I tell you in all honesty that the money that poor widow has just donated has more worth than all of yours.'

I thought by the look on Rabinth's face that he might actually explode with anger.

'Why do I say this?' Jesus went on calmly. 'Because you are wealthy and can spare what you donate; what that widow gave represents all she has to live on today.' With that he moved on but before I could slip away Rabinth turned and came to within three feet of the pillar behind which I was hiding.

'That does it,' he snorted. 'The man must be stopped. He is undermining everything that is sacrosanct, every structure of society, every way that we have done things for generations – he is . . .'

To my relief he spotted a colleague on the far side of the court, giving me the chance to take a quick look around the groups of worshippers in the hope of finding Susanna. That was when I spotted him. The little fellow – Reuben – the guy whose life I'd saved. I couldn't believe it – if anyone knew where Esther was, he would.

He was tagging along a few feet behind the last of the disciples when I caught up with him and tapped him on the shoulder. I shouldn't have been so thoughtless; he spun round, a look of terror on his face.

'Reuben, it's OK, it's only me – Seth, remember?'

His shoulders dropped and he visibly relaxed.

'You gave me the fright of my life,' he said.

'You – you just spoke!' I gasped.

'Oh yes you probably don't know about that,' he said. 'Jesus did it.'

'That is so cool!'

Reuben nodded. 'Things aren't exactly cool now though,' he murmured. 'Look – I am not being rude, or ungrateful, but well, the bottom line is . . .' He looked at the ground. 'You're the son of a Pharisee, aren't you?'

'Yes – so?'

'I know it's not your fault who your father is but I'm on Jesus' side,' he blurted out. 'And before you ask, so is Esther!'

It was as though he could read my mind and I felt the colour flood my cheeks.

'Is she OK?'

It struck me afterwards that it was odd that I had asked that question before springing to the defence of my father or, for that matter, myself.

'She's fine,' Reuben replied curtly. 'She is here somewhere, praying with Mary Magdalene and Susanna. They are worried about . . .' He stopped. 'I must go,' he said.

'Wait! Please!' I put my hand on his shoulder. 'Listen, I can't say much but believe me, not every Pharisee believes the same thing.'

'Huh!'

'Are you saying that every person in Capernaum believed Jesus was the Messiah?'

'Well, not at first,' he admitted.

'Exactly!' I stressed. 'This is not a sensible place to talk – my father says there are eavesdroppers everywhere – but please believe me. My father doesn't want anything bad to happen to Jesus.'

Reuben said nothing but at least he didn't interrupt.

'Look,' I said, 'if you'll just show me where you are all staying, then we can find somewhere safe to talk.'

Reuben stared at me.

'You must think I'm mad,' he said. 'I tell you where we are – you send soldiers to drive us away . . .'

'Reuben, that is crazy!' I shouted. 'OK, don't believe me, I really don't care. Pity you're not following Jesus, though.'

'I am so!' Reuben stormed. 'He gave me back my voice so that I could . . .'

'Slag off other people's fathers? I thought his message was that we should love our neighbours as ourselves.'

I turned and walked away, burning with anger. I should have left the little sod to die on that hillside if that was all the thanks I got for saving his life. Perhaps my father was right; those people were no-hopers . . . The thought that hit me was so horrifying that I stopped dead in my tracks.

I was doing what I'd accused Reuben of doing. Slagging him off, just because he hadn't agreed with me; echoing my father's past words without thinking whether I truly believed them. That's what Joseph and my father complained about certain of their friends doing – making judgements because they weren't open-minded enough to see the other side of the story.

I turned – and found Reuben hard on my heels.

'I'm sorry,' we spoke in unison and then grinned at one another.

'It's this city,' Reuben said apologetically. 'I hate it – it brings out the worst in me. Last night . . .' He paused. 'Anyway, I just want to be in the open country or down by the lake where I belong. I'm scared all the time – go on, laugh, I know it's silly . . .'

'No it's not,' I said seriously. 'I'm scared too. Everyone is on edge – I've never known the city like it and I've lived here all my life.'

Reuben nodded. 'Come on then,' he said beckoning me to follow him.

'Where are we going?' I asked, not daring to hope.

'To see Esther,' Reuben grinned. 'That's the only thing that will shut you up, isn't it?'

There she was, standing near the Beautiful Gate, with Mary, Susanna and a crowd of other women.

'I can't believe this, I thought I'd never see you again!' she cried, and then checked herself, dropping her eyes as Susanna threw her a warning glance.

'This is Seth,' she said politely to the other women. 'You remember I told you about him – how he came to Reuben's rescue when he got hurt.'

I could have hugged her. At once, the faces of the other women softened and Susanna immediately smiled.

'Of course I remember,' she said. 'I didn't recognise you at first – I guess our minds are all over the place,' she sighed.

'We're waiting for Jesus,' she went on. 'Do you know of his teaching?'

Whether it was a test or not, I shall never know. I just said the first thing that came into my mind, and it wasn't until the words were out that I realised how true they were.

'Not enough,' I admitted. 'But he's the Messiah, isn't he? And I have to find out more.'

'For whom?' one of the women asked abruptly.

'Salome, hush,' Mary said.

'It's OK,' I replied. 'For me. Not because my father's a Pharisee, or because someone has told me to but because the kindest people I've ever met believe in and follow Jesus. And I want to follow him too.'

'Then come with us,' Esther urged. 'We can tell you loads of things and . . .'

'Esther, wait!' Mary said. 'Seth has a home, people who will be worrying about him.'

She turned to me. 'We are camped at Bethany,' she said.

'That's two miles away,' I gasped.

'Yes, but if you really want to learn . . .'

'I do,' I said hastily.

'So if your family are happy for you to visit us, then we would be thrilled to share everything we know with you. But first, you must go and seek their permission.'

I nodded. 'There won't be a problem,' I assured her. 'I'll go now and . . .'

'Wait,' Esther said. 'Look, Jesus is coming! At least stay and listen to him for a bit.'

Jesus was walking briskly and while he smiled at the women he didn't slacken his pace. We all followed him, me as eagerly as the rest. After we'd milled through the Gate and out onto the street, one of his disciples caught up with him.

> Jesus left the temple and was walking away when his disciples came up to him to call his attention to its buildings. 'Do you see all these things?' he asked. 'I tell you the truth, not one stone here will be left on another; every one will be thrown down.'
>
> *Matthew 24:1, 2*

'Aren't these buildings amazing, Master? I've never seen anything so grand and ornate in my life!'

Jesus paused, frowning, 'You're not blown away just because of its size and gaudiness, are you?' he asked. 'I'm telling you, there isn't a single stone in that building that will be left standing; everything will end up as a pile of rubble.'

'What does he mean?' I asked Mary. 'Is he predicting an earthquake? Is there going to be a war?'

Mary shook her head, 'I don't know the answer to that,' she confessed. 'But I'll tell you what – you go home and if you're allowed to join us, you can ask Jesus to explain it himself, can't you?'

The thought of actually speaking face to face with Jesus was enough to have me running full tilt for home.

My father wasn't at home. Zerah, the steward said he had gone out with Joseph and another friend, Gamaliel, on urgent business.

'To do with this troublemaker prophet, I guess,' Zerah sniffed. 'Still, the master will sort it, I'm sure of that.'

I smiled and said nothing.

'In that case, I think I will go and visit my cousins,' I told him. 'I'll be home before dark.'

'Your father said you were to study,' Zerah replied.

'Oh yes, I know,' I replied glibly. 'That's why I need the help of Telah – my cousin's so much cleverer than me.' And before he could argue, I picked up my wax tablet and a couple of scrolls and hurried off.

So what has that got to do with me?

1. The more we learn about Jesus the more we are forced to look at things differently. Can you think of ways in which you have felt the need to re-think your opinions and attitudes since becoming a Christian? Are there areas of your life that you feel are 'out of sync' with following Jesus? Don't worry; most people can give a list of things that need to be changed – the first step is acknowledging what they are!
2. 'They don't teach God's law the way they should – as something you can feed on and be nourished by and gain joy from. No, they just wrap it all up in a whole heap of their own rules and regulations, burdening you with stuff you can't possibly carry.' Have you ever felt that way about the church today? Do you think the church meets you where you are? What, if anything, puts you off going to church? Have you ever thought of trying out lots of different churches until you find one where you feel at home? One size doesn't fit all!
3. Judging people because of their race, creed or colour is wrong. Period. What standards should we use to measure people by? What standards would we want people to use when forming judgements about us?
4. A phylactery was a strip of parchment inscribed with passages from Exodus 13 and Deuteronomy 6, enclosed in a black calfskin case and fastened by thongs either to the forehead or left hand or arm. The bigger they were the more people would notice them. In what ways do some people today try to draw attention to the fact that they are religious?
5. The lepton was the smallest and lowest denomination coin that circulated in Jerusalem in Christ's lifetime. They were thin and crudely struck, about 10mm in diameter and sometimes as small as the size of a pencil eraser. Their value was based on combined weight with other coins and not on individual coin value. The coins donated by the widow were in themselves insignificant; her donation was massive. What cutbacks might she have had to make in order to give to the Temple?

CHAPTER FORTY-FOUR

Night terrors

Esther

'Esther, what are you doing? It's the middle of the night!'

Mary Magdalene, wrapped in her blanket and shivering slightly in the chill air, crept over to where I was sitting, my knees up to my chin.

'I can't sleep,' I murmured. 'I'm scared.'

'Of the wild animals?' she asked 'There's no need. We've kept the fires burning and some of the men are on guard.'

'It's not that,' I admitted. 'It's what Jesus said.'

'I know, it's terrible – but I can't believe they'll let it happen. There has to be good people in Jerusalem who will stop it.'

'The destruction? The end of time?'

'No, no – not that. He said he'd be put to death.' Her voice broke. 'It can't happen, we won't let it happen. There are enough of us who know and love him – we can stop it. So don't worry.'

I didn't say anything.

'That is what is frightening you?'

'Well, yes of course,' I stammered. 'But also – all this talk of destruction and the end of time – I don't want to die yet!'

As Jesus was sitting on the Mount of Olives, his disciples approached and asked him, 'Tell us, when are these things going to happen? What will be the sign of your coming, that the time's up?' Jesus said, 'Watch out for doomsday deceivers. Many leaders are going to show up with forged identities, claiming "I am Christ, the Messiah." They will deceive a lot of people. When reports come in of wars and rumoured wars, keep your head and don't panic. This is routine history; this is no sign of the end. Nation will fight nation and ruler fight ruler, over and over. Famines and earthquakes will occur in various places. This is nothing compared to what is coming.

'They are going to throw you to the wolves and kill you, everyone hating you because you carry my name. And then, going from bad to worse, it will be dog-eat-dog, everyone at each other's throat, everyone hating each other. In the confusion, lying preachers will come forward and deceive a lot of people. For many others, the overwhelming spread of evil will do them in – nothing left of their love but a mound of ashes. Staying with it – that's what God requires. Stay with it to the end. You won't be sorry and you'll be saved. All during this time, the good news – the Message of the kingdom – will be preached all over the world, a witness staked out in every country. And then the end will come.'

Matthew 24:3-14, The Message

I didn't add that seeing Seth had made me long for a future that I knew could never happen; but the truth was that sitting next to him, listening to Jesus earlier that afternoon, had made me realise that I didn't want my life to always be as it was now. I was after all sixteen years old; and still not married. I longed for a house of my own, for a husband I could cook for and care for, children who would run around and call me Mummy. I'd been daydreaming about a life like that when Jesus started talking about what was going to happen in the future. And it sure wasn't the kind of future I wanted to be part of. Sitting beside Seth as he scribbled the odd word on the wax tablet that he told me he had brought with him as his alibi, I wondered whether now wasn't the time to ask Susanna to find a husband for me. At least then, when the awful things Jesus talked about actually happened, I wouldn't be alone.

Now in the middle of the night, echoes of his words were going round and round in my head, driving away any possibility of sleep. 'Watch out that no one deceives you,' he had said. 'There will be famines and earthquakes . . . reports of wars . . . nations fighting nations.' That was scary enough but what followed was even worse.

'People will hate you because you follow me,' he'd said. 'Some of you will be tortured and killed; many will turn away from faith in me and my Father and everyone will be at one another's throats, full of hatred and bitterness.' I remember Seth muttering something along the lines of 'it's beginning already' and I looked at him for reassurance; but he was engrossed in what Jesus was saying.

'What you need to be aware of,' he warned, 'is that in the middle of all this confusion, people will start taking advantage of the situation – some will set themselves up as preachers, spouting a lot of lies and deceit; and love will be in short supply.'

Sitting with Mary with only the flickering of flames from the fire for light, I dared to voice what I'd been thinking for hours.

'The worst bit was when he said that we had to head for the hills when they come to destroy the Temple,' I stammered. 'He said we shouldn't take anything, and he said . . .'

I didn't know whether to continue, but Mary squeezed my hand and I knew I had to get it off my chest.

'He said that pregnant women and nursing mothers would have it worst,' I said. 'That could be me – I mean, if by then I'm married and . . .'

'Esther, Esther,' Mary said, wrapping her arms round me. 'You're focusing on the bad bits – but remember, he said that if we stay loyal and true to his teaching we will be saved.' She sighed. 'I'm not pretending I understand it all, because I don't,' she went on. 'And right now, all I can think about is him, here, now. I love him so much, Esther.'

She took a deep breath. 'But Jesus said that the good news of his kingdom is going to reach everyone in the whole world and that it's only when that's happened, that the end time will come.'

She gave me a hug.

'And to be honest, sweetheart, I think that's going to take a lot longer than my lifetime, or even yours!'

'Yes but what if I'm one of the ones who's not good enough and gets killed off?' I asked.

'What do you mean?'

> The arrival of the Son of Man will fill the skies – no one will miss it . . . But the exact day and hour? No one knows that, not even heaven's angels, not even the Son. Only the Father knows . . . Two men will be working in the field – one will be taken, one left behind. Two women will be grinding at the mill – one will be taken, one left behind. So stay awake, alert. You have no idea what day your Master will show up, but you do know this: you know that if the homeowner had known what time of night the burglar would arrive, he would have been there with his dogs to prevent the break-in. Be vigilant just like that. You have no idea when the Son of Man is going to show up.
>
> *Matthew 24 passim*

'Jesus said that there might be two women grinding corn, and one will die and the other will live,' I persisted. 'It sounds like God's just going to do some kind of lucky dip and I don't want . . .'

'Stop it!' Mary said shaking me gently. 'Remember what Jesus said about the ten virgins?'

I was glad it was dark because I could feel my face flushing. I remembered the story word for word, but probably not for the reasons I should have done.

'God's kingdom is like ten young virgins who took their oil lamps and went to meet the bridegroom,' Jesus had said. *'Five were on the ball and with it, five were totally ditsy and silly. The silly ones took their lamps but forgot to take extra oil, while the smart ones took jars to refill their lamps. The bridegroom was late appearing, and they all fell asleep.'*

'If I was a bridegroom, I wouldn't be late,' Seth had whispered in my ear. 'Not if my bride was as pretty as you.'

His lips had hardly moved and he had kept his eyes looking straight ahead; no one would have noticed anything unseemly. The fact that his thumb brushed my little finger was known only to the two of us.

'In the middle of the night,' Jesus had continued, *'the cry went up that the bridegroom was on his way. The ten virgins got up and prepared their lamps.*

'"Oh no, our lamps are going out!" the silly ones shrieked. "Lend us some of your oil!"'

Jesus' mimickry of panicking girls was so spot on that everyone burst out laughing.

'But the sensible virgins refused on the grounds that if they shared their oil, there might not be enough to go round. They sent the silly girls out to buy more oil, but while they were gone the bridegroom arrived. When all the guests had gone into the wedding feast, the door was locked.'

'And the stupid ones were shut out!' someone interjected with a laugh.

'*Exactly,'* Jesus had agreed. *'They came back, hammered on the door and begged to be let in but the bridegroom was adamant that he didn't have a clue who they were. So let that be a warning to you: stay alert. You never know when the Son of Man will return.'*

'So don't you see, Esther,' Mary said. 'No one knows the future except God. What we must do is stay alert so that in every situation we try to do what Jesus has taught us to do, to behave the way he does. We can't do any more; we can't change the future, but we live today in the best way we can. Live it for him.'

'So is that what he meant when he talked about feeding the hungry?' I asked.

When the Son of Man comes in his glory and all the angels with him, he will sit on the throne of his glory. All the nations will be gathered before him, and he will separate people one from another as a shepherd separates the sheep from the goats and he will put the sheep at his right hand and the goats at the left. Then the king will say to those at his right hand, 'Come, you that are blessed by my Father, inherit the kingdom prepared for you from the foundation of the world, for I was hungry and you gave me food, I was thirsty and you gave me something to drink, I was a stranger and you welcomed me, I was naked and you gave me clothing, I was sick and you took care of me, I was in prison and you visited me.' Then the righteous will answer him, 'Lord, when was it that we saw you hungry and gave you food, or thirsty and gave you something to drink? And when was it that we saw you a stranger and welcomed you, or naked and gave you clothing? And when was it that we saw you sick or in prison and visited you?' And the king will answer them, 'Truly, I tell you, just as you did it to one of the least of these who are members of my family, you did it to me.' Then he will say to those at his left hand, 'You that are accursed, depart from me into the eternal fire prepared for the devil and his angels; for I was hungry and you gave me no food, I was thirsty and you gave me nothing to drink, I was a stranger and you did not welcome me, naked and you did not give me clothing, sick and in prison and you did not visit me.' Then they also will answer, 'Lord, when was it that we saw you hungry or thirsty or a stranger or naked or sick or in prison, and did not take care of you?' Then he will answer them, 'Truly I tell you, just as you did not do it to one of the least of these, you did not do it to me.' And these will go away into eternal punishment, but the righteous into eternal life.

Matthew 25:31-45, NRSV

'Because that's what Susanna did for me – she took me in, gave me a job, fed me, bought me new clothes . . .'

'Yes – and by doing that for you, she did it for Jesus,' Mary explained. 'And you're doing it right now for Ziva.'

I jerked away and stared at her.

'It's OK, Esther – we know she disappears; we know that sometimes she is tempted to slip back into her old ways,' she murmured. 'But we've seen you go after her; heard you talking to her and telling her over and over, that she has a life with us now, and that she doesn't need to look for security anywhere but here, with Jesus and us. When you do that, you're doing what Jesus wants; sharing his love.'

She patted my arm. 'Now come back and get some sleep,' she encouraged. 'After all, you don't want to look pale and tired tomorrow, do you?

'What's happening tomorrow?' I asked.

'If I'm not very much mistaken, your friend Seth will be back,' she laughed. 'Not that you'd be interested in that, would you?'

I wish she hadn't said that. All the next day, in between fetching water, and going into the city for food, and mending the tear in Susanna's robe, I scanned the crowds for his familiar face. But he never came.

So what has that got to do with me?

1. Jesus said, 'watch out that no one deceives you'. In what ways can we be deceived today and by whom? What are the signs that someone is trying to deceive us? How can we test that what they say is for real?
2. What does it mean to live life for Christ? Is it just some religious holy-speak? Is it just about going to church and reading the Bible? Or is there more? What have you done today that has been an example of living for Christ? And if you say nothing, I bet you are wrong! Sometimes we fail to realise that the smallest acts of kindness are a joy to Jesus.

CHAPTER FORTY-FIVE

Off the fence

Seth

'I am displeased. Extremely displeased.'

It was late in the evening, far later than I had intended, when I reached home. At the sound of my footsteps my father emerged from his room and even from the doorway, I could sense his simmering anger.

'Just where have you been?'

'To see my cousin Telah,' I said – and the instant the words were on my lips, I regretted them.

'So – you compound your stupidity and your disobedience by lying, do you?' my father raged. 'I happen to know you went to the Temple, which in itself I could excuse; but then you followed Jesus out of town to the Mount of Olives. Have you taken leave of your senses?'

'I just wanted . . .'

'You wanted what? To be marked down as a follower of the man that three quarters of the Sanhedrin want to kill? Or perhaps you want to bring shame on me? Have me labelled as a father who lets his son run riot with Gentiles and fishermen and . . .'

'Father, that's just not fair!' I shouted. 'You're always telling me to search for truth, to form my own judgements, to take responsibility as an adult – and then when I do just that, you tell me I'm wrong.'

'I . . .' my father began, but now that I had had the courage to speak my mind I wasn't about to stop.

'You went to see Jesus ages ago, late at night – you told me so. You said you really wanted to find out more about him. Well, that's all I was doing.'

'You ran great risks.' My father's voice was still stern but his anger appeared to be abating. 'No one can be trusted at the moment; no one is sure whose side their friend is on. It was Rabinth who saw you at the Temple; he followed you – and now . . .' He sighed. 'Now he has me labelled as a supporter of Jesus.'

I stared at him. I knew that if I said any more I was at risk of being punished, but I couldn't let the moment pass. 'But father,' I said as politely as I could. 'You *are* on Jesus' side – aren't you?'

My father took a deep breath. 'I want to see justice done,' he replied. 'And yes, I believe that Jesus is – could be – might well be . . .' He faltered. 'The more I consider the evidence, the more I think he may well be the Messiah.'

'So why are you angry with me for going to listen to him teach?'

'As I have told you many times, it is one thing to believe in something,' he sighed. 'And quite another to come out and admit it.'

He rubbed a hand wearily over his eyes.

'I'm sorry I shouted at you,' he apologised. 'It's just that I love you so much and I was frightened for your safety.'

He patted my shoulder and gave me a quick hug.

'Listen,' he said briskly, 'several of us have met with Caiphas, the high priest. All the most vocal, outspoken ones were there – Annas, Nathaniel, Archelaus, of course – and things got pretty heated. The long and the short of it, Seth, is that they are out for Jesus' blood.'

'What? You mean . . . ?'

'They want to kill him.'

'You can't let that happen,' I cried.

My father turned to face me again and I swear there were tears in his eyes. 'I know,' he nodded slowly. 'I am very much afraid that the day of reckoning has come.'

He took my hand in his. 'I, and Joseph, and maybe a couple of others have agreed. We will do all in our power to see that justice is done. But you have to understand this, Seth: we are in a minority and our stance won't make us popular.'

'It'll be OK,' I murmured, realising even as I made the remark how childish and shallow it sounded.

'One thing will be OK,' my father said with a tired smile. 'Whatever the outcome, you – my dear, dear son – will know that in the end his father got off the fence and did what was right. And that is enough for me.'

So what has that got to do with me?

1. Why do you think Nicodemus was worried that Seth might openly admit he was following Jesus?
2. What was brave about Nicodemus' words to Seth and his decision to get off the fence?
3. Are there any issues in today's society that you would like to take a stand against but feel uncertain of how your friends or family would react? How do you work out the best way forward?

CHAPTER FORTY-SIX

Not to be served but to serve

Caleb

'Well, go and ask him then! Time's running out – Passover meals don't prepare themselves.'

'He'll have a plan, he always does.'

'That's all very well, but we need to know what we're doing!'

It was very early on the morning of the first day of the Feast of Unleavened Bread and the disciples were anxious. No one knew quite what was happening and like all good Jews, it was vital to them that nothing went wrong on such an important day.

For me things had already started going wrong. Judas had been really off with me the previous evening, and for no reason at all. All I had done was ask him where he was going when I saw him leaving the village after dark.

'Is it any of your business if I want to take a walk?' he had snapped. 'I have things on my mind and I need peace and quiet so just get off my back and stop following me round!'

With that he had set off at a furious pace down the path that led into the city. I stayed awake for a long time but he didn't come back.

Then Satan entered Judas, called Iscariot, one of the Twelve. And Judas went to the chief priests and the officers of the temple guard and discussed with them how he might betray Jesus. They were delighted and agreed to give him money. He consented and

> watched for an opportunity to hand Jesus over to them when no crowd was present.
>
> *Luke 22:3-6*

I needed to make peace with him. For one thing, he of all the disciples was the one who made me feel important and for another he had money.

But that wasn't the only cause of my unease. Early the previous morning, someone had spread the news that Pontius Pilate, the governor, had arrived in the city in preparation for the Passover. That was no surprise; it happened every year, and yet when Joanna heard the news, she began visibly to tremble.

'Jesus mustn't go,' she said over and over under her breath. 'Mary, tell your son he must not go into the city now.'

'My son,' Mary said softly, 'will do whatever God ordains. But Joanna, what do you know? What is troubling you so much?'

'Chuza, my husband' she whispered, 'says that Pilate is fearful for his own position and that Herod knows he can manipulate him in whatever ways he wants. If Herod feels threatened, it will be Pilate who is called on to act – and if the crowds we've seen follow Jesus into the city, then . . .' she faltered, '. . . then Chuza says they will be regarded as rebels and treated accordingly.'

I had heard how the Romans suppressed uprisings and I felt a shiver of fear ripple through my body. Now, as the disciples were muttering about Passover plans, I hoped that Jesus would turn his back on the city and head for the calm and peace of Capernaum. Even Judea would be preferable to facing the wrath of the Romans.

'There's the lamb to buy, the herbs to pick, the bread . . .' My thoughts jolted back to the present as Mary Magdalene listed the jobs to be done. 'And only a few hours to do it all.'

'I don't think you need to worry,' Susanna began calmly but Mary cut her short.

'Susanna, you're always so laid back,' she sighed. 'I suppose you think that providing a Passover meal for all this lot is just going to happen, do you?'

Susanna smiled but said nothing.

'I'll go and ask Jesus what he wants to do,' Peter said.

Just then, Judas appeared looking like death. His eyes were bloodshot and he was struggling to stifle his yawns.

'You OK, Judas?' Thomas asked. 'You look dreadful.'

'Bad night,' Judas replied curtly. 'What's going on?'

Thomas was about to answer when Peter reappeared. 'John, he wants you to come with me,' he said eagerly. 'We're to go into the city where a man carrying a water jar will meet us.'

'You mean a woman surely?' Judas asked incredulously. It would be a strange kind of guy who would walk the streets doing such a womanly task.

'No, he definitely said a man,' Peter retorted curtly. 'He will take us to a house and we have to ask the owner to show us to the guest room.'

'Whose house is it?' Judas asked eagerly. 'Does Jesus have relations in the city?'

Peter shrugged. 'I don't know,' he said. 'All Jesus would say is that the owner will take us to a big room upstairs and that's where we have to get to work to prepare the meal.'

'Then we must come with you,' Susanna insisted. 'There's far too much work to be done for just the two of you.'

'My son wants to eat the Passover meal with his closest friends,' his mother said softly.

'I understand,' Susanna said. 'But trust me – there's a place nearby where we can eat our own meal and still be on hand to help. That is what you want, isn't it?'

Mary smiled gratefully and nodded.

'Right, I'll tell Esther and Ziva what the plan is and then we can leave.'

She hurried off.

'John,' Peter urged. 'Let's hit the road.' He then turned to Joanna. 'Jesus and the others will go to the Temple to sacrifice the lamb, and then bring it to us for roasting. Judas – we need money for the food.'

Judas opened his money bag and handed them some coins.

'This won't be sufficient,' Peter said.

'No – I will get you more,' Judas said. 'I don't keep it all on my person when I go into – well, anywhere really. It's far too risky.' He paused and glanced at me.

'You go on ahead, and I'll send Caleb to catch you up with the rest of the cash,' he declared.

My heart soared. This is was real proof that finally, after three whole years, I was in, judged one of the select few to be trusted with money.

At the time, I thought that was all there was to it.

I ran on ahead of the women and could easily have caught up with Peter and John way before they reached the city gate, but instead, I timed it so that I didn't make my presence known until they had been led by the water carrier up a narrow winding street to a house on the corner. It was clear in an instant this was the home of someone with money; the limestone walls were immaculate, with no sign of a crack in them, the windows all had shutters and the door was of solid oak. If this was where we were all going to share the Seder meal, I was very happy.

Just as Peter and John were being ushered into the house, and before the steward could shut the door, I called out to them, 'Wait! I have the money!'

John turned and smiled at me. 'Good,' he said. 'We were beginning to think you would never come. There's so much to do.'

'Let me help,' I said hastily. 'At least until the women get here. I could go to the market, I could help cook – I used to work as an under steward . . .' OK, so I promoted myself but I just wanted to be in on the action.

'Well,' Peter replied thoughtfully. 'We could do with an extra pair of hands. OK, stay. Thank you.'

The room to which we were shown was large, with the door in one corner and two small shuttered windows. There was plenty to do; I swept the floor, I set cushions and platters in place, and lit oil lamps. It seemed strange that such a house shouldn't have servants, but even the steward disappeared the moment he had shown us where to go and we never saw him again.

After a while, the women arrived carrying baskets of herbs and the dates, olives and figs for the *haroset* and Esther and Susanna set about making the *matzo,* the unleavened bread we always ate at Passover. Peter sent me out to get wine and more lamp oil and it was as I was hurrying back that I heard the trumpet sounding from the pinnacle of the Temple, summoning people to the slaughter of the lambs. From the Nikanor Gate I could hear snatches of a song: '*I will offer thee the sacrifice of thanksgiving . . .'* Somewhere from the deep recesses of my memory I heard my father's voice chanting those same words, with me gripping his hand in a crowded synagogue. I must have been very young, because my mother was there, and my father still loved me.

A little later, Bartholomew and Thomas arrived, carrying the lamb, its head still attached and the women began the process of roasting and basting and smothering with herbs. Eventually, everything was ready. The women left and I looked round the room, wondering where I should sit.

'Thanks, you've been a great help,' John said, turning to me. 'You better go now.'

'Go?' I gasped. 'But the meal . . .'

'Jesus made it quite clear to me,' John said firmly. 'The meal here is just for him and the twelve of us,' he said.

'Don't worry,' Bartholomew called. 'Susanna has made arrangements. You do realise this is one of her family's houses, don't you?'

'One of them?' I gasped.

'The other is just down the road, the home of her sister. You'll find it easily – there's a marble urn in the courtyard – and you can celebrate the feast there.'

'But . . .'

'Or of course you could return to the camp. I think there will be enough food among that crowd for you to avoid starvation!' Then he ushered me out of the door and I heard it shut firmly behind me.

I stomped down the stairs in a foul mood. I simply didn't get it. One minute Jesus was saying that everyone was welcome in his kingdom and the next he was doing the cliquey, 'it's only for the favoured few' thing. Why couldn't we all eat together? It didn't make any sense.

I went into the street, practically deserted now, and filled with the aroma of roasting lamb and bitter herbs. I walked a few paces away from the house and slammed my fist into the wall. So who was I? Pretty obvious, really. I was just Caleb, son of Jonas, servant. Not Caleb the probationary disciple, not even Caleb true follower of Jesus. More like Caleb who could be useful but didn't count for much; Caleb who tagged along because he had once thought Jesus might notice him and like what he saw. Jesus had been kind and said wonderful things to me and I had really thought that he meant them all, but how come there were only twelve people he really thought suitable to stay close to him all the time? I had so wanted to be one of them; for the wrong reasons at the start, sure, but now . . .

Well, stuff that. It was never going to happen. As soon as the seven days of Passover had ended, I'd leave and go in search of a proper job. What's more, I'd suggest to Esther that she come too. Esther. My heart did that strange somersault again. If I left, and she wanted to stay with Susanna, that would mean I might never see her again. But perhaps Susanna could find work for me and I could ask Esther to . . .

My thoughts were running away with me. I turned round and began walking towards the house Bartholomew had described. At least for this evening, I could be with her and worry about the future in the morning.

'He said the first would be last and the last would be first,' I muttered out loud, raising my eyes heavenward. 'Easy to say but proof would be better and I don't see any signs of that.'

That's when I saw them all coming up the road. Thomas, Andrew, Philip – all of the other disciples, with Jesus leading them. And he saw me.

'Caleb! You are still with us?'

'Of course, Master – I've been helping John and . . .'

Jesus held up his hand. 'It is the fact that you're here, not what you've been doing, that matters,' he said. 'You will wait on us this evening?'

'Me, Master? But Bartholomew said . . .'

'Caleb, I am saying I would like you to wait on us tonight.'

'Yes – oh yes, please.'

'Then go into the house and prepare the water for washing and bring it to us,' he said and turned back to his friends.

'Come,' he said. 'It is time to eat.'

My hands were shaking as I carried the pitcher of water, carefully balanced in a large bowl, up to the guest room. I nudged the door open with my elbow, and hesitated on the threshold uncertain quite what to do next.

Jesus walked over to me, took the towel, which I had flung over my shoulder, and gestured to me to put the pitcher and bowl on the end of one of the low tables. As I did so, he took off his mantle and wrapped the towel around his waist. I couldn't understand what he was doing: if I was to wash the guests' feet, a job I'd done a hundred times before back in Cana, I needed the towel, not him.

And then he did the most astonishing thing. He poured the water into the basin, knelt down on the floor in front of Philip and began tenderly washing his feet, drying them carefully with the towel. Then he moved on to Thaddeus, then Thomas and then Judas. I couldn't believe it: foot washing was the job of the lowest of all house servants and yet here was Jesus, the Messiah, taking on the role that even I had relinquished in my last few months at Cana.

I wasn't sure what to do. The eyes of the disciples were fixed on Jesus and no one noticed me still hovering in the doorway.

Suddenly, as Jesus reached Peter's place at the table, Peter jumped to his feet.

'Master, *you* washing *my* feet? It's all wrong, it's . . .'

Jesus smiled. 'You don't understand what I'm doing right now, but later on you will realise the significance of it.'

Peter shook his head. 'No Master, no way can I let you wash my feet!'

Jesus sighed. 'If I don't do it, then you can't be a part of my work here.'

Peter slumped back down onto his cushion. 'In that case, Lord, wash my hands, my head – all of me! Scrub me clean.'

Jesus cradled Peter's calloused left foot in his hand, as tenderly as a mother cradling her baby's head. 'Peter, this isn't about hygiene, it's about holiness. Now you are cleansed – well, not every one of you actually.'

I guess he realised that he had another four pairs of feet to deal with. When he had finished, he stood up and gestured to me to remove the soiled towel and grimy water. As I left the room, he began to speak, and I confess I left the door just slightly ajar so that I could hear what he was saying. I've never forgotten his words.

'Do you understand what I've just done for you?' he asked them. 'You call me Teacher and Lord and that's right because that is what I am. So if I, your Lord and teacher, washed your feet, you must now do the same for one another. Follow my example; remember that no servant is greater than his master, no messenger more important than the one who sent him. Serve God, serve one another, serve those you meet in days to come – and in doing so you will be truly blessed.'

It struck me that when Jesus talked about being a servant, the job didn't seem as insignificant and lowly as I'd always thought it was. He even managed to make it sound special.

'Caleb, is that you?'

'What are you doing here? Why aren't you with the others?'

I almost dropped the bowl of water as two figures emerged from a small unlit room at the foot of the stairs. As they stepped out of the shadows, I realised it was Mary Magdalene and Susanna.

'Jesus asked me to wait on them,' I told them proudly. 'Truly – I mean it, I'm not lying . . .'

Mary laughed. 'Why would we think you were?' she asked.

'Are you here to eat with them?' I queried.

Susanna shook her head. 'That's not our place,' she sighed. 'But – well to be honest, it's my house and I've used that as an excuse to be down here. I pretend it's to check on all this . . .' She waved her hand towards the dishes of matzo and haroset that they'd prepared that afternoon. 'But really, it's because we want to be near to him – just in case . . .'

'In case what?'

'Let's just say,' Mary interrupted, 'that whatever happens, we want to be as close to Jesus as we can possibly get. And now you'd better get back upstairs – Jesus has need of you.'

Never in my life had five words given me such joy.

I went up and down the stairs, carrying the platters of matzo, the bowls of haroset and refilling pitchers of wine.

As I placed the last dish on the table, Jesus turned and smiled warmly at the disciples.

'I've looked forward so much to sharing this Passover meal with you before my time of suffering begins,' he said. 'I will not eat it again until we all share it in the kingdom of God.'

I picked up a pitcher that needed refilling and moved as silently as I could towards the door. But as I opened it, I nearly dropped the pitcher.

'One of you will betray me,' Jesus said, his voice trembling. Was he thinking of me? Did he somehow know that I'd been thinking of chucking it all in, leaving him and the rest of them to get on with it and going off to do my own thing?

But no. His next words made me sigh with relief.

'One of you who at this moment is seated round this table will be the one,' he said.

'No!'

'That can't be, none of us would . . .'

'Who is it?'

All the disciples were talking at once. I knew I must hurry to refill the wine but for a moment, I lingered outside the door.

'Is it I, Master?' The voice was familiar and I smiled to myself. As if! Judas was the one who had asked me to keep my ear to the ground in case anyone was plotting against Jesus.

> Jesus was troubled in spirit and testified, 'I tell you the truth, one of you is going to betray me.' His disciples stared at one another, at a loss to know which of them he meant. One of them, the disciple whom Jesus loved, was reclining next to him. Simon Peter motioned to this disciple and said, 'Ask him which one he means.' Leaning back against Jesus, he asked him, 'Lord, who is it?' Jesus answered, 'It is the one to whom I will give this piece of bread when I have dipped it in the dish.'
>
> *John 13:26-28*

'It's the one to whom I will give this piece of bread,' Jesus said. There was silence; well, of course, I couldn't see who he'd given it to and besides I needed to get going. But the idea that anybody in that room would possibly want to betray Jesus was ludicrous; those twelve loved him, hung on his every word, had spent three years traipsing round the countryside after him. No way would any of them give up on him now. Would they?

'So do what you have to do but do it quickly,' I heard Jesus say as I tiptoed down the stairs to the wine store.

As Susanna helped me to refill the pitcher, I heard the outer door close with a thud. Glancing through the open shutter, I saw a man hurrying down the street. For a moment, he paused, and turned back towards the house. A shaft of lamplight lit up his face and my heart missed a beat. It was Judas.

He couldn't be – no, it was unthinkable. Jesus must have told him to do something quickly – something else, getting more wine, more oil . . . but no we had plenty and . . .

'Caleb, the wine!'

I'd been so taken up with watching Judas that I hadn't realised when the pitcher was full. Wine was pouring down the sides and onto the table staining the linen like fresh blood. When I looked up again, Judas had disappeared into the blackness of the night.

I stood in the serving alcove ready to replenish the matzo bread from the basket I had brought upstairs with me. The mood in the room had changed; there was little, if any, conversation and the disciples, reclining round the table, looked thoughtful and reflective. Jesus was watching them, his eyes full of sadness. Then he picked up one of the matzo loaves and stood up. Everyone became more alert, shifting their position, leaning on their elbows to hear what he would say.

Jesus held up the bread and blessed it. Then he broke it in half and handed one half to John, who was sitting beside him and the other to Peter. 'Take and eat,' he said. 'This is my body given for you. Do this regularly to remember me.'

I could see that at least three disciples opened their mouths to speak but then thought better of it. Each one of them broke off a piece of the loaf and then passed it to their neighbour, chewing slowly and thoughtfully. Then he took the cup of wine that I had recently filled and raised it up, blessed it and passed it to John.

'Drink this, all of you,' he said. 'This is my blood. God's new covenant poured out for many people for the forgiveness of sins.'

The forgiveness of sins. In an instant I was back on that hillside sitting at Jesus' feet, hearing those words. '*Caleb, it is in the past, it is forgiven, it has gone. And you must understand one thing above all else: I do want you. I need you.*'

And tonight, he had said he needed me to serve – but now, just as I'd got the message, and realised that I could perhaps do something with him, for him – he was talking of leaving us all.

He watched as one by one the disciples drank from the cup and then he turned and looked at me as I stood in the corner by the door.

'Come, Caleb,' he said.

I went to the table expecting to be asked to refill the wine. Jesus broke off a piece of bread and handed it to me.

'Eat,' he said. 'For all are welcome at my table.'

Our eyes met. Slowly I put the bread in my mouth as Jesus picked up a cup of wine.

'Drink this,' he said. 'It is my blood which is shed for everyone, not just the special few.'

It was as though he had read my mind. As the wine touched the back of my throat, and his warm hand took the cup back from me, I understood.

He did need me. He needed all of us. So much of what he said went over my head, but that didn't matter. It was who he was that was important. As I swallowed hard in an attempt to hold back the wave of emotion that threatened to choke me, I knew beyond every shadow of doubt that I would do whatever it took to help other people feel what I felt that evening.

It took me several minutes to regain my composure after I had retreated to my corner by the door. When I was calmer, I tried to focus on what Jesus was saying to the disciples.

'I'm telling you the truth,' he said, 'I won't drink wine again with you until I drink it with you in my father's kingdom.'

He sat down and rested against John's shoulder. 'My dear, dear friends,' he said. 'I can only be with you for a little longer. You'll search for me but as I have said before, where I'm going, you cannot come.'

Perhaps, I thought, he was going to make his escape, go to some distant country and lie low until all the trouble was over. Maybe that was what he meant when he said that no one else could go with him. Except that I knew that wasn't the case. Jesus would never run away. Jesus was going to die.

'Before I leave you, I have another commandment for you and it is this. You are to love one another in just the same way as I have loved you. Do that, and people won't fail to realise that you really are my disciples because love shines out in the darkness and people can't ignore it.'

'But Master,' Peter asked, 'where exactly are you going?'

'Somewhere you can't follow,' Jesus replied gently.

'But Master, why not?' Peter protested. 'I'll go anywhere, I'll do anything. I'd die for you!'

Jesus looked at him long and hard, an expression of deep sadness on his face. 'Would you, Peter? Would you really die for me?'

'I would, I would,' Peter exclaimed.

'Let me tell you something,' Jesus sighed. 'Before the cock crows in the morning, you will disown me three times.'

'Never! Never!' Peter cried, as all the other disciples began protesting that none of them would ever forsake Jesus.

'When I sent you all out,' Jesus went on, 'and told you to take nothing with you, did you go without? Did you lack anything?'

They all shook their heads.

'Well, I'm changing the rules now,' he said. 'Now you need to be prepared for whatever the world may fling at you. If you have a purse, take it and also a bag; and if you don't have a sword, sell your cloak and buy one.'

Now that was a shock. Was this the same Jesus who preached peace, and love, and turning the other cheek?

'You will have read in the Scripture, *"he was counted in with the criminals"*? Well, it's all coming true in me right now.'

'This is awful!' It was Philip who broke the silence.

'Despite all that I've said,' Jesus replied, 'I don't want you to be thrown into a state of panic or fear. Trust me just as you trust God. In my Father's house, there's room for everyone – why else would I tell you that I am going ahead in order to be there to welcome you. And you already know the way to the place I'm going.'

'No we don't!' Thomas protested. 'We don't have a clue because you're talking in riddles. How can we possibly know the way?'

'Thomas, I am the Way, and I am the Truth and I am the Life. No one comes to God except through me. Know me, and you know my Father – and you do know me, and you have seen the Father!'

'Master, if you'd just let us see the Father, then we could rest easy and understand a bit better,' Philip said, echoing my own thoughts.

'You've been a follower for three years, Philip, and you still don't get it?' Jesus sighed. 'You've seen me; that means you've seen the Father. I am in him and he is in me. I don't just talk on and on about anything that comes into my head; everything I say comes from my Father; he lives in me, and I am part of him.'

Jesus bit his lip. 'When I have left you, my Father will send his Holy Spirit to dwell in you, to guide you, teach you and remind you of everything I have said to you. The Spirit will be your counsellor, always there, always on your side. For as long as you love me, and do the things I have taught you, my father will love you and we will both be with you and in you and work through you. But if you stop loving me, you'll stop living the way I have shown you – and if that happens, then we become separate from one another.'

> The Counsellor, the Holy Spirit, whom the Father will send in my name, will teach you all things and will remind you of everything I have said to you. Peace I leave with you; my peace I give you. I do not give as the world gives. Do not let your hearts be troubled and do not be afraid.
>
> *John 14:26-28, NIV*

He stood up, and gestured to the others to do the same. He opened his arms wide, swallowed hard and took a deep breath. 'Peace I leave with you now,' he said softly. 'My peace is my gift to you. It is a gift the world cannot offer you. Don't be anxious, don't be afraid. I have told you I am going away but I will come back. When the things I have spoken of happen, you will believe.'

He dropped his hands. 'Come,' he said. 'It is time to leave.'

So what has that got to do with me?

1. Judas had decided to betray Jesus yet he still shared the meal with him. We might think this is great hypocrisy but our challenge is to look at ourselves. Do we ever profess one thing and do another? Do we deny Christ by doubting him, disobeying his teaching?
2. Caleb thought that the twelve were the inner circle and that Jesus had no use for him. Jesus proved him wrong. He uses all of us but his timing and his plans may not always coincide with what we imagine we want!
3. By washing his disciples' feet, what example was Jesus setting? Why did Peter react the way he did?
4. The Eucharist is central to Christian worship, commemorating and re-enacting the Last Supper and the death and resurrection of Christ. We do it in remembrance of Christ just as he commanded.
5. Why do you think the author allowed Caleb to receive bread and wine from Jesus?
6. Christians commemorate and re-enact the Last Supper in the Eucharist. Bread is taken, blessed, broken and shared. The cup of wine is blessed and shared. How was Jesus' life taken and blessed and broken and shared? How does God take, bless, break and share us in our lives today?
7. 'I have another commandment for you . . . love one another in just the same way as I have loved you.' What do those last five words tell us and how does this make the commandment hard to follow all the time?
8. Make a list of all the parts of the Holy Communion or Eucharist that you don't understand. Ask questions and find out what they mean.

9. Explanation of old and new covenant: The old covenant involved forgiveness through the blood of animal sacrifice; the new covenant was made by Jesus offering himself as the final sacrifice for sins and his blood sealed the new covenant between us and God. Through Jesus every one of us can come to God in the certain knowledge that he will welcome us and forgive our sins.

CHAPTER FORTY-SEVEN

The letter

Seth

I suppose it happens to everyone; that moment when you realise that suddenly you have grown up. For some of my friends, it happened at their bar mitzvah, but not for me. For me it happened the day I found the letter.

It was the evening of Passover and I should have been with my father eating Seder meal with his brother, my uncle, and his family. But I had been ill the night before with sickness and although I seemed cured, the thought of facing a meal was too much. So I remained at home, with just my mother and her maid for company.

I was in my father's room – not his bedroom, but the room he withdrew to when he wanted to read or pray or simply be alone. I shouldn't have been there, of course; but my mother, who was having one of her more lucid days, was beginning to get agitated because she couldn't find her harp. My mother had a gift for music; it was the one thing that could calm her and when her fingers were plucking the strings, her whole body relaxed.

I knew that my father often removed the harp into his study on days when my mother was particularly out of it; she was prone to throwing things and to damage the instrument would have been catastrophic.

His room was cluttered; scrolls lay all over his table, wax tablets were piled in one corner and his old sandals had been randomly kicked into the middle of the floor. Sure enough, in the far corner, stood my mother's harp and it was as I passed my father's table that my name jumped out at me from a sheet of papyrus parchment. I stopped and began to read.

> For my son Seth from his father Nicodemus. The fifteenth day of Nisan
>
> I am writing this to you, my dear son, that in this time of great rumours and intrigue, you might know the truth, not only of what occurs, but of my part in it. If all ends well, you will never read this; if, as I fear, the forces of evil overtake this great city and the last-minute, half-hearted efforts of cowards like myself do not bear fruit, then I pray when you do read it, you will understand a little more of the trials and dilemmas that face those of us in positions of authority.
>
> Tonight they will arrest Jesus of Nazareth.

'No!' I think I must have shouted the word out loud, because at once my mother called from her room at the rear of the house.

'Seth! Seth!'

Her voice was high pitched and whining, a sure sign that I needed to return to her at once. I snatched up the harp and hurried to her room.

'Mother, shall I call Rebekah? You can play to her.' On days when she was able to recognise people, my mother was very affectionate towards her maid, largely because of her exquisite singing voice.

'Yes, Rebekah. And you – go now! Who are you anyway?'

If I hadn't had the letter to go back to, her words might have hurt more.

> These last few weeks have been agonising for me and I do not use that word lightly. I have always believed that we, the members of the High Council, had the respect of the people, knew their needs, could decree how they lived. But we don't: we sit in our rarified atmosphere in the Hall of the Hewn Stones and pontificate about minor details in age old

laws – but do we understand the feelings of the people we legislate for? I don't think so.

But one thing I do know: the people love Jesus because he understands them. And because he understands them they listen to him and take on board what he is saying far more readily than they would ever do with us.

I said as much in the meeting of the High Council yesterday, and I was shouted down. Some of my colleagues looked at me as if I had taken leave of my senses, saying that Jesus was just a novelty, a new prophet – a fake even – who admittedly could heal on occasion but who was also a blasphemer, a rebel and a troublemaker. Joseph of Arimathea was on my side: he stood up and said that we were a crowd of hypocrites, saying with one breath that we wanted to soak up Scripture and learn more of God's will for Israel, and then shunning anyone who came up with a new vision of how God's purposes could be fulfilled.

Here there was a huge ink blot – perhaps his stylus had split too far, or perhaps something or someone had made him jump. There were several words I could not read, smudged as they were, and then the writing became less tidy and more of a scrawl, as if he had been writing at great speed.

Then I did it. Where I found the courage I don't know, and somehow I fear I may live to regret it. But I stood up and said that perhaps they should all take a few minutes to consider that far from being a blasphemer, Jesus of Nazareth was indeed the Messiah. I told them that when I heard him preach (I didn't mention my face-to-face conversation, of course – I wasn't that brave!) – I was touched in a way I could not describe, and that somehow I felt God was speaking through him, trying to reach out through him to us.

They shouted at me, but a few – a very few – told them to let me continue. That's when I said that we all anticipated the coming of the Messiah – it was the very core of our faith and always had been – so why did we find it so difficult to accept that he might just be here, now, among us.

Rabinth shouted that a carpenter's son was hardly likely to be the Messiah – but Joseph cut in and reminded them that David had been a humble shepherd.

For a moment, I thought – I hoped – I might have convinced them, or at least made them reconsider their stance. But then Caiphas had his say and of course, being the chief priest, everyone took note. And he is a much better speaker than I.

'It isn't the miracles he performs, and it isn't the words he says, or even the fact that he stirs up a frenzy wherever he goes, that is the point,' he said. 'It is that he dares – he has the audacity, the temerity – to say that he is the Son of God.'

Then he marched over to where Joseph and I were standing and asked whether we, learned, respected, educated – all that patronising stuff – whether we really believed that Jesus was the Son of God.

I said nothing. I would have done, I was trying to frame my words but that was the moment when Caiphas, who's known for his sense of timing, said that if he wasn't the Son of God, then he was a false prophet. Only God can forgive sins, he said; our law says false prophets should die and surely, he asked yet again, it would be better for one man to die than for a whole nation to perish?

Well, you know – or at least I hope you do if you have retained a fragment of what your tutors have taught you – that under Roman occupation the people of Israel aren't allowed to put anyone to death, so I thought that at least Jesus' life was not in danger. But then Archelaus said he had to be charged with a crime so that the Romans would find him guilty and they would deal with him.

That did it. I found my voice. I demanded that they see sense; that Jesus hadn't even had a hearing in front of

> us and that we couldn't hand anyone over to the Romans until we had first interrogated them. I thought I'd done well; several other members agreed that to hand over a fellow Jew to the Romans would be immoral. Joseph suggested that he should be allowed to invite Jesus to come before the Sanhedrin once Passover had finished and explain himself, and Caiphas agreed. I thought we were home and dry.
>
> I was wrong. And now I believe they will take him and the only thing I can do is . . .

The letter ended. I didn't know what my father planned to do, or indeed whether there was anything he could do. But one thing I did know for sure.

I respected him now more than I ever had before.

So what has that got to do with me?

1. Why do you think Seth respected his father more than ever after reading the letter? What elements of Nicodemus' behaviour do you admire?
2. Do you find it hard to imagine Jesus coming again among us? If he did tomorrow, how do you think he would be received?

CHAPTER FORTY-EIGHT

The moment of truth

Caleb

I followed them.

I couldn't help it.

It was as though something unseen was pushing me to stick close to Jesus.

I thought they'd be heading back up the Mount of Olives to the patch where we'd set up camp earlier in the week.

They didn't.

They went to the Garden of Gethsemane.

I hesitated.

I almost walked on by and went to search for the other followers.

I wish I had.

I really wish I had.

CHAPTER FORTY-NINE

Shock

Esther

'No! No-ooo!'

'Take me to him!'

'You should have stopped them, you could have . . .'

I sat bolt upright, sleep shattered by the frantic screams all around me. In the dim light I could see two men crouched in the crowd, and Mary and Susanna, their shawls wrapped tightly around them, beside them, their shoulders shaking.

'What is it? What's happened?' I cried rushing over to them.

'They've arrested Jesus,' Susanna sobbed. 'They've taken him away.'

CHAPTER FIFTY

The kiss

Reuben

If I hadn't drunk so much at the feast I wouldn't have got up to relieve myself and then God knows what would have happened to him.

But I did get up and I did walk a little way away into a grove of trees.

And there he was.

I thought he was a ghost. His face was white in the moonlight and he was trembling from head to foot.

'Caleb?' I muttered. 'Caleb!'

Nothing. Not a flicker of recognition.

I walked up to him and gripped his shoulders.

'Caleb, it's me. Reuben. What's happened? What's wrong with you?'

Slowly, so, so slowly, he blinked and turned his head to look at me.

'He kissed him,' he murmured. 'And then they came.'

'Who kissed who? Who came?' I asked, as Caleb lurched forward as if about to throw up.

'Soldiers, priests,' he said, his voice breaking.

He gripped my arm.

'They've taken Jesus away,' he said. 'And no one did anything to stop them.'

So what has that got to do with me?

1. Why do you think the followers were so shocked by Jesus' arrest? After all, he had warned them. Why do you think they didn't really believe it could happen?
2. Why was Caleb so badly affected by witnessing Judas' betrayal? What thoughts do you think might have been going through his mind?
3. 'No one stopped them.' Could anyone have stopped it happening? Was it predestined or could someone have changed the course of events?

CHAPTER FIFTY-ONE

Why? Why? Why?

Caleb

Then Jesus went with his disciples to a place called Gethsemane, and he said to them, 'Sit here while I go over there and pray.' He took Peter and the two sons of Zebedee along with him, and he began to be sorrowful and troubled. Then he said to them, 'My soul is overwhelmed with sorrow to the point of death. Stay here and keep watch with me.' Going a little farther, he fell with his face to the ground and prayed. 'My Father, if it is possible, may this cup be taken from me. Yet not as I will, but as you will.'

Then he returned to his disciples and found them sleeping. 'Could you men not keep watch with me for one hour?' he asked Peter. 'Watch and pray so that you will not fall into temptation. The spirit is willing but the body is weak.' He went away a second time and prayed, 'My Father, if it is not possible for this cup to be taken away unless I drink it, may your will be done.' When he came back he again found them sleeping, because their eyes were heavy. So he left them and went away once more and prayed the third time, saying the same thing.

Then he returned to the disciples and said to them, 'Are you still sleeping and resting? Look, the hour is near, and the Son of Man is betrayed into the hands of sinners. Rise, let us go! Here comes my betrayer!'

Matthew 26:36-46

I guess no one slept any more that night, not after I'd told them what I'd seen. Certainly Mary, Susanna and the other women, along with Cleopas and several of the newer disciples were all for going straight into the city and confronting the authorities there and then, but Thomas and Andrew persuaded them to wait until morning.

'Inflame the guards now,' Andrew said, 'and we'll all be arrested and then what use will we be to Jesus?'

'So tell us,' Mary sobbed. 'Tell us exactly what happened.'

Thomas and Andrew looked at one another and hesitated. I wasn't surprised; from what I saw, standing way back in the olive groves, they'd been fast asleep most of the time despite the fact that Jesus had specifically asked them to keep watch while he prayed. I say pray, but to be honest he looked to be in total agony, kneeling on the ground, rocking back and forth the way you do when you've got a pain so bad you can hardly breathe, and muttering words I couldn't hear but which seemed muffled by sobs.

Twice he went back to the disciples and woke them up but they were out of it. I assumed they'd drunk rather more than their share of the wine at supper; when I'd cleared the tables there wasn't a drop left.

'It was Judas,' Thomas said suddenly. 'He betrayed Jesus. He kissed him and the soldiers appeared . . .'

'But he knew,' Andrew burst out, his face twisted with anger. 'He said, *"here comes my betrayer"*. If he knew he was doing that, why didn't he get away while he had the chance?'

'And the others? They've gone with him?' Susanna asked urgently.

Thomas shook his head. 'I haven't a clue where they are,' he said. 'We all just ran for it . . .'

'You did what?' Mary cried. 'You left him?'

Sure they did – fled in all directions like chickens at the first sight of a fox.

'Well, not at first, of course,' Thomas replied defensively. 'But after Peter had sliced off the ear of a servant of the high priest . . .'

'Typical Peter, act first, think later,' Andrew sighed. 'But you know what, despite the fact that he was being pushed and shoved and manacled and manhandled, Jesus reached out and touched the injured guy and his ear was as good as new.'

'Then we came here to tell you all what had happened,' Thomas said. 'And to work out what to do next.'

Andrew sat back on his haunches and put his head in his hands. 'I was so jealous,' he whispered. 'As usual it was Peter and James and John that he took with him deep into the grove of olives and I so wished that just once, it could have been me. When I saw my brother and the other two had fallen asleep, I crept nearer to where Jesus was praying. I heard what he said.'

'What was it?' Seeing Andrew's distress, Mary touched his hand lightly.

'He said, "Father, you can do anything. Please take this cup away from me."'

Andrew took a deep breath. 'And then he said, "But it mustn't be the way I want it to be – it has to be your way."'

He thumped the ground with his balled fist.

'So are you telling me God wants Jesus to die at the hands of the Romans? Why? Why? What possible good can the death of a man like him do for anyone?'

So what has that got to do with me?

1. Why did the disciples desert Jesus? How do you think they justified their actions to themselves and one another? Were they sensible under the circumstances? Remember that we know the end of the story and they didn't – they were living the horror minute by minute.

CHAPTER FIFTY-TWO

The postscript

Seth

I woke to the sound of voices. It was still pitch dark but from the entrance hall lamplight flickered. I got up, wrapped a blanket round my shoulders and made my way into the hall. My father was standing in the doorway of his room, already dressed, and Joseph was with him.

'Father, what's wrong? Is Mother . . . ?'

'No, son, your mother's sleeping. But I have to go out at once – to the Council chamber.'

'Why? What . . . ?'

'Wait.' He walked over to his table, picked up the parchment I had read the day before and thrust it into my hands.

'I hoped you wouldn't need to read this yet,' he said, 'but now it is important that you understand.' With that, he and Joseph disappeared into the night.

I glanced at the parchment, knowing every word that was written. Every word that is until a couple of hastily scrawled lines at the very bottom.

> It is too late. They have taken him. Pray God that there will be enough of us to stop this evil being perpetrated. For if they kill him, they may well find that nothing will ever be the same again.

So what has that got to do with me?

1. How correct was Nicodemus' postscript to the letter? Think hard about the question and explore all the interpretations! He thought that if Christ was killed, nothing would ever be the same again. What would have been different if somehow he had managed to stop the crucifixion from happening?

CHAPTER FIFTY-THREE

The denial

Esther

The following morning before first light we set off – about two hundred of us, the ones who hadn't suddenly realised they needed to go back home or stay well clear of the city. We women were the first to get going, along with Caleb, Reuben, Cleopas and quite a few of the newer disciples; and it was as we drew near to the city gates early the following morning that I saw my sister Ziva running towards us. Despite all the misery and fear of the past few hours, my heart lifted – at least she was safe and I would try not to think about what she might have been doing in the city these past few days.

'Ziva! Where have you been? We've been so worried,' Susanna exclaimed and not for the first time I was amazed at her patience and her love.

'I've been looking for a job,' she confessed, 'and before you ask, I mean a proper job.' She glanced at Susanna. 'To be honest, I'm tired of travelling around all the time, and I love the city – the countryside is too dull and . . .'

'So you must know what's happened?' I blurted out. 'They've arrested Jesus!'

'I know,' Ziva nodded.

'And we don't know what's happening, and all the disciples have disappeared and . . .'

'Not all of them,' Ziva replied. 'I saw Peter only an hour ago.'

'You did?' Mary cried. 'Where? What was he doing?'

'Pretending not to be himself, actually,' Ziva laughed. 'He was sitting with some of the soldiers round the fire in the courtyard at the high priest's house, and one of the other servants – a girl called Anna, she's really nice and she's going to see if she can find me a job there and if not there, maybe with . . .'

'Yes, get on with it!' I snapped and then, seeing the look on her face, instantly regretted it.

'Anna was desperate to find out what was going on – she's going to marry one of the grooms who works for the Romans – so she went up to Peter and said she'd seen him with Jesus,' Ziva said. 'And you know what? He denied it – said he had never met the man.'

'That can't be right,' Salome protested. 'He's been with him from the very start, just like my boys. Perhaps the girl misheard him.'

'Well, I didn't,' Ziva replied. 'When Anna told me what he'd said, I went up to him and said that I'd seen him with Jesus loads of times – I even began to say that I knew all of you, but he swore at me – really loudly. He said it was nonsense; that I clearly had mistaken him for someone who looked like him. He got up and stomped towards the gateway, and one of the soldiers shouted after him saying that he didn't know why he was trying to hide the fact, because his accent gave him away every time he opened his mouth.'

'So where did Peter go?' Salome asked urgently. 'Have you any idea?'

Ziva shrugged and shook her head. 'To be honest, I think he might have lost it,' she confided. 'Because as he was leaving, the cocks starting crowing – they make the most infernal noise every morning – and he clamped his hands to his ears, and shouted something about not meaning it to be like this and then ran off.'

She brushed a fly off her forehead. 'So – what are we going to do?'

'We?' I asked abruptly. 'I thought you were job hunting.'

She took my hand. 'I was, and I will again,' she said. 'But right now, the more of us who stick with Jesus the better. The bigger the protest, the more they'll have to take notice. They can't get rid of someone that everyone loves, can they?'

It didn't strike me until sometime later that no one had answered her question.

So what has that got to do with me?

1. Was Peter a coward to deny Jesus? Or did he perhaps have a reason? Did he think he could rescue Jesus if no one realised who he was? What had Peter done at the time of Jesus' arrest that suggests he was not of a cowardly nature?

CHAPTER FIFTY-FOUR

The beginning of the end

Seth

At first I thought it was the crowing of the cockerels that had woken me, although heaven knows I'm used to the sound and normally managed to sleep through it. But then I heard something else; a rhythmic banging coming from my father's room down the passageway and interspersed with the bangs, long low moans.

I ran towards his study. Was he in pain? Ill? Had the old trouble recurred before he'd been able to call for one of the servants?

I knocked on the door but didn't wait for an answer. My father was pacing the room – the rhythmic banging I had heard was his stick, which he had used intermittently since his illness, thudding on the ground.

'Why? Why?' he muttered under his breath.

'Father – are you ill?' It was still my deepest fear – fear that the person I loved more than any other in the world would one day not be there.

'Seth!' He turned round, startled. 'No, no – I'm not ill, I'm just in despair.'

'Is it because of what you wrote in the letter?'

'You read it, then? I'm glad,' my father nodded, easing himself slowly into his chair. 'I've been in a meeting all night with Caiphas, the high priest and all the elders. They brought us Jesus.'

'So they did arrest him!' I gasped.

'Arrested him and dragged him before us like a common criminal, hands bound behind his back!' my father shouted. 'I couldn't stand it; I defied them and undid the ropes.'

For a moment a faint smile twitched the corners of his mouth. 'And no one stopped me.'

'I said they'd take notice of you,' I grinned.

'Oh but that's where you are wrong, son,' he sighed. 'Such stupidity, such short-sightedness, from men who profess to have wisdom and understanding.' He slammed his fist onto the top of his table with such force that his stylus and wax tablet were thrown to the floor.

'I discovered that it was one of his own followers who led them to him,' he told me. 'A man called Judas apparently. Archelaus was chuffed to bits, pompous ass – said that this Judas thought that the elders wanted Jesus in order to give him a fair trial, to hear what his plans were for our nation.'

He shook his head. 'Poor, trusting, misguided soul!'

I frowned. 'So what did you all want?'

'Me – I wanted him left alone,' my father said. 'Joseph too, and a couple of the others. But as for the rest of them, they wanted evidence, something they could latch on to that would justify killing him and for a while it looked as if they wouldn't find it. In fact, at first I thought Caiphas was seeing reason because he asked Jesus to explain the nature of his teaching.'

'Great – so did he tell them . . . ?'

'All Jesus would say was that he'd taught quite openly in the synagogues and in the Temple, he'd done nothing in secret. Then he asked Caiphas why he was asking the question of him, when he should be asking all the people who'd heard him preach. They, he said, are my witnesses.'

Again he banged his fist on the table.

'And I am a witness,' he cried. 'And I did try. For a long time, Joseph and I between us were able to counter all their arguments. But then . . .' He put his head in his hands. 'Then Ezechiel stood up and said that Jesus had declared that he would destroy the Temple and within three days build another. That did it: Caiphas marched over to him and asked him why he didn't defend himself.'

'What did he say?' I asked.

'Nothing, not a word,' my father replied. 'Joseph tried to explain that his words were symbolic, but no one was listening. The fact that

Jesus didn't speak incensed Caiphas, who has a short fuse at the best of times. He poked Jesus in the ribs and he shouted at him. *"I ask you now; are you the Christ, the son of the Blessed One?"* The whole room fell silent; it was as if every person there was holding his breath.'

'What did Jesus say?' I murmured.

'His exact words?' My father turned and walked slowly over to the window. 'He said, "I am. And you will see the Son of Man sitting at the right hand of the Mighty One and coming on the clouds of heaven."'

'He actually said that to the high priest?' I was incredulous. Did the man want to die? Did he think the laws of blasphemy wouldn't apply to him?

My father nodded. 'Caiphas grabbed the lapels of his high priestly robes and ripped at the cloth, flinging his arms wide so that no one could mistake his meaning. He said that we had all the proof we needed to send him for trial before Pontius Pilate.'

He rubbed his eyes and I could see they were bright with unshed tears.

'And there was nothing I or Joseph could do about it.'

So what has that got to do with me?

1. Jesus was not going to deny who he was. He was not going to deny the role that he had to accomplish. We might be tempted to suggest that if he had refused to be called by that title, he could have lived a long time and done a lot of good work and taught thousands more people. But he was not prepared to deny either who he was or the mission that his Father had sent him to fulfil. How do you think Jesus felt, standing there in front of the Sanhedrin? Remember, he became human for us – he had no magic button to switch off human pain.

CHAPTER FIFTY-FIVE

Waiting

Reuben

I had never been so terrified in my life. I was being jostled, knocked over, pushed and shoved; I had a foot in my face, someone shouting at me in a dialect I didn't understand and now, to complete the horror, I'd lost my companions.

It was my own fault; I should never have agreed to come into this hateful city again. I knew that if I had any chance of avoiding real injury I would have to let myself be swept along with the crowd, although I didn't have a clue what was happening. All I caught were snatches of conversation as I struggled to peer between the sea of legs and keep upright.

'They've taken him to Pilate . . .'

'He'll get what's coming to him now . . .'

'I believed him at first but of course now I see that he was just a liar and a con artist . . .'

Suddenly the pace slowed, the people around me stood still, necks craning at something I couldn't see. I took a chance; I began edging forwards through the crowd, nudging knees and thighs, knowing that if anyone looked down to challenge me, they'd recoil and pull away which for once would be very helpful. It took a long time, and I was spat on twice, but eventually I found myself on a slope leading up to a wall that overlooked what I could now see was the procurator's house. I climbed the slope and scrambled up onto the wall. I scanned the crowd but there was no sign of Esther or the other women. All I could do was wait.

CHAPTER FIFTY-SIX

The choice

Caleb

As soon as we realised Reuben was missing, I said I would go to look for him. We all knew, although no one actually put into words, the risks a little chap like him would face in this mob – and believe me, by now they were on the rampage. Not only did he risk being trampled underfoot, but there were enough anger-crazed hotheads about who would welcome the chance to vent their fury on someone as vulnerable and defenceless as Reuben. There were hundreds of zealots, shouting about freedom and liberation and some guy called Barabbas who they obviously thought was a hero. The numbers of soldiers had trebled in the last half hour, all of them trying – not very effectively – to hold back the swarming masses from rushing up the steps of Pilate's palace.

I was pushing and shoving my way through the crowd, intent on finding Reuben, when I spotted one of the men who had been with the seventy that Jesus sent out to spread the word. I didn't know his name but he had a livid red scar on his cheek which made him kind of memorable.

'Sir, excuse me, but you're a follower of Jesus, right?' I said.

'Who wants to know?' The fear on his face was unmistakeable.

'Another follower – me,' I said. 'I've been with Jesus for ages . . .'

'I don't recall you,' he muttered and turned away. I grabbed his sleeve.

'Then maybe you remember my friend, Reuben,' I persisted. 'He's very small, and he has bad legs and Jesus . . .'

'The one who was mute and then Je— He got his voice back?' he muttered. 'I do remember – but for heaven's sake, don't you realise that speaking openly about a certain person in a mob like this is the best way to find yourself clapped in chains?'

He looked back towards Pilate's palace. 'I would give anything to know what was going on in there,' he muttered. 'But I've got a good idea it won't be pretty.'

Then they led him to Pilate and they began to accuse him saying, 'We have found this man subverting our nation. He opposes payment of taxes to Caesar and claims to be Christ, a King.'

So Pilate asked Jesus, 'Are you the king of the Jews?'

'It is as you say,' Jesus replied.

Then Pilate announced, 'I find no basis for a charge against this man.'

But they insisted. 'He stirs up the people all over Judea by his teaching. He started in Galilee and has come all the way here.'

On hearing this, Pilate asked if the man was a Galilean. When he learned that Jesus was under Herod's jurisdiction, he sent him to Herod, who was also in Jerusalem at that time.

When Herod saw Jesus he was greatly pleased because for a long time he had been wanting to see him. From what he had heard about him, he hoped to see him perform some miracle. He plied him with many questions but Jesus gave him no answer. Then Herod and his soldiers ridiculed and mocked him. Dressing him in an elegant robe, they sent him back to Pilate.

Luke 23:1-11

The man looked furtively over his shoulder and leaned towards me. 'If you take my advice,' he muttered, 'you'll lie low till all this is over. Let's face it, we can't influence the outcome but we can save our own skins.' With that, he pulled his head covering down over his face and hurried away.

I didn't know what to do. On the one hand, I was desperate to find Reuben and stop anything awful happening to him; forgiven or not, memories of Kizia never left me. On the other hand I felt I should get back to the others and warn them about what the guy had told me. I was still dithering when a burly man started shouting a few feet away from me.

'Listen you lot – the Romans have got to follow our custom of releasing a prisoner at Passover, right! Because if they don't they know that we'll storm the palace, we'll cut them down, we'll . . .'

'Like we could do that!' somebody yelled back.

'Well, I'll tell you this,' the first man snarled. 'You shout for Barabbas to be released or it will go badly with you. Get it?'

'Sure, we need Barabbas, he's a true patriot . . .'

'He should never have been taken in the first place . . .'

'Get him out and we can reassemble, make plans . . .'

I was just pushing past them when the burly speaker grabbed my shoulder.

'And you – foreigner are you?'

I nodded.

'Never mind, you've got a voice,' he laughed. 'You shout for Barabbas – 'cos if I hear anyone shouting for the upstart preacher, they'll be sorry. And I've got my spies so don't think it'll go unnoticed, OK.'

I said nothing.

'I said, do you get it? God, even deformed dwarves have got my message and you . . .'

'You've seen him? The little guy with the limp? Where is he?'

'What's it to you?'

'He's my . . . brother.'

'So are you going to shout for Barabbas?'

'Yes, sure,' I lied.

'He's up on the wall by the courtyard gate,' he sniffed. 'But if you take my advice . . .'

I didn't wait for him to finish his sentence. I skirted round the back of the crowd who were by now pressing like a great rolling sea towards the steps to the palace, and there I saw him, sitting hunched on the end of the low wall.

'Reuben!' I grabbed his hand. 'Thank goodness – we've been worried sick about you. Come on, we need to get back to the others before things kick off. I have a horrible feeling it's going to get pretty dangerous round here.'

'Caleb, you found him! Thanks be to God!' Susanna clasped Reuben's hand. 'We were so worried, things are so awful, gangs of men are trying to make everyone promise to shout out for the release of some criminal who's committed murder and . . .'

'I know, they tried it on me, but . . .' I began. My words were drowned by the sound of a trumpet followed by a roar from the crowd. I turned and instantly saw the cause of the excitement. Pontius Pilate had appeared on The Stone Pavement of the palace accompanied by six Roman guards in full uniform, their burnished breastplates glinting in the early morning sun. With him were two of the priests and a number of important looking elders.

Pilate raised a hand. The crowd fell silent.

'We know that it is your custom at Passover to request the release of one prisoner. And our Emperor has graciously consented that this custom may continue.'

'So he damn well should!'

'Let him try stopping it!'

The soldiers who had been patrolling the crowds began prodding the protestors with their spears. It's a fairly effective way of shutting people up.

'We have two prisoners,' Pilate continued and paused as an attendant appeared at his side, bowing low and murmuring something in his ear.

While Pilate was sitting on the judge's seat, his wife sent him this message: 'Don't have anything to do with that innocent man, for I have suffered a great deal today in a dream because of him.'

Matthew 27:19

Pilate nodded, stood up and continued addressing the crowd. 'As I say, two prisoners. Jesus, who is called Christ . . .' He nodded and beckoned to a guard, '. . . and Barabbas, a man accused of sedition and murder.'

The guard brought both men out into full view of the crowd. Barabbas, a great giant of a man in a filthy loin cloth, stood defiantly, nodding as the crowd called out his name. Jesus, his grey tunic covered by a purple robe, stood motionless, his face without expression or emotion.

'Which one,' Pilate called over the clamour of the mob, 'shall I release to you?'

'Barabbas, Barabbas!' the crowd shouted.

'Jesus, Jesus, Jesus,' Mary yelled.

'Bar-ab-bas, Bar-ab-bas . . .'

'Jesus, Jesus . . .'

We might as well have stayed silent. I reckon three thousand voices were shouting for Barabbas and only our couple of hundred for Jesus.

'Where's Peter, and James and all the others?' I asked Esther, in between yelling Jesus' name.

She shook her head. 'None of us have seen them since last night,' she replied. 'I just hope they haven't been captured.'

The shouting died down as Pilate again held up a hand for silence. 'I ask you again, do you want me to release to you Jesus, the King of the Jews?'

'No, no, no. Bar-ab-bas, Bar-ab-bas . . .'

'And what then,' Pilate shouted, 'shall I do with Jesus, who is called Christ?'

'Crucify him!' someone shouted.

'Yes, crucify him!'

The noise was deafening, and you could smell the bloodlust of the supporters of Barabbas.

'No, no!'

'They can't!'

The two Marys clung to one another, trembling.

'Crucify!'

'Crucify!'

'Stop!' Pilate shouted. 'What crime has he committed that you should demand his death?'

'Crucify, crucify, crucify . . .'

The crowd began storming up the steps, brandishing staffs and shouting abuse. More soldiers appeared from within the palace, spears crossed to form a barricade.

'Cease!' Pilate shouted. He gestured to a servant who returned with a basin of water. 'I take no responsibility for this,' he shouted, washing his hands and holding them up for the crowd to see. 'I am innocent of this man's blood. On your heads be it!'

He turned to the guards. 'Release Barabbas,' he shouted and the crowd broke into ecstatic cheering.

'And have Jesus flogged and then crucified.'

'No – dear God no, save him, no . . .' Mary Magdalene collapsed at the feet of Cleopas, who was weeping openly. Susanna retched and clamped a hand in front of her mouth. Esther was sobbing uncontrollably and Joanna and Salome clung to one another, wailing loudly. Only Mary, Jesus' mother, stood, swaying slightly, her eyes lifted to heaven. She seemed to be talking to herself. I edged closer, frightened that she might pass out.

'And a sword,' I heard her whisper, 'will pierce your own soul too.'

So what has that got to do with me?

1. Pilate says that the death of Jesus is not his responsibility and that he is washing his hands of it. Was he responsible? What could he have done? Or was God's purpose being fulfilled so that nothing could have changed Pilate's behaviour?
2. Why do you think the crowd were so eager to have Barabbas released? Try to put yourself in their place – a country under foreign occupation.
3. Mary remembers the words 'and a sword will pierce your own soul too'. Where did she first hear them spoken and by whom?

CHAPTER FIFTY-SEVEN

The atrocity

Esther

Even if I live to be an old, old woman, I will never ever forget how awful it was. Soldiers, dozens of them, got hold of Jesus and took him off to the Praetorium. Every step of the way they prodded him with spears, hit him over the head and round the legs with their staffs, till the blood ran into his eyes, and his legs began to buckle under him. We followed, crying, wailing, and still shouting to the guards.

'He's done no wrong!'

'Spare him, spare him!'

But we knew it wasn't up to them. They were just guards doing whatever they were paid to do. The die had been cast.

We followed them all the way to the Praetorium, cutting round a back route that Cleopas knew until we reached the gates to the courtyard.

We were at the front, the two Marys, Susanna, Salome and I; our faces were pressed up against the cold metal of the gates and we were pinned there by the weight of the people behind us. The guards were shouting at Jesus, shoving him into the middle of the courtyard as more and more soldiers poured out from the barrack rooms.

'Hey look!' one of the soldiers jeered. 'He's wearing a kingly robe – oh, Your Majesty, but you don't have a crown!'

'I'll get him a crown!' yelled another, striding over to the back wall where thorn bushes protruded through the crumbling stonework. Donning his leather gauntlet gloves, he wrenched at one of the bushes and twisted the branches into a crude crown.

'All hail, King of the Jews!' he mocked, and slammed the crown onto Jesus' head. He flinched as the thorns penetrated his scalp and eyelids, but he didn't make a sound.

'Come on guys,' yelled one of the centurions, 'let's pay homage to this oh so mighty king!'

With that they all fell to their knees, jeering and spitting on his feet. Some of them stood up and began hitting him round the head with wooden sticks, driving the thorns deeper into his scalp so that the blood ran into his eyes.

A centurion strode over to them and for a minute I thought he was going to put a stop to all this horror.

'You were ordered to flog him!' he shouted. 'Now get on with it or be flogged yourselves!'

There was a pole in the middle of the courtyard to which they tied him. They stripped off his clothes so that only his loincloth remained and then two soldiers bearing long whips appeared from a side room. The whips had balls of lead attached to the long leather strands and the soldiers were wielding them round their heads and taunting Jesus.

'No!' Mary Magdalene breathed. 'Please God, no. Stop them, stop them!'

The sounds of the lashes will never leave me. The sound of flesh being ripped open, of Jesus' agonised choking cries, the change in tone as the whips hit bone rather than flesh.

I knew what was about to happen, but I had nowhere to run. I struggled against it but it was no good. I threw up, the vomit spurting through the gaps in the iron gate onto the courtyard floor. Susanna put an arm round my shoulders; her sleeve was wet with her tears.

It seemed as though the lashing would never stop but eventually the centurion stepped forward. 'Thirty-nine! Enough!' he shouted. Two guards undid one of the straps which bound Jesus' hands to the pole and he fell back, limp, supported only by the one remaining strap, great flaps of flesh hanging off his back, his eyes rolling back into his head.

'Put his clothes on and take him to Golgotha,' the centurion ordered. 'Let's get this over and done with.'

I don't know how we got there. All I have in my memory are disconnected pictures seen through a blur of tears. Jesus, staggering, stumbling, falling with this huge unwieldy wooden crossbeam roped to his outstretched arms. The blood from his cuts leaving a trail behind him, flies settling on the wounds.

Jesus falling again, struggling to get up, his legs buckling under him. Two burly soldiers grabbing hold of a dark-skinned man in the crowd and flinging him towards Jesus, ordering him to help support the weight of the wooden beam.

And ourselves, Mary his mother, his aunt, another Mary who lived in Jerusalem and who had come the moment she heard the news. Mary Magdalene, Susanna, Joanna, my sister and me along with at least thirty other women; all sobbing, wailing, calling his name. I know now that Reuben and Caleb were there but I have no memory of them, nor of Cleopas or John, who Reuben told me later joined them on the way; all I remember is us women clinging to one another as we walked through a waking nightmare.

I hear the taunts and jeers of the onlookers mixed with the wailing of those of us who really knew him. I remember a point on the way when his knees buckled and Simon – I learned his name much later – had to catch him to prevent him falling to the ground.

'Master, my Master!' Mary Magdalene howled.

I remember Jesus, his eyes bloodshot, lips swollen so that he could hardly form the words, turning and looking directly at us.

'Daughters of Jerusalem' he said, 'don't cry for me – cry for yourselves and for your children. A time is coming when people will say that the women who never conceived, who never gave birth or suckled a child, are the lucky ones. If they are doing this to me, who comes in peace, what will they do to those who come waging war and destruction?'

I remember another woman, a stranger, stepping forward and mopping the blood and sweat from Jesus' face with a linen cloth, and then pressing it her breast as she sobbed.

I remember the place. Golgotha, they call it – the Place of the Skull: a windswept hillside with rows of scaffolds. There were two men already hanging there when we arrived; I couldn't look at them.

The soldiers pushed Jesus over so that he was lying on his back with his shoulders against the shaft of wood. And then they picked up the nails – huge iron nails, bigger even than the hateful, calloused hands that held them.

One of the men picked up a hammer. With one hand holding the nail against Jesus' wrist, he swung his other arm back and smashed the hammer onto the head of the nail.

Jesus' shriek of agony splintered my heart.

They did the same to his right hand, and then they attached ropes to the plank of wood, levered it upright and hoisted him onto the scaffold.

It was when they began hammering nails into his feet that I passed out.

So what has that got to do with me?

1. The violence and torture to which Jesus was subjected horrifies us – but there are still areas in the world where people undergo huge suffering for their beliefs. When Jesus came to earth in human form, he took on all our frailty so the pain he suffered was as intense as it would be for us. That is why whatever and however we suffer, Christ understands and shares our anguish.
2. The women who watched Jesus being flogged were powerless to do anything about it. Is there anything we can do today about injustice in the world and if so what?
3. Why did Jesus say that the women without children were the fortunate ones?

CHAPTER FIFTY-EIGHT

Forgive them

Reuben

It didn't matter that I was crying. Caleb was too, in between retching and gagging at the horror in front of our eyes.

He hung there, this wonderful man who had made me feel worth something, who'd brought people back to life, and he wasn't doing anything to save himself. The Romans had hung a sign above his head.

'What does it say?' I asked Caleb, ashamed that I couldn't read it myself.

'I don't know,' he confessed. 'It's in Roman-speak.'

'It says,' laughed one of the soldiers who was standing nearby, "Jesus of Nazareth, the King of the Jews". Some king!'

He strode off to join the other guards who were swigging wine and arguing over Jesus' clothes.

'Why doesn't he do something?' I stammered, swallowing back tears. 'Why doesn't he prove it to them?'

'He will.'

'Get real,' I snapped. 'It's too late – look; he's struggling to breathe.'

Caleb said nothing but moved forward, nearer to the foot of the cross. Fists clenched against his side, he gazed up at the broken body.

'Come on,' he whispered. 'Come on, save yourself, please, please, for our sake. You can do it.'

A couple of bystanders, who seemed to be actually enjoying the spectacle of murder in front of them, laughed out loud.

'Yeah, do like he says!' one of them shouted. 'After all, aren't you the guy who was going to destroy the Temple and rebuild it in three days? Should be a doddle to get yourself down from the cross then, shouldn't it!'

'Dead right,' yelled the other. 'Come down – if you really are the Son of God!'

Suddenly Jesus moved. Slowly, agonisingly, he turned his head and looked at them. His lips began to move.

'He's going to do it,' Caleb breathed, gripping my hand so tightly I had to clench my teeth to avoid crying out. 'Look!'

Jesus opened and shut his mouth as if struggling to get enough breath to speak.

'Father,' he began.

'Yes, yes,' Caleb whispered. 'This is it. He's going to ask God to save him.'

'Father,' Jesus said, 'forgive them. They don't know what they are doing.'

So what has that got to do with me?

1. Why didn't Jesus save himself and come down from the cross? What would have been the impact? What has been the impact of his death on the world for 2000 years?
2. How do we react when everything seems to go against us?
3. Have you ever been falsely accused and punished for something you didn't do? How did it make you feel?

CHAPTER FIFTY-NINE

The question

Caleb

I wanted to hit them, spit on them, snatch his clothes away from them, throw their dice in their faces. What did I do? Nothing. I stood there, staring at them as they gambled to see who should have his cloak, who should win his mantle, and I was too scared to move. I guess it was because it had just hit me. From now on, there would be no Jesus. No one to follow. No one to strive to be like, no more dreams of becoming a proper disciple.

'Caleb, I need you.' Those words of his seemed to come from another lifetime, a time when anything was possible, a time when he was going to set up a kingdom that would be like no other, where people like me and Esther and Reuben and Ziva would be as welcome and as important as all the clever intellectuals and the moneyed aristocracy.

Now, looking at his body, discolouring before my very eyes, I realised it was all a fantasy. Jesus was going to die and that would be that.

'Jeeeee-sus!'

I turned round at the sound of a strangled cry. People were pointing up to the cross where one of the criminals was hanging.

'Aren't you the Christ?' the man rasped, his breath coming in short spurts. 'Save yourself – and us!'

The criminal on the other side of Jesus turned his head.

'Have you no . . . fear . . . of God?' The man struggled to get enough breath to speak. 'We deserve this – he doesn't.'

His face crumpled and tears filled his eyes.

'Aaargh!' His face contorted with pain as he tried to lever his weight upwards.

'Je . . . sus, remember me . . . when you come . . . come into your kingdom,' he gasped.

The expression on Jesus' face, just for a fleeting moment, reminded me of the way he'd looked at me when I had told him about Kizia.

'Today,' Jesus said to him, 'you will be with me in Paradise.'

So that really was it. He wasn't going to save himself. He wasn't going to set up any kingdom. He was leaving us.

So just what had been the point of it all?

So what has that got to do with me?

1. Why did the authorities place Jesus between two criminals? What point were they trying to make?
2. Why were the religious leaders so eager to get rid of Jesus?
3. Imagine yourself at the foot of the cross? What would your thoughts have been?
4. Caleb wonders what was the point of it all? What do you think? Jesus died for us. Because he took the weight of our sins, we can live free of the burden of guilt. He made the greatest sacrifice anyone can make – he gave his life. How can we live in a way that shows in some tiny measure our thankfulness for his precious gift?

CHAPTER SIXTY

It is finished

Esther

It seemed as if time had ceased to have any meaning. Watching Mary, the mother of Jesus, lying face down, clawing at the earth, then clutching the foot of the cross, face upturned to her dying son, my mind flew back to that courtyard in Cana, to the gentle, quiet Mary who had seen, not just my bruises, but the pain I hid.

As Mary Magdalene tore at her clothes, and pulled her hair out in handfuls, wailing and pleading, I remembered that evening round the table at Susanna's house when she had told her story – the story of how Jesus had banished her black moods, driven out her demons and saved her from taking her own life.

I watched Salome, the mother of James and John, torn between grief over Jesus and worry about James, of whom there had been no sign all day.

I turned to look at my sister standing wide-eyed and silent beside me. She was Jesus' gift to me. If he hadn't forgiven her, saved her from suicide, she wouldn't have come looking for him and I wouldn't have found her again. I had had plans for her; I'd been going to ask Jesus to finish what he'd started, to take away her fear of being rejected, which I knew was the reason that from time to time she ran off, tempted to go back to her old way of life. I had been going to ask him to send her a good husband, someone who would make her feel valued and treasured and now I couldn't. I'd never be able to ask him anything else again.

'What will we do now?' It was as if Ziva had been able to read my mind.

'We must stick together and make a life for ourselves,' I whispered.

'A life without Jesus,' she said dully. 'How do we do that?'

I said nothing. I had no answer. Not then.

'My son, my child, my baby . . .'

Mary's cries made even the Roman centurion standing guard by the cross bite his lip and bow his head. John, the only disciple who had shown up, crouched down beside her as she lay prostrate on the ground. Gently he raised her to her feet and she leaned against him, burying her face in his shoulder. They were both shivering even though it was the middle of the day. Black clouds blotted out the sun and the temperature was dropping sharply. In the distance, thunder rolled and the wind grew stronger.

'Dear woman . . .' Jesus, his head lolling to one side, his tongue protruding swollen from his mouth, gazed down at her.

'Dear woman, here is your son. John, she is now your mother.'

John nodded slowly and drew Mary closer to him. Together they stood there and wept.

'It's so horrible!' Ziva sobbed. 'If they had to kill him, couldn't they have done it quickly? Why does he have to suffer like this? It's just not fair.'

Three hours had passed. Three hours in which we sat watching his agony. Three hours in which no one did anything to relieve it. We women, all of us except Jesus' mother, her sister, John and Mary Magdalene, had moved away from the cross and were standing slightly apart, leaving them to the last few moments with Jesus on their own.

From time to time we thought he was already dead and then suddenly his body would twitch and writhe in agony and gurgling noises would splutter from his throat as he fought for air.

'Aaargh!' Suddenly he screamed, a great howl like a tortured animal. 'My God, my God, why have you abandoned me?'

'Yes, God, why, why?' The tears I had been trying to contain spilled over. Some God to let his own son suffer like this. It made my father look positively upright by comparison. I couldn't help it; I ran forward towards the cross.

'Jesus, Jesus,' I sobbed. I looked up at him hanging there, sinews bulging purple against his bloodstained flesh.

'I am thirsty.'

A soldier shoved a stick with a posca-soaked sponge against his lips but for some reason he didn't drink it.

'Father,' he gasped, 'into your hands I commend my spirit.'

A great wail rose into the air as the women at the foot of the cross stretched up their arms as if to pull him down to them.

'It . . . is . . . finished.'

A great death rattle shook his whole body. His head drooped forward. A flash of lightning lit up his limp, battered, prone form.

He was dead.

So what has that got to do with me?

1. Esther felt that she would never be able to ask Jesus anything again. Was she right?

2. How do you think Mary felt as she saw the soldiers gambling for her son's clothes? Jesus' garment is described as a single, seamless piece of cloth – which is exactly what the high priests wore. A priest was a go-between between God and the people; Jesus was a go-between between God and his people.

3. Was anyone to blame for Jesus' death?

4. Why do you think Jesus told John to regard Mary as his mother, and Mary to look on John as her son? Mary had other sons to care for her. What might his reason have been?

5. Jesus cried out 'My God, my God, why have you forsaken me?' Have you ever felt rejected and forgotten by God? By other people? Jesus knew that his death was essential for restoring the relationship between God and his people but that didn't make the feeling of isolation go away. It didn't deaden the physical pain or the emotional anguish. Because Jesus suffered as he did, we will never experience true isolation from God – he is always there, waiting for us to turn to him.

6. Years later, Peter would write a letter in which he would say 'Although he (Jesus) was abused, he never tried to get even. And when he suffered, he made no threats. Instead, he had faith in God, who judges fairly. Christ carried the burden of our sins. He was nailed to the cross so that we would stop sinning and start living right. By his cuts and bruises, you are healed.' How do those words make you feel?

7. Jesus said he was thirsty. What references to water had he made during his ministry?

8. When Jesus said 'It is finished', to what do you think he was referring?

CHAPTER SIXTY-ONE

What else is there to do?

Seth

Now it was the day of Preparation, and the next day was to be a special Sabbath. Because the Jews did not want the bodies left on the crosses during the Sabbath, they asked Pilate to have the legs broken and the bodies taken down. The soldiers therefore came and broke the legs of the first man who had been crucified with Jesus, and then those of the other. But when they came to Jesus and found that he was already dead, they did not break his legs. Instead, one of the soldiers pierced Jesus' side with a spear, bringing a sudden flow of blood and water. The man who saw it has given testimony and his testimony is true. He knows that he tells the truth, and he testifies so that you also may believe. These things happened so that the scripture would be fulfilled: 'Not one of his bones will be broken,' and as another scripture says, 'They will look on the one they have pierced.'

John 19:31-37

I was there.

I saw him die.

I saw the soldier pierce his side with his spear and I saw the blood and water gush out.

I saw my father's tears; I heard Joseph of Arimathea moan and bow his head.

I saw them break the legs of the two thieves to speed up their death before the Sabbath began and I saw how, when they reached Jesus, they left his legs intact because he was already dead.

I saw the sun blotted out and darkness fall hours before it was time. I felt the earth shake beneath my feet and I saw rocks split open.

I saw all of it and I was terrified.

But what remains in my memory more than anything else, more even that the smell of blood and the sight of swollen bodies, is the image of my father, Nicodemus, respected elder of the Sanhedrin, walking away from the group of elders who had come to witness the crucifixion, and leaning against a tree, eyes upturned to heaven, tears pouring down his wrinkled cheeks. I went over to him, fearful for his health, but he didn't see me. He stood there, shaking and reciting the Scriptures.

'He was despised and rejected of men, a man of sorrows and acquainted with grief . . . he was brought as a lamb to slaughter and as a sheep before its shearer is dumb.'

His eyes were fixed on the lifeless body of Christ. In my mind I can still see Joseph moving closer to him and taking up the chant.

'He was wounded for our transgressions, he was crushed for our iniquities; the punishment that brought us peace was on him and by his wounds we are healed.'

His voice broke. I looked from him to my father and back again, these two men who were everything to me.

'We all like sheep have gone astray,' I whispered, taking my father's hand. '*Each of us has turned to his own way; and the Lord has laid on him the iniquity of us all.'*

My father squeezed my hand and drew me to him. We clung together as the thunder crashed and the rain began pouring down, drenching everything within minutes. After a while, I became aware that the Roman centurion who had been at the foot of the cross was striding towards us.

'Father,' I whispered. 'Look.'

'They tell me your people want the bodies taken down before your Sabbath,' the centurion said gruffly. 'We have sent to Pilate for permission.'

'Thank you,' Joseph murmured. 'We appreciate that.'

'I had a job to do,' he went on. 'But I'll tell you something. I am certain now that Jesus of Nazareth is – was – really the Son of God.'

It was as we were leaving, my father and Joseph deep in conversation, that I saw Esther. She was with a group of women huddled near the cross of Jesus, torn apart with grief. I wanted to rush over to her but how could I? I knew from listening earlier to the comments of people standing nearby that one of the women was Jesus' mother. For me to intrude now would be unthinkable. And yet, I so wanted to see Esther. After everything that had happened, she would surely go back to Susanna's house in Capernaum, and since my father and his friend Simon had fallen out big time, I might never see her again.

'I shall go to Pilate now,' Joseph said. 'And you, Nicodemus, will take care of the rest?'

'I will,' my father said. 'At once.'

'What are you going to do?' I asked, still looking over my shoulder at Esther.

'Care for Jesus now in a way we never did when he was alive,' Joseph said. 'Bury him with dignity before the Sabbath. Come, I need your help.'

'We have permission.'

It was more than an hour later when Joseph sent word for us to meet him at the bottom of the hill leading to the Place of Skulls. There was no time to be lost; it was past four in the afternoon of the Day of Preparation and the special Passover Sabbath would begin at sunset. My father had explained that Joseph wanted to lay Jesus in his own new, unused tomb and that he had gone to get Pilate's permission.

'He's a brave man,' my father stressed. 'Not only is he defiling himself by entering the house of a Gentile, but also everyone knows he supported Jesus – I just hope none of the Council members get wind of what he's been doing.'

'But if Pilate says that he may have the body, no one would dare argue, would they?'

'Oh believe me, they would argue black is white given the opportunity,' my father said. 'But time is on our side; at least the Romans respect our Sabbath traditions.'

We found Joseph, accompanied by three Roman soldiers carrying the body of Jesus in a linen shroud. They lifted it onto a donkey cart that Joseph had ordered and together we walked to the cemetery on the hillside outside Jerusalem.

'Why are the soldiers coming with us?' I murmured to Joseph.

'It seems Pilate has authorised a guard to be stationed at the tomb,' he replied. 'To make sure that nobody tries to steal the body.'

I couldn't imagine why anyone would want to and said as much to my father.

'Jesus taught that after three days he would rise again,' Joseph explained. 'None of them believe that, of course – they think his disciples will try to steal the body and then pretend he's risen.'

When I laughed Joseph turned and gave me a penetrating glare. 'How many of the Scriptures have been fulfilled thus far in the teachings and life of Jesus?'

I was saved from replying by my father's exclamation of surprise: 'Are you saying – do you believe that . . . ?'

'I am saying,' Joseph replied calmly, 'that there are yet more prophecies to be fulfilled. Come, we have work to do.'

The tomb was hewn into the limestone rock, a fair way into the burial garden. My father had brought myrrh and aloes with him to rub onto Jesus' battered body. Their smell reminded me of days when I was small and fell and injured myself; for aloe is one of the quickest healing herbs there is and my mother, in the days when she was in charge of such things, used it for all of us, even the servants when they cut themselves on kitchen knives.

A small group of the women who had watched Jesus die were clustered back by the gates to the burial garden, silently watching and weeping as Joseph and my father began to unwrap the bloodstained linen cloth and replace it with the fresh shroud.

'Father, you'll be unclean – don't touch him!' I cried as my father tenderly raised Jesus' head.

'Unclean?' my father sighed. 'Oh I think in the eyes of most people we've done more to make ourselves unclean than touching the Son of God could ever do.'

The linen cloth fell off the body. I turned away. And I didn't turn back until I heard the guards grunting and groaning as they heaved the stone into place in front of the tomb.

The soldiers positioned themselves in front of it, looking, I must say, somewhat fed up with the task they had been allotted and my father and Joseph went to speak to the women. As they moved into the shelter of some olive trees, I saw her. Esther. She was with another, older girl, and she was staring into space as if in shock.

I saw my chance. Checking that my father was still otherwise occupied, I ran over to them.

'Esther? Remember me?'

'Seth!' she gasped. 'What are you doing here?'

For a moment she looked really pleased to see me but then her face clouded.

'You're not spying on us, are you?'

'Don't be ridiculous,' I exclaimed. 'My father's . . .'

'A Pharisee, I know,' she retorted. 'I used to think Caleb was wrong about you lot but now . . .'

'Hang on! Just stop right there!' I butted in. 'Let me put a few things straight, OK?'

I dropped my voice, fearful of being overheard. 'One – my father's friend Joseph has given his tomb to Jesus because he believes in him. Two – my father's here to help because he has spoken with Jesus and what's more he stood up to all the other elders in the council. And three . . .' I paused. Actually I couldn't think of number three.

'I'm sorry, Seth,' she murmured. 'Really. It's been so horrible, and everyone is looking over their shoulders, not sure who to trust.'

At that moment, my father called to me.

'I have to go,' I said, 'but tell me – what are you all going to do now?'

Although it made no sense, I needed to know what was going to happen to her, even if I could do nothing about it.

She sighed and shook her head. 'I don't know,' she murmured, her voice breaking. 'I guess we'll go back with the other women to Susanna's house and then back to Capernaum. What else is there to do?'

So what has that got to do with me?

1. Seth's father had come a long way; from visiting Jesus by night for fear of being seen to openly burying his body. Had it been an easy journey? What were the things that repeatedly made him think long and hard about who Jesus was and what his message was for the people? Do those issues apply to us today?

CHAPTER SIXTY-TWO

The betrayer's end

Caleb

They'd all left. The bodies had been taken away and the soldiers had marched back to their barracks.

John had led a weeping Mary away and Salome had gone in search of James and the other disciples and Reuben was all for going with them.

'They'll be sure to go back to Capernaum as soon as the Passover's finished,' he reckoned. 'We can go too.'

'And what would be the point of that?' I snapped. 'You might be content to lead a dead end life but I'm not.'

'I didn't mean . . .'

'Just leave me alone, OK?' I asked. 'I'll catch up with you later. Please?'

Reuben shrugged his shoulders and set off in the direction of the city.

I looked back at the outline of the cross, stark against the shafts of light between the billowing clouds.

'Caleb, I need you.'

Why couldn't I get his voice out of my mind? He didn't need me now, did he, lying there in a tomb, stiff and cold, ready for the worms to eat his flesh.

'Caleb, I need you.'

I broke into a run as if speed and sweat could eliminate the sound of his voice. I crashed through a thicket of trees, slipping and sliding on the mud and splashing through puddles left by the torrential downpour. The path became steeper, and I felt myself falling. I reached out and grabbed at an overhanging branch. As it bent towards me, something hit me between the eyes.

It was a foot. I screamed and looked up into the tree.

He was hanging there. Judas. Quite, quite, dead.

I just had time to acknowledge what I'd known to be true ever since the meal in the upper room – and then the world turned black.

So what has that got to do with me?

1. Caleb found it hard to understand that Jesus' need for him was eternal – the fact that Jesus had died didn't alter the need for Caleb to follow him. He couldn't get the sound of Jesus' voice out of his head – Jesus saying how much he needed Caleb. Do we listen to Christ's voice? Sometimes he will speak to us through the words of others, sometimes through our own hearts and consciences. Sometimes it is difficult to work out whether it is his voice, or our own – or Satan's! At times like that, it is good to share our thoughts and anxieties with someone who is a dedicated Christian.

2. Judas killed himself but there would have been a better way to go. What could he have done? Life is God's precious gift to each one of us and in times of despair or guilt, we need to remember that there is always help and forgiveness to be found.

CHAPTER SIXTY-THREE

It can't be true – can it?

Reuben

When Caleb reached the house long after the start of the Sabbath, I hardly recognised him. He was caked in mud, there was a gash across his cheek and he was walking like a man in a trance. The disciples were all closeted together in the upper room; the women were downstairs huddled together hardly speaking.

'Caleb! What's happened to you? Was it one of the soldiers?' Salome gasped, taking his arm and leading him gently to a place by the fire.

'He's dead, he's dead,' he groaned.

'I know, I know,' Mary Magdalene sobbed. 'Tomorrow we will go and embalm him and . . .'

'No, no,' Caleb muttered.

'Yes, Caleb, that's the custom,' Mary, Jesus' mother whispered. 'And my friends will do this last thing for him – and for me.'

'It's my fault, I should have stopped him,' Caleb stammered.

Mary put an arm around his shoulder. 'Caleb, what could you have done? How could you have saved Jesus?'

'Not Jesus. Judas,' Caleb stammered. 'He's dead.'

'Judas is dead? The betrayer has been killed? Who did it?' Joanna gasped.

Caleb turned and for the first time his eyes seemed to focus, not on Joanna, but on some unseen horror.

'He did, he killed himself,' Caleb whispered. 'I saw him hanging there on the tree, a rope tight around his neck.'

He closed his eyes. 'There was money all around him on the ground,' he said. 'More money than I've ever seen.'

'Did you collect it?' Ziva asked.

Caleb looked at her in disgust. 'I didn't touch it,' he said. 'I've done some bad things in my time but blood money – never!'

And then his face crumpled and he began sobbing like a baby. 'Why did he do it? Why? Why?' he repeated over and over.

Mary wrapped her arms around him and rocked him gently. 'I think it was the work of the devil,' she replied. 'I can't believe that deep down he was a bad man. I think perhaps it was beyond his power to understand the big picture. I think he was unable to resist – he was just a tool of the devil himself.'

All that night I tossed and turned. Whenever I managed to doze off, my dreams were so terrifying with their images of nails and blood and thorns and men hanging on ropes, that I preferred being awake. Eventually, worn out and with legs in such pain that I thought I might be sick, I fell asleep.

I dreamed of Jesus. But this time there was no cross, no blood, no nails. Just his face smiling down at me on a sunlit hillside and his words, repeated over and over in the softest, most gentle of voices.

'You must speak of me to those who do not know.'

By morning, I knew what I had to do. I didn't have a clue how it would work; after all, the people I spent all my time with knew all about him already. And who wants to hear about a guy whose best laid plans came to nothing?

But he'd given me a voice and told me to use it and I couldn't ignore that. I just wished he had thought to give me a few more details.

I wanted to talk to Andrew. After all, he was the one who had taken me under his wing, and always looked out for me. What's more I was fairly sure he wouldn't laugh at me for sharing my thoughts with him.

It was still dark when I heard people moving about in the house – it was so crammed with people that I was sleeping in the servants' quarters with Caleb, under strict instructions to keep a careful eye on him. I waited until it was fully light and then, checking that he was at last sleeping peacefully, I got up, climbed the stairs – well, OK, sat on my bottom and heaved myself up them because it was a very bad leg day – and knocked on the door.

'Who is it?' Peter's voice was full of suspicion.

'Me – Reuben,' I muttered.

The door opened and Peter let me in.

Now I was here I felt tongue-tied. Not literally any more of course, but I just didn't know how to say what was on my mind. The men looked so downcast, so haggard from lack of sleep and at least two of them had clearly been weeping. Suddenly my idea seemed childish, ludicrous and arrogant beyond belief.

'Did anyone see you coming here?' Philip snapped.

I shook my head. 'I've only come from the courtyard . . .'

'Oh, and you think walls don't have eyes and there aren't eyes prying into every corner,' Thomas snapped.

'The Romans have posted soldiers all over the city and beyond,' Philip added. 'I just think we should get out of here as fast as we can. For as long as we hang about, we're in danger.'

'Anyway, what was it you wanted, Reuben?' Andrew asked anxiously.

I was about to fabricate some excuse and make a hasty retreat when there was a furious hammering on the door. Philip leapt to his feet, Bartholomew grabbed his staff and Peter snatched up the sword that was leaning against the wall.

'Who is it?'

'It's me, Mary! Let me in, let me in!'

Peter unbolted the door, opened it a chink and then, shoulders sagging with relief, let Mary Magdalene into the room.

'Peter! John! The Master – he is risen!'

They stared at her as if she had taken leave of her senses.

'I went to the tomb with Salome and the other Mary and the stone had been rolled away,' she panted, beads of perspiration forming on her forehead.

'So you mean – someone has stolen his body?' Peter groaned.

'No, no, that's not it,' Mary gabbled, clutching at his sleeve. 'A man standing nearby asked me what I was doing looking for the living among the dead. And then he said, "He's not here, he is risen!"'

She ran from one disciple to the other, shaking them, repeating over and over again, 'He is risen, don't you see?'

Andrew stepped forward and gently took her arm. 'Mary, you're grieving, you've hardly had any sleep . . .'

'You don't believe me, do you?' she shouted. 'I'm telling you – it's true. Salome was with me – ask her! The man reminded us of Jesus' words when we were still in Galilee – surely you remember?' She stared wildly round the room. No one had appeared to notice that I was still there, no one that is except Mary.

She walked up to me. 'Reuben, you remember don't you? When he said, '*"The Son of Man must be delivered into the hands of sinful men, be crucified and . . ."*'

'On the third day,' I whispered, 'be raised again.'

The disciples looked at one another, then at Mary and finally back to me.

'That's what he said,' I ventured. 'And if he said it . . .'

'I want to see for myself,' Peter cried. 'Who's coming with me?'

'And risk bumping into a legion of Romans?' Thomas mocked.

'I'm with Thomas,' Thaddeus nodded. 'I thought we were trying to keep out of trouble, not invite it in.'

'I'm coming,' John said. 'There has to be some explanation. Perhaps the Romans took the body and this man was planted to spin you a yarn.'

'There's only one way to find out,' Peter urged, 'and it's not by standing here talking.'

So what has that got to do with me?

1. The author has suggested, through the words of Mary, that Judas was the tool of the devil. What do you think? Could he have acted differently or was it all predestined? If so why?
2. Jesus had told the disciples he would rise again but they had never managed to get their heads around it. What amazing things have you been told about Christ that you simply cannot take on board? Is it the magnitude of his love? The impact of his sacrifice?
3. At first the disciples didn't believe Mary Magdalene – they assumed she was mad with grief. How ready are we to believe the testimony of others when it comes to their experience of the Risen Christ?

CHAPTER SIXTY-FOUR

He is risen!

Esther

I so wanted to believe what Mary Magdalene was saying and yet I couldn't help thinking that Peter was right. If Jesus really had come back to life why wasn't he here, with us? Why would he appear to Mary and not to Peter, or John or James, who let's face it had always been his favourites?

'She's deluded,' Thomas confided in Joanna. 'The grief has turned her brain.'

What had happened was this. Peter and John had come back from the tomb and confirmed that it was indeed empty, the linen cloths lying on the stone slab. Mary wasn't with them.

'She insisted on staying behind,' John said, 'and to be honest, it seemed best to leave her be. I think she was trying to come to terms with the fact that perhaps the man she spoke to was just leading her on.'

That theory didn't last long. Within minutes, Mary had burst into the room where everyone had gathered together to make some kind of a plan about getting out of Jerusalem, her eyes bright and a huge smile on her face.

'I've seen him! I've really seen him and what's more I've spoken to him!'

'Now this is getting ridiculous,' Thomas began.

'Tell us.' Jesus' mother's voice was firm enough to silence Thomas.

'After Peter and John had gone, I just knelt there by the empty tomb, weeping,' she began. 'Someone came up behind me, and asked me why I was crying. I told them it was because they'd taken the Master's body and I had no idea where he was. I asked him if he knew and if so, would he tell me. Of course, all this time I didn't look at him; I was trying to control my tears.'

'And what did he say?' Joanna urged.

'He just said "Mary",' she whispered. 'And I turned round and it was him. I cried out, "Rabboni! Teacher!" and flung my arms around him.'

'Was he a ghost? Did he disappear?' Caleb asked.

'No,' Mary shook her head. 'He told me not to cling on to him because he hadn't yet gone back to his Father. He told me to come and tell all of you what I'd seen, and to say that he was going back to his Father, who is our Father too, to his God, who is our God.'

Jesus' mother closed her eyes and mouthed a silent prayer.

'Well, I'm telling you this,' Thomas blurted out. 'I don't believe a word of it. And I shan't believe it until I see him face to face – and what's more put my hands in those dreadful holes and wounds . . .' His voice broke and he turned away in embarrassment.

Peter had been standing to one side, deep in thought. 'We must make a plan,' he said suddenly. 'Jesus would not have wanted us to skulk in the shadows like frightened sheep. We have to carry on with our lives; we have to try to make sense of all of this . . .'

'And I must get home,' Philip said. 'Pick up the threads of the old life, I guess.'

'Me too,' Bartholomew nodded.

'And I shall head home to Emmaus today,' Cleopas said. 'No point hanging around in this godforsaken city.'

One by one, people began gathering their few belongings, while Reuben, Caleb and I looked at one another anxiously but it was Reuben who voiced what was in all our minds.

'What if,' he said under his breath, 'it really is true? What if Jesus has risen from the dead?'

CHAPTER SIXTY-FIVE

Wisdom of the traveller

Caleb

'Sir,' I said to Cleopas later that morning (I always think it's worth being polite when you want something badly), 'I couldn't help overhearing when you said that your steward had died.'

'Indeed yes,' Cleopas replied, 'and now I have to return to a house in heaven knows what state,' he sighed.

'My wife will go back to Capernaum to stay with Zebedee and Salome for a while,' he said. 'Her nerves have been shattered by the events of this past week and I don't want to put her under any more stress.'

'So – you will need to find a new steward?' I ventured.

'I suppose so,' Cleopas sighed. 'Although to be honest, I don't have the will or the energy to look further ahead than the next hour. What is the point? I believed – we all believed – that my nephew was going to change the world.' He turned to me, his eyes rheumy and pink. 'I guess we left home to follow a lost cause,' he sighed. 'But Jesus did do wonderful things and we must be glad we were there to see them.'

He coughed and hammered his chest. 'I guess I'm too old for all these wanderings,' he said. 'But you – what will you do? You're young and . . .'

'Well, sir,' I intervened hastily. 'I left my last job because I wanted to follow Jesus . . .'

OK, so that was the edited version, but I wasn't about to ruin my chances before I'd started.

'I didn't miss working as a – an under steward,' I went on, stressing the last two words, 'because we were all in it together and I thought I'd end up as a proper disciple. But now . . .' I left the words hanging in the air just long enough for Cleopas to cotton on, '. . . now, with Jesus gone, I don't know what to do. I'm useful, I can cook, I know about husbandry . . .'

I was relieved when he interrupted. There was a limit to how much I could boost up my qualifications. 'Am I right in thinking you are asking for a job?' Cleopas smiled.

'Sir, even for a week or two, just until your wife returns . . .'

'Come back with me today,' he suggested. 'See how things go.'

'Sir, I'm so grateful,' I said as humbly as I could, and dashed off to tell Esther how she fitted into my plan.

'Leave Susanna? You must be mad!' Esther exclaimed. 'Why would I do that?'

'To stay close to me,' I suggested. 'You could get a job in Emmaus – that's where Cleopas lives and there must be people needing maids and . . .'

'I have a job, and I have a home with Susanna,' Esther said gently. 'She's already told me of some of her plans for the future and the amazing thing is, I'm part of them. I'm sorry, Caleb, and I really hope you'll be happy and that everything will work out for you, but I can't be part of it.'

'So you don't care about me at all?'

Esther squeezed my hand and dropped her eyes. 'I care about you a lot, of course I do,' she said. 'You helped me get away from Cana and I'll never forget that, and we've been through a lot together.'

'But that's all?'

'Yes,' she whispered. 'I'm sorry, Caleb, that's all.'

'So we won't see each other again?'

'Who knows? Cleopas might decide to visit Galilee again and bring you with him!'

At the time, that wasn't much consolation.

Emmaus was a seven-mile walk from Jerusalem and it would have taken me only a couple of hours, but Cleopas was old and a slow walker who needed frequent stops. Luckily he was a far better companion than I had thought he would be; he questioned me on what I thought about the past three years and he seemed really interested in my replies. I even found myself telling him about my foolish idea of Jesus accepting me as a proper disciple, about getting drunk at Matthew's house and about the awful incident with the pigs. He listened, occasionally quoting some of Jesus' teachings, and as we walked I realised how much grief he was suppressing; he spoke of Jesus as a little boy, and of his brother Joseph's pride in him; of how one of the main reasons he and his wife decided to shut up their house and follow Jesus was because it was what Joseph would have done had he still been alive.

'And,' Cleopas admitted, 'because somehow the way Jesus taught the Scriptures was so fresh, so new and so much more relevant to the struggle I was having with my own faith.'

I wanted to ask more about that – struggle was something I knew a lot about – but just then, when we were about two miles from his village another traveller caught up with us.

'I couldn't help hearing snatches of your conversation,' he said. 'Tell me, what were you discussing?'

'Sir,' Cleopas said, 'I guess you must be a visitor from a long way away, if you are not aware of everything that's happened in the city these past few days.'

'What things?' he looked puzzled.

'About Jesus,' I butted in. 'He was a prophet, and he did the most amazing things, and told wonderful stories and taught – I don't know how to put it . . . a new way of living, I guess.'

'But they crucified him!' Now the grief that Cleopas had been struggling to keep at bay spilled out. 'Those brutes tortured and crucified him – and all our hopes with him! We thought he was the One – the Redeemer of Israel!'

The man said nothing but appeared to be listening intently.

'And you know what?' I went on. 'Some women who were with us went to his tomb this morning and said they couldn't find his body and that just makes it worse because . . .'

'You really are foolish, aren't you?' the man interrupted suddenly. I couldn't believe how rude he was; what did he know about it, a foreigner who hadn't even heard the first thing about Jesus.

'Have you never read the Scriptures?'

'Well, yes, of course,' Cleopas said, rightly sounding somewhat offended.

'So don't you believe everything that the prophets of old have predicted? Don't you realise that the Christ, the Messiah, had to suffer and die before he could enter into his glory? Let me explain . . .'

And he started to talk about the law of Moses and the teachings of all the prophets, flagging up everything that referred to Jesus' life and ministry. He didn't have a single scroll with him; yet he could quote great chunks of the Torah from memory.

I don't usually enjoy deep and learned conversations but I found myself hanging on his every word as he spoke about the day when God delivered our ancestors from the angel of death in Egypt. I knew the story of course – but when he asked us what God was trying to teach us at that time, I realised I hadn't a clue. I thought it was all about our people getting away in the night while the Egyptians got sick and died.

'What about the victim, the innocent victim?' the man said. 'The lamb that was slain? Don't you think that was a sign that if sinners were to be allowed to go free, an innocent substitute had to be found?'

Then he quoted passages from the prophet Isaiah, phrases I had heard in the synagogue but never understood.

'*God will make him a guilt offering for the sins of his people . . . bruise his servant . . . by his stripes we are healed.*'

On and on he talked, and although I didn't understand all of it, I felt as if I wanted to. I began to wonder whether Cleopas might arrange for me to study under a rabbi, now that Jesus was gone.

When we finally reached Cleopas' house, the man made to continue down the road.

'Sir, wait!' Cleopas cried. 'It's late and getting dark. Stay and eat with us, please.'

We had brought bread and curd cheese, barley cakes and olives, as well as some figs and pomegranates with us from Jerusalem. The house was a mess; but I grabbed a broom, swept the floor and scrubbed the table and within minutes we were sitting down to eat.

I reached out to pass the platter of bread to Cleopas so he might bless it but the stranger had already taken a loaf and was holding it up high. He broke it and gave it to us.

'Take, eat,' he said.

And I knew. We knew.

'Master!' Cleopas cried and fell to his knees.

'It's you – Jesus!' I gasped. 'You're here! You're alive!'

We looked at one another, each of us I guess wanting reassurance that the other had seen the same thing. Then we turned back to face him. But he had disappeared.

'It was him, wasn't it?' I said a moment later.

'Yes,' said Cleopas, tears in his eyes. 'It was the Lord. I should have realised by the way I felt when he was talking about the prophecies. Come, eat – we must go back to Jerusalem.'

'Now?'

'Of course now,' he said. 'This changes everything. Can't you see that? We have to tell them. We have to tell everyone. Jesus the Christ really has risen from the dead!'

So what has that got to do with me?

1. Jesus talked about the Scriptures – the Old Testament. He reminded Cleopas and Caleb of all the prophecies that had been made about him. Sometimes the Old Testament can seem difficult and challenging to modern – and particularly to new – Christians. Try reading The Message translation – you will discover that the Old Testament is packed full of stories of every kind – adventure, horror, romance – and The Message uses accessible language to help you understand them!

2. Cleopas couldn't wait to get back to Jerusalem to tell the others the wonderful news that Christ had risen from the dead. Think of all the times when you've been bursting to tell someone an amazing piece of news. Do you ever feel that way about the Good News of Jesus? Does the church burst with joy and energy when it speaks about Christ? What type of worship enables you to 'let rip' with the joy of knowing Christ? If you are still new to faith, what are the easy and what are the difficult elements of worship?

CHAPTER SIXTY-SIX

No more doubts

Reuben

The plan to leave straight away bit the dust pretty quickly when we saw just how many soldiers were patrolling the streets. Thaddeus, who had ventured up the street to the house of Susanna's sister, where some of the gang were staying, overheard the reason for the sudden influx of Roman guards.

'They think there will be a riot because Jesus' body is missing,' he said. 'They've heard the rumour that he's risen from the dead and they are determined to quash it – by force, if necessary.'

That's when Peter said we should bolt the door and stay put till things had died down.

'Thomas isn't back yet,' Bartholomew reminded him.

'So he'll knock and we'll let him in,' Peter replied. 'We can't keep open house here – we have to watch our backs, right?'

I retreated to a corner of the room, hoping that no one would realise I was still there. Sadly, Philip saw me and nudged Andrew.

'Can I stay here?' I asked, and then ashamed at the fear in my voice added a quick excuse. 'I could be useful if you needed . . . anything.'

'Of course you must stay,' Andrew said. 'Your friends are safe – Caleb's with Cleopas in Emmaus and Susanna will be sure to look after Esther and Ziva.'

He gave me a friendly shove on the shoulder. 'So I guess it's up to me to keep an eye on you, isn't it?'

To say I was relieved is an understatement. Now that Jesus was dead, I knew that how I was, was how I would always be and if I was going to make a living I would need the protection of someone like Andrew. In the cold light of another day, my idea of speaking to people about Jesus seemed crazy. Folk want stories with a happy ending; and telling them what he did for me, would only make those who were still dumb, or deaf, or blind or plagued with demons, feel worse than ever.

'You must speak of me to those who do not know.'

I wished I could get his voice out of my head.

Jesus came and stood among them and said, 'Peace be with you!' After he said this he showed them his hands and side. The disciples were overjoyed when they saw the Lord.

John 20:19, 20

'Peace be with you!'

It was the cries of the others in the room that made me look up. He was there. Jesus.

He stood there, in the middle of the room, with his hands outstretched, palms upwards, just as he had so many times before. On his wrists were the holes where the nails had been driven through his flesh.

'Lord!'

'Master!'

'Is it really you?'

The disciples were laughing, crying, hugging one another, falling at Jesus' feet, calling his name over and over.

'Listen to me,' Jesus said and one by one they fell silent. I sat in the corner, holding my breath, praying he wouldn't notice me and send me away.

'In the same way as my Father sent me to you, so now I am sending you.'

He took a deep breath and, walking round the circle of men, he breathed out on each one of them.

'Receive the Holy Spirit,' he said. 'If you forgive someone's sins, they will be over and done for good. If you choose not to forgive them, then the burden of them will remain.'

And then he was gone.

'It was him!'

'Mary was right . . .'

'I never really doubted it for a minute . . .'

The disciples were still in a state of delirious joy when there was a hammering at the door.

'Thomas?' Peter called. 'Is that you?'

'It's Cleopas, let us in – quickly!'

Philip rushed to the door and slid the bolt. Cleopas, out of breath and with sweat pouring down his face, burst in and to my delight, Caleb was hard on his heels.

'We've seen him,' Peter burst out before Cleopas could draw breath. 'The Lord! He came to us – he is risen!'

'I know, I know,' Cleopas cried. 'We've seen him too – he broke bread with us – we didn't know at first it was him, but then we realised – and oh! Tell me, tell me, did he speak with you?'

While Peter and John were recounting the story, with the others chipping in every few seconds, I reached out and touched Caleb's leg. He turned, his eyes widened and he grinned from ear to ear.

'Hey, you!' he said, dropping down on his knees beside me. 'Were you here? Did you see him too?'

'Yes,' I said. 'I saw him. He didn't see me though. And now, I do so wish he had.'

For a week we stayed in the house, and I really came into my own. Ironically, it was a lot safer for me to go to the market for supplies than it was for the disciples. Masquerading as a beggar every time I saw a soldier, I was able to move around freely, not just to the traders' stalls but to the other two houses where our motley crew were hiding out. I felt needed and useful; and there was another bonus to it all. Esther did the shopping for the women and while occasionally Susanna was with her, there were several occasions when we were on our own.

On one such occasion, she seemed quiet and withdrawn and I asked her what was wrong.

'You've seen Jesus, Caleb's seen Jesus, so has Mary and Salome – I wish I could see him too,' she sighed.

'But you do believe me?'

'Oh yes, of course I do,' she replied. 'It's just that to see him alive and risen might blot out that awful memory of his poor battered, bruised, broken body. I see it every time I close my eyes at night. I just want to forget it and if I saw him whole again, then I could.'

I don't know what made me say what I did – I don't even know where the words came from.

'I don't think,' I said as gently as I could, 'that any of us are meant to forget. Ever.'

The atmosphere wasn't brilliant among the disciples. Thomas took every opportunity of deriding them for what he called their 'visions' of Christ and as each day passed and Jesus didn't appear, he became more and more convinced that it had all been a delusion.

'And was Christ's visit to my home a delusion?' Cleopas demanded. He had decided to remain with us now that Miriam his wife had gone home with Salome; he said that he felt sure the story wasn't over after all, and that it was only just beginning.

'Listen,' Thomas ranted. 'Unless Jesus appears before me, and not just as some flimsy ghost, mind you, but alive and breathing as you seem to think he is – unless that happens, and I can put my hand into the holes where the nails went, I won't believe it.'

It was about a week after we'd seen Jesus, and at last it seemed safe to leave the city. The furore had died down, the numbers of soldiers on the street had reduced dramatically and everyone felt ready to go home.

I had been to the market to get provisions for the journey and was in the kitchen with Susanna, Esther and Ziva when Andrew came running down the stairs, followed by Peter and Thomas.

'He believes – at last, Thomas is onside!' Andrew cried. 'Jesus came to us again, just like before!'

'Praise be!' Susanna cried. 'Thomas tell us, what happened?'

'It was just as they all said it was,' Thomas replied slowly. 'He stood there, as real and as solid as we are. And he must have known . . .' He faltered.

'Known what?' Ziva asked.

'That I wanted proof,' Thomas replied. 'He turned to me and told me to put my finger in his wounds. I felt so ashamed; he knew all along about my doubts.'

'So you put your finger in the holes?' Ziva shuddered as she asked the question.

Thomas shook his head. 'No,' he said. 'There was no need. I knew all I needed to know – that my Lord and my God is alive!'

At that Esther, who was packing a basket with fruit and cheese, looked up.

'I so wish I could see him,' she murmured.

Thomas smiled at her. He wasn't a guy I often saw smile which made its effect doubly surprising.

'Do you know something?' he said. 'Jesus was right. I believed only after I had seen him. He told me that it is the people who believe in him without ever having seen him, or witnessed a miracle, or been healed – it is those people who are truly and eternally blessed.'

He took a step closer to Esther. 'Do you believe that Jesus is the Son of God?'

'Oh yes, yes of course I do,' she declared.

'Then,' Thomas said, 'you too are truly blessed.'

So what has that got to do with me?

1. 'If you forgive someone's sins, they will be over and done for good. If you choose not to forgive them, then the burden of them will remain.' What does this tell us about bearing grudges? Who suffers when sins are not forgiven? Is it just the person who needs forgiveness?
2. Esther wanted to see the risen Christ so that she could blot out the memory of his body hanging on the Cross. Reuben was right when he said we were not meant to forget – ever. Those who had seen him saw that the marks of the nails were still visible. We need to remember the Cross in order to appreciate that Jesus died in order to save us; and as we rejoice in the Resurrection, to understand that without the Cross our sins could not have been forgiven.

CHAPTER SIXTY-SEVEN

The eternal promise

It was so strange to be back. In many ways, life at Capernaum fell into the old pattern – Peter, Andrew, James and John fished every night and Philip grumbled every morning about having to find an easier way to earn a living. I still helped with the boats, Esther continued to work as Susanna's maid and Caleb was learning to be a fisherman. Of course, being Caleb, he was already talking of owning a fleet of boats, and then buying a repair yard . . . well, you get the picture!

Cleopas had come back with us to fetch his wife, and was still staying with Zebedee and Salome, enjoying as he put it the fresh air of Galilee after the oppressiveness of Jerusalem. As for Ziva, she had taken a fancy to a potter in Capernaum and Esther had high hopes that something might come of it. Susanna did say that she sincerely hoped it would because it was amazing how many jars and pots had accidentally been chipped or smashed in the three weeks we had been home. Life jogged on.

Yet in many ways everything had changed. It was as if the old ways weren't enough: there was a restlessness in everyone, a feeling that we were all marking time, not sure what to do with the rest of our lives. I found myself thinking about that day three years before when I'd first seen Jesus; and I realised I was a different person from that angry, thieving, hurting boy. It wasn't just that now I could speak; the scars on my arms and thighs had disappeared, and I hadn't felt an urge to slice my skin for so long that I found it hard to imagine how I had ever done it. I wasn't even resentful that Jesus had left me with twisted feet and limbs that ached more with every passing month. Something inside me that had raged for as long as I could remember had calmed. I was different. And I wanted to live differently, but I didn't know where to begin.

And then he came back again.

The disciples had been fishing – not just Peter and Andrew and Zebedee's sons, but Thomas and Nathaniel and Philip. Caleb went too; Philip was teaching him the ropes, and teased him that maybe he could take over his boat and free him to do something more exciting.

I was on the beach early in the morning waiting for them to come back. It was a beautiful morning, the sun just rising and the air already warm. The beach was deserted apart from one man lighting a fire a few hundred yards away.

Cleopas loved fish and Salome, who enjoyed fussing over her visitors, wanted me to clean and gut the first of the catch to be landed.

As it turned out, she was out of luck. As the boat drew closer I could see that the nets were empty. This was not going to be a good day.

'Hey there!' The man near the fire was shouting to the disciples. 'So – haven't you got any fish?'

'No!' Peter called back, and I could just imagine him muttering under his breath. 'Does it look like we have any?'

I guessed that the guy had wanted to buy some fish to cook.

'No problem,' he shouted back. 'Throw your net over the right side of the boat and you'll get plenty.'

In that moment, my heart stood still. I was back on the beach – way back – watching nets that split because there were so many fish . . .

Didn't they get it? It was him. It was Jesus.

I ran towards the water's edge. They were hauling a net crammed full of wriggling fish, just as they had two years before. Only this time the nets didn't tear.

If I didn't act now, while the disciples were wrestling with the net, it would be too late. Any minute now they would realise just who it was standing by the fire.

'It's the Lord!' John's voice rang out over the waves.

I had to do it. There wasn't a moment to lose.

'Master.'

Jesus turned and looked at me. 'Reuben,' he said. 'You know me.'

'Of course I know you, Master – I've followed you for a long time.'

'Yes you have,' Jesus replied gently. 'You've seen me, you've talked to me, you've fed people for me. But today you have come to know me.'

His eyes held mine and I felt love like I'd never known existed. His love for me and mine for him – it was as if the sparks from the fire were warming the very core of my being. I felt a burst of energy coursing through my body.

'Lord, I . . .'

'Master! Master!'

The moment was broken as Peter came splashing through the water and rushing up to him. The others beached the boat, and came rushing over, Caleb among them.

'Well, here you all are at last,' Jesus laughed. 'Come and have some breakfast – I thought the fish would be charred to a cinder by the time you lot got here!'

I was shaking from head to foot, wanting to laugh and to cry all at the same time. He'd noticed me. He'd spoken to me. He understood.

'Can you believe this?' Caleb whispered in my ear. 'You and me, here, with him.'

'Someone's missing though,' I said. I knew what I had to do: I had to fetch Esther from Susanna's house, and bring her to him. I knew how much she wanted to see him alive.

I got up and broke into a run, heading for the path that led to the barrel maker's street and then stopped dead. Cautiously, I walked, then jogged, then ran as fast as I could. My feet were straight and the pain had gone.

'Where is he? Where's Jesus?'

Esther and I had run all the way back to the beach, but there was no sign of Jesus. Susanna, Mary and a crowd of other villagers were hard on our heels, as the news that the Lord was on the beach spread from house to house.

'He's gone,' Peter said quietly. 'Or at least, we can't see him any more.'

I thought Esther was going to burst into tears, and to be honest, I was pretty disappointed myself.

'But I wanted to thank him,' I blurted out. 'Look!'

The expression on the faces of the disciples when they saw my two straight feet was worth the stitch in my side.

'Wow!' Caleb said. 'So how come he didn't make your arms . . .'

One look from me shut him up.

'Will he come back?' Esther asked Peter shyly.

'I don't know,' he answered. 'What I do know is that I have to share something with you – all of you.'

He gestured to Susanna and the other women, to the men who had left their nets and their shops to see what all the commotion was about, and took a deep breath.

'That day when they crucified Jesus, I did a terrible thing. I can hardly bring myself to confess it . . .'

'You mean, when you pretended you didn't know Jesus?' Andrew asked.

'You knew?'

'We heard about it,' Philip said. 'Esther's sister saw you.

Slowly Peter nodded.

'When I saw the charcoal fire just now, and Jesus standing beside it, everything came flooding back – the fire in the courtyard of the high priest's house, the people bombarding me with questions and all the time, the knife-like fear that if I told the truth, they might kill me too.'

He shook his head. 'All this time,' he said, 'I have felt such pain, such shame . . .'

'We were as bad,' his brother said. 'We all hid away – how many of us stood at the cross? These kids were more loyal than we were.'

'Which is why I need them to hear this too,' Peter replied. 'Just now, when Jesus took me to one side he asked me if I loved him more than all this.'

He waved a hand towards the boat and over to his house. 'And of course, I said that I did. And you know what he said? He said, "Feed my lambs."' He bit his lip. 'But he asked me again, a second time. Do you really love me more than all these things? And again, I said I did and he said again, "Feed my lambs." When he asked me a third time, I got pretty irritated if I'm honest.'

'What did you say?' Andrew asked.

'I asked him why he was still posing the same question. I told him that he knew everything there is to know and therefore he must know just how very much I love him. That's when he told me to be a shepherd to his sheep.'

'So you are what he said you were,' John declared. 'The rock on which he is going to build.'

'He said that from now on, I would be led – sometimes to places I didn't even want to go – but that I should follow him.'

Then he turned to John. 'When he told me to follow him, I asked him what about you? I mean, I didn't add this bit, but I knew that you've been his favourite all the way through so I asked what was going to happen to you.'

'And?' John asked, a little anxiously.

'He said something very strange,' Peter replied. 'Basically that it was none of my business and that if he decided that he wanted you to live until he came again, then that's how it would be. Then he put an arm round my shoulder and said . . .'

He paused, and I could have sworn his eyes filled with tears.

'He said again, "You Peter, you follow me," and he pointed up the mountain. I thought that's where he wanted me to go, but then suddenly – he'd vanished.'

Esther stared at him. 'But if Jesus was pointing there, then surely that's where we should be going,' she cried.

'She's right,' John urged. 'After all, how many times has Jesus taken us up the mountain when he had something important to say?'

It was as though John's words had shone a light straight into Peter's eyes. I could have sworn they glowed.

'The mountain!' he breathed. 'Remember when the three of us went up and saw Moses and Elijah . . .'

'He told us not to talk about that,' James cut in.

'He said we were to tell no one until . . .' Peter hesitated as if trying to remember Jesus' words.

'. . . until the Son of Man is raised from the dead,' John finished. 'And we didn't get it, did we? He told us as plainly as that – and still we didn't understand.'

'So why are we hanging about here?' Esther burst out. I'd never heard her be so forthright – well, not since the little matter of Seth and Caleb on that very same stretch of beach a lifetime ago.

She began running up the beach and onto the path that led round the back of the village and up the hillside.

'She's right!' Peter cried. 'Come on, follow me!'

I had always found the climb up the hillside a real struggle but not this time. My legs felt strong as if new muscles had grown to replace the old twisted worn out sinews, and I found I could stride out with best of them which was just as well because the clouds were low and before long we were walking through mist. The only way to keep warm was to move fast.

'It's a miracle,' Susanna exclaimed as I scrambled over the rock-strewn path like a mountain goat. 'The Lord is still working his wonders.'

'Do you think we will see him?' Ziva asked.

'If he told Peter to go up the mountain, there must be a reason,' Mary replied. 'And whatever it is, we're just doing what he said.'

'My Lord! Jesus! I can see you!'

Esther's voice rang out through the mist. Then, quite suddenly, the fog lifted and there, in a thin shaft of watery sunlight, was Jesus. He smiled and opened his arms wide as if to catch us all in one huge embrace.

'My dear friends,' he began, before anyone could speak. 'The time has come for me to leave the world again and go to my Father.'

'Lord, no,' John cried out.

Jesus beckoned the eleven closer.

'As my Father sent me to you, so I am now sending you out into the world.' He turned and looked straight at us – me, and Caleb and Esther, the three of us clinging to one another under a gnarled and bent old olive tree.

'I am sending you *all,*' he smiled. 'Go and make disciples wherever you find yourselves, baptising them in the name of the Father, and of the Son, and of the Holy Spirit. Teach them everything I have taught you.'

'Lord, don't leave us,' Peter groaned. 'We can't do all that on our own.'

'Don't be afraid,' he said gently. 'Remember what I have taught you. Love one another as I have loved you.'

He raised his eyes towards heaven, and then slowly opened his arms and looked from one to another, until each of us had looked into his eyes.

'My children, whatever else you forget, remember this: I am with you always, every day, even to the end of time.'

As the cloud came down, he raised his arms and it seemed that the wind was lifting him off his feet. We didn't see him again. But he has never really left us – and I know he never will.

Freely, freely you have received,
freely, freely give.
Go in my name and because you believe
others will know that I live.

So what has that got to do with me?

1. What is the difference between knowing *about* Christ and knowing Christ?
2. Why do you think Jesus waited until now to straighten Reuben's feet? Why was the time now right?
3. Jesus sends all of us who believe in him – sends us out into the world to share this amazing love story with others. And that doesn't mean we all have to be missionaries in far flung places, or priests in churches, or teachers of RE. It means that we take a very deep breath, set our fear of being teased or ridiculed to one side and tell others about what it means to have Jesus in our lives. Even if you've only just come to know him, or are putting a very tentative toe in the water, every time you feel that surge of joy, or that comforting hand, or that word in your ear that lets you know he is right beside you – *share it*! You could transform someone's life without ever knowing it.

Author's note

This has been a book about the journey of four young people – all fictitious, yet all real; young people with disabilities, abusive pasts, lonely lives and prejudiced upbringings – whose futures were transformed by the love of one man. My prayer for every reader of this book is that they too may come to know that Jesus is their friend, brother, Lord and Saviour, as alive and passionate about them as he was about Reuben, Esther, Caleb and Seth; and that they may discover for themselves the joy and the strength that comes from following the Risen Christ.

Sources

One of the great joys of writing this imaginative retelling of the Gospels has been reading and absorbing the thoughts and experiences of others – Christians, academics, new believers, old scholars – all readily available on the wonderful worldwide web. My thanks are especially due to contributors to the following websites:

www.bible-lands.net – About the people and cities of the Bible.
www.gobible.org – Bible-based sermons and studies by lay pastor and published author Bruce Cameron.
www.jesuswalk.com – In-depth Bible studies.
www.wordlibrary.co.uk – Christian resource.

The following books have proved invaluable:

Morgan, Alison, *The Wild Gospel*, Monarch Books, Oxford, UK, and Grand Rapids, MN, 2004
Pritchard, John, *Living Jesus*, SPCK, 2011
Stott, John R. W., *The Cross of Christ*, Varsity Press, 25th anniversary edn, 2006 (first published in 1981)
Vamosh, Miriam Feinberg, *Food at the time of the Bible*, Palphot Ltd, Herzlia, Israel
Verney, Stephen, *Water into Wine*, Fount Paperbacks, 1985, reprinted 1999 by Darton Longman and Todd
Wright, Tom, *Luke for Everyone*, SPCK, 2001
— *Mark for Everyone*, SPCK, 2001
— *John for Everyone*, SPCK, 2002
— *Matthew for Everyone*, SPCK, 2002

The writings of Philip Yancey and John Ortberg, too numerous to mention, have inspired and urged enquiry for many years.

I have used several translations of the Bible, but have as always returned time and again to the New Standard Version, The Message by Eugene H. Peterson, and the NRSV Life Application Study Bible and the New Century Version of The Youth Bible.

Acknowledgements

I am deeply grateful to the following people without whose patience, love, support and wisdom I would never have found The Way, come to realise The Truth, or continued, with many trippings up and fallings down, to do my best to walk in The Way. Thank you is simply not enough.

To Mary Potter, for beginning it all

To The Revd Canon Alison White for shining the light

To The Revd Canon Clive Evans for opening new windows on the Word

To The Revd Canon Margaret Johnson for her wisdom, endless patience and understanding

To Revd David Kirby for allowing time to write and making time to listen

To Revd Colin W. Wake for opening doors and having faith in me and for putting up with endless garbled emails

To Rt Revd Donald Allister for encouragement

To Cindy, Lorraine, Ginny and Pamela who know why

To Christina Dickens, William Fazackerley, Rachel Halstead, Rosalind Martin, Hannah Needham, Dominic Leatherland, Harrison Cook and Adam Shaw for saying how it is to be a teenage follower of Christ today

To the family of St Peter's, Weston Favell, past and present, for more than words can ever express

To Kevin Mayhew for having faith in the idea

To Paul Tompsett and Ronnie Hanna at Free Range Book Design & Production Limited

. . . and above all, to Niki, Sally and Caroline for loving me through the dark days and making them light